MAKING WESTERN CANADA

MAKING WESTERN CANADA

Essays on European Colonization and Settlement

Edited by Catherine Cavanaugh & Jeremy Mouat

Garamond Press, Toronto

Printed and bound in Canada

Copy editors: Melodie Mayson-Richmond and Ted Richmond
Typesetting and Design: Robin Brass Associates
Publisher: Peter R. Saunders

Garamond Press
77 Mowat Avenue, Suite 403
Toronto, Ontario
M6K 3E3

Canadian Cataloguing in Publication Data

Main entry under title:

Making Western Canada: essays on European colonization and settlement

Includes bibliographical references.
ISBN 0-920059-45-7

1. Canada, Western – History. I. Cavanaugh, Catherine Anne, 1945– . II. Mouat, Jeremy, 1950– .

FC3206.M35 1996   971.2   C96-930613-X
F1060.M35 1996

We acknowledge the support of the Canadian Studies Directorate of the Federal Department of Canadian Heritage in the publication of this book.

Contents

Contributors

Lyle Dick lives in Victoria and is Senior Specialist, Cultural Resource Management (Pacific & Yukon Region), with the Department of Canadian Heritage. He is the author of *Farmers "Making Good": The Development of Abernethy District, Saskatchewan, 1880-1920* (Ottawa: National Historic Parks and Sites, Canadian Parks Service, 1989).

Sarah A. Carter teaches history at the University of Calgary and is the author of *Lost Harvests: Prairie Indian Reserve Farmers and Government Policy* (Montreal: McGill-Queen's University Press, 1990).

Elizabeth Jameson teaches history at the University of New Mexico and co-edited *The Women's West* (Norman: University of Oklahoma Press, 1987). She has written extensively on the history of women in the North American West, and was a co-founder of the Coalition for Western Women's History.

Tina Loo teaches history at Simon Fraser University and is the author of *Making Law, Order and Authority in British Columbia, 1821-1871* (Toronto: University of Toronto Press, 1994).

Richard Rajala teaches history at the University of Victoria and is the author of *The Legacy and the Challenge: A Century of the Forest Industry at Cowichan Lake* (Victoria: Beach Holme Publishers, 1993).

Mark Leier teaches history at Simon Fraser University and is the author of *Red Flags and Red Tape: The Making of a Labour Bureaucracy* (Toronto: University of Toronto Press, 1995).

Cecilia Danysk teaches history at Dalhousie University; her most recent publication is *Hired Hands: Labour and the Development of Prairie Agriculture, 1880-1930* (Toronto: McClelland and Stewart, 1995).

Catherine Cavanaugh teaches women's studies and history at Athabasca University and co-edited (with Randi Warne) *Standing on New Ground: Women in Alberta* (Edmonton: University of Alberta Press, 1993).

Timothy J. Stanley teaches education foundations at the University of Ottawa. His articles have appeared in *Canadian Historical Review*, *BC Studies*, and *Historical Studies in Education/Revue d'histoire de l'éducation*.

Jeremy Mouat teaches history at Athabasca University and is the author of *Roaring Days: Rossland's Mines and the History of British Columbia* (Vancouver: University of British Columbia Press, 1995).

Preface

The photograph on the book's cover shows two young women in Athabasca in 1911, dressed in men's clothes. Likely the pose was no more than an impulsive gesture of fun, but the pipes in their mouths and the garb of the Mounties offered a sly challenge to the dominant symbols of their world. We chose the picture to underline our own approach in this book. We also want to challenge some of the myths of the Canadian West.

Our challenge is to the books and articles that still dominate the historiography of Western Canada. Much of this work adopts an uncritical stance, providing readers with narratives of railways and Mounties, settlers and politicians. This literature assumes that the story has an obvious logic: all that happened was bound to happen. From this perspective, the historian's role is simply to embellish the chronicle with an appropriate scholarly apparatus: the precise date, the exact archival reference, the complete bibliography. This mythic history of Western Canada emphasises peaceful relations with Native peoples and celebrates rugged (male) pioneers, fur traders, explorers, and law & order heroes – usually police officers or judges. History is reduced to no more than a preordained march to the present, with actors displaying a seemly Canadian sense of peace, order and good government. The focus on personality and politics means that important aspects of the past are devalued. And this traditional view rarely acknowledges the difficulties that confront the historian: the ambiguities, the silences, and the too loud voices of the powerful.

The essays in this volume demonstrate the research interests of a new generation of scholars. For us, the past of western Canadian history is more complex than its depiction in the traditional literature. Our emphasis is on the ways in which society has been made: the extent to which it was and is the product of human agency, rather than having an intangible existence (and history) beyond the interaction of groups of people. These themes recur throughout the following chapters.

Our hope is that this book will be read by people in western Canada and that it will stimulate further interrogation of our past. The complacent narratives of an earlier period stand in need of revision, a process which will continue to engage our energy and imagination for some time to come. Many friends and colleagues are similarly engaged on the revisionary project; this collection is illustrative of much contemporary work but it is by no means definitive. We could have included the work of many other authors, some of whose work will be found in the bibliography at the end of the book. If there is a single obstacle to be overcome, it is that of apparent disinterest. While the "New Western" history in the United States has generated a great deal of controversy (and an impressive number of thoughtful books), in Canada people have been reluctant to engage in a similar searching critique of the myths of our western past. Clearly there is much work to be done.

We wish to thank our colleagues for agreeing to participate in this book, especially American historian, Elizabeth Jameson, for her thoughtful commentary. We are also grateful to Melodie Mayson-Richmond and Ted Richmond, our editors, and to Peter Saunders and staff at Garamond Press for making the production of this book relatively painless. Finally, we extend our sincere thanks to the various journals and publishers who permitted us to reproduce articles and chapters. (Sarah Carter's and Richard Rajala's essays have not been published before.) Lyle Dick's article is reproduced by kind permission of the Canadian Historical Association; it was originally published in the *Journal of the Canadian Historical Association/Revue de la Société historique du Canada*, New Series/Nouvelle Série, Vol. 2 (1991): 91-113. Tina Loo's article was published in Hamar Foster and John McLaren, eds., *Essays in the History of Canadian Law, Volume VI, British Columbia and the Yukon* (Toronto: University of Toronto Press, with the Osgoode Society, 1995), pp. 128-70, and we are grateful to the editors for allowing us to reprint it here. Mark Leier's article was originally published in the *Journal of History and Politics/Revue d'Histoire et de Politique*, Vol. 10 (1992): 87-108. Cecilia Danysk's essay is based on several chapters of her recent book, *Hired Hands: Labour and the Development of Prairie Agriculture, 1880-1930*, Toronto: McClelland and Stewart, 1995. Catherine Cavanaugh's article was originally published in the *Canadian Historical Review*, Vol. 74, #2 (June 1993): 198-225. Tim Stanley's article first appeared in *BC Studies*, #107 (Autumn 1995): 3-29. Jeremy Mouat's article was originally published in *Prairie Forum*, Vol. 17, No. 1 (Spring, 1992): 79-96. Again, our thanks to all of the above for granting us permission to reprint the essays in this volume.

CATHERINE CAVANAUGH & JEREMY MOUAT

Introduction

ELIZABETH JAMESON

M aking *Western Canada* challenges uncritical histories of a peaceful, orderly, and Anglo-centric Canadian West. Collectively, its authors suggest the potential of more inclusive histories based in the social relationships that knit the region's history. As a historian of the American West, I read these essays eagerly for the perspectives they bring to my own work. The new Canadian scholarship suggests comparative frameworks from which to consider common themes and questions.

What do we share, in our western histories and as historians, and where do our paths diverge? I think about these questions from a distant vantage on western Canada. Albuquerque, where I teach and live, began as a colonial settlement on the northern Spanish Mexican frontier. Herbert Eugene Bolton opened the study of the Spanish borderlands for American historians over seven decades ago, but the Canadian border has not, so far, generated an equivalent school of history.[1] What I know about the Spanish borderlands I learned largely because those borders shifted with the Mexican-American War, when northern Mexico became the southwestern United States. I know a bit of the history of the Canadian West, largely because some of the westerners I study have taken me there as they moved back and forth across the border. For the most part, however, my "expertise," such as it is, stops at the national boundary lines. Ecosystems, kin groups, economies, and people all cross those borders. Defining history as the story of nation states generates remarkable ignorance of our connected pasts.

I ponder all this from the New Mexico desert, wondering what I might possibly say to Canadian readers. James Keelaghan, fittingly enough, plays in the background.

Take a walk under my skies
Try to see it once the way I do
If you look out through my eyes
You'll find a different point of view[2]

How different? My Albuquerque skies this January morning are deep blue and sunny. Logging onto e-mail, Jeremy Mouat tells me the skies are overcast in Athabasca, but the weather has moderated from yesterday's forty below zero to a balmy minus twenty. That's as useful a metaphor as any to begin linking our histories. What is common under our western skies? Where do we offer one another a different point of view? Where do we draw the boundary lines – geographic, social, historical – of our respective Wests?

The western skies as metaphor, like the new western histories in this volume, invite us to examine the myths that have passed as the past. As a child, I learned to sing of a mythic "home on the range" where "the skies are not cloudy all day." That idyllic image entered the collective imagination as a vision of what made America and Americans. Under sunny western skies, the story went, rugged pioneers found a land of opportunity that nourished independence and democracy. Those opportunities constituted a national heritage, a common legacy, like the cloudless, open, western sky and the sun that shone down equally on all the rugged western folks.[3]

In a more sophisticated form, western opportunity anchored a major narrative of American history, Frederick Jackson Turner's "frontier thesis," still heatedly contested among adherents of the "new" and "old" western histories. American history, Turner announced in 1893, was "in a large degree the history of the colonization of the Great West. The existence of an area of free land, its continuous recession, and the advance of American settlement westward, explain American development."[4] What of Canadian development? Settlers' encounters with the land were not entirely different on the plains of North Dakota, Montana, Manitoba, and Saskatchewan. The underground workings of Butte and Cripple Creek were not wholly unlike the Rossland mines. The forests of Washington and Oregon bore some resemblance to British Columbia timbers. The same sun, presumably, sometimes shone on both sides of the border.

So what of Keelaghan's skies? Take a walk under *my* skies. What does the "my" mean? I can think of several interpretations, based in different definitions of western particularity. The first, which traditional historians of the American West eagerly claimed, had to do with the distinctiveness of westerners and the West. Turner's frontiers made westerners more individualistic, rebellious, and democratic than easterners. The frontier explained western lawlessness, western labor radicalism, woman suffrage, and a host of other "exceptional" behaviors. The West was different, too, because it was environmentally distinct. Aridity, in particular, defined the eastern boundary of the West.[5] These "exceptionalist" perspectives made "*our*" skies special because the West was different from the East.

New western histories challenge this simple story and emphasize a different sort of particularity, grounded in the diverse experiences of various westerners. The new West offers "different points of view" because differences of race, class, and gender gave people distinct perspectives on their pasts, and on the social and economic relationships that linked them. The authors of this anthology want to challenge a mythic Canadian West that resembles in many respects the mythic U.S. West. Both were, apparently, demographic anomalies, inhabited by a peculiarly limited cast of characters. Turner's sequence of frontiers – the dividing lines between "savagery and civilization" – belonged to Indian traders, hunters, soldiers, ranchers, miners, and farmers. The perspective was unremittingly white and masculine. There was no missionaries' frontier, no chicken raisers' or butter churners' frontier, and certainly no American Indian or Hispanic frontier.[6] The mythic Canadian West was not much different in its cast of fur traders, Mounties, judges, and homesteaders. If women or people of color appeared in these stories, they played supporting roles at best. More often they were acted upon by white men, who became the agents of progress, Manifest Destiny, and the inevitable triumph of civilization over savagery. The first challenge for new western historians in both countries was simply to include all the players, to cast indigenous peoples, ethnic immigrants, workers, and women as actors in their own lives.

In the United States these concerns led historians to focus on particular histories – *The Black West, Becoming Mexican American, Asian America, Peoples of Color in the American West, The Women's West.* The unequal power relationships that connected different "westerners" prompted us to reinterpret western history as *The Legacy of Conquest* or *The Roots of Dependency*. Richard White summed some of these power relationships in the old cowboy song he chose to name his recent synthesis, *"It's Your Misfortune and None of My Own"*.[7]

The new western histories emphasize diversity, difference, inequality, and power. The essays in this volume are diverse in their subjects, analytic strategies, questions, and conclusions. They emphasize human agency, plural perspectives, and daily processes of social construction. Most fundamentally, they question the partial histories we inherited. Lyle Dick begins with the issue of perspective. The same events appear different to different actors. Dick illustrates this point through multiple accounts of the Seven Oaks incident as told from Métis and Anglo-Canadian perspectives. Seven Oaks and the captivity narratives Sarah Carter explores help us to see how different histories supported changing historical and political agendas. We see, too, how race and gender function in different histories.

Catherine Cavanaugh and Cecilia Danysk elaborate the significance of class and gender, to analyze how homesteading differed for women and men, landowners and wage workers. Class analysis provides the framework for Richard Rajala's account of mechanization in the timber industry from the perspectives of workers and corporate managers. Mark Leier explores how the class perspectives of socialists and labor leaders generated differences about labor leadership and working-class policies. Timothy Stanley and Tina Loo analyze how racism separated the historical experiences of Anglo Canadians from those of Chinese Canadians and native peoples, and how the stories change when told from the perspectives of people of color.[8]

These diverse subjects make a larger point. The seemingly universal dome of western skies looked different from different social and historical perspectives. The West was different for the hired hand working a twine binder, the homesteader plowing his own field, and the woman fueling a prairie cookstove with buffalo chips. It was different for the miner toiling in darkness underground and the prostitute who toiled in a different darkness above, for Chipewyan fur trappers or Lakota buffalo hunters and the Chipewyan and Lakota women who tanned the hides, for Métis children, European fathers, and Native mothers. From each "point of view" we see a different slice of western sky.

Such diverse perspectives stretch the limits of older histories and their plots of inevitable progress. Analyzing differences of race, class, and gender is a hallmark of the new social history. These categories invite us to compare common themes and questions in the U.S. and Canadian Wests. We begin with the people who do not fit the western stories we inherited.

Canada and the United States were both colonized by Europeans whose perspectives defined our histories. More inclusive narratives would start with the native peoples whose histories predate national boundary lines. Some of the most stimulating scholarship for comparative purposes explores Indians' roles in the U.S. and Canadian fur trades, and different state policies toward native peoples.[9] We need to extend these efforts. We must move beyond European and national frameworks to compare the particular migrations that created our racially and ethnically diverse Wests. French and Ukrainian immigrants, for instance, were proportionately more significant in Canada; Spanish-Mexican and Mexican-American settlement was more important in the U.S.; Asian immigration was more significant on both west coasts than further inland. Some migrations engendered similar racist reactions, such as the U.S. and Canadian Asian Exclusion laws and Japanese internment during World War II.[10] Others, like the United States' Mexican immigration policies, defined regional particularities. These topics invite comparisons of how our respective Euro- centricities were enacted in the histories of western race relations, of what brought peoples from different parts of the world to the American and Canadian Wests, and how immigrants forged new identities and options for themselves.

The ways we have defined race offers another topic for comparison. Spanish and Canadian racial categories appear less dichotomous, from my outside viewpoint, than the racial system that was enacted in the U.S. West. Spain recognized a variety of racial categories to describe mestizo (mixed-race) peoples, just as Canada recognized Métis as a particular racial category.[11] U.S. racial policies more often assigned minority racial status to a person with any "colored blood." These differences emphasize that race is not "natural," but a social creation, and invite further comparative analyses of how we have constructed race and race relations.

The new histories of western women suggest similar topics for comparative gender analysis. The mythic Wests marginalized women and defined their roles from Euro-American and Anglo-Canadian assumptions about domesticity. If women achieved "western opportunity" in these stories, they did so in political terms, because women voted first in western states and provinces. Western women's historians advocated broader frameworks, that include women of all races and that focus less narrowly on Anglo pioneers.[12] Even those pioneers of the traditional West might benefit from comparative analysis, however. Western women's historians have begun to explore women's own activism for the vote. We could gain a great deal from a comparative analysis of suffrage campaigns throughout the West, and from comparing the politics of western race and gender. It would be instructive, for instance, to explore when various states and provinces enfranchised women, African Americans, native peoples, and Asian immigrants, and when national legislation was required.

Several of these essays suggest further comparisons. Catherine Cavanaugh opens the subject of women's comparative access to western lands. The U.S. Homestead Act of 1862 allowed women, for the first time, to acquire an independent stake in the land by permitting women to homestead on the same terms as men, if they were single women or heads of households.[13] Canadian women could homestead independently only in extremely limited circumstances. We have yet to explore how these differences affected women's organizing in both countries, or the ways that women understood the value of their own labor on western farms. Cavanaugh's focus on the Homestead Dower opens an important area for comparative analysis. Cecilia Danysk suggests the largely unexplored subject of how masculinity was constructed in the western U.S. and Canada, a topic with enormous potential to challenge the mythic characters of all the old Wests. Sarah Carter suggests a further possibility in her analysis of how race and gender functioned in particular histories. Images of frail white women and rapacious Indian men, for instance, justified narratives of conquest and colonization in both Canada and the United States.

Mark Leier and Richard Rajala suggest comparative class analyses. Rajala emphasizes labor and management strategies that were implemented throughout the western lumber industry, in Oregon and Washington as well as British Columbia. Leier engages a debate about western labor radicalism that parallels a U.S. discourse about the exceptional "radicalism" of western labor. His class analysis of the socialist and labor leaderships suggests a fruitful approach for the United States. By following workers and capital across national boundaries, we may explore how common industries and economic relationships affected western development. In the process we should discard western exceptionalism, since the same "exceptional" qualities were ascribed to Canadians and Americans alike, and provoked the same challenges.[14] Commonalities in our regional economies and class relationships suggest instead that we explore what the Canadian and U.S. Wests shared, and what distinguished them both from central Canada and the eastern United States.

We approach the possibilities of new histories through the old ones we have learned. In traditional western histories, the stories of state and nation diminish the agency of the diverse peoples who forged regional identities and social relationships. We might usefully compare the place that western settlement occupies in our national histories. There is, so far as I know, no Canadian equivalent to the Turnerian narrative, no interpretation that suggests that the Canadian character was shaped by the availability of free land on the western prairies and beyond. Because the West has not "explained" Canadians, there has been, apparently, less controversy, rancour, and interest regarding the new western histories in Canada than in the United States.

We need to analyze how our mythic Wests differed. The American West, for instance, was characterized as wild, lawless, and disorderly; traditional histories of the Canadian West emphasized peace and order. Were these differences real, or were they narrative strategies to explain national development? Order and lawlessness may distinguish our different routes to independence. They may also reflect the fact that state power largely preceded white settlers in the Canadian West, and followed Euro-American settlement in the U.S. Whatever their origins, these values create interesting differences among the characters of mythic western narratives. The "civilizer" role assigned white women in the U.S. West appears to characterize Canadian men as well, like the judges and Mounties who enforced civilized behavior. Did these idealized traits reflect actual lived experience? Was the Canadian West in fact much more peaceful and orderly than the American West? Were Canadian men, for instance, less likely to fight or beat their wives than American men, or more apt to face community censure if they did? How do regional histories illuminate the connections between idealized national characteristics and daily behaviours?

Mythic histories of westward movement served the metaphorical purpose of separating us from our European roots. Turner's frontier theory was a direct challenge to histories that located the "germs" of American institutions in Europe. The mythic westward journey did not take us, however, to the diverse people who settled the West, or to the tangled roots of western communities. Instead, the old histories gave us a single narrative from which to construct a new and common national identity. The limits of those national creation stories open new possibilities for more inclusive western histories that cross our national boundary lines.

New western historians have all challenged the mythic histories we inherited. We now face the difficult task of imagining new narratives of diverse and plural Wests. We might begin, as Jeremy Mouat suggests, by examining the work of artists who have explored new forms for western stories. Before there was a new western history, there was a new western literature. Its authors, too, grappled with issues of perspective, diversity, chronology, causality, and asked which stories are important to write into our collective memory.[15] They offered stories of accommodations and limits, and crafted pessimistic counterpoints to the mythic West. One of the leading new western authors was Wallace Stegner, whose own journey crossed our national borders, and whose words in *Wolf Willow* inspired Keelaghan's western skies. Stegner, who celebrated the West as "the native home of hope," encouraged us to abandon the old West. "The West does not need to explore its myths much further; it has already relied on them too long."[16]

Our western myths are, increasingly, common caricatures. As Tina Loo suggests, the Lone Ranger and Tonto are part of a Canadian cultural legacy, just as Sergeant Preston and King are part of mine. *Making Western Canada* takes us far beyond the limits of common myths and stereotypes. Its authors suggest many possible routes to more accurate and inclusive histories of the Canadian West. A number of those routes link our histories. Big Bear, Theresa Delaney, bachelor farmhands, migratory lumberjacks, and many others we meet in these pages moved back and forth across our borders. We might well join them. They pose enough interesting questions to fuel our conversations for years to come. They may lead us to the Wests that we inherit. They may help us find our ways home.

Notes

1. See especially Bolton's *The Spanish Borderlands: A Chronicle of Old Florida and the Southwest* (New Haven: Yale University Press; Toronto: Glasgow, Brook; London: H. Milford, Oxford University Press, 1921), and for recent scholarship, see David J. Weber, *The Idea of the Spanish Borderlands* (New York: Garland, 1991).
2. James Keelaghan, "My Skies," words and music © James Keelaghan. Thanks to Jeremy Mouat, who sent me the CD and introduced me to Keelaghan.
3. Western skies are in vogue these days in western history circles. Two recent books are William Cronon, George Miles and Jay Gitlin, eds., *Under An Open Sky* (New York: W.W. Norton, 1992) and Donald Worster, *Under Western Skies: Nature and History in the American West* (New York: Oxford University Press, 1992).
4. Frederick Jackson Turner, "The Significance of the Frontier in American History," in Martin Ridge, ed., *History, Frontier, and Section: Three Essays by Frederick Jackson Turner* (Albuquerque: University of New Mexico Press, 1993), p. 59. Turner first delivered "The Significance of the Frontier" as a paper at the American Historical Association meeting in Chicago, July 12, 1893.
5. John Wesley Powell, the 19th century explorer who became the country's most thoughtful interpreter of the arid West, placed its boundary at the 100th meridian. A number of historians subsequently explored how westerners adapted to the treeless and arid Plains. See particularly Walter Prescott Webb, *The Great Plains* (1931; New York: Grossett and Dunlap, 1971). Aridity, a measure that excludes the Pacific Northwest, engendered considerable controversy about environmental definitions of region. We have not, so far, followed the Canadian example of separating the prairies and British Columbia as regions. Instead, American historians debated the relative merits of frontier and region as organizing principles for our histories, and devoted considerable energy to drawing the precise boundaries of "the West." A comparison of the Canadian and U.S. Wests would surely address these questions of regional definition.
6. Turner, pp. 66-71. William Cronon, Howard R. Lamar, Katherine G. Morrissey, and Jay Gitlin called attention to the ways that male work roles defined American frontiers. Women's work never became the basis for a frontier classification, so we do not speak of a "chicken frontier" as we do of a "cattle frontier," though there is no logical reason not to. See Cronon, et al, "Women and the West: Rethinking the Western History Survey Course," *Western Historical Quarterly* XVII: 3 (July 1986): 269-90, 272-73.
7. William Loren Katz, *The Black West* (Garden City, N.Y.: Anchor Press, 1973); George J. Sánchez, *Becoming Mexican American: Ethnicity, Culture and Identity in Chicano Los Angeles, 1900-1945* (New York: Oxford University Press, 1993); Roger Daniels, *Asian America: Chinese and Japanese in the United States Since 1850,* (Seattle: University of Washington Press, 1850); Sucheng Chan, Douglas Henry Daniels, Mario T. García, and Terry P. Wilson, eds., *Peoples of Color in the American West*

(Lexington, Mass.: D.C. Heath and Company, 1994); Susan Armitage and Elizabeth Jameson, eds., *The Women's West* (Norman: University of Oklahoma Press, 1987); Patricia Nelson Limerick, *The Legacy of Conquest: The Unbroken Past of the American West* (New York: W.W. Norton & Company, 1987); Richard White, *The Roots of Dependency: Subsistence, Environment, and Social Change among the Choctaws, Pawnees, and Navajos* (Lincoln: University of Nebraska Press, 1983); Richard White, *"It's Your Misfortune and None of My Own": A New History of the American West* (Norman: University of Oklahoma Press, 1991).

8. For more on these issues in the American West, see Elizabeth Jameson and Susan Armitage, eds., *Writing the Range: Race, Class, and Culture in the Women's West* (Norman: University of Oklahoma Press, forthcoming 1997).

9. See especially Sylvia Van Kirk, *Many Tender Ties: Women in Fur Trade Society, 1670-1870* (Norman: University of Oklahoma Press, 1983); Jennifer S. H. Brown, *Strangers in Blood: Fur Trade American Families in Indian Country* (Vancouver: University of British Columbia Press, 1980); William R. Swagerty, "Marriage and Settlement Patterns of Rocky Mountain Trappers and Traders," *Western Historical Quarterly* 11:2 (April 1980): 159-80; Jacqueline Peterson and Jennifer S. H. Brown, *The New Peoples: Being and Becoming Métis in North America* (Winnipeg: University of Manitoba Press, 1985); Jacqueline Peterson, "Ethnogenesis: Settlement and Growth of a 'New People'," *American Indian Culture and Research Journal* 6 (1982): 22-64; Jacqueline Peterson, "The People in Between: Indian: White Marriage and the Genesis of a Métis Society: Society and Culture in the Great Lakes Region, 1680-1830," (Ph.D. dissertation, University of Illinois at Chicago Circle, 1981).

10. See Sucheng Chan, ed., *Entry Denied* (Philadelphia: Temple University Press, 1991); Roger Daniels, *Concentration Camps USA: Japanese Americans and World War II* (1971; New York: Holt, Rinehart and Winston, 1981); Roger Daniels, *The Decision to Relocate the Japanese Americans* (Philadelphia: Lipincott, 1975).

11. In the Spanish colonies, an intricate system of ethnic designation connected class and race. Among the "Spanish Mexican" colonizers were people of Spanish, Indian, and African ancestries. Their colonial system recognized a variety of racial-ethnic categories, including a variety of mixed-race categories that testified to the intermingling of all these groups: mestizos (persons descended from Spaniards and Mexican Indians), coyotes (Spanish and New Mexican Indian), mulatos (usually African and Spanish, but sometimes used to designate Spanish and Indian), lobos (a racial mixture), color quebrado (a racial mixture, possibly of any combination of white, Indian, and African descent) and genizaros (de-tribalized Indians). See Virginia L. Olmsted, Introduction to the 1790 Spanish colonial census of the Province of New Mexico, together with the 1823 and 1845; Fray Angelico Chávez, *Archives of the Archdiocese of Santa Fe, 1678-1900* (Washington, D.C.: Academy of American Franciscan History, 1957), p. 201.

12. Armitage and Jameson, *The Women's West*; Lillian Schlissel, Vicki Ruíz, and Janice Monk, eds., *Western Women: Their Lives, Their Land* (Albuquerque: University of New Mexico Press, 1988); Joan M. Jensen and Darlis A. Miller, "The Gentle Tamers Revisited: New Approaches to the History of Women in the American West," *Pacific Historical Review* 49:2 (May 1980): 173-213; Elizabeth Jameson, "Toward a Multicultural History of Women in the Western United States," *Signs* 13:4 (Summer 1988): 761-91.

13. Sheryll Patterson-Black, "Women Homesteaders on the Great Plains Frontier," *Frontiers* 1:2 (Spring 1976): 67-88; H. Elaine Lindgren, *Land in Her Own Name: Women Homesteaders in North Dakota* (Fargo: The North Dakota Institute for Regional Studies, North Dakota State University, 1991); Paula Nelson, "No Place for Clinging Vines: Women Homesteaders on the South Dakota Frontier," (M.A. thesis, University of South Dakota, 1978).

14. The origins and consequences of radicalism in western hardrock mining have been much debated. See especially Vernon H. Jensen, *Heritage of Conflict Labor Relations in the Nonferrous Metals Industry up to 1930* (Ithaca, New York: Cornell University Press, 1950); Melvyn Dubofsky, "The Origins of Western Working-Class Radicalism, 1890-1905," *Labor History*, 7 (Spring 1966): 131-154, and Richard E. Lingenfelter, *The Hardrock Miners: A History of the Mining Labor Movement in the American West, 1863-1893* (Berkeley: University of California Press, 1974). Scholars have advanced various – often competing – explanations, including frontier lawlessness, the lack of a stabilizing middle class, social isolation, and responses to rapid and dislocating industrialization. Works that question the characterization of the union as radical – on various grounds and to varying degrees – include James C. Foster, "Quantification and the Western Federation," *Historical Methods Newsletter* 10 (Fall 1977): 141-48, esp. 143; Richard H. Peterson, "Conflict and Consensus: Labor Relations in Western Mining," *Journal of the West* 12 (January 1973): 1-17; and Mark Wyman, *Hard Rock Epic: Western Miners and the Industrial Revolution, 1860-1910* (Berkeley: University of California Press, 1979). For a Canadian challenge to exceptionalist interpretations see Jeremy Mouat, "The Genesis of Western Exceptionalism: British Columbia's Hard Rock Miners, 1895-1903," *Canadian Historical Review* 71:3 (September 1990): 317-45.

15. I am thinking, for instance, of the work of William Kittredge, M. Scott Momaday, Louise Erdrich, Denise Chàvez, Rudolfo Anaya, Maxine Hong Kingston, Sallie Tisdale, Leslie Marmon Silko. To name a few. For a recent history that grapples with postmodern perspectives in a historical narrative, see Joan M. Jensen, *One Foot on the Rockies: Women and Creativity in the American West* (Albuquerque: University of New Mexico Press, 1995).

16. Quotes from Stegner's obituary, *The New York Times*, April 15, 1993. Keelaghan quotes from *Wolf Willow* on the notes to *My Skies*: ". . .over the segmented circle of the earth is domed the biggest sky anywhere. . . ."

1

The Seven Oaks Incident and

the Construction of a Historical

Tradition, 1816 to 1970

LYLE DICK

Voulez-vous écouter chanter
Une chanson de vérité?[1]

PIERRE FALCON, "CHANSON DE LA GRENOUILLÈRE," 1816

Each [the historian and the poet] is a maker of myths, only the historian has ne-
glected his job of making myths in this decadent, analytical age.[2]

W. L. MORTON, 1943

It is to be regretted that in a war of this kind, a very painful duty devolves on the
narrator . . . for lawyers and commissioners will not be satisfied with "I was in-
formed of this," or "I was told of that," but, "Who were the persons that in-
formed you," is the point in question.[3]

COLIN ROBERTSON TO PETER IRVING, DECEMBER 1818

In 1891, the Manitoba Historical Society dedicated the province's first historical monument, a stone cairn to commemorate the Seven Oaks incident, a violent clash in 1816 between a group of Hudson's Bay Company (HBC) officers and Selkirk settlers and a party of Métis traders from Red River and the upper Assiniboine. The monument's brief inscription contrasted with a growing body of writings on this controversial event, a collection made larger by the society's simultaneous release of a pamphlet to mark the occasion.[4] The pamphlet included excerpts from previously published accounts of the battle or its contexts by two prominent Manitoba historians of the period – George Bryce, an academic, and Charles N. Bell, an amateur. The combination of these excerpts had a retrospective historiographical significance: it was the last time that two competing interpretations of Seven Oaks appeared under one cover, the last time that one version was not rewritten, overwritten, or erased by its rival.

The pamphlet's publication simultaneously marked the eclipse of one tradition of English-language writing on Seven Oaks and the inauguration of another. The outgoing tradition. represented by Bell's text, comprised a series of writings on the event by amateurs with ties to Old Red River or witnesses with direct knowledge of the event. The ascendant tradition, represented by Bryce's version and his academic successors in the West, drew instead from treatments earlier advanced by Lord Selkirk, the Hudson's Bay Company, and their sympathizers, and now promoted to orthodoxy by the newly dominant Anglo-Canadian immigrant group in the West. Yet Bryce's and Bell's texts contrasted in more ways than the interpretative conclusions they drew from the event. They differed sharply in techniques of collection, evaluation, and presentation of empirical evidence; in the handling of contradictory or contentious material; even in the definition of what constituted appropriate empirical evidence. Further, the selection of particular structures of historical representation revealed the diverging ideological positions of these authors. The differences between Bryce and Bell in methodology, interpretation, and form bear upon larger issues than the reconstruction of the Seven Oaks incident and go to the root of history-making in Western Canada. They chart a trajectory from the raw pluralistic origins of prairie historiography in the early nineteenth-century controversies over Seven Oaks to the polished hierarchical structures of twentieth-century historical writing. An intensive investigation of treatments of this single event reveals much about the historiographical process in Western Canada, and about the role of history in the construction of cultural traditions.

Such a reconsideration also occasions a reexamination of the respective roles of amateurs and professionals in Canadian prairie historiography. In

The Writing of Canadian History, Carl Berger argues that serious written history only began with the creation of an academic discipline.[5] Nineteenth-century "clergymen, lawyers, and journalists" wrote history "to amuse themselves, to commemorate the eminent, to strengthen patriotism, or to draw morals from the past"; twentieth-century professionals practised the "critical study of the Canadian past." For Berger, these developments represent "a decisive change in the nature of historical study." Similar arguments have been advanced by other Canadian intellectual historians. M. Brook Taylor argues that nineteenth-century historical writing was characterised by amateur partisanship,[6] while A. B. McKillop credits the late nineteenth-century academics George Wrong at the University of Toronto and George Bryce at the University of Manitoba with initiating a "serious attempt to examine original sources" and "introducing principles of historical criticism into Canadian historiography."[7]

None of these writers devotes much attention to the actual *writing* of history: methods of research, forms of argument, or structures of historical representation. Instead, these works are thematic discussions of the subjects Canadian historians choose, combined with group biographies of its practitioners. There is no substantive discussion of how these new twentieth-century professionals improved the techniques of the nineteenth-century amateurs.

A historiographical reconsideration of the Seven Oaks incident presents a rare opportunity to test Berger's thesis. With the exception of Bryce's early writings, all of the texts on the battle written before the 1890s were prepared by amateurs, while the English-language texts of historiographical significance thereafter were by professionals. Moreover, the survival of oral tradition on Seven Oaks, specifically Pierre Falcon's "Chanson de la Grenouillère," affords the opportunity for alternative perspectives on the event from outside the realm of the written word. The presence of oral tradition and amateur texts outside the mainstream historiography facilitates an interrogation of long-standing notions about the boundaries of legitimate historical discourse in Canada.

Rather than provide a historiographical survey, culminating in an improved, factual reconstruction, this paper proposes to deconstruct the various versions of Seven Oaks by drawing on basic methods from literary and linguistic criticism, and focusing on the relationships between "story" and "discourse,"[8] two narrative functions integral to any historical reconstruction. Contemporary theorists have argued that all forms of historical narrative constitute a content independent of the "facts" they subsume.[9] An analysis of writing on Seven Oaks suggests that literary strategies not only influenced the writers' selection and ordering of particular historical data, but actually required both the production of supporting "facts" and the negation or omission of alternative "facts." Moreover, the inherently allegorical character of historical discourse inevitably generates meanings on both literal and metaphorical levels.[10] This paper will also consider the extent to which the discourse on Seven Oaks could be explained by the concept of "master narrative," an overarching cultural allegory which explains an entire tradition of writing on the event.

That said, history itself is not a text, though it is accessible mainly through the spoken or written word. There is an obvious need to investigate the existing literature and the primary sources to establish the reported facts or basic "story" from which the discourse on Seven Oaks has been constructed.

Most writing on Seven Oaks occurred in the period of controversy immediately following the event, and later in the hundred years between 1870 and 1970. The enormous volume of literature of the early period largely falls under the rubric of partisan pamphleteering by the contending parties or their representatives.[11] The primary source materials also include the transcripts of subsequent trials of participants in the battle,[12] the surviving sworn depositions of various witnesses to Seven Oaks and related events,[13] and a voluminous correspondence between government officials and representatives of either Lord Selkirk or the principals of the North West Company (NWC).[14] Finally, the period record includes the report of William Bachelor Coltman, the principal commissioner appointed to investigate the Seven Oaks incident and other violent episodes associated with the fur companies' rivalry.[15]

Coltman's report in particular warrants close attention. The most detailed and comprehensive analysis ever prepared on the Seven Oaks incident, it has been largely ignored in the dominant Anglo-Canadian historiography. Its neglect in its own period might be attributed to several factors, beginning with the multipurpose mandate accorded Coltman and his fellow commissioner, John Fletcher, and its frosty reception by the Selkirk side. In his instructions to the commissioners, Governor Sherbrooke charged them with a number of roles, to serve, alternately, as investigators, enforcers, and peacemakers.[16] It was Coltman's prosecution of these latter powers as a justice of the peace which occasioned an almost immediate and continuing series of attacks on his impartiality by the Selkirk party.

Coltman's peacemaking and law enforcement roles apparently also disqualified his report from the serious attention of Anglo-Canadian historians after 1870. Not until 1910, when George Bryce praised the report as "admirable" and "fairly impartial," was it mentioned in the literature.[17] In summarising its contents in 1939, A. S. Morton stated that "the detailed report describes the acts of violence with great particularity, on the whole accurately and with a great show of impartiality."[18] Even John Morgan Gray, who was critical of Coltman's role as commissioner, endorsed aspects of his report.[19] When it came to Seven Oaks, however, these historians utilised neither the report's data nor its conclusions. Bypassing as well the original testimony on which it was based, they chose instead to rely on mediations of these sources, that is, on representations of representations.

Coltman's research methodology derived from his legal experience as a justice of the peace,[20] and more generally from the inductive approach of Baconian science. To establish the facts of Seven Oaks and related incidents, he or his colleague, John Fletcher, examined under oath a large selection of witnesses. Each voluntary deposition[21] was transcribed, sworn, and signed. Of the thirty-three depositions or statements concerning Seven Oaks which were identified by name, sixteen were taken from Selkirk settlers or HBC employees, and seventeen from Métis or NWC witnesses. Coltman therefore appears even-handed in the compilation of evidence and in bringing all of it forward in his analysis.[22]

Beyond the adducing of evidence, Coltman's techniques of examination were derivative of contemporary British courtroom practice. He endeavoured to determine the credibility of the individual witnesses by examining their depositions for internal consistency, or by comparing their statements on specific points made on different occasions. In keeping with contemporary civil procedure, he also made an effort to establish the relative weight of evidence. He operated according to the convention, current in eighteenth-century civil jurisprudence, that stress must be placed on the character of the witness.[23] Regarding evidence submitted by the fur companies, he was more sceptical. His approach was to consider these writings as "moral evidence," useful in establishing admissions by these parties, but not to be taken as proof.[24] Various legal issues pertaining to the broader conflict of which Seven Oaks formed a part were also discussed at length in both this report and in a shorter, confidential memorandum he sent to Sherbrooke a week before formally submitting the *Statement*.[25]

Coltman's reconstitution of Seven Oaks comprises a massive discussion in its own right. Here it is useful to focus only on those contentious points which have been most prominent in the event's subsequent historiography. These include the issues of which party fired the first shot, the extent to which the battle was a premeditated "massacre," the allegations of "finishing-off" the wounded, the alleged mutilation and plunder of the bodies, and the claim that the Métis abandoned them on the field to be devoured by wild animals.

Coltman unambiguously concluded that the first shot was fired by the Selkirk party. He referred to testimony by two Métis witnesses that a member of Semple's party fired the first shot at François Boucher, a ball which passed so close that it caused him to fall off his horse. Joseph Pelletier also claimed that the Semple side fired a second shot at an Indian in the Métis camp, before the firing became general.[26] Three other witnesses gave similar testimony.[27] The Selkirk witness Michael Hayden disputed their testimony, but acknowledged that Lieutenant Holte of Semple's party had fired a shot beforehand by accident.[28] Coltman concluded that the weight of evidence obliged him to reject the allegation of a precipitous Métis attack.

On a strict examination of the evidence, the commissioner also concluded that the battle could not appropriately be considered a "massacre." Noting that the Semple side had begun the battle, he surmised that it continued until "the whole either fell or ran off." In his opinion the casualties on the Hudson's Bay side had been increased by their "standing together in a crowd, unaccustomed to the use of fire-arms, or any of the practices of irregular warfare," while their opponents were "all excellent marksmen, advantageously posted in superior numbers around their opponents, and ac-

customed as huntsmen, and from the habits of Indian warfare, to every device that could tend to their own preservation, or the destruction of their
enemy."[29]

On the other hand, in considering whether the wounded had been "finished off," Coltman found it self-evident that scarcely one half of those
killed would have been mortally wounded by the first volley. He therefore
concluded that the wounded must have been "finished off" after the outbreak of hostilities. Coltman judged that the evidence pointed to the northern members of the fur brigade; specifically mentioned were François
Deschamps, a French-Canadian living in the Northwest, and three of his
sons as the individuals responsible.[30] He attributed their actions to a Native
custom of taking no prisoners, and suggested that a mercenary approach
was the only security available to individuals operating in this context.

Coltman examined the issue of whether the wounded members of the
Selkirk party tried to surrender, and concluded that the only two men to
have done so were Pritchard, who was spared, and Rodgers, who was not.
He noted that a number of Métis witnesses acknowledged that Rodgers had
been finished off while pleading for mercy, but they identified "Grossetête,"
a son of Deschamps, as the guilty party. Coltman noted that Hayden also
gave contrary testimony, alleging a general massacre of wounded men trying to surrender, but he found Hayden to be an inaccurate witness.

Regarding the mutilation and pillaging of the dead bodies, Coltman concluded that these alleged occurrences were established by a "mass of evidence"; he cited nine depositions as proof. Yet, here again, he found it important to distinguish between the actions of particular individuals and the
conduct of the group, as only a few persons were said to have "partaken of
these spoils." The Deschamps were identified as the men carrying off the
largest share of the plunder, although witnesses also claimed to have seen
others with articles of clothing or arms.[31]

Coltman also examined the allegations of Frederick Damien Huerter
that the Métis left the dead bodies of their fallen adversaries on the field for
an extended period to be preyed upon by birds and animals. He referred to
evidence to the contrary from both the Selkirk and Métis sides, which
tended to confirm that the bodies were duly buried.[32] He therefore considered Huerter's testimony to be coloured by "exaggeration," and also ques-

tioned this witness's reliability in that he had abandoned the service of one employer, the NWC, to become "an open and active partizan" of the HBC.[33]

These highlights of Coltman's treatment of Seven Oaks hardly do justice to his extremely comprehensive analysis. Whatever his personal biases or the constraints of his mandate, his assemblage of a myriad of reported facts on Seven Oaks established most of the evidentiary base available to subsequent histories of this event. These data comprise much of the "story" to be considered in evaluating the "discourse" of the event's historians. His methods of collection, adducing, and evaluation of evidence also set a standard of historical research against which his successors might fairly be judged.

The indigenous historiography of Seven Oaks in Western Canada begins with Pierre Falcon's "Chanson de la Grenouillère," said to have been composed by a Métis witness immediately following the battle. Throughout the Red River period, and long afterward, the predominantly oral culture of the Métis preserved its memory of Seven Oaks by singing this song as an expression of ethnic pride and national identity.[34] Despite its status as an eye-witness account, or at least a version based on eye-witness accounts, it was almost never cited as a source in reconstructions of the event.[35]

With regard to its content, the song presented information on both the historical background and the event itself. Falcon treated the English as having come to pillage their country; he acknowledged that, prior to the engagement, the Métis had taken three prisoners; and he related that they discerned Semple's party as coming out to attack them, and that they turned to meet their adversaries. He stated that Semple ordered his men to fire on them, and recounted a number of other details, including an admission that the Métis killed most of Semple's men, chasing them from mound to mound.

On the level of discourse, Falcon's song made few concessions to rhetoric to enlist its audience's concurrence with its claims. The 1816 version was quite unpolished, showing irregular metrical patterns, imperfect rhyming, and an absence of alliteration. The contents of this hastily composed account evidently were determined more by the desire to relate particular details than the discourse needs of a particular literary structure.

Jan Vansina has drawn attention to the pitfalls of relying exclusively on oral tradition as historical evidence. In being passed on from the original observer to others by word of mouth, a story is reinterpreted by each performer in the chain of transmission.[36] Yet Falcon's song is a rare example of oral tradition on a historical event for which there is also voluminous textual evidence. Note that, in a number of its details, it corresponds closely to sworn testimony at the trials in central Canada and depositions taken by Commissioners Coltman and Fletcher. Its significance as a historical source derives principally from its status as an authentic expression of Métis perceptions and attitudes toward the events of 19 June 1816.

Alexander Ross's 1856 book *The Red River Settlement* is the first published account by an author from the region. Moreover, it is apparently the first account to rely largely on written evidence: the only specific references he cites are to a published transcription of the trials. Ross also pioneered in making Seven Oaks an episode in a structured version of the region's history, and in self-consciously employing literary models to this end.

Ross's interpretive framework is uncomplicated: it is a straightforward expression of the theme of "civilisation versus savagery" which was to become so prominent in Western Canadian historiography. On the critical issue of who initiated hostilities, Ross asserted that "there has never been a shadow of doubt . . . that the North-West Company did unquestionably fire the first shot, and almost all the shots that were fired."[37] As evidence, he cited both the testimony of Michael Hayden at the Seven Oaks murder trials in Canada, and Chief Justice Powell's charge to the jury, in which Powell is said to have accepted Hayden's testimony that the Métis fired the first two shots. (Ross here seems to have misread the transcript. Powell clearly states that the evidence on this point is contradictory.[38]) There is no reference to Coltman's report or any suggestion that Ross read it.

What Ross's account lacked in empirical data it made up in imaginative conjecture. The final "proof" offered of the North West Company's guilt was the author's assertion that twenty-six of Semple's opponents at Seven Oaks subsequently met violent or sudden deaths. Ross took their supposed fate as confirmation of a kind of divine retribution on sinners.[39] His foray into occult models of historical explanation has been reproduced occasionally over the course of Seven Oaks historiography, in books by J. J. Hargrave, Mercer Adam, George Bryce, A. C. Garrioch and, most recently, Peter C. Newman.[40]

Ross's account of Seven Oaks cannot be separated from the overall narrative structure of his book. For him, Western Canadian history began with the granting of the Hudson's Bay Company charter in 1670, while he hailed the "real object" of Selkirk's scheme as "the pious and philanthropic desire of introducing civilization into the wilderness."[41] The remainder of his book elaborated this theme. It was a sustained effort by Ross to privilege his own European ethnicity in opposition to the posited savagery of all Native peoples within the Red River settlement, including persons of mixed race.

The narrative purpose of these assorted characterizations becomes apparent at the end of the book, when a discussion of the Pembina Métis functions to set off the hero of Ross's narrative, the entrepreneur Alexander McDermot. The Métis are presented as creatures of whim, contrasting with the purposeful entrepreneurship of McDermot.[42] These depictions function as a backdrop to Ross's advocacy of several causes, including an enforced dispersal and separation of Native groups from the colony and the transfer of oligarchic control from the HBC to a core of formally educated residents such as himself.

Ross's partisan conclusions could command credibility because the book was published in London for an audience with little knowledge of the region or people he was writing about. The subordination of Seven Oaks to ideological imperatives far removed from the original disputes within which it occurred was a tradition which prevailed after 1870. While Ross was not an academic, his interpretations were embraced by post-Confederation professional and popular historians alike, and provided the basis for many of the stereotypes of the Métis that would be reproduced over and over again, to infinite regress.

A contemporary of Ross, Donald Gunn took a different approach to the representation of Seven Oaks. While Gunn's account was not published until 1880, it reflected local knowledge of the event and belongs to Red River historiography rather than the Canadian period after 1870. Gunn's career in Red River paralleled Ross's in a number of respects, in that he settled there in the 1820s, served as a teacher and magistrate in the community, and was critical of the Hudson's Bay Company's role in the settlement.[43] Unlike Ross, however, he did not aspire to political dominance in the community, and his writing reflects his more populist sympathies.

Gunn's *History of Manitoba*[44] differs from Ross's treatment in more than its interpretive conclusions. It reflects a completely different approach to collecting and presenting evidence and to the ways in which the author inserted Seven Oaks into his larger text. Gunn presented the battle as the culmination of a series of aggressions committed by the HBC on the NWC. Noting an initial lack of animosity between the NWC and the Selkirk settlers, he attributed the deterioration in their relations to attempts by Selkirk to use Red River as a base from which to destroy the Nor'-Westers' trade. Among the listed HBC "outrages" was Miles Macdonell's "Pemmican Proclamation" which, in his view, inflamed the situation to the point of confrontation.

Regarding Seven Oaks, his approach was to present two versions of the event – one from the HBC sympathizer John Pritchard, and the other from the North West Company side. He referred to evidence assembled after the coalition of the two companies: "When party interest required no longer to be propped up by any fabrications that would serve that purpose, all parties agreed in acknowledging that the first shot was from Lieutenant Holt's piece, which went off accidentally."[45] Gunn limited himself to a discussion of actions, without resorting to ontological explanations of innate Native savagery, as in Ross's account. Nor is there an obvious "point" to his history, which simply ends in 1835 without interpretive conclusions.

Gunn's more pluralistic approach was echoed by one other Red River historian, J. J. Hargrave. The son of Chief Factor James Hargrave and himself an employee of the HBC,[46] Hargrave, unlike Ross or Gunn, was a HBC sympathizer. His account of Seven Oaks reflected the company's viewpoint, although his relegation of the discussion to an appendix suggests the minor significance attributed to the event in the Red River era.[47] Hargrave summarised the respective versions of both sides of the conflict and also reproduced Falcon's song, observing that it "gives, I have no doubt, a truthful description of the light in which the author, along with doubtless the majority of his comrades, regarded the appearance and intentions of Governor Semple and his followers."[48] Never again was Falcon's song accorded credibility as a legitimate account of the Seven Oaks incident. Nor, with the exception of Ross, were any of the other amateur versions from the pre-1870 era given legitimacy as historical accounts.

In 1870 the HBC ceded Rupert's Land to Britain, Britain transferred it to Canada, and the Red River colony ceased to be. Within only two decades, the large-scale influx of Anglo-Ontarian immigrants radically altered Manitoba's ethnic mix from a mixed-blood majority of Red River settlers with approximate parity in numbers between French and English, to the overwhelming dominance of the white, Anglo-Canadian newcomers. These new arrivals rapidly became the region's ruling group. While they claimed the region's best farmlands[49] and established their business dominance in the cities,[50] they nevertheless lacked the cultural traditions that could legitimise their political and economic power. Their writers, and particularly their historians, played a key role in constructing these traditions, and Seven Oaks figured prominently in their work.

In constructing a historical role for the Anglo-Canadian newcomers, no other writer matched the contributions of George Bryce. The first professional historian in Western Canada, the founder of Manitoba College, cofounder of the University of Manitoba, Moderator of the Presbyterian Church of Canada, the first president of the Manitoba Historical Society and, later, president of the Royal Society of Canada,[51] Bryce was positioned to rewrite the region's history from the perspective of his own ethnic group and class. He wrote for a mass readership across the new Dominion of Canada. His work represents a formal departure, as it constitutes the first fully realised integration of the event within the narrative structures of European literature.

The quantity of texts Bryce produced on Seven Oaks and the Selkirk settlement reveals the enormous significance he placed on this event and period. He left six published accounts of the incident, more than any other historian.[52] To Bryce, Seven Oaks was "the most notable event that ever occurred on the prairies of Rupert's Land or in the limits of the fur country,"[53] and "the most shocking episode that ever occurred in North-Western history."[54]

Seven Oaks assumed significance in Bryce's books to the extent that his narrativisation of Métis violence and lawlessness in 1816 functioned to explain the conflicts of 1869-70 and 1885. In a paper read only a few weeks after Louis Riel's execution, Bryce stated:

Having tasted blood in the death of Governor Semple they were turbulent ever after. Living the life of buffalo hunters they preserved their warlike tastes . . . it needs not that I should recite to you the doings in the rebellion of 1869-70, it was simply the outbreak of the "Seven Oaks" and "Sayer" affair again. A too generous Government overlooked the serious nature of those events. It was reserved for what we may trust may be the last manifestation of this unruly spirit existent for three quarters of a century to show itself on the banks of the Saskatchewan in 1885.[55]

Bryce's plot form is the romance, a construction of the region's past as a struggle between forces of light and darkness.[56] In his narratives, Selkirk and his settlers were the un-problematic heroes, and the North West Company and the Métis the villains, under-scored by their putative role at Seven Oaks.[57] Bryce's approach to historical evidence was also quite straightforward: in researching Seven Oaks, he simply looked for testimony from the Selkirk side alleging Métis savagery, quoted it at length, and ignored contrary evidence. His reliance on three witnesses in particular suggests that he found all he needed in a collection of partisan testimonies compiled by John Halkett,[58] Selkirk's brother-in-law and ghost writer.[59] By quoting testimony from only one side, Bryce was able to rewrite the history of Seven Oaks to incorporate all of the old Selkirk party's allegations which had been rejected by Coltman and called into question by the Red River historiography. For example, he revived the charge that the Métis fired the first shot,[60] and Huerter's assertions that the Métis deliberately left the bodies on the field for the scavenging animals.

The allegorical function of these details was revealed in the concluding chapters to Bryce's books, as he introduced the collective hero for whom the Selkirk settlers were earlier stand-ins: "What, then, is to be the future of this Canadian West? The possibilities are illimitable. The Anglo-Saxon race, with its energy and pluck, has laid hold of the land so long shut in by the wall built around it by the fur traders. This race, with its dominating forcefulness, will absorb and harmonize elements coming from all parts of the world. . . ."[61] This justification for conquest explains Bryce's narrativisations of Seven Oaks. Just as a heroic role needed to be accorded Anglo-Canadians and their imaginary ancestors, the Selkirk settlers, so the Métis needed to be presented as lawless, violent, unstable, and irresponsible – in short, as embodying the attributes considered antithetical to the new Anglo-Canadian business civilisation. Representing Seven Oaks as a "massacre" was therefore integral to the construction of a new master narrative of progress in the West.

Bryce set the tone for the subsequent English-language historiography of Seven Oaks. With the notable exception of the amateur Charles Napier Bell,[62] Bryce's Anglo-Canadian contemporaries adhered to his interpretation, and it became entrenched as the orthodox version in academic, popular, and novelistic treatments of the event.[63]

With the work of Chester Martin, the academic historiography of Seven Oaks moves from the overdetermined figural language of Bryce and his contemporaries to the assumed neutrality of the plain prose discourse.[64] Born in Nova Scotia, Martin established the Department of History at the University of Manitoba and taught there until 1929. His obituary in the *Canadian Historical Review* in 1958 characterised him as "a disciple of the school of 'objective history'."[65] Yet Martin was also identified with the revival of British imperial sentiment in the early-twentieth century.[66] His choice of the biographical form for his book *Lord Selkirk's Work in Canada*[67] and his presentation of Selkirk as an unproblematic hero were evidence of the continuation of the romance genre even within the school of "scientific history."

Martin's work on Selkirk was extensively footnoted and was written in a measured, apparently nonrhetorical style. Its hidden rhetoric can only be apprehended by a careful reading of its textual signifying practices. Martin structured the paragraph comprising his narrative of Seven Oaks into a sequence of sentences which individually and cumulatively signify aggression by the Métis and passivity on the HBC–Selkirk side. For example, he referred to Semple's seeing the "formidable numbers and attitude of his opponents," while "panic-stricken settlers" confirmed an impending Métis attack on the colony. The statement that "Semple soon found himself surrounded" reinforces his party's implied passivity, while the passive voice was also used to refer to the outbreak of gunfire: "There was a shot and then a general fusillade. The first to fall was Lieutenant Holte of the colony, but in a few minutes," says Pritchard, "'almost all our people were either killed or wounded'."[68]

This construction avoided the issue of who fired the first shot. The implication of the second sentence is that the Métis not only fired the first shot, but immediately followed with a coordinated round of gunfire, a predetermined military manoeuvre which explains the heavy casualties. This implication contrasts with one of Martin's footnotes, which referred to "the usual conflict of evidence regarding the first shot" but acknowledged that it was fired by one of Semple's men, "perhaps accidentally."

Martin's book on *Selkirk* provided an academic justification for the standard Anglo-Canadian interpretation of the battle. While he avoided the use of the term "massacre," his grammatical and syntactical techniques of representation pointed to this conclusion. The apparent contradictions between his text and footnotes suggest the author's unconscious ambivalence toward his own reconstruction; yet readers were left with their pre-conceptions of the battle essentially undisturbed.

Outside the Anglo-Canadian discourse, an alternative historiography on Seven Oaks emerged in this period in French-language accounts by Franco-Manitoban and Métis amateur historians. These writers included Louis-Arthur Prud'homme, a francophone judge who wrote extensively on Métis and other aboriginal topics from the time of his arrival in St. Boniface in 1880,[69] and Auguste-Henri de Trémaudan, whose *Histoire de la Nation Métisse*[70] was commissioned by the Union Nationale Métisse Saint-Joseph de Manitoba. Both of these accounts relied heavily on the Coltman report. Prud'homme's article in particular was a closely reasoned analysis, with little overt use of rhetoric.[71] As in Bell's pamphlet, the paper ended with a discussion of his sources, directing attention back to its evidentiary base. Neither of these works appears to have figured in any of the subsequent accounts of Seven Oaks.

De Trémaudan's book received a mixed review in the *Canadian Historical Review* in the same issue in which a very positive review of George Stanley's *The Birth of Western Canada* appeared.[72] Unlike the two francophone accounts, this latter book was to have a major impact on the historiography of the Métis. In uncritically reproducing stereotypes from Alexander Ross,[73] Stanley helped perpetuate the conventional wisdom of Métis inferiority in Anglo-Canadian discourse. He referred to Seven Oaks as a "massacre" and, like Martin, avoided assigning responsibility by resorting to a passive construction: "A gun was fired." As with Bryce, he was principally concerned with impressing on readers a connection between Seven Oaks, Métis "turbulence," and 1885: "Seven Oaks was only the first of several demonstrations by the half-breeds against the settlement of their country by the whites, and was, in consequence, the forerunner of the Riel Rebellions of 1869-70 and 1885."[74]

In 1939 the Hudson's Bay Record Society published the HBC trader Colin Robertson's correspondence book from 1817 to 1822, edited by the distinguished British economic historian E. E. Rich. This was the first time since Seven Oaks that Hudson's Bay Company documents pertaining to the event were published for general research use. Their interest resides in Rich's conclusion that the evidence confirmed that the HBC party initiated the shooting. Among the documents he published was a letter by Robertson, dated December 1818, in which he referred to "the accidental shot from the musquet of the deceased Maroni."[75] In the footnote to this statement, Rich identified "Maroni" as Patrick Marooney, a member of the Semple party who was killed at Seven Oaks. He added that "this reference would seem to point to Patrick Marooney as firing the first shot." Rich also quoted from a contemporary report by the HBC Factor James Bird, who wrote of the altercation between Boucher and Semple: "the insolence of this man [Boucher] so irritated some of the party which accompanied Mr. Semple that they rashly fired on the Half-breeds who stood round and who had hitherto remained quiet spectators of the scuffle with Boucher."[76] These testimonies are conspicuous by their absence in the subsequent historiography of Seven Oaks.

In 1945, Marcel Giraud published his monumental doctoral thesis, *Le Métis canadien.*[77] It has long been held that this study presented a more sympathetic portrait of the Métis than had appeared in Anglo-Canadian writing. Reliance on Hudson's Bay Company primary sources and secondary works by Ross, Bryce, Agnes C. Laut, Martin, A. S. Morton, and Stanley helped ensure, however, that his interpretations were in the mainstream of the Anglo-Canadian discourse.

The consistency of Giraud's interpretation with Anglo-Canadian writing on the event is immediately suggested in his terminology. Where Martin had been careful to avoid the loaded term "massacre," Giraud underlined this interpretation by entitling a chapter section "Le Massacre De La Grenouillère," and repeatedly invoking the term throughout his discussion.[78] These lexical signifiers were reinforced by grammatical use. Specifically, on the question of the first shot, Giraud obfuscated. After describing the angry exchange between Boucher and Semple and the governor's seizing Boucher's bridle, he stated that at this moment "des coups de feu éclatèrent." As with Martin and Stanley, he resorted to a passive construction to sidestep the problem of attributing responsibility and added that since the eye-witness testimony was contradictory, it was impossible to verify where the shots came from. He supported his equivocation by referring to four sources: John Bird's "Edmonton Report" and depositions by Michael Hayden, John Pritchard, and Joseph Pelletier. Of these witnesses, Pelletier attributed the first shot to the Semple party, Bird's report was a tacit admission from a HBC employee that his own side fired first, and Pritchard testified that he could not tell which side initiated the gunfire. This leaves only Hayden (who had been discredited as an unreliable witness by Coltman) asserting that the Métis fired the first shot. Giraud then focused on the supposed inability of the Métis to restrain innately savage impulses, reflected in alleged mutilation of the bodies: "l'action une fois engagée, ces natures simples, dépourvues de conviction réligieuse, parurent donner libre cours a l'instinct sauvage que les North-Westers avaient éveillé en eux. Leur barbarie s'exprima dans la mutilation des cadavres."[79]

Presenting Seven Oaks as a manifestation of instinctive Métis savagery was consistent with English-language versions from the time of Bryce. Giraud's contribution was to give renewed credibility to the old stereotypes by providing both extensive foot-noting and the scientific gloss of eugenics theory.[80] In spite of the trappings of academic references and the use of pseudo-scientific language, Giraud's thesis of the Métis as the inherently flawed product of an unsound racial mixture was derived entirely from the encrusted prejudices of half a century of Anglo-Canadian writing on this Aboriginal group.

The Anglo-Canadian historiography of Seven Oaks culminates in the work of W. L. Morton. Morton was the most prominent post-Second-World-War historian in and of Western Canada, and he was the only regional historian to whom Carl Berger devoted an entire chapter in his *The*

Writing of Canadian History. Morton wrote two versions of the battle, a shorter account in his survey history of Manitoba and a more substantial narrative in a book on Cuthbert Grant.

Recent scholarship has credited Morton's account in *Cuthbert Grant of Grantown* with being the "most detailed reconstruction of Seven Oaks,"[81] but it is consistent with the version in his provincial history, albeit with more detail and footnotes. As with Martin, Stanley, and Giraud, he employed passive constructions and apologies to soften the impact of the Semple party's firing the first shot, while shifting the emphasis to an assumed coordinated response. Morton discussed the killing of Semple and correctly attributed it to either Deschamps or Machicabou, an Indian. Nevertheless, he proceeded to extend the responsibility for this "savagery" to the entire group of Métis: "This piece of savagery was matched elsewhere. The wounded were knifed and tomahawked, the dead stripped and ripped up after the Indian fashion. The wild blood of the *brûlés* was boiling, and it was some time before Grant could check their savagery." Grant's entire party was also presented as a wild group of plunderers.[82]

Beyond attributing savagery to the entire group, the author presented them as a continuing menace to the colonists. He referred to the settlers' "terror-stricken night"; the "horrors of the massacre"; and the "horror of the colonists."[83] Morton asked: "What pity for man or woman could be expected from these savages?" Grant was presented as mercifully in control of his men; otherwise, it was implied, they would have massacred the entire settlement. Morton also discussed the appearance of the bodies after they were brought in: "Some of them were naked, some mutilated, all rent by spear or knife. The spectacle completed the terror of the colonists."[84]

Morton's views on the Métis role at Seven Oaks are clear enough from his reconstruction in *Cuthbert Grant of Grantown* but, as a collaborative text, the book does not reveal his reasons for this interpretation. An answer is found in his *Manitoba: A History,* in which a similar version of Seven Oaks was narrativised as part of a much larger interpretive framework.

Here, the selected form of emplotment was the epic, essentially a monumental prose poem narrating the progress of a hero. While the epic form all but disappeared in Europe with the rise of professional history in the early-nineteenth century, in North America it was given new life by the nation-building preoccupations of the occupying Anglo-Saxon groups in the United States.[85] In a similar way, Morton's book represents the deployment of an antiquated literary form to advance the historical role of his ethnic group, class, and profession.

Morton plotted *Manitoba: A History* as a succession of dialectical struggles between what he considered to be the progressive and reactionary forces at each stage of the historical process. In each successive era, the mode of production and social organization considered to advance society swept away the old order. For example, the Métis were accorded a role in the Red River period but, by 1870, they were viewed as resisting progress, and had to be turned out. This narrative structure required that the Métis be presented in a negative light before the reader reaches the critical years of 1869-70 in the text. Accordingly, they were thematised as wild men throughout the approximately eighty pages devoted to the Red River period. This was achieved through the simple device of applying a large number of adjectives signifying their alleged unruliness and irresponsibility.[86]

The function of Seven Oaks within the larger narrative is revealed when Morton referred to the "sudden and deadly burst of passion" at Seven Oaks, a foreshadowing of the subsequent reference to the execution of Thomas Scott as a "sudden return to violence by Riel." He asked: "Why the resistance, hitherto so restrained rose so suddenly to this pitch of brutal violence, is an obscure and complex question," and then answered by attributing the violence to "the divisions and instability of his [Riel's] own people."[87] He thereby echoed the interpretation he advanced in reviewing Giraud's book in 1950: "it was their tragedy that the instability and violence of Riel, reflecting the inherent instability and ready violence of his own uncertain people, ruined his achievement and destroyed his nation."[88]

Morton's narrativisation of Seven Oaks can therefore be seen as integral to the discrediting of the legitimacy of the Riel Resistance and, by extension, the Métis rights it represented. Here Giraud's assertions of an inherent Métis instability and tendency to violence provided Morton with all that was required to justify their suppression in 1870 and, by implication, 1885.

Morton's version of Seven Oaks reveals a deeper allegorical structure beyond these narrative functions, which it shares with the broader Anglo-Canadian discourse. One has only to compare the optimistic tone of the

conclusions to Bryce's books with the pessimism evident in Morton's concluding jeremiad to perceive that a very different conception is at work.
That his text went beyond the agendas of the Anglo-Canadian discourse is
also evident from a comparison of stereotypes in the respective accounts.
Where such writers as Ross, Bryce, and Stanley presented the Métis in terms
of both positive and negative stereotypes as a combination of Wild Man and
Noble Savage, Morton's characterization was almost uniformly negative.

Why Morton resorted to such hyperbole might well have had less to do
with the Métis than a preoccupation with a perceived decline in the position of his own ethnic group and profession in the twentieth century. Morton's uneasiness with the increasingly multicultural composition of the
province after 1900 is reflected in the statement that "many of them were
to be alien in origin and of faiths and traditions unknown to the West, and
with their coming was to begin a testing of the Canadian nationality such
as it had not yet undergone." Here "Canadian nationality" signifies Anglo-
Canadian nationality. Later, he referred to the "the gulf between the immigrant and the Canadian-born generation breaching family ties, delinquency
among the younger generation, the decline of politeness, the debasement
of English speech," and so on. Similarly decried was the decline in status of
the academy: "The decadence of intellectual standards, the maintenance of
which was the greatest need of a society emerging from pioneering, was increased by the contempt in which a materialistic community held the teaching profession. The really fine achievement of the University of Manitoba
in its first generation was similarly threatened." Just as he wistfully recalled
the leading role of the university in Bryce's day, he nostalgically looked
back to the privileged role of Ross and other retired fur traders, men of
"prestige and means" and "the natural aristocracy of the primitive community of Red River" in their own era.[89]

These assorted statements point to the author's deeper narrative purpose.
In his statement quoted at the beginning of this paper, Morton suggested
that historians had neglected their responsibility to produce "myths" to
counter the "decadence" of the age. His own narrativisation of Seven Oaks
approached the mythical in *Manitoba: A History*, a romantic epic in which
the role attributed to the Métis functioned to set off the text's implied hero,
an Anglo-Canadian aristocracy for the West.

Morton's account of Seven Oaks in *Cuthbert Grant of Grantown* was apparently the last detailed treatment of the event by a Manitoba-born Anglo-Canadian. Its status as the last archivally based version has ensured a continuation of elements of the Anglo-Canadian tradition in historical writing to the present. Morton's interpretation of a "massacre" survived in Frits Pannekoek's recently published study on the origins of the Red River Resistance,[90] and a current francophone history of St. Boniface relied on Giraud and Morton as sources on Seven Oaks.[91] In varying degrees the Anglo-Canadian version is also in evidence in current survey textbooks in Canadian history.[92]

Some regional histories of the fur trade or Western Canada have been more discriminating but they, too, reveal the influence of this tradition. For example, in his book on the Western Canadian fur trade, Daniel Francis reproduced the passive equivocation ("A shot was fired"),[93] as did Gerald Friesen in his textbook on prairie history. In chiding other writers for their use of the term "massacre,"[94] Friesen has been more judicious than most. Friesen's and Francis's treatments do not consciously conform to the master narrative but, as syntheses of secondary materials, these versions are unavoidably dependent on the existing literature.

Today, exaggerated accounts of Métis "savagery" persist only in popular works by authors such as George Woodcock or Peter C. Newman,[95] or in fictional accounts, as in a particularly lurid version in a recent romance novel.[96] Writing on Seven Oaks appears to have come full circle. Anglo-Canadian academics seized control of the incident's historiography from Red River amateurs in the period between 1870 and 1970 but, in the last twenty years amateurs have returned to the fore. Where the nineteenth-century writers exemplified *vernacular* or grass-roots approaches to historical writing, however, the more recent amateur historians fall into the category of *popular* writing, essentially comprising the popular reproduction of conventional wisdom.[97] In stretching the gulf between story and discourse to absurd lengths, the popular historians have only extended a process of textual reification, pioneered by the Anglo-Canadian academics and entrenched in a discursive tradition of a hundred years' duration.

The voluminous literature on the Seven Oaks incident illuminates far more than the event of Seven Oaks, and broadly bears on the practice of historical writing as it evolved in Western Canada. In different but comple-mentary ways, each of the nineteenth-century amateur texts on Seven Oaks, apart from Ross, contributed suggestive models as to how writing on history within the region might otherwise have developed. Coltman contributed the judicial techniques of comprehensive compilation and review of all the available evidence and subjection of the data to the rigorous standards of courtroom examination. Falcon's "Chanson de la Grenouillère" constituted both an eye-witness account and a folk memory of one of the groups par-ticipating in the event. Gunn and Hargrave acknowledged the existence of more than one viewpoint on the event, while C. N. Bell took the remark-ably progressive step of letting eye-witness representatives from both sides of the conflict speak for themselves. In the twentieth century, they were joined by Louis-Arthur Prud'homme and Auguste-Henri de Trémaudan, who preserved the memory of alternative perspectives on Seven Oaks in the French language.

Yet the amateur historical writings were virtually without impact on the post-Confederation historiography of the battle. In the hundred years be-tween 1870 and 1970, writing on Seven Oaks was dominated by profession-als who proceeded to rewrite its history to reflect the ideological impera-tives of their ethnic group, the newly dominant Anglo-Canadians on the prairies. With the passage of time, the new tradition of writing became en-trenched as "truth," while the more pluralistic Red River amateur accounts passed into oblivion. The problem was that the academics' forms of writing often owed more to the structures of the fictional genre than to scientific analysis, while their contents were based less on empirical research than on discursive tradition.

The Anglo-Canadian discourse on Seven Oaks might be best understood by referring to the concept of master narrative, an overriding interpretive paradigm informing an entire body of writing. After 1870, the master narra-tive of progress was apparent in the Anglo-Canadian erasure of Métis tradi-tions and the rewriting of the historiography of the battle, as attested to by the works of Bryce, Martin, and a host of other historians and novelists. In these works, the year 1870 simultaneously heralded the end of a long period of stagnation for Red River, its rescue through Canada's acquisition of the region, and the introduction of an integrated national market economy. As a society of new-comers, however, prairie Anglo-Canadians needed to establish cultural traditions to justify their assumption of dominance in the region. A key element in their programme consisted of the Canadians' adoption of the Selkirk settlers as imagined ancestors in the West. Whatever shortcomings they might have perceived in them, these Scots were the only full-blooded European, anglophone settlers from the early-nineteenth century available for the purpose. Selkirk's claims to the occupation of Western lands therefore needed to be valorized, and rivals discredited. The narrativisation of Seven Oaks as a flashpoint in the imagined struggle of civilisation versus savagery was essential to promoting the legitimacy of these adopted ancestors.

In the context of the new master narrative of progress, however, it was important that the Métis assume broader allegorical roles. This was so because the Anglo-Canadians were essentially in competition with the Métis for lands to which this Western Native group held a prior claim, a fact which the resistances of 1869-70 and 1885 had made all too clear. The Métis needed to be seen as violent, volatile, easily led astray, and lacking in judgement – -in short, as the antithesis of qualities considered essential to the development of a stable free market economy in the West. Seven Oaks provided a convenient vehicle for the presentation of an alleged Métis weakness of character, implicitly justifying the dispossession of their lands. The preoccupation with this event probably also had as much to do with the construction of Euro-Canadian identities in the West as with the discrediting of the Métis. The representation of a savage Métis "Other" was integral to the inculcation of a kind of "morality tale" in which the chain of stereotyped characteristics of the Métis functioned to set off all the attributes valued by the new capitalist order in the West.

The discourse on Seven Oaks also raises some questions regarding the master narrative of the Canadian historical profession, which interprets the professionalization of the discipline around 1900 as having enabled critical methods to supersede the partisanship of nineteenth-century amateurs. With specific reference to Western Canada, the intellectual historian Doug Owram has correctly identified Bryce with a major historiographical shift, focusing on the rehabilitation of the role of the Selkirk settlers. Yet this shift was not rooted in "a sense of alienation from the East"[98] so much as it reflected the demonstrable need of an immigrant group aspiring to preeminence in the West to establish a blood line of succession. This study of Seven Oaks also challenges Owram's conclusion that the "major proponents of this increasingly romantic view of life in Red River were those older settlers who had actually experienced life in the settlement before 1870 and their descendants,"[99] as opposed to Bryce and his successors.

The historiography of Seven Oaks suggests that it was actually the other way around. The romance form was essential to the Anglo-Canadians' construction of a history favourable to their claims to dominance, and survivors of Old Red River acquired a romantic sensibility from newcomers such as Bryce, rather than *vice versa*. A case in point was Roderick G. MacBeth, an amateur historian and descendant of Selkirk settlers, whose life spans the transition from the Red River colony to the Canadian period after 1870. An indication of the shift in his own writing is provided by the titles of two of his books, *The Selkirk Settlers in Real Life*, published in 1897, and *The Romance of Western Canada*, published some twenty years later. The titles are also indicative of their contents; on Seven Oaks, MacBeth moves from a neutral, more realistic treatment in the earlier book to a romantic representation of a massacre, based on Bryce, in the second.[100]

What we witness in most of the Anglo-Canadian versions, then, is less a reconstruction of the Seven Oaks incident than the construction, through historical discourse, of the self-image of prairie Anglo-Canadian society. Bryce and his successors brought about the transformation of Seven Oaks historiography from Red River pluralism to Anglo-Canadian romance, while Morton presided over its final elevation to the realm of myth. As current writing on the event suggests, when the weight of discourse compresses its sedimentary layers into an ideological bedrock, such myths have been stubbornly resistant to revision.

Notes

1. Canada. National Archives (NA), Selkirk Papers, MG 2, A 1, fols. 9207-08.
2. W. L. Morton, comment on R. G. Trotter, "Aims in the Study and Teaching of History in Canadian Universities Today," Canadian Historical Association, *Annual Report* (1943): 61.
3. E. E. Rich, ed., *Colin Robertson's Correspondence Book, September 1817 to September 1818* (London, 1939), 28.

4. "Seven Oaks," Historical and Scientific Society of Manitoba, *Transactions* 43 (1891-92).
5. Carl Berger, *The Writing of Canadian History* (Toronto, 1976). The following quotations are from page 1 of this text.
6. M. Brook Taylor, *Promoters, Patriots and Partisans: Historiography in Nineteenth-Century Canada* (Toronto, 1989).
7. A. B. McKillop, "Historiography in English," *Canadian Encyclopedia*, rev. ed., 993.
8. "Story" is defined as a sequence of events to which historians refer in constructing their narratives, while "discourse," or plot, is a particular version of the referred-to events. See Wallace Martin, *Recent Theories of Narrative* (Ithaca and London, 1986), 108-29.
9. The narratological study of historical texts comprises a growing subdiscipline within the field of historical criticism. Among various works now published in this area, see Hayden White, *Metahistory* (Baltimore, 1973); Dominick LaCapra, *Historical Criticism* (Ithaca, 1985); Sande Cohen, *Historical Culture: On the Recoding of an Academic Discipline* (Berkeley, 1986); and Hans Kellner, *Language and Historical Representation* (Madison, 1989).
10. See Hayden White, *The Content of the Form* (Baltimore, 1987), 26-57.
11. The published sources are listed in W. S. Wallace, "The Literature Relating to the Selkirk Controversy," *Canadian Historical Review* 13:1 (March 1932): 45-50.
12. A. Amos, ed., *Report of the Trials in the Courts of Canada Relative to the Destruction of the Earl of Selkirk's Settlement of the Red River with Observations* (London, 1820), and *Report of the Proceedings Connected with the Disputes Between the Earl of Selkirk and the North-West [sic] Company at the Assizes Held at York, in Upper Canada, October, 1818, From Minutes Taken in Court* (London, 1819).
13. See NA, Records of the Provincial and Civil Secretaries' Offices, Québec, Lower Canada, and Canada East, 1760-1867, RG 4, B 46, "Lower Canada, Commission of Enquiry into the Red River Disturbances, 1815-21," Vols. 1-5 (hereafter "Commission of Enquiry"); Manitoba. Provincial Archives, Hudson's Bay Company Archives, E. 8/5, "Papers Relating to Disturbances Forwarded to Lord Bathurst, 1815-1819," and E. 8/6, "Papers Relating to Disturbances, 1814-1819"; McGill University Libraries, Department of Rare Books and Special Collections, Selkirk Papers, MS 403/12 and 403/13.
14. In addition to the assorted correspondence reproduced in *Papers Relating to the Red River Settlement*, see the original letters in NA, RG 4, B 46, "Commission of Enquiry," and NA, Colonial Office Records, MG 11, CO 42, Vol. 181.
15. "A General Statement and Report Relative to the Disturbances in the Indian Territories of British North America by the Undersigned Special Commissioner for Inquiring into the Offences Committed in the Said Indian Territories and the Circumstances Attending the Same." Two manuscript copies of the report were examined, in NA, Colonial Office Records, MG 11, CO 42, Vol. 181, fols. 74-232 and in NA, Fur Trade and Indian Records 1763-1867, MG 19, E 2, "Red River Settlement," Vol. 1. Both copies contain essentially the same text as the published version in Great Britain. Parliament, House of Commons, *Papers Relating to the Red River Settlement*, Paper 18, No. 584 (London, 1819), 165-250. This version has been republished in *Collections of the State Historical Society of North Dakota* 4 (1915): 451-653.

16. Instructions to W. B. Coltman and John Fletcher by Sir J. C. Sherbrooke, 11 November 1816, reprinted in *Papers Relating to the Red River Settlement*, 64.

17. George Bryce, *The Remarkable History of the Hudson's Bay Company* (3rd ed., Toronto, 1910), 255.

18. A. S. Morton, *A History the Canadian West to 1870-71* (Toronto, 1939), 599.

19. John Morgan Gray, *Lord Selkirk of Red River* (Toronto, 1963), 320-21.

20. Roy C. Dalton et al, "William Bachelor Coltman," *Dictionary of Canadian Biography (DCB)* 6: 166.

21. W. B. Coltman to the agents of the North West Company, 27 December 1817, reprinted in *Papers Relating to the Red River Settlement*, 127.

22. For Coltman's defence of his approach to evidence, see NA, Colonial Office Records, MG 11, CO 42, Vol. 181, fol. 254, W B. Coltman to Earl Bathurst, 30 November 1819.

23. See Sir William Holdsworth, *A History of the English Law* (London, 1926), 9: 210-11.

24. W. B Coltman to the agents of the North West Company, 27 December 1817, reprinted in *Papers Relating to the Red River Settlement*, 127.

25. NA, Colonial Office Records, MG 11, CO 42, Vol. 181, fols. 3-17, W. B. Coltman to Sir J. C. Sherbrooke, 14 May 1818.

26. *Papers Relating to the Red River Settlement*, 190.

27. *Ibid.*, 188.

28. At the Seven Oaks trials at York, two Selkirk settlers, Winnifred McNolty and Hugh Bannerman, testified that Hayden had admitted to them that his own side fired the first shot. Amos, ed., *Report of the Trials*, 315-16, and *Report of the Proceedings Connected With the Dispute*, 192.

29. *Papers Relating to the Red River Settlement*, 192.

30. *Ibid.*, 219-20.

31. *Ibid.*, 187, 191, 192, and 193.

32. NA, Fur Trade and Indian Records 1763-1867, MG 19, E 2, fols. 285-89, W. B. Coltman, "A General Statement and Report Relative to the Disturbances. . . ."

33. *Ibid.*, fols. 290-91.

34. Margaret Complin, "Pierre Falcon's "Chanson de la Grenouillère"," *Transactions of the Royal Society of Canada*, Section 2 (1939): 49-58.

35. Numerous renditions of this song have followed its publication in the Québec folklorist François Larue's 1863 compilation, *Chansons populaires et historiques*. For historiographical purposes, an early handwritten copy and an 1871 published version transcribed from a performance by the author may be considered to be the most authentic. The handwritten version was among papers seized by Lord Selkirk at Fort William in 1816 and now found in NA, Selkirk Papers, MG 2, A 1, fols. 9207-08; the 1871 published counterpart is found in Joseph James Hargrave, *The Red River* (Montréal, 1871), 488-89.

36. Jan Vansina, *Oral Tradition as History* (London, 1985), 29.

37. Alexander Ross, *The Red River Settlement: Its Rise, Progress, and Present State, With Some Account of the Native Races and its General History, to the Present Day* (London, 1856), 36-37.

38. Amos, ed., *Report of the Trials*, 173-74.

39. *Ibid.*, 37-40.

40. Hargrave, *The Red River*, 489-91; G. Mercer Adam, *The Canadian North-West: Its*

History and its Troubles: The Narrative of Three Insurrections (Toronto, 1885), 123; George Bryce, *Mackenzie, Selkirk, Simpson* (Toronto, 1909), 184; A. C. Garrioch, *The Correction Line* (Winnipeg, 1933), 39-41; and Peter C. Newman, *Caesars of the Wilderness* (Toronto, 1987), 175.

41. Ross, *The Red River Settlement*, 18. Ross's constructions of the Métis role at Seven Oaks and on other occasions reveal the "cultural ambivalence" that Sylvia Van Kirk has described in an insightful article on his family; see ""What if Mama is an Indian?": The Cultural Ambivalence of the Alexander Ross Family," in *The Developing West: Essays in Honour of L. H. Thomas*, ed. John E. Foster (Edmonton, 1983), 125-36.

42. Ross, *The Red River Settlement*, 404 and 401.

43. L. G. Thomas, "Donald Gunn," *DCB* 10: 324.

44. Donald Gunn and Charles R. Tuttle, *History of Manitoba* (Ottawa, 1880).

45. *Ibid.*, 107-08 and 149.

46. Glen Makahonuk, "Joseph James Hargrave," *DCB* 12: 408-09.

47. Hargrave, *The Red River*, 485-91.

48. *Ibid.*, 487-88.

49. See Lyle Dick, *Farmers "Making Good"* (Ottawa, 1989), Chap. I, and "Factors Affecting Prairie Settlement: A Case Study of Abernethy, Saskatchewan in the 1880s," *Historical Papers/Communications historiques* (1985): 11-28.

50. See Alan F. J. Artibise, *Winnipeg: A Social History of Urban Growth* (Montreal, 1975), 23-37.

51. Henry J. Morgan, ed., *Canadian Men and Women of the Time* (Toronto, 1912), 163-64; George Bryce, *A History of Manitoba, Its Resources and People* (Toronto/Montreal, 1906), 689-92.

52. Bryce's versions of Seven Oaks appear in the following: *Manitoba: Its Infancy, Growth, and Present Condition* (London, 1882), 213-35; *Mackenzie, Selkirk, Simpson*, 177-84; *A History of Manitoba, Its Resources and People*, 80-85; *The Remarkable History of the Hudson's Bay Company*, 3rd ed., 229-37; *The Romantic Settlement of Lord Selkirk's Colonists (The Pioneers of Manitoba)* (Toronto, 1909), 117-32; and *The Life of Lord Selkirk: Colonizer of Western Canada* (Toronto, 1912), 67-73.

53. *A History of Manitoba, Its Resources and People*, 80.

54. *The Romantic Settlement of Lord Selkirk's Colonists*, 133.

55. George Bryce, *The old settlers of Red River, a paper read before the Society on the evening of 26th November 1885* (Winnipeg,1885), 6. In 1903, he reiterated this interpretation: "their attack on Fort Douglas, in 1816, gave them a reputation for turbulence, which again showed itself in the rebellions of 1849, 1869, 1885." See his "Intrusive Ethnological Types in Rupert's Land," *Transactions of the Royal Society of Canada*, Section 2 (1903): 412. Contemporaries who also attributed the conflicts of 1869-70 and 1885 to the unleashing of Métis turbulence at Seven Oaks include John Reade, "The Half-Breed," *Transactions of the Royal Society of Canada*, Section 2 (1885): 12 and G. Mercer Adam, *The Canadian North-West*.

56. For a discussion of the formal characteristics of the romance genre, see Northrop Frye, *The Secular Scripture: A Study of the Structure of Romance* (Cambridge, Mass., 1976).

57. Essentially, the Métis role is constructed from stereotypes originating with Ross. See *Manitoba: Its Infancy, Growth, and Present Condition*, 200 and 204.

58. *Narratives of John Pritchard, Pierre Chrysologue Pambrun and Frederick Damien lit perter, Respecting the Aggressions of the North-West [sic] Company Against the Earl of Selkirk's Settlement Upon Red River* (London, 1819).

59. W. S. Wallace, "Lord Selkirk's Ghost Writer," *The Beaver* 271, No. 2 (September 1940): 31.

60. See, for example, *Manitoba: Its Infancy, Growth, and Present Condition*, 223; *Mackenzie, Selkirk, Simpson*, 181; *A History of Manitoba, Its Resources and People*, 81-82.

61. Bryce, *A History of Manitoba, Its Resources and People*, 306.

62. Emigrating from Perth, Ontario to Manitoba in 1870, Bell was a cofounder and president of the Manitoba Historical Society and a fellow of various geographical societies in the United States and Europe. His account of Seven Oaks appears in his pamphlet, *The Selkirk Settlement and the Settlers. A Concise History of the Red River Country From its Discovery, Including Information Extracted from Original Documents Lately Discovered and Notes Obtained From Selkirk Settlement Colonists* (Winnipeg, 1887). Basing his conclusions on oral and documentary research, he acknowledged that "it is difficult to get at the exact truth of what followed this meeting of the rival traders" (17). He therefore quotes representative eye-witness accounts from both sides - -the familiar testimony of John Pritchard favoured by pro-Selkirk historians, and a statement by François Firman Boucher of the North West Company. He added that "many of the settlers are of the opinion that the first shot fired was by Lieut. Holte, whose gun went off by accident, thus precipitating the conflict" (19).

63. See Alexander Begg, *History of the North-West* (Toronto. 1894), 183; F. H. Schofield, *The Story of Manitoba* (Chicago, 1913), 1: 138; Robert B. Hill, *Manitoba: History of Its Early Settlement, Development, and Resources* (Toronto, 1890), 50-56; Louis Aubrey Wood, *The Red River Colony: A Chronicle of the Beginnings of Manitoba* (Toronto, 1915), 91-107; and John Perry Pritchard, *The Red River Valley, 1811-1849: A Regional Study* (New York, 1942), 162-80. Among the many fictional accounts acknowledging their debt to Bryce or reproducing the essentials of his accounts include Agnes C. Laut, *Lords of the North* (Toronto, 1900), v; 1. H . McCulloch, *The Men of Kildonan: A Romance of the Selkirk Settlers* (New York, 1926), vii; Frederick Niven, *Mine Inheritance* (London, 1940), 285-88; John Jennings, *The Strange Brigade: A Story of the Red River and the Opening of the Canadian West* (Boston, 1952), 367; and 1. W . Chalmers, *Red River Adventures: The Story of the Selkirk Settlers* (Toronto, 1952), 99-103.

64. See Robert Adolph, *The Rise of the Modern Prose Style* (Cambridge, Mass., 1968), and Hayden White, *Tropics of Discourse* (Baltimore, 1978), 94-95.

65. *Canadian Historical Review* 39:3 (September 1958): 264.

66. Carl Berger, *The Sense of Power* (Toronto, 1970), 215.

67. Chester Martin, *Lord Selkirk's Work in Canada* (Oxford, 1916).

68. *Ibid.*, 111.

69. L'abbé Elie-J. Auclair, "L'honorable Juge Prud'homme," *Mémoires de la Société Royale du Canada*, Section 1, Série III, 35 (1941): 135-40; Morgan, *Canadian Men and Women of the Time*, 921.

70. Auguste-Henri de Trémaudan, *Histoire de la nation métisse dans l'ouest canadien* (Montréal, 1935), 105-12.

71. L.-A. Prud'homme, "L'engagement des Sept Chênes," *Mémoires de la Société Royale du Canada*, Section 1, Série III, 12 (décembre 1918/mars 1919): 165-88.

72. *Canadian Historical Review* 17:4 (December 1936): 452-54 and 454-57.
73. George F. G. Stanley, *The Birth of Western Canada* (Toronto, 1936), 6-9.
74. *Ibid.*, 11 and 12.
75. E. E. Rich, ed., *Colin Robertson's Correspondence Book, September 1817 to September 1822* (London, 1939), 27.
76. *Ibid.*, 27, n. 2.
77. Marcel Giraud, *Le Métis canadien: son role dans l'histoire de provinces de l'Ouest* (Paris, 1945).
78. *Ibid.*, 1: 591, 594, and 596.
79. *Ibid.*, 1: 594 and 596.
80. Eugenics, an ideology and programme of fostering racial betterment by genetic manipulation, generated an enormous literature in the early-twentieth century. See Samuel J. Holmes, *A Bibliography of Eugenics* (Berkeley, 1924).
81. J. M. Bumsted, "Introduction," *The Collected Works of Lord Selkirk, 1810-1820* (Winnipeg, 1987), 2: lxxxix, n. 285. The narrative in *Cuthbert Grant of Grantown* has been attributed incorrectly to both Morton and his coauthor, the amateur historian Margaret Arnett MacLeod. In the preface to the second edition, Morton disassociated himself from what he considered MacLeod's overly romantic view of Grant as a "heroic" figure, and he assumed sole responsibility for authoring various chapters, including the one which treats Seven Oaks. See W. L. Morton, "Introduction to the Carleton Library Edition," in Morton and MacLeod, *Cuthbert Grant of Grantown* (Toronto, 1974), ix-xv.
82. Morton and MacLeod, *Cuthbert Grant of Grantown*, 49.
83. *Ibid.*, 51 and 52.
84. *Ibid.*, 51-52.
85. At least five leading American historians of the nineteenth century wrote epic histories to reflect the national experience of the United States. See Ernst Breisach, *Historiography: Ancient, Medieval, and Modern* (Chicago, 1983), 255-56.
86. W. L. Morton, *Manitoba: A History* (Toronto, 1957). The adjectives used to depict the Métis include six applications of the term "wild" – twice on page 51 and on pages 56, 62, 65, and 70; one instance of "half-wild" (56); one case of "Ishmaelite wildness" (67); four instances of "turbulent" (56, 70, 102, and 119); another of "turbulent and lawless" (82); and references to "barbarism" (56 and 62), "but half-won from barbarism" (39), and "slovenly barbarism" (90). Other modifiers used for the Métis include "slovenliness" (65), "volatile" (77), "fickle" (63), "careless and amiable" (63), "restless" (102), "reckless" (145), "insouciant" (66), and "lawless" (61 and 64). He also refers to their "divisions and instability" (138) and to their "primitive and slovenly agriculture" (88), and speaks of "a lazy fecklessness a Métis could not have exceeded" (67).
87. *Ibid.*, 54, 136, 138, and 137.
88. W. L. Morton, "The Canadian Métis," *The Beaver* 281 (September 1950): 7.
89. Morton, *Manitoba: A History*, 274, 467, and 67.
90. Note Pannekoek's reproduction of Morton's terminology ("the horrors of the Seven Oaks Massacre") in *A Snug Little Flock: The Social Origins of the Riel Resistance of 1869-70* (Winnipeg, 1991), 76.
91. Luc Dauphinais, *Histoire de Saint-Boniface*, tome I, *À l'ombre des cathédrales* (Saint-Boniface, 1991), 45-46.

92. For example, the revised edition of J. M. S. Careless's *Canada: A Story of Challenge* (Toronto, 1974) characterizes Seven Oaks as a "massacre" (143), while Desmond Morton's *A Short History of Canada* (Edmonton, 1983) perpetuates the image of the Métis as North West Company dupes who "shot down twenty-one men from the colony and mutilated some of the corpses" (66). Even J. L. Finlay and D. N. Sprague's *The Structure of Canadian History* (Scarborough, 1979), an account generally sympathetic to the Métis, states that the incident is remembered as an "atrocity" and a "massacre" (104).

93. Daniel Francis, *Battle for the West* (Edmonton, 1982), 121.

94. Gerald Friesen, *The Canadian Prairies: A History* (Toronto, 1984), 78-79.

95. George Woodcock, *The Hudson's Bay Company* (Toronto, 1970), 115-16; Newman, *Caesars of the Wilderness*, 173-75.

96. Alfred Silver, *Red River Story* (New York, 1988), 382-84.

97. For a discussion of the character of Canadian popular history writing, and of the approach of Peter C. Newman in particular, see Lyle Dick, "Renegade in Archives: Peter C. Newman and the Writing of Canadian Popular History," *Archivaria* 22 (Summer 1986): 168-81.

98. Douglas Owram, *Promise of Eden: The Canadian Expansionist Movement and the Idea of the West 1856-1900*, (Toronto, 1980), 203.

99. *Ibid.*, 208.

100. R. G. MacBeth, *The Selkirk Settlers in Real Life* (Toronto, 1897), 26 and *idem.*, *The Romance of Western Canada* (Toronto, 1918), 42-43.

The Exploitation and Narration

of the Captivity of Theresa Delaney

and Theresa Gowanlock, 1885

SARAH A. CARTER

"A thrill of pleasure will influence every Canadian man and woman on learning that Mrs. Delaney and Mrs. Gowanlock have escaped from the Indians safe and uninjured. The news will give as much genuine cause for congratulation as that of the success at Batoche." The same day that this item appeared in *The Free Press* of Ottawa, June 8, 1885, two telegrams from the North-West were read in the House of Commons, conveying the glad tidings that the two women were no longer prisoners of Big Bear.[1] As though returning to a close and affectionate family circle, the widows were sympathetically greeted particularly by other women well-wishers at various stops along their trip east from Swift Current, and upon their arrival in Toronto in mid-July they were "treated with the consideration and attention which might be awarded to honoured rulers in the land." One of the city's newspapers pointed out that the two women had endured "for nearly three months the severest trials of any concerned in the whole of the rebellion in the North-West."[2]

The fate of the two women attracted national attention in the spring of 1885, during what became known as the second Riel Rebellion and the North-West Campaign, after their husbands and seven other men were killed at Frog Lake (Alberta). During the women's two months captivity with the Cree, rumours that they had been ill-treated and killed served a wide range of often contradictory political, economic, social and military purposes. After their release, the news that the women had not been harmed was put to a variety of other uses. Their book, *Two Months in the Camp of Big Bear: The Life and Adventures of Theresa Gowanlock and Theresa Delaney*, published in November 1885, claimed to be a truthful and accurate rendition, but it too was carefully constructed to serve certain interests and purposes while condemning others. The original statements that the women made describing their experiences differ in important respects from the version that appeared in their book. This article is less an examination of the actual experiences of the women than an analysis of the Gowanlock and Delaney phenomena and the ways in which their captivity was represented, exploited and manipulated.

Not many "captivity narratives" emerged from the Canadian West; *Two Months* may be the only one from the late nineteenth century, although among the non-Aboriginal population there were periodic rumours and anxieties about possible "captivities," especially when children went missing, or when "white" children were spotted in Aboriginal settlements.[3] The fact that there are few examples from the Canadian West is perhaps best explained by the relative lack of violent confrontations between Aboriginal and Euro-Canadian as captivity was most often a function of warfare, and Aboriginal people were not the only perpetrators of this practice.

In the United States however, captivity narratives were a popular form of literature from colonial times on. Studies of this genre attest to the complexity of understanding both the experience and narration of captivity. As texts that shed light on Aboriginal lifestyles and cultural values these narratives have generally been regarded with suspicion because of their ideological underpinnings and privileging of the centre. Often Aboriginal people are cast as savage, sadistic and irrational. In a recent study however, Colin Calloway argued that some of these narratives may be seen as rare sources from "inside" Aboriginal societies, that eighteenth-century narratives from New England display a keen sense of toleration for cultural differences.[4] The same argument could well be made for many of the passages in *A Narrative of the Captivity and Adventures of John Tanner*, who spent thirty years among the Anishinabe (Ojibway) of what became southern Manitoba.[5] By virtue of his lengthy familiarity with Aboriginal lifestyles and language, Tanner's narrative is a useful source of information. The term "captive" remains problematic for Tanner however, as for many years he had no desire to return "home." Not all captivity narratives provide such insight.

From the time of earliest European settlement in the United States, captivity narratives have proved repeatedly useful; they were exploited for a wide range of purposes, and were often edited, adjusted or meddled with to more perfectly advance certain points. They were used as a means of rallying newly-formed communities around their commitment to their errand in the wilderness, their obligations to settle and subdue. These narratives allowed the intruders in Aboriginal territory to appear as the innocent victims, the wronged, who were subject to injustice and misrule. They could be used to show the great need for non-Aboriginal settlement and possession of the land and resources. In *The Legacy of Conquest: The Unbroken Past of the American West*, Patricia Limerick wrote that "The idea of captivity organized much of Western sentiment. . . It was an easy transition of thought to move from the idea of humans held in an unjust and resented captivity to the idea of land and natural resources held in Indian captivity – in fact, a kind of monopoly in which very few Indians kept immense resources to themselves, refusing to let the large numbers of willing and eager white Americans make what they could of those resources."[6]

These narratives were especially useful when the protagonists were women. As they tended to stress physical discomforts and distress in a vast, inhospitable wilderness, the female captive was the more affecting image as she appeared more vulnerable.[7] In a study of American captivity literature from 1607 to 1870 June Namias argued that the image of the frail and vulnerable female captive did not always prevail, that the nature of these narratives changed over time, reflecting prevailing social beliefs regarding women. She identified three female models: the "Survivor" of the colonial period; the "Amazon" of the revolutionary era and early republic, and the "Frail Flower" of the "era of expansion" of 1820 to 1870.[8] While the earlier literature had portrayed women captives as physically and emotionally tough, as adapting and surviving, and as courageous, fierce defending mothers, even warriors, the Frail Flower was a poor hapless woman, shocked, distressed and disgusted by her capture, she was paralysed and unable to adapt. A culture of delicate and frail femininity had so permeated the ideology of white middle-class womanhood in the nineteenth century that the loss of a protective husband supposedly left them defenceless and powerless. The brutality of Aboriginal people, their threat to white women as nurturers and protectors was a central theme of these nineteenth century narratives.

In a recent article Carroll Smith-Rosenberg suggests further dimensions to an understanding of the American Indian captivity narrative.[9] She contends that Euro-American women helped to create an American national identity as this identity was primarily defined by drawing boundaries differentiating new nationals from the indigenous people. "Euro-American women played a complex role in the construction of the American Indian as savage and inhuman and hence of European residents in America as True Americans," Smith-Rosenberg argues, and they did so "by assuming the role of innocent victims of barbarous savagery, by assuming the role of authoritative writers, and by authorizing themselves as an alternative white icon for America."[10] The women authors of these narratives are seen as vital agents in the construction of an American national identity, rooted in an imagined community which involved the marking of boundaries which established who was "one of us" and who was excluded.

All of these scholars study white captives solely from the viewpoint of non-Aboriginal society. Few have considered such issues as what Aboriginal Americans thought of these captives, or of the uses to which these societies put captivity narratives. It has recently been suggested that attention must be paid to what Aboriginal groups thought of the experiences of their people who were much more frequently taken captive, and that accounts of time spent in residential schools for example, or some of the "as-told-to" autobiographies of people captive on reserves should be seen as "reverse" captivity narratives.[11] In a sense the "stolen women" narratives of many Aboriginal societies are similar to the captivity narratives of Euro-Americans.[12] Both reflect ideals of suitable roles for women although quite different ideals, and both functioned as teaching texts, serving educational purposes much larger than imparting knowledge of actual incidents. Some were accounts of authentic experiences, others were wholly or partly invented. In stolen women narratives, women are abducted, or lured away by enemies or by supernatural forces. The women use their practical survival skills, their resourcefulness and ingenuity to outwit or escape their captors, and return to their families. These stories were used to educate especially young women as to how problems are solved, how they might apply their skills to different predicaments, and what pitfalls to avoid. Admiration is expressed for those women who are capable of surviving on their own, without the assistance of men.

By contrast, narratives such as *Two Months* emphasized the helplessness and vulnerability of women in an inhospitable wilderness, how they were unable to cope without their husbands as they entirely lacked ingenuity and wilderness skills. They had no ability to outwit their captors, and had to be rescued. Although this was not the impression Theresa Delaney and Theresa Gowanlock gave to correspondents on the scene in June of 1885, this is clearly the image that pervades their written accounts. Stress upon the vulnerability of white women in the West served as a rationale for those who wished to secure greater control over the Aboriginal population. Their harrowing experience of captivity, their need of protection especially from Aboriginal men suggested that boundaries between people needed to be clarified. The experiences of the women were exploited to serve a variety of purposes that were clearly useful to powerful interests. In *Two Months* the government was praised for its benevolent administration, although again this was not clearly reflected in original statements of the women to the press. Several of the Métis that the two women praised for their conduct immediately upon their return from the Cree appear in a sinister light in the written account. An enormous amount of money had been spent and young lives lost waging war on the Métis, and images of Métis heroes were not especially palatable.

Emphasis in the narratives of Delaney and Gowanlock upon the constant threat of the "fate worse than death" carried the clear cautionary message that unions between white and Aboriginal were an abominable business, particularly as such unions created the menacing Métis. The November release of the book coincided with the hanging of Riel in Regina, and of eight Aboriginal men at Battleford, and the book served as a reminder of how justifiable these actions were. Like stolen women narratives, captivity narratives functioned to make certain instructional points. The imagined experiences of the two women were exploited for a wide variety of purposes from the time that news of their capture became public.

The two women who emerged so dramatically and fleetingly from obscurity in the spring of 1885 were the only "white" women from eastern Canada in the village of Frog Lake, about thirty miles from Fort Pitt, ten miles north of the North Saskatchewan. Theresa (Fulford) Delaney arrived in the settlement in August 1882 as the bride of government farm instructor John Delaney. She was from the lumbering and farming community of Aylmer, Quebec, not far from Ottawa, and until her marriage she lived at the home established about 1812 by her grandfather who was originally from Massachusetts.[13] Theresa Delaney was the eldest daughter of a family of several brothers and sisters and was described as between thirty and forty years of age in 1885. Her husband was from Nepean Ontario, and he had worked as a foreman for different lumber firms before his appointment as farm instructor in 1879. As the wife of the farm instructor Theresa Delaney was assigned duties as "farm instructress" and she gave lessons to the women in baking, milking, churning, making butter, knitting and dressmaking. Theresa Mary (Johnson) Gowanlock arrived at Frog Lake Creek, two miles from the settlement of Frog Lake in December of 1884 following her marriage in October of that year at age twenty-one to John Alexander Gowanlock, who had secured a government contract to build a combined saw and grist mill.[14] She was from a Loyalist family and was born at Tintern (Lincoln) Ontario. John Gowanlock was originally from Stratford Ontario, and he had worked as a farmer, speculator, surveyor and store-keeper in the Battleford district before securing the contract for the Frog Lake mill. The Gowanlocks spent the first months of 1885 on the construction of the saw mill, assisted by the Cree who were assigned this among other work in return for their rations, and it was completed by mid-March.

Although generally presented in contemporary non-Aboriginal accounts as a remote, isolated village, Frog Lake and district was relatively well-populated as it was in the heart of Woods Cree territory, there were three reserves nearby and indeed the settlement existed only because it served the neighbouring Aboriginal population. Frog Lake appears on Captain John Palliser's map of 1859, and the name of the lake is a translation of the Cree "Ah-Yik sa-kha-higan."[15] The settlement grew up around a Hudson's Bay trading post founded in 1883, and by 1885 the village consisted of the HBC post, the buildings of the Indian agency, the Roman Catholic mission, the store of "free" trader George Dill, and a six-man detachment of the North-West Mounted Police (NWMP). Although often portrayed in non-Aboriginal histories of 1885 as a "white" settlement or enclave in the wilderness, this was not quite the case. Frog Lake was settled by people from a variety of backgrounds. Among the residents of Frog Lake were John Pritchard, the Métis interpreter for the government Indian agency, his wife Rose (Delorme) and their eight children Salomon, John, Marie Rose, Amelia, Adeline, Ralph, Alfred and Margaret. The Pritchards also kept a rooming house and store. HBC trader James K. Simpson, and his wife Catherine lived at Frog Lake as did Catherine's grown-up sons, Louis and Benjamin Patenaude. Simpson was a son of Sir George Simpson and Mary Keith, while Catherine was a sister of Gabriel Dumont.[16] All of these people were also among the many captives in 1885, as was the wife and daughter of subagent Thomas Trueman Quinn. Quinn, who was part Dakota, was married to a woman from Big Bear's band named Owl Sitting or Jane Quinn. There was also a "poor house" or old people's home at Frog Lake, possibly attached to the mission, a small one-room shack into which nineteen persons were crowded.[17]

This was the parkland belt, where the Woods Cree met the Plains Cree, and where many groups before the 1870s had developed a transitional economy that had drawn on the resources of both plains and parkland. There were four bands of Woods Cree in the Frog Lake district who were adherents to Treaty Six: Chief Machaoo (Mahkayo) of 108, Chief Nepawhayhaw of 65, Chief Puskaahgowin of 31, and Chief Keehewin of 138.[18] In the early 1880s, these groups put in crops of wheat, barley and root crops but had limited success; well over half the population regularly fished and hunted off their reserves.

In the fall of 1884, the population of the Frog Lake district was augmented and the resources considerably strained by the arrival of Big Bear's band of Plains Cree. The new arrivals numbered 504, almost equal to the combined populations of the reserves at Onion Lake, Frog Lake and Long Lake.[19] Big Bear, a chief of the Fort Pitt district renowned for his visions, medicine, and political skill had refused to sign Treaty Six in 1876 and had pursued a strategy aimed at preserving the autonomy and integrity of the Cree and a treaty revision.[20] After several years of severe hardship for his followers first in the United States, and then in the vicinity of Fort Walsh in the Cypress Hills, Big Bear's authority and stature among his own people was considerably diminished as his followers were not permitted the rations and supplies allowed to the treaty bands. In 1882, faced with the anger and impatience of even his own family, Big Bear had no choice but to accept the treaty, or his followers would starve. As his last negotiating point, Big Bear refused to select a reserve site for his band, as he believed that government officials would have to meet with him as long as he held out, but this tactic too generated anger and discontent among many of his followers. A reserve site was under negotiation in the district of Frog Lake for Big Bear's followers in the fall of 1884. When his requests for extra rations were turned down, Big Bear delayed moving to the proposed reserve site. Government officials also favoured a delay, as they wished to assess the reserve land.[21] That winter the band received some rations in return for work such as cutting cordwood, but it was a time of great poverty and hardship. Many members of the fractionalized band were angry to learn that they would be without a reserve and the promised extra rations that winter. The Frog Lake district at that time was almost entirely devoid of game and the winter was an extremely cold one with deep snow. Just at this time, officials of the Indian department were instructed from Ottawa to cut costs and to reduce rations.

The events that took place at Frog Lake in the spring of 1885 have been told in great detail in many accounts reflecting a wide variety of perspectives, of which the slim volume by Gowanlock and Delaney is but one.[22] The earliest contemporary non-Aboriginal accounts tended to stress the innocence, good intentions, and martyrdom of the Euro-Canadians at Frog Lake and laid the blame variously upon the nefarious influence of Louis Riel and his Métis messengers, upon the supposedly fierce, unpredictable savage temperament of Aboriginal people who could not resist the contagion of revolt, upon the notorious Big Bear and his malign influence upon the whole district, upon the perfidy and collusion of the Hudson's Bay Company, upon critics of the government who pandered to Aboriginal people in their outrageous demands and misled notions, and upon the maladministration of Indian affairs in the North-West.

Accounts from the perspective of Aboriginal people stress the frustration with government policy and employees, as well as the conditions of poverty and starvation in the district and the multiple tensions that had built up in the community. There was never enough food that winter, and for the meagre rations that they received debilitating work had to be performed in sub-zero temperatures, and with threadbare clothing.[23] Thomas Quinn was inflexible, lacked tact and had an explosive temper. Despite his Cree wife, Quinn regarded the Cree with contempt, and enjoyed saying "no" to all of their requests.[24] Quinn's parents were said to have been killed during the 1862 "Sioux Uprising" in Minnesota, and it is ironic that his behaviour so closely mirrored that of the hated Indian agent there who told the Santee that they could eat grass. John Delaney was disliked by many. In 1881 a man named Sand Fly accused him of stealing his wife. Delaney responded by charging this man with assault and then theft, resulting in a prison sentence of two and a half years, which was generally seen as an action taken by Delaney in order to allow him to cohabit with the prisoner's wife. Delaney, along with Quinn, was also thought to have deliberately persecuted Big Bear's band because they were camped on land that the two men had hoped to profit from.[25] Mary Dion, a young Métis girl living in Frog Lake in 1885, recalled many instances of the casual cruelty of the white people in the settlement, their disdain and contempt, and their merriment at the sight of human misery. News of the confrontation at Duck Lake between the Métis and the NWMP on March 26 during which ten policemen died also excited and inspired some of the young men in Big Bear's camp who were impatient with his leadership. Louis Riel had proclaimed a new Métis provisional government in mid-March, 1885, had moved to seize arms and ammunition at the store at Duck Lake, and the police had ridden out to prevent this.

In the aftermath of Duck Lake, Inspector Francis Dickens of the NWMP at Fort Pitt suggested that the non-Aboriginal people at Frog Lake ought to move to the safety of the Fort, but this proposal was rejected, although it was decided that the police should evacuate Frog Lake for reasons that remain obscure. On the morning of April 2 under the leadership of war chief Wandering Spirit and Ayimasis, one of Big Bear's sons, some of the Cree began to remove items from the stores at Frog Lake and to round up prisoners including Quinn, the Gowanlocks, Delaneys and Pritchards. They were ordered to move with the Cree to a new camp on Frog Creek, and Big Bear agreed to the move, only on the condition that the whites not be harmed. Quinn adamantly refused and he was shot in the head by Wandering Spirit. In very short order, Charles Gouin, the Métis Indian agency carpenter, Delaney, Gowanlock, Father Adelarde Fafard, and Father Felix Marchand, (visiting from Onion Lake), John Williscraft, Fafard's lay assistant, George Dill and William Gilchrist, Gowanlock's clerk, all met the same fate.

The only "white" people to survive that day in Frog Lake were William B. Cameron, an HBC assistant to James Simpson and the widows of Gowanlock and Delaney. Catherine Simpson was credited with the survival of Cameron as she disguised him with a blanket. Mrs. Gowanlock and Mrs. Delaney were hastily and unceremoniously pulled from their dead husbands, most likely in the interests of saving their lives.[26] From this point on, it is impossible to know for certain the exact circumstances under which the lives of the two women were spared, or indeed whether their safety was ever in danger. According to George Stanley (Musunekwepan), a Woods Cree, the terrified and distraught women were first taken to the tepee of his father, Chneepahaos, who assured them they would not be harmed and whose wife gave them water.[27] Stanley remembered that his father informed the women and Cameron that "Neither you nor these two women shall be killed. I will speak for you."[28] Big Bear set aside a tent for the two women, and he ordered John Pritchard and another Métis interpreter he identified as Budreau, to keep watch over them. At a meeting of Plains and Woods Cree, Stanley's father as well as Big Bear warned the people of the dangers should the prisoners be harmed, and it was decided that close guard should be kept over them by Pritchard, Budreau, as well as Isadore Moyah, John Horse and Yellow Bear. Other Aboriginal accounts credit the persuasive skills of the Woods Cree for arranging that the women prisoners be placed in the safe custody of John Pritchard and the other Métis who were assigned to this task.[29] In W. B. Cameron's first statements to the press he too credited the Woods Cree with saving the women, but in his account published years later *Blood Red the Sun* (1926) he described at length how Pritchard and Adolphus Nolin cleverly outwitted the Cree and purchased Mrs. Delaney from her Cree captors. He also claimed that Pierre Blondin had a role in securing the safety of Mrs. Gowanlock, but that Blondin's later conduct was not praiseworthy.[30] In his memoirs Métis Louis Goulet described how he persuaded Pierre Blondin to assist him in the purchase of Gowanlock by donating his horses, and that Goulet then left her in the care of Pritchard. When they first emerged from their ordeal the two women credited Pritchard, Nolin and Blondin for their safety, but in the written account Blondin appears as a villain, responsible, it is suggested for the murders, interested in acquiring Mrs. Gowanlock only for his own sinister purposes, and taken to parading before her in her dead husband's clothing.[31] It is far from certain then just how the women came to be in the protective custody of John Pritchard but it is clear that they remained with the Pritchard family for the rest of their captivity.

For the next three months this group of Cree, more aptly described as fugitives than warriors, and their white, Métis and Aboriginal hostages, mainly attempted to evade detection and capture by troops through an exhausting routine of travel through swampy and bushy country. It appears the function of the captives or hostages was to help ensure the safety of the group and perhaps to win better peace terms. After the fall of Batoche and Riel's surrender by mid-May, there were four footsore and weary columns in pursuit of Big Bear, struggling across creeks and sloughs dragging their heavy guns and wagons. The troops found this last phase of the North-West campaign exhausting and tiresome, and they were galvanized only by reminders of the white prisoners.[32] As it turned out none of the hostages were heroically "rescued" by the North-West Field Force, or by the NWMP – they either escaped on their own in groups or individually, or were allowed to leave. Nor was Big Bear ever "captured." He surrendered at the HBC post Fort Carlton on July 2, 1885, about a month after Major General Middleton abandoned the blundering pursuit.

In the first weeks after Frog Lake, the camp was considerably augmented by other hostages. In need of supplies and equipment such as wagons, by mid-April the Cree camp moved from Frog Lake to the Hudson's Bay Company's Fort Pitt which was under the supervision of chief trader W. J. McLean. McLean, born in Scotland, had served twenty years with the Company at Fort Qu'Appelle and at Isle a la Crosse. His wife Helen was the daughter of Alexander Murray, founder of Fort Yukon. Her mother Anne

Campbell was the daughter of Chief Trader Colin Campell of the Athabasca district.[33] Helen McLean was in her mid-30s in 1885 and was expecting another child. The three eldest McLean sisters, Amelia (18), Eliza (16), and Kitty (14) were well-educated as they had attended boarding schools and were musical, but they could also ride, shoot and were fluent in Cree and Saulteaux.

Fort Pitt consisted of little more than a huddle of six buildings arranged in a square, and was without a palisade. Nonetheless much of the white population of the district had sought refuge there after learning of the events at Frog Lake, and there were 44 civilians and 23 NWMP in the Fort, including those who had earlier evacuated Frog Lake. Among those who had arrived were Reverend Charles and Mrs. Quinney, and farm instructor George Mann, his wife and five children all from the Onion Lake agency. Steps were taken to barricade and fortify, and sentries were posted with the McLean sisters taking their turn on duty. When the Cree slowly and silently assembled on a ridge overlooking Fort Pitt on April 14, W. J. McLean agreed to meet with them at their camp. McLean was well-acquainted with Big Bear – they had met that winter on several occasions. Negotiations broke down however, on the second day when two NWMP, earlier assigned to locate the Cree, were sighted returning to Fort Pitt. Believing they were under attack, the Cree shot at the two policemen. Constable David Cowan was killed, and Constable Clarence Loasby was seriously wounded, but was brought into Fort Pitt when Amelia McLean among others provided covering fire. Three Cree were also killed during this confrontation. The terms eventually agreed to between McLean and Wandering Spirit after this turmoil were that the civilians would join the Cree camp, while the police were to be allowed two hours to evacuate the fort, leaving behind their weapons, ammunitions, horses and supplies. McLean decided that he was willing to accept the protection of Big Bear for all of the civilians. As these details were being worked out, Amelia and Kitty walked into the circle unescorted – they had simply left the fort and walked toward the camp as they insisted upon seeing how their father was being treated, while their mother and Eliza tended to Loasby's wounds. According to McLean family accounts, their bravery astonished the Cree, and when the sisters were asked if they were afraid, Amelia replied "Why should we be afraid of you? We have lived together as brothers and sisters for many years. We speak the same language. Why should we be afraid of you?"[34] The civilians at Fort Pitt then unanimously accepted Big Bear's protection and in this way Big Bear's entourage expanded considerably, as did their supplies and number of waggons. The Mounties escaped on a scow amidst the icy floes of the North Saskatchewan River under cover of darkness, and although shots were sent their way none were wounded.

It took eight days for news of the "massacre" at Frog Lake to reach a wider public and for most of April details remained sketchy as to what had happened, who had been killed and exactly who was part of the fugitive Cree camp. Even as late as April 22 there were "authoritative" claims that the massacre was a "canard."[35] The earliest reports included the name of Mrs Gowanlock among the dead. She was described in one account as having pinioned the arms of the man who had killed her husband as he aimed his rifle at another; the man shook her off and fired, killing her instantly.[36] It was the police who escaped from Fort Pitt who reported that Mrs. Gowanlock was alive and with the Cree.[37]

Gradually it became apparent that a great number of people from a variety of backgrounds, Euro-Canadian, Métis and Aboriginal, were part of Big Bear's camp. (It was at first unclear whether members of the McLean family were "prisoners," since evidence suggested that they may have opted for the protection of the Cree. A letter came to light in which McLean asked his wife and children to join him in the Cree camp; this did not match public images of white people being dragged from burning homesteads.[38]) Public attention focused primarily on the two widows, rather than upon the pregnant Helen McLean and her daughters, or the widowed Jane Quinn and her daughter, the widowed Mrs. Gouin, or any of the Métis or Aboriginal women. Jane Quinn was suspected of having been aware of the intended Frog Lake murders.[39]

The Métis women and children of Batoche who experienced death, hardship, hunger, and the loss of their property and belongings because of Field Force looting and destruction never became the objects of public concern. At the end of June, when hostilities had ceased, the Manitoba *Free Press* gave but one example of the "horrors of war" by reporting on the sufferings of the Tourond family of Fish Creek, originally from the parish of St. Francois-Xavier Manitoba.[40] Madame Tourond was a widow with a family of five boys and two girls. During the fighting their home was attacked by cannon and sacked by Middleton's troops. During this time the two Tourond girls, aged 18 and 20 feared for their lives and escaped into the woods with a Miss Gervais. They were never found again, and without doubt perished from cold and hunger. Two of the Tourond boys died at Batoche, one was seriously wounded, and two were prisoners at Regina. It was reported that Madame Tourond was alone without a dwelling or any means of subsistence. A small item that appeared in the Ottawa *Free Press* for example on July 27 1885 made it clear that there was much distress and suffering among Métis families, that two women had recently died of exposure, and several were so sick that they were not expected to live. Such reports were not circulated during the weeks of conflict, when the impression was left that Métis women and children were humanely cared for, in contrast to the treatment of Gowanlock and Delaney. An illustration in the Montreal *Star* of May 30 was designed to leave the impression that General Middleton had compassion for the families of "dead rebels" after the battle of Batoche. The caption read that "He contemplating their wretchedness reassures them, they are in no danger of injury." Other news reports complimented the troops for the "respect, courtesy, and kindness with which the men, flush with victory, treated the women . . . had they been their own mothers, sisters or wives, they could not have shown them greater consideration."[41] Recent research, however, suggests that these reports too were very exaggerated and that some Métisse were sexually assaulted.[42]

During the month of May, the fate of Gowanlock and Delaney attracted much anxiety and rumours abounded as to the treatment of the women. By mid-May it was reported that Delaney had been bartered several times, that she had repeatedly suffered "a fate worse than death" and would soon die, and that she was ill-treated more than Gowanlock because John Delaney was much disliked.[43] Some papers refused to publish these rumours, generally those that supported the government, while others were willing to seize upon all evidence to criticize the actions of the government gave grim details. The Toronto *Daily Mail* for example insisted that there was little fear that the women might be ill-treated, as "outrages of this sort has never been, and is not now, an Indian habit," but other papers emphasized the horrors of the "fate worse than death."[44]

Until the turning-point of the campaign at Batoche on May 9-12, when the North-West Field Force under the command of Major General Frederick Middleton successfully assaulted the Métis settlement, the Métis and to some extent the Cree, had succeeded in dealing Canadian authorities a series of devastating blows at Duck Lake, Fish Creek, and Cut Knife Hill. There was also the events at Frog Lake, and the "fall" of Fort Pitt. Terrified settlers at Battleford, believing themselves to be under seige had deserted their homes and taken refuge in the police barracks. There were rumours of an "Indian Rising," that they were gathering in large numbers and planning other massacres. After the police's disastrous encounter with the Métis at Duck Lake the Canadian government mobilized over 5,000 men for the North-West Campaign. Over 3,400 men were transported from the East, from as far away as Halifax.[45] An image of the brutal treatment of the hapless brides, now widows, from the East was clearly used to galvanize the troops, to strengthen the determination of not only the men but also the mothers, wives and daughters, whose contribution to the war effort was considerable. By the end of May, with Riel and Poundmaker in custody, the last task of the field force, the column under General Strange, was to bring in Big Bear and secure the safety of the hostages. There was criticism in some quarters of Strange's delay, and hints at his incompetence. The Toronto *News* claimed that this was "scandalous apathy" and a discredit to humanity that so little was being done to release the captives form their "inhuman custodians."[46] It would surely encourage similar atrocities on defenceless women. The Field Force must "impress upon the Indians that the honour of a white woman is sacred." Strange's reputation did not improve after he fought an inconclusive battle with the Cree at Frenchman's Butte on May 27, with the hostages securely protected in hastily-constructed earthworks in the woods.

On May 20, it was widely reported that Mrs. Delaney had been killed, that she had been the "victim of foul outrages on the part of Indians, and torture on the part of squaws."[47] This report was attributed to Adjutant La Touche Tupper, with Col. Smith's Battalion. It was also reported some days later that Mrs. Gowanlock's mutilated body had been found dumped in a well. Although Lt.-Gov. Edgar Dewdney denied these as sensational stories, stating on May 29 in Regina that there was not one reliable word yet received regarding Delaney or Gowanlock, such rumours flourished.[48] They served to galvanize troops still in the field. After learning of these reports there was "fearful excitement" among the volunteers under Strange, and "threats are freely made that if the abuse of the women is confirmed a war of extermination will be waged against the Indians under Big Bear."[49]

The account of Charles R. Daoust, who was with the 65th Montreal battalion, gives some insight into how these rumours flourished, among the French-speaking as well as the English-speaking soldiers, and the functions the rumours served among men who had marched five hundred miles and literally "tramped the soles off their boots."[50] Daoust describes how, while they were encamped at Fort Pitt late in May, the reports of the scouts did much to "excite the impatience of the soldiers to again engage the enemy. Here is what was reported to the soldiers concerning Madame Delaney: "after cruelly maltreating her the Indians stripped off her clothes, bound her feet, dislocated her hip joints, and then in turn outraged her until she was dead. They continued as long as her body was warm."[51] The scouts also informed the 65th that two of the McLean girls were slaves of the lesser chiefs, and Daoust wrote that "Hearing these stories the spirits of the soldiers were very high. They found a shirt in a meadow bearing the initials of one of the McLean girls. It was torn to the shoulders and the sleeve was spotted with blood. There was no doubt that the young girls had suffered the final outrage." Dr. John P. Pennefather, a surgeon with the Alberta Field Force wrote in his 1892 book that the "revolting" stories of the fate of the women wound the "whole force up to a pitch of fury" and he had no doubt that "Had Big Bear and his band fallen into our hands while these reports were credited, I do not think man, woman, or child would have been spared." When the rumours, which Pennefather described as having been "industriously circulated" proved false, "the interest of the campaign died away."[52] Editors of the Toronto *News* wrote on May 21 that once the captives had been delivered safely into the hands of their friends, "our troops may find no other course open than the exaction of a blood atonement from Big Bear and his gang." After describing how Mrs Delaney purportedly met her end, the editor of the Macleod *Gazette* asked "Will you blame us if we kill, men women and children of such an outfit?" "No but we will never forgive you if you don't."[53]

These reports not only served to steel military resolve in the campaign against the Cree, but they also served the purposes of those who wished to condemn the government's administration of the Northwest. For example, the Moosomin *Courier* suggested that the government should get an "illuminated copy of the account of Mrs. Delaney and Mrs. Gowanlock's treatment at the hands of Big Bear's band, nicely framed and hung conspicuously in the Legislative Hall in memoriam of the hellish effects of their "Dishwater Administration" in the North-West Territories."[54]

Delaney and Gowanlock were also dragged into the midst of a debate about the Macdonald government's 1885 Electoral Franchise Act. As initially introduced on March 19, 1885, the Act was to provide that persons occupying real property of a value of $250.00 or more in rural areas were eligible to vote. The act originally provided that Indians, as well as widows and unmarried women who met the necessary property qualifications would be granted the franchise.[55] The bill was the subject of heated debate in the House of Commons and in the press during the course of the resistance in the North-West. Indeed it was suggested at the time and since that the franchise bill was a diversionary tactic that drew the attention of the House away from the events in the North-West and helped the Prime Minister to appear enlightened on Native issues at a time when his policy was under attack.[56] While the extension of the franchise to widows and unmarried women was soon dropped from the bill the question of the "Indian vote" remained before the House during the weeks of military engagement in the North-West. The Liberal opposition objected to the franchise bill on the grounds that most were "pagan," illiterate, and did not have sufficient intelligence to wisely use the vote. One Member of Parliament declared "that to give the franchise to women would interfere with their proper position, that it would be a burden instead of a benefit to them. This, I believe, to be exactly the case as regards the Indians. . . it will be doing him an injury rather than a benefit to give him a power which neither by training, education nor instinct he is able to appreciate and to wisely exercise."[57]

Opponents of the Franchise Act also seized upon events in the North-West to argue that Macdonald was prepared to give the vote to a horde of "bloody vindictive barbarians," who were ready, "on the slightest pretext, to return to their ancient habits of rapine, pillage and murder."[58] Throughout the month of May, newspapers showered scorn on what was described as "one of the most monstrous propositions ever submitted to a free legislature... [as] Piapot, Poundmaker, White Cap and their horde of savages who have been butchering women and children, and devastating their homes with fire, will be entitled to the elective franchise."[59] Often it was pointed out how unfair it was that those "massacreeing [sic] white people" would be qualified voters, while white women, and younger white men - many of whom had been sent out west to restore law and order- were not so entitled. The Ottawa *Free Press* declared on May 1 that "The Tory majority in the House of Commons have refused to bestow the power of voting upon the intelligent white women of Canada; but they decided to enfranchise Poundmaker and the other reserve Indians of the territories whose hands are red with the blood of white men and white women."

Sensational fabrications about the fate of Mrs. Delaney circulated during the last part of May were used as ammunition against the franchise bill. Readers of the Ottawa *Free Press* were warned that Sir John's franchise bill "would confer the ballot upon the wretches who dishonored Mrs. Delaney, till her death mercifully relieved her of the sense of the ignominy to which she had been compulsorily and brutally subjected."[60] The issue of woman suffrage and the "Indian" franchise was often linked. This same editorial was critical of the bill which would give the vote to the "savage" who had "violated the unfortunate woman until she died, but refuse it to the intelligent women of Canada, who might use their ballots to avenge their sister's wrongs." This volley of fire met its mark and on May 26, the Prime Minister Macdonald introduced an amendment disqualifying the Indians in Manitoba, Keewatin and the North-West Territories (as well as those anywhere who had failed to improve their distinct tracts of land by the value of $150.00). The opposition also demanded that the disqualification extend to British Columbia and the Prime Minister acceded to this demand as well. Two days later he introduced an amendment to his own amendment, adding B.C. to the list of exempted provinces.[61] Criticisms mounted against the Aboriginal people of British Columbia also centred upon their treatment of women – that they were "notoriously among the most degraded and lowest type of Indians in the world... Lust and licentiousness are their ruling passions. Chastity and morality are unknown to them."[62] The act that was passed gave the federal vote to all adult male Indians in Eastern Canada who met the necessary property qualifications.

It was with profound relief, as well as shamefacedness in some quarters, that the world learned on June 8 that Gowanlock and Delaney were safe. The women arrived at Fort Pitt on June 5, along with a large party of Métis men, women and children, including the Pritchards, who had escaped with them. Although it was widely proclaimed that they had been "rescued," this large group had in fact themselves parted company with Big Bear's camp.[63] Under the cover of heavy fog one morning, their party had fallen to the rear of the main group and they struck off to the east. For three days they travelled in many directions through the bush to avoid being discovered when police scouts stumbled upon them.

The women announced that they had been treated well, and that no "indignities" were offered them.[64] There were occasions when menacing behaviour made them fear for their lives and their "virtue," but they were well-protected, and had met with little suffering and had plenty to eat. They had cooked and laundered, but were not forced to do these tasks, rather they did them of their own accord, and did not mind as it had given them some occupation. Their principal trouble was loneliness, as neither spoke Cree or French. Unlike most of the others in the constantly-moving camp such as the McLeans, the two women did not have to walk; instead they rode in the Pritchard's wagon. Once or twice they had walked off together when their cart was not ready, but were never compelled to walk on foot. John Pritchard often made his children walk so that the two might ride.[65]

A group of 24 including the McLeans and the Manns were allowed to leave the Cree camp on June 17 as food supplies were low. They were provided with horses and flour and set adrift arriving at Fort Pitt on June 22. In W. J. McLean's first statement, to a reporter from *The Globe*, he too testified that they were not badly treated: "Of course we underwent a great deal of hardship, the nature of our wanderings made that unavoidable, but otherwise we were treated with the greatest respect. Nothing in the nature of an insult was ever offered us. The only reason the Indians kept us was to protect themselves in case they were cornered. I was never as much as asked to do any work."[66]

One of the McLean girls told a correspondent that while she was glad to have her life among the Indians at an end, she had "rather enjoyed the trip as a whole. She appeared inclined to look upon their experience as a joke."[67] Amelia McLean was praised for her courage, especially for having shouldered a Winchester and taken her turn at sentry duty at Fort Pitt.

Gowanlock and Delaney reserved their highest praise for their Métis benefactors, Pritchard, Adolphus Nolin, and Pierre Blondin. Both credited them, especially the Pritchards, with having saved them from hardship and suffering, as well as from the menacing behaviour of certain Plains Cree men. According to the women, Pritchard and Nolin had given a horse each for Mrs. Delaney, and Pierre Blondin gave two horses for Mrs. Gowanlock, and through this bargain they had been allowed to remain with them.[68] Nolin and the Pritchards also had to give up other of their possessions from time to time, such as blankets and dishes to ensure the safety of the women. Delaney was distressed to learn that Nolin was a manacled prisoner and pleaded for his immediate release. He had left the Cree camp on the pretence of acting as a scout for the Cree but had instead gone to Prince Albert for assistance, where he was immediately arrested, as no one believed his story that he had helped the two women.[69] Although charged with treason, Nolin was released on 22 July 1885 because of his efforts in securing the safety of Gowanlock and Delaney.[70]

Military and police authorities, as well as the correspondents on the scene, appeared uncertain as to just how to regard Pritchard and the other Métis as they were all viewed as hostiles. To say the least, the honesty of their intentions was questioned. Pritchard's heroism for example was celebrated only to a most modest extent. An editorial in the *Globe* praised the noble and chivalrous conduct of the "French Halfbreeds" who incurred grave personal danger, in order that two English-speaking women might be shielded from the "nameless horrors which threatened them." The men were nonetheless portrayed as "our foes," whose arms were "turned against us."[71] In the weeks that followed, Pritchard's image was increasing sullied by a public that seemed unable to perceive a "Halfbreed" in a noble and chivalrous light. In a July 1885 letter to the Toronto *Mail*, a reader suggested that Pritchard and the other Métis could only have purchased the women for their own "vile use." In a reply on August 8, John Pritchard defended himself against this and other charges that he collaborated with the Cree, that he had received payment for keeping the women, and that he had used stolen oxen and provisions.

When the news of the safety of the two widows first became public, there had been some talk of a reward for Pritchard and Blondin.[72] In *The Week* of Toronto on June 18 it was declared that "A woman proposes that every one of her sex who is able to do so should contribute twenty-five cents with which to form a fund to reward the men by whom the liberty of the captives was purchased. Should the sisterhood act upon the suggestion, John Pritchard and Pierre Blondin will not go unrewarded." The sisterhood did not act upon the suggestion and the Métis benefactors were never rewarded in any way.

The glad tidings of the safety of the women was used as evidence to both condemn and condone the government. An editorial in the Regina *Leader* of 23 June, 1885, proclaimed that the fact that all the prisoners were restored without having been ill-treated, "shows that the past policy of kindness to the Indians has not been in vain." "The way Big Bear's band treated Mrs. Gowanlock and Mrs. Delaney shows the civilizing influence of kindness," and it was the "white scoundrels" who invented the stories of abominable atrocities, who "should never be allowed to put their foot in decent society again." P.G. Laurie, editor of the *Saskatchewan Herald* of Battleford, who had ceased publishing for several weeks while barricaded with the other citizens in the police barracks, took great exception to such complimentary statements about the treatment of the hostages. "Big Bear," Laurie wrote, "had sold the unfortunate women just as he would horses, regardless of what fate might be in store for them," and it was heartless to "say that two months imprisonment of these ladies in the camp of savages is neither injury nor ill treatment."[73] Others were quick to blame the government for having allowed the hideous reports as to the women's fate to circulate. The Toronto *News*, which had not hesitated to print any and all rumours, proclaimed that it had been natural to conclude that an even worse fate than the victims of Frog Lake had befallen the captives, and blamed the government for the lack of reliable information, and for not having made greater exertions to rescue the women.[74] Critics of the administration of the North-West also drew upon statements made by Mrs. Delaney who "has laid to his [Edgar Dewdney's] door the greater portion of the blame for the Indians' antipathy to the instructors, and to his door, a share in the causes that led to their massacre."[75]

Gowanlock and Delaney spent two weeks with the P.G. Laurie family of Battleford, sharing their accommodation at the police barracks as the Laurie home was in ruins, while arrangements were made for their transportation to their former homes. They were accompanied on the trip by Mrs. Laurie and her daughter Effie.[76] In Winnipeg the women stayed at the home of Mrs. C. F. Bennett who had been moved to write them a letter on June 8 just after her husband had informed her that the two were safe. Mrs. Bennett invited them to stay in her home, and informed them that "their sufferings have given you a sister's place in every heart," and that "*every one in Winnipeg would be deeply disappointed if you did not give them an op-portunity of expressing their deep sympathy and regards.*"[77] The women were described as "weary and worn looking, dressed in black" when they walked down the gangway of the steamer Alberta on to the wharf at Owen Sound. They were met there by Andrew Gowanlock of Parkdale, brother-in-law of the widow, who accompanied them to Toronto.[78]

Andrew Gowanlock was an owner of the Parkdale Times of Toronto that published the book *Two Months* in swift order. The book consists of two separate accounts. According to some descendants of Mrs. Delaney's fam-ily, she was pressured into preparing her account by the Gowanlock family, and both women were reluctant to criticize government actions or policies for fear of jeopardizing their hoped-for pensions from the government.[79] They likely also had their own reasons for wishing to publish the account as the rumours that had circulated about their suffering "the fate worse than death" would have made it difficult for them to socially function upon their return to central Canada.

The story presented in *Two Months* differs in significant respects from some of the statements made to correspondents immediately upon their release from detention. It is squarely within the "frail flower" mould as it emphasizes the "untold suffering and privations" they experienced at the hands of "savages" as they wandered amid the "snow and ice of that track-less prairie." (While there may have been some snow and ice at the outset, this was after all April, May and June.) The women do not cope but are prostrated by their bereavement, by fatigue, exposure and by "the constant dread of outrage and death."[80] Mrs. Delaney wrote that "There is no possibility of giving an idea of our sufferings. The physical pains, exposures, dangers, colds, heats, sleepless nights, long marches, scant food, poor raiment."[81] This impression of suffering, of frailty and incapacity was not the feeling they conveyed to the several correspondents on the scene at the time of their escape. *Two Months* does not mention that they never had to walk but rode in a wagon; instead the impression is left of difficult travel on foot through mud and water, with thin shoes and while "the Indians were riding beside us with our horses and buckboards, laughing at us with umbrellas over their heads and buffalo overcoats on."[82]

In *Two Months* John Pritchard is praised, especially by Mrs. Delaney for his role in saving her "from inhuman treatment, and even worse than a hundred deaths."[83] She does however suggest several pages earlier that on the morning of April 2 at Frog Lake, Pritchard was involved with Ayimasis in the theft of horses from the Indian agency that had helped to incapacitate the white settlers at Frog Lake.[84] There is more than a hint throughout that the Pritchards were not entirely trustworthy. On the morning that they were found by scouts, Mrs. Pritchard is depicted as saying "with unfeigned disgust, 'that the police were coming,'" clearly drawing into question the idea that the Pritchards ever were truly captives.[85] Both Delaney and Gowanlock stressed that even with Pritchard's protection during their ordeal they were not safe, and never knew what minute might be their last. Although the women had claimed initially that they had not been forced to do any work, the Pritchards are depicted as wanting "to work us to death."[86] They had to bake, cut wood, carry water, and sew for the nine children with fabric and clothing that originally came from their own homes. "Not work enough, after walking or working all day, after dark we were required to bake bannock and do anything else they had a mind to give us."[87]

Gregory Donnaire and Pierre Blondin are two Métis who are especially vilified in *Two Months* for their treachery, despite that fact that the women initially voiced their appreciation for Blondin in particular. Mrs. Gowanlock included an elaborate story of Blondin's pre-meditated plan to acquire her as well as all of the Gowanlock possessions. At the commencement of the massacre she claimed, Blondin had gone to their house to gather up all the furniture and possessions. "The wretch was there with evil intent in his heart. . . . Why did he go down to our house when that dreadful affair was going on? Why did he help himself to our goods? Oh! God I saw it all. He had everything arranged for me to live with him. All my husband's things; all my things; and a tent."[88]

In each of the narratives the description of days before the events of April 2 focus upon the fertility and potential of the land, their own domestic happiness, the peaceful tranquillity of the Frog Lake, the sterling qualities of their husbands, and the placid contentment of the local Aboriginal population. Mrs. Delaney especially emphasized that Aboriginal people were treated with generosity and kindness by government, in contrast to her initial statements. She wrote "there is one thing I do know and most emphatically desire to express and have thoroughly understood and that is the fact, *the Indians have no grievances and no complaints to make.*"[89] The government is portrayed as sparing no effort to make them adopt an agricultural way of life, and Mrs. Delaney noted that reserve farmers had many advantages over English, Scotch or Irish farmers striving to take up a farm for themselves. They never went hungry. Mrs. Delaney wrote that her husband was respected and beloved by all. Evil-minded people had instilled into excitable heads the false idea that they were persecuted by the government.[90] The true villain in Mrs. Delaney's account is the Hudson's Bay Company whose interests were completely at odds with those of the government. While the government wished to enlighten and civilize, the Company wished to keep Aboriginal people in a state of "savagery." The HBC did not wish to see Indians farming, according to Delaney, as the Company got less fur. Nor did the HBC favour rationing, as this meant the less the Company could sell to them. War paint and feathers were acquired from the HBC posts. Mrs. Delaney claimed that rebellion served the interests of the HBC.[91]

Much of the published narrative dwells upon description of Aboriginal people as "vicious, treacherous and superstitious," as "murderers of defenceless settlers, the despoilers of happy homes, the polluters of poor women and children."[92] (Both women made distinctions however between Woods and Plains Cree, with the former quiet and industrious, and the latter idle, worthless and cruel.) There was a particular focus upon the mistreatment of Aboriginal women within their own society. Many of Mrs. Gowanlock's first pages are devoted to this theme, of how Aboriginal women functioned as "beasts of burden," which is the caption beneath a sketch of a woman carrying wood on her back. Gowanlock was astonished to see women butchering a horse that fell through a bridge onto the ice of the Battle River and to learn that they intended to eat the meat.

Events Mrs. Gowanlock described shortly after her release did not appear in the published narrative, events that might have evoked pity or sympathy for at least some of the Cree. Young Effie Laurie remembered one tragic story that Gowanlock told while she was staying with their family in Battleford, a story that did not appear in the published version.[93] Gowanlock described how near the end of their sojourn, the camp was thrown into disarray by the booming cannons that could be heard. One evening the Aboriginal women in particular were dismayed at the portentous appearance of the clouds. To them it seemed as if the little church at Frog Lake which had been burnt down stood out clearly in the sky. The cloud formation then changed and it appeared as if Father Fafard approached the church, dismounted, and entered the doorway, signalling them to enter. This was interpreted as an omen of their end, and bedlam broke out in the camp that night. "Old women wailed their imprecations on the men of the tribe for the disaster that was overtaking them."

Delaney and Gowanlock received government pensions. By order-in-council dated 14 November, 1885, Mrs. Delaney was granted a pension of $400.00 per annum that was paid to her until her death in 1913. She received the same as military widows whose husbands had died in the line of action, half of the deceased's annual salary.[94] It appears that Delaney lived in relative obscurity following her ordeal. She moved to the Ottawa Valley, and never married again. One relative remembered her as a "broken woman" who supported herself by various means including teaching.[95] Another relative however, the father of editor and journalist Robert Fulford, never mentioned that she was bitter or broken, but "spoke of her with affection, as the family's celebrity."[96] Shortly after her death, members of Mrs. Delaney's family, the Fulford heirs to her estate, applied to the government for compensation for loss of property during the rebellion as they had had to assist Mrs. Delaney "with money and in other ways."[97] This application for compensation was denied, as the Commission on Rebellion Losses had long since been dispersed. It is perhaps this denial that a member of Mrs. Delaney's family was recalling when she claimed that the widow never received a pension.[98] The Delaney house at Frog Lake, along with the other Indian agency buildings that were destroyed, was government property and Mrs. Delaney was not eligible for compensation from these losses.

Mrs. Gowanlock however was allowed $907.00 from the Rebellion Losses Commission, and she eventually also secured a pension of the same amount as Mrs. Delaney, although this was not granted her until May of 1888.[99] Mr. Gowanlock had not been employed by the government, and for this reason her eligibility for a pension was in greater doubt. She died at the home of her parents in Tintern, Ontario in Sept, 1899.[100] It is quite possible that for both women and their families, the necessity of securing a pension, and for Mrs. Gowanlock a rebellion losses claim, may have been in mind when *Two Months* was prepared. Even Mrs. Delaney was not granted her pension until after this published version of events appeared in press.

It is interesting to compare these pensions with that granted Jane Quinn, whose husband was also killed, and who had held a government position superior to that of John Delaney. The Quinns also had a child, while the other women had no children. Jane Quinn was granted "$12.00 a month upon the understanding that she would lead a moral life."[101] This amount was not paid to her for some years when she left the Blood reserve where she resided after 1885 and for a time went to live in Montana. Upon her return in 1912, she applied for her pension and enquiries were duly made as to whether she was leading a "moral" life. When it was reported by the Chief of Police at Fort Macleod that Mrs. Quinn was a "hard working woman with a good reputation in the district," her pension was resumed. Cheque No. 4540 for $12.00 arrived at Macleod on the day the woman died in January 1913.[102]

In the months that followed the events in the North-West, grand panoramic paintings of the major confrontations were reproduced in colour and widely distributed throughout Canada and Britain. Although they were loosely based upon sketches of soldiers who saw action, they skewed both the landscape and the position of the combatants.[103] The Field Force is consistently shown as decisive and orderly in their actions, which was far from the case. The enemies are depicted mostly as "savage Indians" rather than the Métis whose dress was more Euro-Canadian. Just as these visual images were carefully altered to support the ideology, cultural values, and the forms of artistic expressions of the dominant society of the time, so too were the original stories of Gowanlock and Delaney altered to fit existing stereotypes and images of women, Aboriginal and Métis people.

In the case of Gowanlock and Delaney, it is possible to locate an initial first-hand story, just as one is able to find the sketches soldiers made at the time and at the site of the battles. But the stories that were initially told would not have fit the stereotypes, myths and established narratives of Aboriginal and Métis people of the West. Indeed the metanarratives of "progress" and "development" portrayed those who stood in the way of Anglo-Canadian settlement and "civilization" as "backward," "indigent," and "savage." Demonizing imagery of Aboriginal and Métis people dominated the popular press in both written and visual form during the 1885 resistance. Visual images of Aboriginal people were consistently presented to the public at eye-level, as immediately threatening to them, as menacing – a people that had to be dealt with by force. The story that the women originally told was revised to reinforce the dominant myths. To sustain the myth of savagery such facts as the reasonable treatment of the women by the Cree would have to be suppressed. Métis such as Pierre Blondin, originally thanked for his kindness and generosity, would have to be recast as sinister. Keeping the image of the "enemy" clear and uncluttered would help sustain the legitimacy of using force and coercive measures. Few readers of the popular press were interested in learning anything good about the Cree or the Métis. Similarly the two women who had coped with their ordeal reasonably well had to be recast as vulnerable and frail. Their defencelessness was necessary as it served many purposes – it justified heroic white male rescue, as well as the hanging of Riel who had to be made to "atone in some small degree for the terrible outrages perpetrated on defenceless women by his Indian allies."[104] It is not surprising that excerpts from *Two Months* were published in papers such as the Toronto *Mail* two days after the news coverage of the hangings of eight Cree at Battleford.[105] These excerpts featured their bereavement, defencelessness and the hardships of their ordeal. The vulnerability of white women was essential to those who sought new prescriptions for securing white control in the West.

Just as the artwork of the battles of 1885 was redrawn by different artists for the desired effect, so were the stories of Delaney and Gowanlock adjusted and meddled with. The complexity of just what happened to these women got in the way of the mythology of savagery in the West, as well as dominant images and prescribed roles of women. Myth and history collided as the complex facts that first emerged about their two months challenged the dominant myths. The final product supported the ideology of those who held power in the East and were about to tighten the reins of power in the West.

Notes

1. Canada. *House of Commons Debates*, Session 1885, vol. 3, 8 June, 1885, p. 2357.
2. *The Globe* (Toronto), 13 July, 1885.
3. Sarah Carter, "A Fate Worse Than Death: Indian Captivity Stories Thrilled Victorian Readers – But Were They True?" *The Beaver*, 68, no. 2, 1988.
4. Colin Calloway, ed., *North Country Captives: Selected Narratives of Indian Captivity from Vermont and New Hampshire* (Hanover, NH: University Press of New England, 1992).
5. John Tanner, *A Narrative of the Captivity and Adventures of John Tanner During Thirty Years Residence Among The Indians of the Interior of North America* (1830: rpt. Minneapolis: Ross and Haines Inc., 1956).
6. Patricia N. Limerick, *The Legacy of Conquest: The Unbroken Past of the American West* (New York: W.W. Norton and Co., 1988) 46.
7. Annette Kolodny, *The Land Before Her: Fantasy and Experience of the American Frontiers, 1630-1860* (Chapell Hill and London: The University of North Carolina Press, 1984), 21-26.
8. June Namias, *White Captives: Gender and Ethnicity on the American Frontier* (Chapel Hill: The University of North Carolina Press, 1993).
9. Carroll Smith-Rosenberg, "Captured Subjects/ Savage Others: Violently Engendering the New American," *Gender and History*, 5, no. 2 (Summer, 1993), special issue on Gender, Nationalisms and National Identities, 177-195.
10. *Ibid.*, 179.
11. See Glenda Riley's review of Namias, *White Captives*, in *American Historical Review*, (April 1994), 645.
12. See Julie Cruikshank, *The Stolen Women, Female Journeys in Tagish and Tutchone, Canadian Ethnology Service*, Paper no. 87 (Ottawa: National Museum of Man–Mercury Series, 1983).
13. Delaney and Gowanlock, *Two Months*, 83-91.
14. *Ibid.*, 9. See also S.A. Martin, "Theresa Mary Johnson (Gowanlock)," *Dictionary of Canadian Biography*, 12, 1891-1900, (Toronto: University of Toronto Press, 1990), 478.
15. *Land of Red and White* (Heinsburg: Frog Lake Community Club, 1977), 25.
16. Douglas W. Light, *Footprints in the Dust*, (North Battleford: Turner-Warwick Pub-

lications Inc., 1987), 208. Also see Guillaume Charette, *Vanishing Spaces: Memoirs of a Prairie Métis* (Winnipeg: Editions Bois-Brules, 1976) 126.

17. Joe Dion, *My Tribe the Crees* (Calgary: Glenbow Alberta Institute, 1979), 91-2.

18. Canada. *Sessional Papers*. For the Year ending December, 1884, vol. 18, no. 3 (1885), 148-9.

19. Hugh A. Dempsey, *Big Bear: The End of Freedom* (Vancouver: Douglas and McIntyre, 1984), 145.

20. *Ibid.*

21. *Ibid.*, 145-6.

22. Many different accounts, including those of William Bleasdell Cameron, George Stanley (Musunekwepan), Theresa Delaney, Theresa Gowanlock, and W. J. McLean, are included in Stuart Hughes, ed., *The Frog Lake "Massacre": Personal Perspectives on Ethnic Conflict* (Ottawa: Carleton Library no. 97, McClelland and Stewart Ltd., 1976). A detailed account of the events and background to Frog Lake is contained in Norma Sluman and Jean Goodwill, *John Tootoosis: A Biography of a Cree Leader* (Ottawa: Golden Dog Press, 1982). See also Dion, *My Tribe the Crees*, Charette, *Vanishing Spaces*, ``My Own Story: Isabelle Little Bear, One of the Last Remaining Links with the Riel Rebellion,'' in Mary Bennett, ed., *Reflections: A History of Elk Point and District* (Winnipeg: Inter-Collegiate Press, 1977), 197-202, and the accounts contained in *Land of Red and White*, (Heinsbury: Frog Lake Community Club, 1977) and *Fort Pitt History Unfolding, 1829-1985* (Frenchman Butte, Fort Pitt Historical Society, 1985).

23. Sluman and Goodwill, 57.

24. *Ibid.*, 59, and Isabelle Little Bear, 199.

25. Charette, 158-9.

26. Bob Beal and Rod Macleod, *Prairie Fire: The 1885 North-West Rebellion* (Edmonton: Hurtig Publishers, 1984), 203.

27. George Stanley (Musunekwepan), "An Account of the Frog Lake Massacre," in Hughes, ed., *The Frog Lake "Massacre"*, 164-5.

28. *Ibid.*, 165.

29. See Joe Dion, *My Tribe the Crees*, and Jimmy Chief's recollections in *Fort Pitt History Unfolding*, 101.

30. *Free Press* (Ottawa), 8 June, 1885. William Bleasdell Cameron, *Blood Red the Sun* (1926; revised edition 1950: Vancouver: The Wrigley Printing Co. Ltd., 1950).

31. Gowanlock and Delaney, 19, 28, 33.

32. Desmond Morton, *The Last War Drum: The North West Campaign of 1885* (Toronto: Hakkert, 1972).

33. Kenneth L. Holmes, "Alexander Hunter Murray," *Dictionary of Canadian Biography*, 10, 1871-1880 (Toronto: University of Toronto Press, 1972), 540-1.

34. Duncan McLean with Eric Wells, published as "The Last Hostage" in Harold Fryer, ed., *Frog Lake Massacre* (Surrey B.C.: Frontier Books, 1984), 81-2.

35. *Daily Mail* (Toronto), 23 April, 1885.

36. *Ibid.*, 14 April, 1885.

37. *Ibid.*, 23 April, 1885.

38. *Ibid.*, 24 April, 1885.

39. Glenbow Alberta Institute Archives, Telegrams Relating to the Riel Rebellion, p. 116, J.S. McDonald to *Sun*, Winnipeg, 12 April, 1885.

40. *Free Press* (Manitoba), 27 June, 1885.
41. G. M. Adam, *From Savagery to Civilization: The Canadian North-West: Its History and its Troubles* (Toronto: Rose Publishing Co., 1885) 365.
42. Nathalie Kermoal, "Les femmes métisses lors des événements de 1870 au Manitoba et de 1885 en Saskatchewan," unpublished paper presented to the Canadian Historical Association, Carleton University, Ottawa, June 1993.
43. *Daily Star* (Montreal), 16 May, 1885.
44. *Daily Mail*, 25 April, 1885.
45. Walter Hildebrandt, *The Battle of Batoche: British Small Warfare and the Entrenched Métis* (Ottawa: Parks Canada, 1985).
46. *News* (Toronto), 25 May, 1885.
47. *Advertiser* (London), 21 May, 1885.
48. *The Free Press*, (Ottawa), 29 May, 1885.
49. *Advertiser*, 21 May, 1885.
50. Morton, 133.
51. Charles R. Daoust, *Cent-Vingt Jours De Service Actif: Récit Historique Très Complet de la Campagne Du 65ième au Nord-Ouest* (1886; English translation by Roberta Cummings, Wetaskiwin: City of Wetaskiwin, 1982), 58.
52. Excerpts from John P. Pennefather, *Thirteen Years on the Prairies* (1892) in Harold Fryer, *Frog Lake Massacre* (Surrey: Frontier Books, 1984), pp. 61, 71.
53. *Macleod Gazette* (Fort Macleod), 6 June, 1885.
54. Quoted in *Ibid.*
55. Richard H. Bartlett, "Citizens Minus: Indians and the Right to Vote," *Saskatchewan Law Review*, 44 (1979-1980), 163-194.
56. D. N. Sprague, *Canada and the Métis, 1869-1885* (Waterloo: Wilfrid Laurier Press, 1988), 176.
57. Quoted in Bartlett, 173.
58. Quoted in *Ibid.*, 179.
59. *The London Advertiser*, 5 May, 1885.
60. *The Free Press* (Ottawa), 22 May, 1885.
61. Bartlett, 180-1.
62. *The Free Press* (Ottawa), 28 May, 1885.
63. *Minneapolis Pioneer Press*, 25 June, 1885.
64. *Ibid.*, and Toronto *Evening News*, 9 June, 1885; Toronto *Globe*, 23 June, 1885; Montreal *Daily Star*, 23 June, 1885.
65. *The Globe*, 23 June, 1885.
66. *The Globe*, 17 July, 1885.
67. *Montreal Daily Star*, 23 June, 1885.
68. *Minneapolis Pioneer Press*, 25 June, 1885.
69. *Globe*, 23 June, 1885.
70. Light, 512.
71. *The Globe*, 24 June, 1885.
72. *The Week* (Toronto), 18 June, 1885.
73. *Saskatchewan Herald* (Battleford), 6 July, 1885.
74. *The Toronto News*, 9 June, 1885.
75. *The Globe*, 1 July, 1885.
76. Glenbow-Alberta Institute, Effie Storer Papers, unpublished manuscript, p. 158.

77. *Two Months*, 56.

78. *The Globe*, 13 July, 1885.

79. Hughes, ed., 1.

80. *Two Months*, 5.

81. *Ibid.*, 119.

82. *Ibid.*, 33.

83. *Ibid.*, 117.

84. *Ibid.*, 110-1.

85. *Ibid.*, 52.

86. *Ibid.*, 36.

87. *Ibid.*

88. *Ibid.*, 60.

89. *Ibid.* 100.

90. *Ibid.*, 101.

91. *Ibid.*, 102.

92. *Ibid.*, 37, 43.

93. GAI, Storer Papers, 148-9.

94. National Archives of Canada. Records of the Department of Indian Affairs. Black Series. Record Group 10. vol. 3719, file 22, 649. L. Vankoughnet to Sir John A. Macdonald, 24 July, 1885, and Order-in-Council, 14 November, 1885.

95. Hughes, 1.

96. Robert Fulford, "Big Bear, Frog Lake, and My Aunt Theresa," *Saturday Night* 91, no. 4 (June 1976), 9-l0. See also Robert Fulford, "How the West Was Lost," *Saturday Night* 100, no. 7 (July, 1985), 5-8.

97. *Ibid.*, Mrs. M.L. Walsh, *et. al.*, to 14 April, 1915.

98. Hughes, 1.

99. *Ibid.*, N. O. Cote, Controller, to W.W. Cory, Deputy Minister of the Interior, 5 May, 1915.

100. *Saskatchewan Herald*, 29 Sept., 1899.

101. NA, RG l0, vol. 3831, file 63,891, Assistant deputy and secretary, to W. J. Hyde, 7 October, 1912.

102. *Ibid.*, E. Forster Brown, to Department of Indian Affairs, 20 Jan., 1913.

103. Walter Hildebrandt, "Official Images of 1885," *Prairie Fire* 6, no. 4 (1985), 31-38.

104. *Free Press* (Ottawa), 2 June.

105. Toronto *Mail*, 30 November, 1885.

Tonto's Due: Law, Culture,

and Colonization

in British Columbia[1]

TINA LOO

A fiery horse with the speed of light, a cloud of dust
and a hearty hi-ho Silver! The Lone Ranger!

Western history, like its films, is full of Lone Rangers; the white-hatted good guys who always triumphed over the forces of evil, singlehandedly ensuring that justice prevailed in the "olde weste." Despite the much commented upon differences between the settlement experiences of the two countries, it appears Canada also had its share of these men. If popular histories are any indication, the Canadian west was largely won by the likes of Matthew Baillie Begbie and Sam Steele, lone rangers who rode north of the forty-ninth, albeit in full-bottomed wigs or scarlet tunics rather than black masks. Begbie and Steele and the many lawmen like them worked their circuits and manned their posts alone or with small complements of equally hardy men, far removed from the centres of settlement. They not only managed to survive the rigors of the harsh environment and the dangers posed by a potentially hostile population (both indigenous and foreign), but to triumph. Both the American and

Canadian wests were conquered, it seems, by great white men doing great white deeds.[2]

Or so we have come to believe.

Despite his appellation, the Lone Ranger did not work alone, nor (and more importantly for our purposes), were the successes he enjoyed due to the combined efforts of white men. Sergeant Preston had Yukon King, and the Lone Ranger had Tonto: the faithful scout whose woodsmanship was at least as responsible as the Ranger's sharpshooting for getting them out of some pretty bad scrapes and for bringing the baddies to justice. For all his efforts, however, Tonto has been overlooked, his contributions erased by his partner-in-justice's very name – the *Lone* Ranger – and further denigrated by his own, for Tonto means "stupid" in Spanish.[3] Moreover, while in the tradition of grade B-westerns, the Ranger was hardly a fully developed character, Tonto was even less so – he was all surfaces.[4] At best, he existed only as a foil, his cigar-store stolidness setting off his partner's flash and derring-do.[5]

For all their dash, we need to shift our attention (our historical attention, anyway) away from the Lone Rangers of western legal history – the heroic European figures – and give Tonto his due, for Tonto-like individuals were very important in establishing *European* dominion in the west. Just as they were crucial to and implicated in the European fur trade, some Native peoples also brokered the extension of European state power in the form of the law well into the twentieth century. In doing so, they helped reproduce the system that contributed so much to their domination. However, their engagement with the law and their victimization by it was more complex than simple, straightforward oppression. The actions of these "Tontos" show how people "make their own history . . . under circumstances not chosen by themselves"; how the powerless can and do act in accordance with their own values and interests in conditions designed to prevent just that, forcing change even as they are oppressed by it.[6] Thus, Native peoples' engagement with the law speaks to and for the ambiguities and contradictions of power, complicating our understanding of agency and oppression and hegemony and resistance.[7] Why these "Tontos" acted as they did and the effects of their participation are also my subjects, but I begin by establishing their presence not just at the sides of the likes of British Columbia's white law men, but at the forefront of "policing a pioneer province" as guides, trackers, and constables, and in the courtroom as interpreters and Crown witnesses.[8]

Chasing the "Wild Boys"; or Giving Tonto his Due

In late 1913 a petition for clemency addressed to the Superintendent of Indian Affairs made its way from British Columbia and across Ottawa to the desk of the Minister of Justice. Despite its unusual authors – twenty-six Chiefs of the Lillooet and Secwepemc (Shuswap) Nations – the rhetoric employed was familiar enough to a man whose office dealt with all persons convicted of capital crimes: "We the undersigned Indian Chiefs and Headmen of the different tribes herewith humbly pray that you will use your best influence on behalf of the two Indian outlaws," they wrote. But the petitioners' deference soon gave way to a sense of betrayal, and then – astonishingly – transformed itself into a threat.

> Our Chief ground for petitioning you on behalf of these two Indians is that we the Chiefs were instructed by the Chief Constable that if we could induce the outlaws to surrender that they would not be hung.
>
> On this ground we took action and when we did locate them, we told them that we had been instructed by the government that if they would surrender peaceably that they would get a fair trial and would not be hung. . .
>
> We, the Chiefs, who were instrumental in getting these two men to surrender, blame ourselves for getting them into the conditions we did, and then for the government not to live up to their agreement.
>
> *We would like to state that if these men are punished as the sentence now stands that we, one and all, will never assist to capture an Indian again.*[9]

The threat was not an idle one. According to one British Columbia provincial police constable, enforcing the "Queen's law" among the province's Native peoples depended on securing their cooperation. By alienating British Columbia's Native peoples as they had done in this case, the province stood to lose "the only reliable way of dealing with Indian wrongdoers in this country."[10] Certainly the events that generated the petition were evidence of the crucial role Native peoples played in law enforcement.

Paul Splintlum, along with Moses Paul, was charged with the murder of Alexander Kindness, a provincial constable. Kindness met his death while pursuing the two Indians – the "Wild Boys" as the Indians called them – who were already wanted for the murders of William Whyte, a miner, and Ah Wye, a woodcutter, both of which occurred near Clinton in 1911.[11] Whyte, it was alleged, had been killed by Moses Paul. Though he was taken into custody, Paul managed to escape from the Clinton lock-up and kill the Crown's only witness, the woodcutter. In both the escape and the murder he was assisted, it appeared, by his friend Paul Splintlum. Both men were well known to the ranchers in the district, having hired themselves out from time to time as labourers during the haying season. Nevertheless, they managed to elude the authorities for well over a year, despite the intensive search that had been launched.

Then, in May of 1912, almost a year after Whyte's murder, they were spotted by Charles Truarn, a local rancher. Truarn, as he later testified, was out riding at dawn, hoping to find some of his horses that had gotten loose from their paddock the previous day. As he rode toward a landmark known as 51 Chasm and what he thought were two horses grazing in the distance, he saw two men making their way towards the animals. Though he did not recognize the horses as his, he did, he thought, recognize the two men who were attempting to put halters on them as Paul and Splintlum, the notorious outlaws. Nonchalantly, Truarn asked the two whether they had seen his horses, and offered them five dollars if they found them and returned them to his ranch. Then he rode off – slowly. When he was out of sight, Truarn tore off towards Clinton to inform the provincial police. In the chase and gunfight that followed, Kindness was killed and another constable wounded. The two Indians – whoever they were – managed to avoid capture.

Spring became fall, and then winter, and still Kindness's killers remained at large, "terrorizing" the district's non-Native population despite the redoubled efforts of the provincial police. Convinced that the fugitives could not have eluded them for so long without the active assistance of their compatriots, the provincials, with the help of British Columbia's Superintendent of Indian Affairs, Thomas Cummiskey, appealed to the Chiefs of the bands around Kamloops for assistance in capturing Paul and Splintlum. Though the request did not elicit an immediate response, in mid-December of 1912 Lillooet Chief Jimmy Retasket (Tyee Jimmy) informed the constable at Clinton that he knew of the whereabouts of the two outlaws and could, if given some leeway, secure their surrender. That leeway amounted to a guarantee of non-interference and a promise that the provincial government would reimburse the expenses of all those involved in the capture. Though concerned about the implications of such conditions, the constable urged his supervisor and the government to agree to Retasket's proposal. They did: effectively, then, Jimmy Retasket, along with the Chiefs of the Kamloops, High Bar, Leon Creek, Pavillion, Canoe Creek, and Clinton reserves – all in the Secwepemc Nation – had secured both control and authority over law enforcement.[12]

Three days after Christmas, the Chiefs summoned Thomas Cummiskey and Kamloops' Chief Constable Joseph Burr,[13] to a meeting in the Ashcroft courthouse. "We Chiefs are sorry for what has happened," the seven informed Cummiskey and Burr.

> . . . A lot of money has been destroyed [i.e. spent] and the boys are not caught. From the way Mr. Cummiskey talked to us we want to give the boys to him and we do not want any reward. To take a reward would be selling the boys and we don't want to do that. Mr. Cummiskey talked to us like Judge Bigby [sic Begbie; i.e. Matthew Baillie Begbie] and Judge Walkem [i.e. George Anthony Walkem] and we want to do right without being paid and we will be glad to be good friends.

In reply, Burr reassured the Chiefs that "we were brothers again," and told them that Paul and Splintlum would receive a fair trial, but if found guilty they would have "to pay the penalty with their own lives."[14] With the preliminaries over, the group proceeded to the nearby Bonaparte reserve, where a crowd of about one hundred Indians had gathered. Cummiskey asked them to "kneel down and give the sign of redemption – the cross – which they did," and after delivering a speech about the ten commandments, he received the "weeping outlaws" into custody – some eight months after Kindness had been killed and almost two years after the deaths of William Whyte and Ah Wye.[15]

Just two weeks short of a year after their surrender, and following not one, but two trials, Paul Splintlum stood on the gallows in the Kamloops jail yard. As the sun rose the drop fell, ending the life of one "Wild Boy" and, to that point, the longest criminal case in the province's history.[16]

While on the surface Paul and Splintlum's story appears emblematic of the triumph of British justice over the hearts, minds, and bodies of the province's Native peoples, it actually reveals the limits of state power. For most of the period under investigation, law enforcement was uneven and often problematic. Professional, uniformed police forces were synonymous with the modern state, but their appearance in Canada was relatively late. For much of the nineteenth century, policing was a "ramshackle affair."[17] Apart from a somewhat more concentrated presence in the capitals of Victoria and New Westminster, formal policing in the period before confederation was carried out by one or two poorly-equipped constables stationed in each of the main settlements of the gold fields, usually under the direction of the district gold commissioner, whose administrative tasks during the height of the Fraser and Cariboo rushes were often more than enough to occupy both his time and that of the officers in his employ.[18] Finances were the chief obstacle to establishing a colonial constabulary and in the name of economy, law officers were charged with a variety of administrative tasks in addition to their judicial ones.[19] When faced with an outbreak of violence, colonial officials often turned to the Royal Engineers or the Royal Navy for help knowing the police were too thin on the ground and too inexperienced to cope adequately.[20] Indeed, as Barry Gough's work shows, the military was not only an aid to civil power in colonial Vancouver Island and British Columbia, but it often was also the only effective form of it.[21] However, calling out the Sappers (as the Royal Engineers were known) or sending one of Her Majesty's gunboats to shell a recalcitrant Native village into submission was costly – both in economic and moral terms.[22] As a result, constables were left to deal the best they could with whatever situations confronted them. That they were able to had, it appears, more to do with the relative lack of violence in the colonies than to the skills and resourcefulness of the law's officers.

Confederation in 1871 did little to alter this situation: in addition to the municipal forces at Victoria and New Westminster, just twenty-two constables served a population consisting of just over 10,000 non-Natives and approximately 26,000 Natives.[23] British Columbia's constabulary grew slowly at first even if its population did not: in 1882, the force was reduced to just nineteen men, though by the end of 1890 it had recovered and grown to twenty-eight. By the turn of the century, however, the force was over one hundred, growing to 208 in 1915.[24] There was a reduction in size after 1919, when the Royal North West Mounted Police were given jurisdiction to enforce all federal laws in the four western provinces.[25] Even with the Mounties, the formal police presence in British Columbia was small, particularly given the size of its population, the scattered nature of settlements, and the sometimes rugged terrain separating them. Of course, both the colonial and the provincial forces augmented their numbers by swearing in special constables.[26] As it turned out, however, that was not always an option they wished to pursue. It was hard enough securing qualified and reliable men to staff the regular force, small as it was. In the colonial period the constabulary was described as "the dumping ground for every young relative or friend newly arrived in British Columbia"; men who, with the first rumour of a rich strike, headed for the hills.[27] It was not until the mid-1880s that the Superintendent of Police reported an improvement in the quality of his recruits.[28] Given these difficulties, swearing in specials was fraught with uncertainty. Faced with doing so in 1912, Clinton's Chief Constable predicted that "in all probability, they would simply go out and hang around and run up expenses without risking their skin or doing anything."[29] He was better off, he felt, relying on the local Indians.

Certainly, without the intervention of the Lillooet and Secwepemc chiefs it is unlikely that the Wild Boys would ever have been tamed. Though the case of Paul and Splintlum was certainly unusual, the province's reliance on the active cooperation of Native peoples in law enforcement was not. The game that was afoot in British Columbia was not only one played by "amateurs" (though ones who were at least as skilled, if not more so, than the "professionals" with whom they worked), but it was also a very old one – so much so that Constable A.N. O'Daunt, one of the Provincials involved in the Splintlum case, deemed it "the practice of years."[30]

Since the days of the fur trade, Indians were both implicated in and crucial to resolving what the legal historian John Phillip Reid calls "international" homicides; that is, homicides involving Native peoples and Europeans.[31] For instance, when fourteen year old Joseph Navarro was killed on the west coast of Vancouver Island in 1792, the Spanish did not take matters into their own hands, perhaps recognizing their powerlessness, but appealed to Chief Maquinna to bring the alleged Native perpetrators to justice. Though a generation later, the English felt confident enough to do what the Spanish had not, and take direct action, the 1828 murder of Hudson's Bay Company (HBC) trader Alexander MacKenzie by members of the Clallum Nation was only resolved when some of the Clallum, in an effort to avoid further hostilities and bloodshed, killed the murderers themselves. When some Secwepemc killed Chief Trader Samuel Black in 1841, the HBC was again assisted in its efforts to capture the perpetrators by Native peoples: this time, Nicola, the chief of the Okanagans, and his family.[32]

Perhaps the best known example of Native policing in the fur trade is provided by Waccan, or Jean-Baptiste Boucher, a mixed blood who came with Simon Fraser to Stuart Lake in 1806 and stayed in the region afterwards, marrying a Carrier in 1811, and finding employment with the Hudson's Bay Company as an interpreter.[33] Unofficially, and more importantly, however, Waccan was, according to historian A.G. Morice, the "Company's gendarme and chief executioner in New Caledonia [mainland British Columbia]."

> He was the official avenger of the killed, the policeman who was dispatched to the villages in order to stir up the natives and send them hunting, or put a stop to the endless gambling parties which prevented them from exerting themselves on behalf of the white traders.

"Chief Factors came and Chief Factors went," observed Morice, "but Waccan stayed under all governments."[34] When Postmaster William Morwick was killed in 1843 by a member of the Babine nation and Alexis Bélanger in 1849, Boucher was dispatched to remedy the situation because "his was, indeed, a name to conjure with among Natives."[35]

Though the fur trade ended, the pattern of Native involvement in dispute resolution did not; it continued into the settlement period. Vancouver Island's Governor James Douglas had hoped that a formally organized Native police force under the direction of the Chief Commissioner of Police would transform the Indian encampments around Victoria into model villages, but his utopian vision was unrealized.[36] Unlike the United States, Australia, or New Zealand, there was no formal, state-constituted Native constabulary on either the Island or the Mainland.[37] However, a volunteer force – the Victoria Voltigeurs – consisting largely of ex-fur trading "French Canadian half-breeds" with a taste for sartorial flamboyance did attempt to carry on the tradition started by their mainland counterpart, Waccan.[38] The Voltigeurs were used as early as 1853 in connection with the murder of HBC shepherd Peter Brown at Cowichan and were on call to deal with any disturbances between settlers living outside Victoria and the local Native population.[39]

Despite the presence of the Voltigeurs, it appeared that effective law enforcement in cases involving disputes between Indians or between Indians and whites depended on the active and independent intervention of Native peoples. Though the Voltigeurs were involved in the apprehension of the alleged killers of Peter Brown, the dispute was resolved only when the Cowichan themselves decided to hand over one of their own.[40] Other instances of Native involvement included the Penelekut band's capture of eighteen Lemalchi following the deaths of the Marks family in 1863;[41] the Secwepemcs' capturing Moise, who was implicated in a number of murders around Williams Lake, in the summer of 1863, and then again in 1865 after he had escaped;[42] and the resolution of the infamous Bute Inlet Massacre (1864). Despite the efforts of two expeditionary forces, the perpetrators of the massacre were brought to trial only because they had given themselves up voluntarily.[43]

After confederation, the federal government assumed responsibility for the Native peoples of Canada, including their policing. Indian agents, each responsible for the management of particular territories and the reserves within them, were empowered as justices of the peace and dealt with any disputes arising in their agencies. They also could appoint Indian constables, who held their offices at the agent's pleasure, thus introducing the possibility for the more regularized and formal policing of reserves. Self-policing was the essence of modern liberal governance, and Indians were no exception to this ideal.[44] No doubt, like their counterparts in the United States and Australia, Indian police in Canada were envisioned as "agents of acculturation,"[45] but in discussing the utility of Native police on the prairies, Hayter Reed also revealed another rationale for their creation. He suggested that Blackfoot scouts be attached to the police force, "as a means of usefully employing and enlisting on the side of law & order, other young

Indians, whom to support in idleness is not only costly, but fraught with danger to themselves and to the country."[46] Native policing thus would not only aid in the assimilation of Indians to Canadian law, but it would also keep young idle male hands and minds safely busy.

However, not all agents made use of their powers, and because Ottawa neither checked nor insisted constables be appointed, it is difficult to get a sense of how large the force was. We do, however, have a letter from British Columbia's Superintendent of Indian Affairs, I. W. Powell, that indicates what its ideal size was to be. Writing in late 1884, perhaps in response to the spate of disputes between Indians and whites on the northwest coast, Powell suggested that Ottawa "might undertake to supply badges for all the Indian policemen of the province,"[47] who, "after all give their services for little remuneration."[48] Though he recommended 200 badges be struck off, four years later (when nothing had been done), he reduced his figure by half, asking for between seventy-five and one hundred.[49] The kinds of activities Indian constables were engaged in or their effectiveness is also somewhat elusive. If Joe Cawston's career is any indication, Indian constables seemed to have been largely occupied dealing with drunkenness and violations of the liquor laws. Cawston was an Okanagan, employed on the Penticton reserve in 1910 perhaps because of the rising level of drunk and disorderly behaviour there. By all accounts, though he was considered competent, he could not singlehandedly combat the problems on the reserve, unsupported as he was by those he policed, the agent and provincial police.[50]

In 1888, perhaps because of the ineffectiveness of policing on reserves, Ottawa transferred responsibility for "the administration of justice and the preservation of peace among the Indians of the province" to Victoria.[51] Rather than do so directly by expanding the provincial police force, however, the province chose to give provincial constable status (but no pay) to the already existing Native police appointed by the agent.[52]

Despite the redrawing of jurisdictional lines, then, the policing of Indians remained unaffected. The Indian constables appointed by the agent were assisted by specials sworn in by the provincial police – as they had been even before 1888 – as the need arose. Though Joe Cawston may have had his troubles, from the scraps of evidence available, it does appear that Indians were both effective and necessary to law enforcement, assisting in the capture of other Indians implicated in the deaths of both Natives and whites: the McLean brothers in 1880;[53] Jacky and Twentyman in 1882; Ha-at in 1884;[54] Quamlet, the "Seabird Murderers" and Alex McLean in 1887;[55] Emia in 1891;[56] Charlie McGilvery and Henry Aleck in 1910;[57] and in the pursuit of Simon Gunanoot in 1906.[58] And, as Constable O'Daunt remarked in expressing his concern over the petition sent by the Lillooet and Secwepemc chiefs, their involvement did not end with the capture of Moses Paul and Paul Splintlum in 1913, for Indians were largely responsible for the capture of Charlie Perrault in 1914 and Alex Ignace in 1919.[59]

In addition to their involvement in these rather spectacular murder cases, Indian sworn as special constables were also involved in enforcing the law for offences other than murder. For instance, if we take 1882 as an example, Indians Kawaywyix, Michelle, Nellimen, and Billy aided in the pursuit and arrest of Indians Galls and Jules; Indians Joe and Charley conveyed prisoner Graham from Chemainus; Indian Jim assisted in the arrest of Indian Mary at Nicola; Indian Luke performed "unspecified services" at Boston Bar; and Nahamcheen and John arrested and brought George Shuttleworth to Osooyoos.[60] And the list goes on.[61]

As Shuttleworth's arrest suggests, Native specials intervened in cases involving both Natives and non-Natives suspected of crime, the most well known example being the pursuit of American train robber Bill Miner in 1906. Indians, it seemed, were implicated in the extension of state power over non-Natives as well as their own peoples.

Natives acting as specials were only the most visible of an elusive group of "Tontos," for others also participated directly in enforcing the Queen's law by guiding provincial constables through unfamiliar territory, hiring out their horses and canoes to the under-equipped lawmen, serving summonses, procuring witnesses, or acting as messengers.[62] For instance, Secwepemc tracker Philip Thomas was instrumental in providing the material evidence that convicted Paul Splintlum, acting as a modern "expert witness" would by interpreting the significance of his evidence. Thomas, reported the *Inland Sentinel*, "gave an interesting tale of the tracking of the fugitives, describing the movements of the men, their stopping places and how they employed their time in a way that would redound to the credit of the mythical Sherlock Holmes."

He pursued them, deductively, from the time they left on one horse until they captured another and mounted separate horses. He told how they had mended a pair of shoes on a big rock ...

Shown the exhibit pair of shoes, Philip said "These are the shoes which made the marks behind the log from which the shooting took place. We made little sticks and measured the tracks and then measured the shoes."

"How do you know?" queried Mr. Henderson.

"By the way they are worn down in the heels. . .," he replied.[63]

In another case, four Indians were paid to help construct the gallows at Lytton on which convicted murderer Ah Chow was hanged in 1887, while two others were hired to dig his grave.[64] Some even engaged in detective work, helping the crown build its case. After arresting Charlie McGilvery and Henry Aleck on suspicion of murdering John Barrick in 1910, Chief Constable Joseph Burr employed Indians Jimmy Retasket and Saul to listen in on the two as they sat in their prison cell, hoping they would implicate themselves. "As both of them [the accused] speak, not only English, but the Douglas Portage and Lillooet languages," Burr wrote to his superior, "I had to get some one who understood all three languages to hear what was said. I considered the parties I employed were the best I could get and most trustworthy."[65]

In addition to the Native constables empowered by the *Indian Act*, there were also those whose positions and power were created by missionaries. These "Tontos" were less shadowy figures than their secular counterparts, perhaps because they fit into a more specialized, self-conscious, and totalizing system of surveillance and control which rendered them more visible to the historian. At both Metlakatla, the mission settlement founded in 1862 by Anglican lay missionary William Duncan, and at Kamloops in 1878, under the Oblates of Mary Immaculate, Native constables played a central role in imposing a Christian social order on their brethren. Duncan also considered holding such an office to be "good training for the natives – [it] tends to enlist their sympathies on the side of the law – is less expensive to the government, and ultimately will afford a better guarantee of the preservation of the peace than if held by white men in their midst."[66] Under his direction, a volunteer, uniformed police force – in fact, the first uniformed police in British Columbia[67] – grew from ten in 1862 to forty by 1880.[68]

Crime, strictly speaking, was not the only concern of these volunteers, for Duncan's police had wide-ranging powers, from aiding in the prosecution of white liquor sellers, patrolling the village on Sundays to make sure all attended church, to scrutinizing the work habits, marital conduct, and religious devotion of all the residents of his model Indian village. A survey of the parson's civil records as a Justice of the Peace reveals the degree of surveillance and intervention that existed in Metlakatla thanks to the eyes and ears of the Native constables. Apart from sureties encompassing the broad, if vague, category of "good behaviour," others bound the signatory to "conduct myself as a Christian husband to my wife from this day ... ", or "to pay my wife ... the half of every thing I have got & the half of all I earn from this date for her support."[69] It was this kind of intervention that was, according to Jean Usher, "in part responsible for the reputation of totalitarianism that Metlakatla gained in some eyes."[70]

Despite the sectarian differences between the Anglican missions like William Duncan's and those of the Roman Catholic church, a spirit of ecumenism seemed to run through their efforts among British Columbia's Native peoples, for the Kamloops Mission, while not a utopian community like Metlakatla, did share many similarities in both the ends sought and the means employed to realize them. Native peoples at the Oblate-run mission were subject to a disciplinary system not unlike that imposed by William Duncan, and one which was aimed at transforming savages into civilized beings and creating an orderly, Christian community. Under the Durieu system (named after Bishop Paul Durieu), Natives governed themselves according to the precepts of both church and state as well as the bylaws enacted by a local village council consisting of the chief, captain, or sub-chief, and watchmen, who were responsible for the surveillance of conduct – all under the direction of the bishop and the local priests, who retained a seat on it. The council also sat as a court to hear and resolve disputes, meting out punishments that ranged from prayers and working in the mission's fields to fines and whipping. Native police assisted the watchmen in surveillance and enforcement of the law, overseeing everything from marital disputes, child neglect, and rowdyism to murder.[71]

The case of Alex Ignace reveals a history of intervention on the part of the council and the police, suggesting the range and degree of their powers.

Ignace's arrest by Native constables in 1919 and subsequent hanging for the murder of his wife Minnie was only the last in a series of clashes he had had with them. In the investigation which followed the murder, it became apparent that theirs was a troubled relationship, and that the watchmen and police had, on several occasions, intervened to bring Minnie back to the Kamloops reserve from the neighbouring Nicola one, where she was living "notoriously" with other men, forcing her to stay with her husband.[72] Alex proved to be no less of a problem, for the council also exercised its authority to make him live at home to care for his ailing father.[73] According to Indian Agent John Freemont Smith, Ignace, who had a taste for firearms, had been "a terror around the Kamloops Reserve for the past four or five years," committing a series of "minor depredations" for which "he was tried by the Chief, who sentenced him to get wood for his parents and the church for two months."[74]

Short of acting as the actual arms of enforcement, many more Indians aided in the imposition of the "Queen's law" as interpreters and crown witnesses in cases involving both Native and non-Native accused. Just as interpreters were necessary to "giving good measure" in the fur trade, they also enabled people to "talk straight" in the court room.[75] In cases involving Native peoples, rendering decisions, and decisions which were viewed as legitimate, often hinged on the degree to which the parties were able to communicate with precision to an audience who spoke another language.[76] Clarity was thus an important prerequisite for justice. Any uncertainty about the accused's or the witnesses' understanding of what was said to them could be used by a judge in making a case for clemency, as John Hamilton Gray did in *R. v. Wyachute* (1879). Because the most important testimony in the case did not come directly from the witnesses, but through interpreters, Gray told the Minister of Justice he was "not . . . inclined to punish anyone severely . . . on evidence diluted thro' interpretations of languages with which the Court, Counsel, and officers of justice are unacquainted."[77] Defence counsel frequently raised the issue of language in an attempt to cast doubt on the guilt of their clients or the credibility of the testimony of Crown witnesses whose first language was not English. The most striking example comes from the trial of Frank Jones, who stood accused of the murder of Gus Hall in 1916. In cross-examining James

Elsworth Green, Chief Detective of the Provincial Police Force, Jones' lawyer, W. F. Hansford, attempted to demonstrate that his client had not been properly warned upon arrest.[78] The presiding judge was so taken by Hansford's line of questioning he engaged in it himself, and chastised the detective for his conduct: "I will tell you now that you should use very plain language to an Indian. You must remember that they are very ignorant people, and using that formality in the Code would mean nothing to them."[79] Later, when it became clear that the interpreter was having difficulty putting questions to and getting answers from Lucy, an Indian woman, Murphy again intervened, observing that even with a skilled interpreter, "it is impossible to put questions in Chinook with sufficient distinctness to get a proper answer."[80]

As interpreters, then, Native peoples were quite literally the brokers of the Queen's law, their skills making its day-to-day administration possible. Equally important for its longterm legitimacy, any justice that was done and seen to be done through the law rested, to a great extent, on their shoulders.

Important though Native interpreters were to the legal process, their services would not have been necessary were it not for a willingness on the part of other Native peoples to testify as crown witnesses. In all the cases of Native people who were capitally convicted from 1867 to 1930 other Natives testified for the crown. Aboriginal crown witnesses also figured in the prosecution of Europeans and Chinese, particularly those charged with selling liquor to Indians. This should hardly be surprising, for if there were to be any eyewitnesses to a crime involving Indians or Indians and whites it was more likely that they would be Native than not (given the demography and the nature of settlement in the province). In any case, simple proximity to the accused meant they were the people who were most likely to be familiar with him or her and the victim, as well as the circumstances surrounding the dispute. British Columbia may have been a society segmented by race, as Peter Ward argues, but it was not one in which racial boundaries precluded social intercourse of the kind which entangled Indians, Europeans, and Asians in activities which could lead them into its courtrooms.[81]

While it is difficult to generalize about the impact and importance of Native peoples' testimony in shaping verdicts, it is safe to say that without their participation, convictions would have been difficult, if not impossible to secure. The importance of Indian testimony to those charged with the administration of justice is borne out by the debate surrounding it – a debate which began in the fur trade and carried on through the colonial period. In December 1851 Chief Factor James Douglas wrote to Earl Grey, drawing his attention to "a difficulty of some weight" involving "the settlement of disputes between the Colonists and Indians." Douglas had been approached by Tenasman, a Sooke chief, who complained that a white settler, Thomas Hall, had taken his double-barrelled fowling piece and given him an inferior weapon in return. Unfortunately, the only evidence Tenasman could offer was that of another Native, whose evidence could not be entered because he was not a Christian and so could not be sworn by the usual oath. Douglas entertained no doubts that Tenasman had been duped, but was forced to side with Hall for lack of evidence. The incident left him uneasy. It seemed manifestly unjust to "reject the only species of testimony [Indians] may have to offer"; and moreover, he continued, "when offences against the life or property are committed by Indians the only testimony against the offender may be that of their own countrymen." If it were rejected, a conviction would be impossible. In addition to these immediate effects, rejecting Indian testimony also had more far reaching consequences: one could hardly expect Indians to put aside "their own hasty and precipitate acts of private revenge," and submit their disputes to English law if that same law rejected their testimony.[82]

Nowhere was the tension between English law, with its requirement for sworn testimony, and the practical necessity of securing convictions more apparent than in enforcing the restrictions on selling liquor to Indians. Colonial and later Dominion statutes made it illegal to sell liquor to Indians, but because liquor sellers could not be convicted on Indian evidence alone, they continued to engage in their criminal activity "with impunity." As a result of this "strange anomaly," steps were taken to modify legal procedure, allowing Indian testimony to be admitted with a simple affirmation rather than oath.[83]

Native peoples' engagement with the law in British Columbia was thus not limited to standing in the dock or on the scaffold, for some also played a role in its enforcement whether as constables, trackers, guides, interpreters, or crown witnesses. Having established their presence and significance in extending European power – given these Tontos their due in the most basic of ways – the more important questions of understanding the reasons for and meaning of Native peoples' engagement with the "Queen's law" remains, and it is to that I now turn.

Law, Culture, and Colonization

If it is clear that some Natives peoples' engagement with the law took the form of their active participation in upholding it – often against their own people as well as non-Natives – and that such participation was in many cases crucial to the effective extension of state power in British Columbia, their motives for doing so are less apparent and certainly more elusive. Why did they do it? Coercion? Perhaps. Certainly, those who lived under the penetrating gaze of Duncan at Metlakatla or the Oblates at Kamloops must have felt its force, but there are many examples of Native people being somewhat less than overawed by European power.[84] In any case, it was the lack of coercive force on the part of whites throughout the period to 1930 that necessitated Native involvement in law enforcement in the first place. If not coercion, does false consciousness or assimilation to European values explain Native peoples' actions? Again, perhaps, but such an explanation is unsatisfying, chiefly because it denies the possibility that Indians acted strategically and in accordance with their own agenda.

On the basis of the capital cases surveyed, I would argue that some Native peoples engaged the law as they did because they stood to gain from doing so. They used the law strategically and instrumentally as a means of furthering their own material interests and that of the communities they lived in. Murder was, presumably, something both Native and white communities had an interest in resolving – albeit in different ways and for different reasons. That said, however, self-interest is not a sufficient explanation. To understand why Indians like Jimmy Retasket and the other chiefs did what they did also requires us to understand how their self-interest and their choices were structured by both their own culture and the institutions of colonization.

Aiding in the apprehension of suspected wrongdoers quite literally brought material rewards to those who did so. Though bounty hunting was not a common characteristic of law enforcement in British Columbia, there were instances of Native peoples collecting cash rewards for the capture of fugitives from justice.[85] For instance, Chief Louis Good received $100 for the capture and conviction of Indian Antoine in 1885[86]; Iscumera-ha-ha $100 for Kitwancool Jim in 1888[87]; Seamore and Basile $50 each for catching P. Carlson in 1889[88]; and Carmichael and Lizzie $33.33 each for Sing Kee in 1892.[89] As well, working for the colonial or provincial authorities as an interpreter or crown witness brought its own more modest remuneration.

More important perhaps than the material rewards that accrued to those who upheld the Queen's law were the opportunities doing so provided to rid their communities of people they considered troublemakers. For instance, in 1903 the chief and council of Kitkatla had their village's Native constables arrest Daniel Whadiboo for practicing witchcraft and hold him – still handcuffed – in an unheated house for several days in the winter. According to the Anglican missionary there, however, "the said wizard Daniel" was in fact a Christian convert, "more enlightened than any other Kitkatla and consequently much disliked."[90] When it became clear the chief and council had used the legal authority vested in the constables to settle old scores, they were dismissed by the agent, who replaced them with his own interim appointees. In addition, they, along with the constables involved, were arrested, tried for false imprisonment, and fined a total of $700.[91]

While Native constables' use of the Queen's law to imprison Christian converts as witches was a serious enough abuse of power in the eyes of white authorities, even more disturbing was the prospect of innocent men and women being sent to the gallows. In discussing the problems of legal administration in a colony whose indigenous population far outstripped its European one, Attorney General Thomas Wood warned that it would be very easy for Indians, in turning over alleged wrongdoers, to subvert the legal process by sacrificing a slave or two in the place of the real criminal, or – equally worrisome – to appropriate the machinery of British justice for their own ends, using it to rid themselves of disruptive individuals without having to dirty their own hands.[92] It appears that the warning was as prescient as it was apocryphal, for in the period to 1930 there were several cases in which Natives appeared to do just what Wood predicted.[93] Indeed, in Tom Klemadikdinhuhu's 1909 murder trial it was so obvious that the accused was being railroaded by his own people his lawyer made an issue of it in an attempt to discredit crown testimony. Witness this cross-examination of Johnson, a Native from Nahwhittie who testified for the Crown:

Q: What was the relationship between the prisoner and the other members of his tribe? Was he popular? ...

A: No, he is not very popular.

Q: Not very well liked?

A: Not very well liked.

Q: The Indians there would be pretty glad to get rid of Tom, wouldn't they?

A: I believe so, because he bears not a very good character.

Or this cross-examination of Mrs. Peter done through an interpreter:

Q: Ask her what she thinks of Tom, the prisoner.

A: I don't think very much about him.

Q: She doesn't like him, does she?

A: She says, "Why should I like him? I don't know him."

Q: Ask her if the Indians would be glad to get rid of Tom?

A: Well, I know his own people don't wish him to be with them all the time.[94]

Less tangible, but no less compelling than the material rewards and the opportunity for ridding their communities of disruptive individuals, was the status, and hence the power attached to enforcing the Queen's law. The terms under which Paul and Splintlum were surrendered to provincial authorities were indicative of the status attached to upholding the law and how Indians used their engagement with it as a vehicle to gain standing vis-à-vis other Native peoples. Far from wanting to shroud what could easily be read as their "traitorous" actions in secrecy, the chiefs, in their negotiations with the province, agreed that their cooperation and active involvement would be recognized publicly and in perpetuity. To this end, they insisted that "as a Reward for the good services rendered by certain of the Chiefs in procuring the surrender of the Outlaws,"

the Government of BC would have a nice medal struck off, commemorative of the event, with the name of each Chief on it, and the name of his tribe, which could be handed down from Father to Son, showing what the old Chiefs had done in the interest of law and order and to show their loyalty to the Crown.[95]

The Attorney General and Henry Birks complied, fashioning a medal according to Cummiskey's specifications: they were to be made "of silver and of good design and to have a ribbon of red, white, and blue together with a clasp so they can be worn by the chiefs on all great occasions," he suggested. "Each medal [is] to have inscribed on it the King's Coat of Arms, the Chief's name, the band over which he rules and a short statement of the cause for which it was struck."[96]

The fact the chiefs wanted their actions commemorated with medals and that, as Constable Burr recalled, "they were very particular as to who gets them" suggests Retasket and the others hoped to gain some status and power by allying themselves with provincial authorities – and, as what happened in the wake of the arrest of Paul and Splintlum indicates, to gain status within their own communities and vis-à-vis other Native groups. That this was the case is indicated by Constable O'Daunt's report of the disagreements in the Native communities over who deserved credit for capturing the Wild Boys. The Lillooet, wrote O'Daunt, "are sore at having the credit of their deed taken from them in the fashion it has been." Not only had the newspapers been full of what he called "the yarns of various glory-hunting Chief Constables," but many Secwepemc, who were not directly involved in the capture (though it did occur in their territory) were also claiming credit.[97] To add insult to injury, the Secwepemcs' claim was reinforced by the venue of the trial. Despite the Lillooet chiefs' attempts to change it, the Wild Boys stood trial in Kamloops, right in the middle of Secwepemc territory.[98] As "this will not be the last case we shall require Indian help on either it is well to look ahead," O'Daunt felt compelled to make his concerns known. "The only people deserving of any credit in the affair are Tyee Jimmy [Retasket] of Lillooet, Major Churchill of Leon Creek, and High Bar Joe," he wrote.

> The other Indians only came on the scene with Burr and the rest of them once the roundup was complete.
>
> Knowing as you do the high feeling of the Indians over this case you will appreciate the nature of the task Jimmy undertook and you will see that he has good cause to feel sore at the outcome of it.[99]

In this case, Native peoples' engagement with the law might thus be read as a strategic use of state power to gain leverage in civil society, and it is all the more intriguing because of the cross-cultural context in which these events occurred. Jimmy Retasket and his friends may have hoped to use an alien cultural form – European law – as a means to distinguish themselves within their own communities. Moreover, the conflicting claims of credit for the capture of Paul and Splintlum – claims lodged, it would appear, by different aboriginal nations – suggests that some Native peoples might have considered an alliance with provincial authorities as a way of achieving status within their own communities. The law, then, was a recognized source of power that could be deployed by some Native people to serve their own private interests – interests that could be quite separate from those of the state.

There was more to the chiefs' actions, however, than this instrumentalist interpretation allows. Self-interest did not and does not exist outside of particular cultural and historical contexts. To get another angle of vision on their possible motivations, we need to place the chiefs' actions in the context of their own concepts of law. Understanding aboriginal law-ways is difficult at best, and trying to understand them historically is even more problematic. Nevertheless, some recent work by John Phillip Reid provides us with a vantage point from which to view the surrender of Paul and Splintlum. Reid argues that in the transboundary west a "pan-Indian" law of homicide governed the ways *both* Native peoples and European fur trappers thought about killings and their subsequent response to them.[100] Simply put, a homicide between members of the same nation was justly answered by killing either the perpetrator of the deed or a member of his or her family. If, however, the homicide was international – that is, if it involved members of different nations – then it could be avenged by the death of any member of the alleged killer's nation. These "principles of vengeance," as Reid dubbed them, were absolute, as they treated all killings as equal in severity; no heed was paid to the context in which the killing took place. An unprovoked or premeditated murder merited the same response as what we now might deem manslaughter.

However, not all homicides needed to be answered in blood. Compensation in in the form of trade goods was possible, and indeed, it was in negotiating the blood price that the parties involved could in fact take account of the circumstances of the killing. When the price was met, the dispute was considered settled. Compensation not only recognized the differing degrees of responsibility and blame that could be attached to the commission of a criminal act, but it also created a more certain way for the parties involved to go on in their relationships. It was, as Thomas Stone calls it, a "forward-looking" form of dispute settlement.[101] As Reid points out, vengeance, particularly in cases of international homicide, could occasionally result in an escalation of hostilities and an all-out war. By opting for compensation, the parties involved were more likely to be in a position to resume peaceful relations.

When the chiefs turned over Moses Paul and Paul Splintlum to the provincial authorities they did so in a particular cultural and historical context; one in which both Natives and Europeans had shared the same understanding of how to respond to homicide. The principles of vengeance developed during the fur trade continued into the early settlement period. Indeed, their continuity on Vancouver Island was a source of complaint among settlers who had no connection with the Hudson's Bay Company and did not appreciate the relations of ruling developed by their fur trader-governor. James Douglas would have done better, these settlers thought, to make the Indians "smell powder and ball instead of perpetuating the old system of doling out blankets to them."[102] Recent work by Hamar Foster and Jonathan Swainger extends Reid's thesis about principles of vengeance beyond the fur trade period to the end of the nineteenth century, and my own research indicates that such considerations continued to animate the administration of homicide law into the twentieth century, particularly with respect to the appointment of defence counsel and the exercise of the prerogative of mercy.[103] In meeting the chiefs' request that Paul and Splintlum be given a fair trial, Attorney General W. J. Bowser agreed to pay for their defence, and sought the advice of Thomas Cummiskey, the province's Superintendent of Indian Affairs, on the best way of proceeding. The province would do well to furnish counsel rather than allowing the chiefs to employ one of their own choosing, Cummiskey advised. As a matter of policy, the Superintendent "forbid the chiefs to allow their people to pay any money to a lawyer." His reasons for doing so are important for they reveal the province's recognition that the compensation ethic – Indian law – continued to shape the legal process. Allowing Indians to retain counsel would, Cummiskey argued, have a bad effect on the Indian Mind. Many of the Indians would look upon money subscribed as so much towards saving the prisoners and in case they were executed the Indian would feel much injured by the "Whites."[104]

The "Indian Mind" Cummiskey described was, it appears, one which saw money as a just and adequate compensation for harms. Because Native peoples considered payment of money precluded physical punishment, misunderstanding and bad feeling could often accompany the sentencing of a convicted criminal, particularly if the sentence passed was capital.

Judges had often appointed counsel for Indians who appeared in the dock undefended, but Cummiskey's policy was a local variation of a federal one initiated some time around the turn of the century, and designed to regularize the process.[105] Counsel were to be appointed by the Department of Justice before the start of the trial, rather than in court. Theoretically, this would give them more time to prepare and to construct a better defence. However, it also gave the Department of Indian Affairs a degree of control it had not previously had. While neither the province nor the federal government could deny Native peoples their right to counsel, they did attempt to control their legal representation by limiting the pool of lawyers from which Indians could choose and still retain funding. Indians were of course free to retain defence counsel of their choice rather than one deemed suitable by the Department of Justice, but if they did they could not expect the Department of Indian Affairs to pay.

Just as a recognition of the force of Indian law shaped white policy with respect to the appointment of defence counsel, it also left its imprint on the exercise of mercy. Native law-ways were both recognized and taken into account by at least some of British Columbia's trial judges in determining whether a homicide was provoked by the actions of the victim – whether that victim was Native or white. Provocation did not transform guilt into innocence, but it could reduce the crime from murder to manslaughter, and commute the sentence of death to life imprisonment. Qutlnoh (1872), Toby (1878), Tsimequor (1888), Johnny Peters (1904), and Big Alec and Edie (1923) were all tried for murder and had their sentences commuted because the presiding judge held that their actions were provoked by the victim, who in each of these cases was said to be a sorcerer or one who was practicing witchcraft or "bad medicine" against the accused or his family.[106] In Attoo's case (1879), the law, as the Minister of Justice's office phrased it, was "allowed to take its course"; however, in reporting on the trial Begbie did point out that the accused was likely provoked by a "breach of conjugal duty. . . The law of conjugal honor is very severe among the fishing tribes of the north west coast. . . I believe such was the provocation in the present case; and that the woman's life was not worth 5 minutes when the deceased interfered."[107] Henry Crease was more successful in convincing the Minister of Justice that Ha-at, found guilty of murdering white storekeeper Amos Youmans at the Forks of the Skeena in 1884, was motivated by Youmans' failure to respect and observe the Indian law relating to the death of an Indian in his (Youman's) employ.[108] Thus, in dispensing mercy, British Columbia's judges recognized that provocation was culturally constructed. Though their sensitivity did not always result in a commutation, it does underscore the enduring influence of Native culture on the administration of European law.

To the Secwepemc and Lillooet Chiefs, Splintlum's hanging was a breach of this ethic of compensation. Despite Constable Burr's insistence that the guilty parties would hang for their crime, the chiefs felt that their assistance in capturing the Wild Boys would preclude the law from taking its course. Their failure to secure a commutation for Paul Splintlum suggests that there were limits to Native peoples' influence on dispute resolution. While they may have greatly shaped the terms by which international homicides were dealt during the nineteenth century as Reid and Foster argue, such was not the case in later years. Despite the continuity and centrality of their engagement with the law well into the twentieth century, Native peoples were not similarly positioned over time: indeed, the ground on which they stood was literally being eroded under their feet. While Native culture continued to shape their engagement with the law in the manner discussed, other factors were at play; factors which structured Native peoples' ability to act. In just a few generations, Indians went from comprising a majority of the population to a distinct minority as a result of both disease and a massive inflow of immigrants in the late-nineteenth century.[109] This demographic shift was accompanied by a decline – uneven though it was – in the numbers of Indians employed as special constables and in other aspects of law enforcement, as well as the systematic dispossession of Native lands and the imposition of a number of disciplinary regimes by the both the state and organized religion aimed at transforming "savages" into citizens.[110]

It is within this context of colonization that we must situate and read the story of the Wild Boys' capture. Doing so does not deny the argument made thus far about their motives – but it does complicate it. The Lillooet and Secwepemc chiefs' engagement with the law *was* strategic and culturally-conditioned; however, the context in which they acted structured their choices differently than they had been during the fur trade. It was not that Native peoples had agency during the fur trade and then somehow lost it completely with settlement. Agency and oppression – the twin poles around which much of the writing of the history of so-called "marginal" groups has been written – were not discrete and exclusive conditions of being, but instead can only be understood in specific contexts. In the case of the Wild Boys, the institutions and agents of colonial domination reconfigured self-interest: Indians like Jimmy Retasket still made choices strategically, and those choices were still mediated by "culture," but the range of possibilities open to them was, as we will see, different.

The Lillooet and Secwepemc chiefs who brokered the surrender of Moses Paul and Paul Splintlum did so, I've argued, in part for the status it conferred, and they did so within the context of particular cultural conventions surrounding homicide. There was, however, more to the Secwepemcs' actions. Their choice to participate in the capture of the Wild Boys and to perhaps claim more credit than was due them were in part structured by the *Indian Act* and the Durieu system, both of which introduced a greater degree and different kind of political instability and social tension among the bands of the Kamloops Agency than perhaps had existed before their imposition.

The *Indian Act* recognized two kinds of chiefs: hereditary ones, and ones who were appointed by the agent or elected by band members under his direction. Those appointed or elected held their positions at the pleasure of the agent and the Department, who could, at any time, remove them for "dishonesty, intemperance, immorality, or incompetence."[111] In the years preceding and following the capture of Paul and Splintlum, the agent – if his actions were any indication – was mightily displeased. Many of those elected chief were deposed, sometimes against the wishes of the people who had voted for them. For instance, in 1903 agent Irwin deposed the elected chief of the Little Shuswap Lake band, Francois Silpahan. When his replacement, Isaac Thomas, proved unpopular, Irwin was forced to depose him and reinstate Silpahan.[112] Irwin also interfered regularly in the affairs of the Head of the Lake reserve, which, though in Okanagan territory, was also under his charge.[113] The pattern of agent intervention continued among the Secwepemc even after Irwin's tenure, for the Little Shuswap Lake band had five different chiefs between 1912 and 1923, all of whom had been elected at one point and then deposed or forced to resign. Other bands in the Kamloops agency displayed similar, if less pronounced, patterns.[114] Given this instability and the factionalization it produced, perhaps some of the Secwepemc seized the opportunity to solidify their political fortunes by assisting in the capture of the two "outlaws" – who conveniently were not members of their nation – and loudly claiming credit, in an attempt to ingratiate themselves with the agent, who, after all, had their political futures in his hands.

Like the *Indian Act*, the Durieu system provided some Indians with the opportunity to enhance their own power by linking their fortunes to an institution and a set of values which, though inspired by humanitarian impulses, were hostile to many aspects of Native peoples' culture. Prior to the imposition of the Oblate system, Secwepemc social organization was relatively non-hierarchical. According to anthropologist James Teit, there were no nobility or clan divisions, and chieftainship, though hereditary, brought no special privileges. Authority flowed largely from personal esteem and needed to be nurtured constantly through the performance of certain deeds and the display of particular skills.[115] All of this changed under the Durieu system. Secwepemc communities came to be characterized by a more rigid hierarchy consisting of chiefs, captains, and watchmen whose power flowed from priestly sanction. Because consensus no longer underpinned governance to the same extent, the potential for social conflict was heightened. That potential was made all the greater by the need on the part of the chiefs and council to maintain the favour of the Oblates by doing things like assisting in the capture of the Wild Boys. However, winning priestly favour could mean alienating those they governed and increasing the factionalization within their communities – both of which made governance all the more difficult.

Factions and social conflict had always existed within Native communities, but with the injection of a new source of power in the form of the missionary, they intensified, as the fact that some Indians turned to the white man's secular law for relief from the harm inflicted by his ecclesiastical variety suggests. For instance, in 1875, two Lillooet chiefs wrote to justice of the peace E.H. Sanders complaining that the floggings meted out to three Indians for having "illicit connections" were unjust. "I should prefer," one of them wrote, "the Indians be treated as other people and brought before the proper tribunal if they offend – we had no such thing as whipping before the Roman Catholic priests came among us."[116] In 1892 this simmering discontent manifested itself in criminal charges. Lucy, a Native girl, had been brutally flogged not just once but twice for keeping company with a young man, and swore an affidavit to that effect which resulted in the arrest and conviction of Killapowtkin, Etwal, Cultus Johnny, Charley, Joe, *and* Father Eugène Casimir Chirouse, the Oblate priest who allegedly ordered the punishment, for assault. In the aftermath, Agent J.W. McKay reported that the Indians around Kamloops "are evidently becoming alive to the ridiculous position held by their chiefs when they assume without warrants the powers and importance of regularly constituted courts ... The support of the Missioners itinerating amongst them," he concluded, "is the only incentive which keeps alive the usurped authority which has caused the late unpleasantness regarding the girl at Lafountain."[117] Other sanctions, like those imposed on Alex and Minnie Ignace or the public shaming inflicted on sabbath breakers were bound to create tensions similar to the ones that resulted in criminal charges being laid against Chirouse, the chief and his councillors; tensions that were a result of the efforts of some Indians to consolidate and maintain their positions by allying themselves with the Oblates. Priestly power was a significant resource itself, but because the missionaries could also influence band elections, maintaining their favour was doubly important.[118]

The Durieu system may have increased social conflict generally, but Lucy's flogging and the restrictions placed on Minnie Ignace also suggest that some of those tensions were concentrated along particular fault lines –

those of gender. Beginning as early as the 1860s and 70s and particularly in the period from the turn-of-the-century to the first world war, the chiefs and councils of both the interior plateau nations and others around the province asserted their dominion over their "stolen women," insisting they be allowed to rescue these "erring ones" from a "concubinage" imposed by white and Chinese men and to apprehend any children that may have resulted from these illicit unions.[119] Because their wishes coincided with those of the Christian clergy – both Protestant and Catholic – to regulate the morals of their aboriginal charges, they were more readily realized. Armed with the coercive power vested in them by the Oblates, some Native men – the chiefs, watchmen, and police – were able to compel and control Native women in a manner which they may not have been able to do before. Gender conflict, while not created by colonization, was certainly intensified and given a particular form by it.[120]

Both the *Indian Act* and the missionary systems imposed by the Oblates and the Anglicans thus provided additional and alternative sources of power for some Native peoples. Possessed of an authority derived from a source which lay outside their traditional communities, chiefs, councillors, and watchmen wielded a degree of power over their communities they might never have had. As oppressive, destabilizing, divisive, and culturally alien as the legal systems set up by both civil and secular white authorities were, then, they did open up new possibilities for some Indians. The Queen's law, it seemed, empowered some even as it oppressed others.

These new cultural futures were signified by particular artifacts: the silver medals struck by the province to commemorate the chiefs' role in capturing Paul and Splintlum; the silver-tipped staff given to Se-in-shoot, who testified against Kalabeen and Scotha, by Governor James Douglas as a symbol of his favoured status as one of the Queen's People; the framed certificate of merit given to John Wesley Mountain for his role in capturing Ha-at; and perhaps most simply the silver badges handed out by the Indian Agent to those Natives who agreed to act as constables and specials.[121] These artifacts had meaning to their owners; they were status symbols, deployed for the distinction they conveyed. Why else would Se-in-shoot carry his staff into the witness box, gripping it as he gave testimony; or Philip Thomas wear his constable's badge proudly as he did the same in the

Splintlum case; and why would John Wesley Mountain display his certificate of merit on the wall for all to see?

While displaying artifacts like these was an act of distinction, it can also be read as evidence of white hegemony. The practice of awarding "good" Indians material goods as symbols of white favour had its origins in the fur trade with the Hudson's Bay Company's attempts to secure a regular supply of pelts. The limited authority of Native band leaders meant that European traders often were forced to deal with different "trading captains" year after year and, often, to negotiate different terms of trade. In an attempt to stabilize band leadership and thus simplify its trading relations, the Hudson's Bay Company extended both credit and goods to particular trading captains, hoping to increase the authority of these leaders in the eyes of the Natives they commanded, and – because authority was tied to European favour – to thus ensure its supply of furs. The "Captain's Outfit" was particularly important symbol of this new authority. Modelled after European military uniforms, it spoke for both the wearer's new power and his dependency.[122]

However, to take such a view to the exclusion of the capillary level of power would be to overlook the multiple meanings and uneven effects of Native peoples' engagement with the law, an engagement which, as I have discussed, served some individual and community interests and was consistent with their notion of law. It would also be to miss the extent to which their engagement with the law influenced its exercise over them, whether it be in shaping their right to counsel or the exercise of mercy. Finally, focussing on the hegemonic power of the Queen's law over Indians misses the counter-hegemonic possibilities embedded in the ritual display of the artifacts of her favour. In styling themselves as the Queen's People, Retasket, Se-in-shoot, Mountain, Thomas, and all the Native constables who wore their badges with pride did not necessarily see themselves the Queen's ciphers, embodying and celebrating the superiority of European values, for if the missionary William Collison is to be believed, such artifacts could be appropriated by Native peoples and be given new and unexpected meanings. In a letter to the Superintendent General of Indian Affairs in 1925, Collison reported that an Indian chief on the Nass River "had his ticket-of-leave [a document indicating the possessor is a *convict*, though one who was granted leave] framed and placed in a conspicuous place in his house and calls everybody's attention to it because he is so impressed with the signature and red seals on the parchment."[123] Like all futures, the new cultural futures had by engaging the law could be uncertain, surprising, and sometimes subversive – as Gary Larson's Lone Ranger discovered when he finally learned the real meaning of "Kemosabe."[124] There was more to Tonto, it seemed, than met the eye.

Notes

1. This essay is for Lawrin Armstrong and Don Kirschner. An earlier version of this paper was given at the American Society for Legal History Conference, Memphis, Tennessee, 22-23 October 1993, as "Chasing the "Wild Boys": Native Peoples' Engagement with the Law in British Columbia." Thanks to the commentators at that session, John Wunder and Elizabeth Higginbotham, and to Constance Backhouse, John Beattie, Hamar Foster, Robert Fraser, Robert McDonald, John McLaren, and Carolyn Strange.

2. See Pierre Berton, *Hollywood's Canada: the Americanization of our National Image* (Toronto: McClelland and Stewart, 1975) and Keith Walden, *Visions of Order: the Mounties in Symbol and Myth* (Toronto: Butterworths, 1982) on this theme.

3. Thanks to my colleague, Don Kirschner, for pointing this out to me.

4. Tonto was a "caricature" rather than a "character." On "character" versus "caricature" in writing, see James Boyd White, *The Legal Imagination*, Abridged Edition (Chicago: University of Chicago Press, 1985), xiv., 113-114. Character is "the successful rendition of personality: believable, full, complex, living and breathing, and so on. Caricature is the reverse: it is a way of talking about people that reduces them to single, exaggerated aspects, to labels, roles, moments from their lives; it is narrow, two-dimensional, unconvincing. Character is true to life; caricature false to it."

5. Jane Tompkins notes that Indians do not, ironically, figure in Westerns as individuals or a people with a point-of-view. Like women, they are "repressed. . . And when they do appear they are even more unreal."

> At least women in Westerns are not played by men. At least horses are not played by dogs, or cattle by goats. Faked scenery is more convincing than fake Indians are. . . An Indian in a Western who is supposed to be a real person has to be played by a white man. The Indians played by actual natives are extras, generic brand; those with bit parts are doodles in the margin of the film.

> See her *West of Everything: the Inner Life of Westerns* (New York, Oxford: Oxford University Press, 1992), 9.

6. "The Eighteenth Brumaire of Louis Bonaparte," in Robert C. Tucker, ed., *The Marx-Engels Reader*, Second Edition (New York: W.W. Norton, 1978), 595.

7. This is the theme of much recent work in legal anthropology. Two recent collections provide a good introduction to this literature: June Starr and Jane F. Collier,

eds., *History and Power in the Study of Law: New Directions in Legal Anthropology* (Ithaca, N.Y.: Cornell University Press, 1989), and Mindie Lazarus-Black and Susan Hirsch, eds., *Contested States: Law, Hegemony, and Resistance* (New York: Routledge, 1994).

8. This is the title of a recent book on policing British Columbia. Lynne Stonier-Newman's *Policing a Pioneer Province* (Victoria: Harbour Publishing, 1992), while outlining the history of the British Columbia Provincial Police, deals with Native peoples primarily as subjects for surveillance or objects of prosecution.

9. Emphasis added. Memorandum for the Hon. Minister of Justice by Pierre M. Coté, for the Deputy Minister of Justice, 22 November 1913. *R. v. Paul Splintum*, capital case file [CCF hereafter]. National Archives of Canada [NAC hereafter]. RG 13, V. 1463, file 494A.

10. O'Daunt to Campbell, Lillooet, 16 January 1913. *R. v. Paul Splintlum*, CCF.

11. "Wild Boys" from O'Daunt to Campbell, Lillooet, 16 January 1913. *R. v. Paul Splintlum*, CCF. Information on the killing of Whyte and Ah Wye from British Columbia. Attorney General. Documents. R. v. Moses Paul (1913). British Columbia Archives and Records Service [BCARS hereafter]. GR 419, v. 178, 1913, file 184.

12. Forsythe to Campbell, Clinton, 16 December 1912; telegram from Fernie to Campbell, Kamloops, 25 December 1912; and telegram from Burr to Campbell, Ashcroft, 27 December 1912. All from *R. v. Paul Splintlum*, CCF. Information on the national affiliations of Natives in the reserves mentioned taken from Wilson Duff, *The Indian History of British Columbia: volume one, The Impact of the White Man* (Victoria: Provincial Museum of British Columbia, 1965), 30-31.

13. A relation of Raymond Burr, TV's Perry Mason and a British Columbian.

14. Cummiskey to Bowser, Vernon, BC, 4 January 1913. In *R. v. Paul Splintum*, CCF.

15. *Ibid.*

16. "Wild boys" is how the Indians referred to Paul and Splintlum, according to one of the constables involved in their arrest. See O'Daunt to Campbell, Lillooet, 16 January 1914. *R. v. Paul Splintlum*, CCF. Moses Paul was sentenced to life imprisonment. He died at the New Westminster penitentiary in 1917.

17. This is how Allan Greer described the police force in Lower Canada. See his "The Birth of the Modern Police in Canada," in Allan Greer and Ian Radforth, eds., *Colonial Leviathan: State Formation in Mid-Nineteenth Century Canada* (Toronto: University of Toronto Press, 1992), 19.

18. In 1860 Attorney General Cary reported that the Police Department in Victoria consisted of two sergeants of police and five ordinary policemen. Four years later, the two sergeants oversaw eight ordinary policemen for the entire Island. See Cary to Douglas, Attorney General's Office, 11 October 1860; Vancouver Island, Colonial Correspondence. BCARS, GR 1372, box 147, file 48; and Kennedy to Newcastle, Victoria, 7 July 1864, CO 305/22, 314-322.

   In 1865 (just past the height of the Cariboo rush and at the onset of the Kootenay), there were constables stationed at most areas of white settlement. Osoyoos, Kootenay, Columbia, Cariboo, Quesnel, Williams Creek, Alexandria, Bella Coola, Cayoosh, Lytton, Yale, Hope, Fort Shepherd, Douglas, and Derby each had a single constable, while Lillooet boasted three, and Richfield and New Westminster four each. See Stonier-Newman, 26, and Frederick John Hatch, "The

British Columbia Police, 1858-1871," UBC MA thesis, 1955, Appendix B.

19. Chartres Brew, who had come to British Columbia expecting to form and head a colonial police force found Governor James Douglas less than enthusiastic. The costs associated with creating a force of 150 men was too high in the governor's view. He put off its formation and called instead for the Colonial Office to send out 150 members of the Irish Constabulary. The Colonial Office recoiled at having to bear the cost of doing so, and as a result, nothing was done. See Douglas to Lytton, Victoria, Vancouver's Island, 27 December 1858. Great Britain. Colonial Office. British Columbia Original Correspondence. CO 60/1, 534-543. NAC. MG 11, reel B-77. Also see Stonier-Newman, *Policing a Pioneer Province*, Chapter One, and Hatch, "The British Columbia Police," 57-59.

20. On the Royal Engineers, see F.W. Howay, *The Work of the Royal Engineers in British Columbia, 1858 to 1863* (Victoria: R. Wolfenden 1910); Beth Hill, *Sappers: The Royal Engineers in British Columbia* (Ganges, B.C.: Horsdal and Schubert 1987); and Frances Woodward, "The Influence of the Royal Engineers on the Development of British Columbia," *BC Studies*, 24 (1974-5), 3-51.

21. Barry M. Gough, *Gunboat Frontier: British Maritime Authority and Northwest Coast Indians, 1846-1890* (Vancouver: UBC Press, 1984); and his "'Turbulent Frontiers' and British Expansion: Governor Douglas, the Royal Navy and the British Columbia Gold Rushes," *Pacific Historical Review*, 41 (1972): 15-32.

22. Gilbert Malcolm Sproat's criticisms of using gunboats to overawe British Columbia's Native peoples are indicative of the kinds of moral concerns some people had of the practice. "It has long been a matter of regret to me that the Government of the country should have been exhibited to these coast Indians in immediate connection with the idea of force, and no other idea," he told the Superintendent of Indian Affairs in 1879. "I am not prepared to deny that this exhibition of force has had its uses in past times among the wilder tribes and that the Knowledge of the presence of Gunboats in these waters is in some degree useful now, but the question in my mind is whether this display of rude power has not been too frequent and unvaried, and whether it is a practice which the Canadian government will think fit to sanction. . . One objection to the method is that it probably punishes many innocent persons for one who is guilty, and how does the commander know whether there is any proof against the alleged Criminal?

"What would be said if a white Nova Scotian village were bombarded and plundered by one of Her Majesty's ships on the obligation of policemen that they had been roughly treated in attempting to arrest an alleged criminal in the village?" See Sproat to the Superintendent General of Indian Affairs, Gulf of Georgia, 6 September 1879. NAC. Canada, Department of Indian Affairs, RG 10, Black Series, vol. 3698, f 15927, reel C-10122.

23. Jean Barman, *The West Beyond the West: a History of British Columbia* (Toronto: University of Toronto Press, 1990), 363.

24. See British Columbia. Sessional Papers, Public Accounts, 1883, 1890, 1900, 1915.

25. Stonier-Newman, *Policing a Pioneer Province*, 31, 49, 67, 84, 94, 126-129.

26. See British Columbia. Sessional Papers for any of the years under study. The breakdown of yearly expenditures reveals that the number of Specials sworn in over any given year was always greater than the number of regular constables.

27. *Ibid.*, 16; also see Hatch, "The British Columbia Police, 1858-1871," 13. On the

allure of the gold fields and the difficulties of keeping the constabulary staffed under such circumstances, see Begbie to Young, July 1863, cited in Hatch, 59. Governor James Douglas doubted the wisdom of recruiting a force from the miners of the colony, "as the men taking service would probably be composed of the idle and worthless classes." At best, they were "merely birds of passage, and have no view in Fraser's River except the one idea of making their pile of gold and leaving the country." In any case, "to secure the service of active adventurers I fear a very high rate of payment not less than 12 shillings a day including rations would be an indispensable condition, in the outset, and the great expense of such a force, together with its immediate character would be an almost insuperable objection to maintaining it in the field." See Douglas to Lytton, Victoria, Vancouver's Island, 27 December 1858. CO 60/1, 540 for the first and third quote, and Douglas to Lytton, Victoria, Vancouver's Island, 12 October 1858, CO 60/1, 225-226 for the second.

28. Stonier-Newman, *Policing a Pioneer Province*, 49.
29. Forsythe to Campbell, Clinton, 10 December 1912. *R. v. Paul Splintlum*, CCF.
30. Constable A. N. O'Daunt, who had assisted in the arrest of Paul and Splintlum observed that the police had "merely followed the practice of years dealing with native tribes and tried to get at them through the Chiefs." O'Daunt to Campbell, Lillooet, 16 January 1913. *R. v. Paul Splintlum*, CCF.
31. John Phillip Reid, "Principles of Vengeance: Fur Trappers, Indians, and Retaliation for Homicide in the Transboundary North American West," *Western Historical Quarterly*, 24 (1993): 21-43.
32. All these examples are discussed in Hamar Foster, "The Queen's Law is Better than Yours: International Homicide in Early British Columbia," in Jim Phillips, Tina Loo, and Susan Lewthwaite, eds., *Essays in the History of Canadian Law: Crime and Criminal Justice History* (Toronto: University of Toronto Press for the Osgoode Society, 1994), 49-60.
33. A. G. Morice, *The History of the Northern Interior of British Columbia, formerly New Caledonia, 1660-1880* (Toronto: William Briggs, 1904), 58, 249.
34. *Ibid.*, 248.
35. *Ibid.*, 211, 252. Quote from 250.
36. Douglas to Newcastle, Victoria, Vancouver's Island, 7 June 1860. Great Britain. Colonial Office. Vancouver Island Original Correspondence. CO 305/14, 336-338. NAC. MG 11, reel B-241. On Douglas's utopian vision and the assimilationist "system" it was part of, see Paul Tennant, *Aboriginal Peoples and Politics: the Indian Land Question in British Columbia, 1849-1989* (Vancouver: UBC Press, 1990), Chapter Three. From the perspective of the city's non-Native residents, the encampment was a source of disorder, particularly in the summer months, when its numbers were swelled by the less "civilized" and war-like Northern Indians. Numerous examples of the kinds of disorder that characterized the encampment and spilled out into the city can be found from the fur trade to the colonial period. See for instance, Douglas to Barclay, Fort Victoria, 10 April 1851, in Hartwell Bowsfield, ed., *Fort Victoria Letters* (Winnipeg: Hudson's Bay Record Society, 1979), 168; Douglas to Grey, Victoria, Vancouver's Island, 15 April 1852, CO 305/3, 105-106; Douglas to Labouchere, Victoria, Vancouver's Island, 7 June 1856, CO 305/7, 57-58; Pemberton to Douglas, Victoria, Vancouver's Island, 15 May 1859, CO 305/10, 188-189; Douglas to Lytton, Government House, Victo-

ria, Vancouver's Island, 25 May 1859, CO 305/10, 183-186; Douglas to Newcastle, Victoria, Vancouver's Island, 7 June 1860, CO 305/14, 328-343; and Douglas to Newcastle, Victoria, 8 August 1860, CO 305/14, 366-374.

37. William T. Hagan, *Indian Judges and Police: an experiment in acculturation and control* (New Haven: Yale University Press, 1966); Leslie K. Skinner, *Police of the Pastoral Frontier: Native Police, 1849-59* (St. Lucia, Queensland: University of Queensland Press, 1975); and Richard S. Hill, *Policing the Colonial Frontier: the Theory and Practice of Coercive Social and Racial Control in New Zealand, 1767-1867* (Wellington, New Zealand: W. R. Ward, Government Printer, 1986).

38. B. A. McKelvie and Willard Ireland, "The Victoria Voltigeurs," *British Columbia Historical Quarterly*, 20 (1956): 223. According to John Work, the Voltigeurs were "anything but . . . prepossessing." He told William Fraser Tolmie that "on passing Government house I was surprised to see Charbonna on duty as Centinel [sic] with his cap & tassel hatband sky blue Capot, red belt and Moleskin trousers[.] But he had no gun, probably not being able to arm them with anything better than trading guns, horn & pouch, I can scarcely refrain at times from riduculing openly such apery, and I dont [sic] know if I do right in refraining from it." Work to Tolmie, 30 July 1855, cited in *ibid.*, 234-235.

39. Ibid., 229; and James K. Nesbitt, "The Diary of Martha Cheney Ella, 1853-1856," part 2, *British Columbia Historical Quarterly*, 13 (1949): 262n.

40. Gough, *Gunboat Frontier*, 53 and Chapter Four more generally.

41. Foster, "The Queen's Law is Better than Yours," 68.

42. Hatch, "The British Columbia Police, 1858-1871," 89.

43. Tina Loo, "Bute Inlet Stories: Crime and Colonial Identity in British Columbia," in Phillips, Loo, and Lewthwaite, eds., *Essays in the History of Canadian Law: Crime and Criminal Justice History* 112-142; and Edward S. Hewlett, "The Chilcotin Uprising of 1864," *BC Studies*, 19 (1973): 50-72.

44. Graham Burchell, Colin Gordon, and Peter Miller, eds., *The Foucault Effect: Studies in Governmentality: with Two Lectures by and an Interview with Michel Foucault* (London: Harvester Wheatsheaf, 1991).

45. Hagan, *Indian Police and Judges*, and Skinner, *Police of the Pastoral Frontier*, 12.

46. Memorandum for the Department attached to the Commissioner's Letter from Regina, 30 November 1891. Canada, Department of Indian Affairs, RG 10, Black Series, v. 3865, f 84815.

47. I. W. Powell to the Superintendent General of Indian Affairs, Victoria, 22 December 1884. RG 10, v. 3694, f 14665, reel C-10121.

48. Powell to Superintendent General of Indian Affairs, Victoria, 18 May 1888. *Ibid.*

49. Powell to the Superintendent General of Indian Affairs, Victoria, 15 June, 1888. Ibid. The Department complied. See Superintendent General of Indian Affairs to Powell, 6 June 1888. *Ibid.*

50. On the disorder on the Penticton reserve, see *Penticton Herald* 19 November 1910. On the problems policing it, see Bunbury to Hussey, Oroville, Washington, 6 December 1910. BCARS, GR 56, box 9, file 13. Things got so bad that Cawston resigned in June 1911, "through the Indians on the Reserve intimidating him with threats &c, and telling him they would put him off the Reserve &c, this was because the Indian Department had just allowed him $25.00 per month as soon as the Indians heard of this the Whiskey and bad element on the Reserve went to

Causton and told him if he was paid they would not let him stop on the Reserve and said they wanted no police Indian or white to interfere with them, as the priest and Chief could manage the Reserve. Causton informed me he was not sufficiently supported by the Indian Agent at the present time the Indias are of the opinion (the bad element) they have got the upper hand and as there is no one to stop it Liquor is taken on the Reserve at night in large quantities by white men who are making quite a profit disposing of it." Aston to Dinsmore, Fairview, 2 July 1911. BCARS, GR 56, box 9, file 14.

51. Orders-in-Council, 12 March 1888 and 11 December 1890. RG 10, v. 3780, f 39675, pt 1. Cited in Duncan Duane Thompson, "A History of the Okanagan," Ph.D., University of British Columbia, 1985, 81.

52. Ditchburn to the Superintendent of Indian Affairs, 6 January 1911. *Ibid.*

53. Mel Rothenburger, *The Wild McLeans* (Victoria: Orca Books, 1993).

54. Foster, "The Queen's Law is Better than Yours," 41-48.

55. Rothenburger, *The Wild McLeans*, 230-231, and Mary Balf, *Kamloops: a History of the District up to 1914* (Kamloops: Kamloops Museum Association, 1969), 74.

56. Davie to Thompson, Victoria, 7 December 1891. *R. v. Emia*, CCF. NAC. RG 13, v. 1427, file 250A.

57. Burr to Hussey, Ashcroft, 21 June 1910. British Columbia Provincial Police Papers. BCARS, GR 56, box 31, file 3.

58. David R. Williams, *Trapline Outlaw: Simon Peter Gunanoot* (Victoria: Sono Nis, 1982).

59. On Perrault, see Smith to Assistant Deputy and Secretary Department of Indian Affairs, Kamloops, 9 November 1914; RG 10, v. 7472, f 19154-5, pt 1. On Ignace, see Smith to Superintendent General of Indian Affairs, Kamloops, BC, 10 January 1919; RG 10, v. 7472, f 19154-4, pt. 1.

60. British Columbia. Sessional Papers. Public Accounts, 1st July 1882 to 30th June 1883. There are other examples as well from that one year.

61. The yearly public accounts reproduced in the sessional papers are an unexpectedly interesting source for recovering these "Tontos." Unfortunately, about 1915 the province changed its accounting procedures and it was no longer possible to get as detailed a breakdown of expenditures on special constables. But it is for every year up to that point.

62. See Public Accounts, British Columbia Sessional Papers for the years to 1905 or so. Unfortunately, after 1905, the province no longer identified individuals it paid monies to by name, opting instead for the designation 'sundry persons.' The British Columbia Police Papers also give glimpses of the reliance on Native peoples. In 1911, for instance, Constable Gosby at Fort George wrote to Superintendent Hussey explaining the extraordinary expenses attached to his recent investigation: "I immediately set to work to rustle a dog team, and man to accompany me. I did not know the trail and had to have a guide. Owing to the arduous nature of the journey (there was three feet of snow, and an unbroken trail) I experienced very great difficulty in getting anyone to go. I eventually found a half breed named Johnny Pierre Way, who offered to go with me for $10.xx a day for himself and dog team of five dogs, he also provided the tent. This was the very best I could do, and I had perforce to accept his terms, or go by way of Blackwater, and wait there a week for the mail team, going to Fraser Lake, which would have been very

little if any cheaper." See British Columbia Provincial Police Papers. BCARS, GR 56, box 10, file 16. In the same year, Chief Constable Fernie wrote from Kamloops asking that a good boat be purchased "for the use of the Provincial Police at Secwepemc, as at present we have to rely entirely on Indian dugouts, & these are neither safe, nor convenient for police work." See *ibid.*, box 12, file 13.

63. "Over Many Miles of Trail – Indian Trackers tell of the Chase of Moses Paul and Paul Splintlum," *The New Westminster News* 26 June 1913.

64. Public Accounts, 1 July 1887, to 30 June 1888. British Columbia Sessional Papers, 31.

65. Burr to Hussey, Ashcroft, 21 June 1910. BCARS, GR 56, box 31, file 3.

66. Duncan to Ash, 27 January 1875, WD/C2149; cited in Usher, 82.

67. Hatch, "The British Columbia Police, 1858-1871," 94.

68. Usher, *William Duncan*, 82.

69. See for instance the sureties dated 9 October 1875; 26 October 1875; and 24 November 1875 in the "Civil Office – Justice of the Peace, bonds, Sureties, etc., 1871-1883"; William Duncan Papers. NAC, MG 29 D55, reel M-2330, 15659-15661.

70. *Ibid.*

71. According to Father Jean-Marie Le Jeune, "the watchmen's duties are to gather the Indians for the meetings [meetings of Chief and Council], either to the meeting-house or into the church, and they have to go after even those that are unwilling and induce them by all possible means to come and attend. They also see that the Indians are attentive at the meeting and will awaken those who have a tendency to sleep.

"If there are some disorders to redress, the watchmen will bring the guilty ones before the captain or chief, as the case may be, and will even go a great distance to fetch them. In case some are punished the watchmen will see that they perform their penance properly." *Kamloops Wawa* May 1898, cited in Kay Cronin, *Cross in the Wilderness* (Vancouver: Mitchell Press, 1960), 175-176; and 162. Margaret Whitehead described a gathering of bands in the Cariboo in 1895 which provided the Oblates with an opportunities to enforce the Durieu system on a grand scale in which Bishop Durieu "posted watchmen equipped with notebooks and pencils" to watch for those who did not attend the services. "In the evening," Whitehead continues, "a list of all these "delinquents" was tacked on Bishop Durieu's door. All retired at ten o'clock and watchmen were posted to enforce curfew." See *The Cariboo Mission: a History of the Oblates in British Columbia* (Victoria: Sono Nis Press, 1981), 95. Also see Thomson, "A History of the Okanagan," 52-54; John Webster Grant, *Moon of Wintertime: Missionaries and Indians in Encounter since 1534* (Toronto: University of Toronto Press, 1984), 125-126; James R. Miller, *Skyscrapers Hide the Heavens: Indian-White Relations in Canada* (Toronto: University of Toronto Press, 1991), 148-149.

72. See a series of petitions from the inhabitants of the county of Yale, the Indians of the County of Yale, and the Secwepemc Tribe on behalf of Alex Ignace, addressed to the Governor General, May 1919 in *R. v. Alexander Ignace*, capital case file, RG 13, vol. 1502, (1,2), file 627 1/2/CC 114.

73. See the Memorandum for the Hon. the Acting Minister of Justice re: Alexander Ignace, 2 June 1919, *ibid.*

74. John Freemont Smith to Superintendent General of Indian Affairs, Kamloops, BC, 10 January 1919. RG 10, v. 7472, f 19154-4, pt. 1.
75. "Giving good measure" was the phrase used by an Indian trading captain. See Arthur J. Ray and Donald Freeman, *"Give Us Good Measure": an Economic Analysis of Relations between the Indians and the Hudson's Bay Company before 1763* (Toronto: University of Toronto Press, 1978). In making her statement to the RCMP regarding the murder of Moccasin, a suspected witch, at the hands of some Liard River Natives, Lucy Loot insisted that the time had come to "talk straight." See Stikine Agency – Murder of Atol or Moccasin, 1923-1927; RG 10 v. 7473 f 19158-3 pt. 1.
76. Though mixed juries were empanelled in British Columbia, this never happened in cases involving Native peoples. On mixed juries, see Marianne Constable, *The Law of the Other: the Mixed Jury and Changing Conceptions of Citizenship, Law, and Knowledge* (Chicago: University of Chicago Press, 1994).
77. Judge's Report on R. v. Wyachute, Clinton Assizes, 10-12 July 1879, in *R. v. Wyachute*, CCF. NAC, RG 13, v. 1416, file 135A.
78. The entire exchange was as follows:

Q. You used the word evidence three or four times?
A. I think I did.
Q. You do not mean to tell us that the Indian understood that?
A. I believe he did.
Q. Why?
A. Because he speaks good English.
Q. You referred to the word statement as well?
A. Yes, Constable Blue did.
Q. And that he had nothing to hope for?
A. I will not say whether in those exact words.
Q. Are these the words he used: "That he was placed under arrest for the murder of Gus Hall, and for him not to make any statement, and any statement he made would be taken down and used against him, and anything he did say were of his own free will and accord, and in making a statement he had nothing to gain and nothing to fear from any person."?
A. Yes I believe that is correct.
Q. Are you interpolated that the accused understands English thoroughly?
A. Not thoroughly.

. . .

Q. Did you say he speaks English and understands English thoroughly?
A. I suppose I did.
Q. Do you think that he understood what Constable Blue said when he made this statement of his own free will and accord?
A. Yes, I think so, but he probably would not understand accord . . .
BY THE COURT:
Q. He did not say anything?
A. No, I advised him not to say anything.
Q. What language did you say this in?

    A. In English.
    Q. Can you give the words?
    A. I advise you not to say anything.
    Q. Speaking to an Indian is that the best way? Would it not have been
        better to say: Better not talk?
    A. Well, I thought he understood.
    The Court: I will tell you now that you should use very plain lan-
    guage to an Indian. You must remember that they are very ignorant
    people, and using that formality in the Code would mean nothing to
    them. At any rate it amounts to nothing really.

    See *R. v. Frank Jones*, In the Supreme Court of British Columbia, Oyer and
Terminer and General Gaol Delivery. Before Mr Justice Murphy, 7 November
1916. *R. v. Frank Jones*, CCF, NAC, RG 13 vol. 1472 (1,2,3), file 583A/CC7.
Other capital cases in which language was an issue were *R. v. Sulwhalem, alias Jim*,
CCF, RG 13, v. 1320, file 189A and *R. v. Alexander Louie*, CCF, RG 13, v. 1444,
file 349A.

79. *Ibid.*
80. Testimony of Lucy, an Indian woman, *ibid.*. Conversely, in arguing against clemency for Attoo, a Native convicted of murdering a toll collector at Telegraph
Creek in 1879, Matthew Begbie observed that although the accused was unrepre-
sented by counsel, he had been able to make himself understood because "[a]ll
the witnesses and most of the jury underst[ood] Chinook well." There had been
no miscarriage of justice; in fact, the judge considered that "the defence was better conducted than is often the case in Indian cases, the prisoner speaking remark-
ably well." Notes of Trial R. v. Johnson alias Atto (Indian) murder of George
Jenkinson, before Begbie at the Glenora Assizes, Cassiar, 25 August 1879. See *R.
v. Attoo alias Johnson*, CCF, NAC. RG 13 v. 1417, file 137A.
81. W. Peter Ward, *White Canada Forever: Popular Attitudes and Public Policy Toward
Orientals in British Columbia* (Montreal and Kingston: McGill-Queen's University
Press, 1978), 20-22.
82. Douglas to Grey, Fort Victoria, 16 December 1851. CO 305/3, 75-76. NAC. MG
11, reel B-233.
83. Kennedy to Cardwell, Victoria, 4 July 1865. CO 305/26, 25. NAC, MG 11, reel B-
248. The statutory provisions against liquor relating to Indians, 1850-1876 (when
the *Indian Act* was passed) are listed in Gough, *Gunboat Frontier*, 219-223.
84. For instance, the Royal Navy may have terrorized Natives in villages along the
coast by their visits and occasional shellings, but there is at least as much (if not
more) evidence that they frightened the European settlers as well. In 1859,
Augustus Pemberton, the Police Magistrate in Victoria, reported "a serious distur-
bance" at the Songhees encampment between the Haida and Tsimshian in which
six people were killed and six wounded. Pemberton's ten men, armed only with
batons, were confronted with "2000 excited Indians equipped with every kind of
offensive weapon – blunderbusses, long & short muskets, single and double-barrelled rifles, fowling pieces; revolvers & pistols from every nation: [illegible]
Swords, bayonets, dirks, daggars [sic] and Knives of every form size & shape. They
are also said to have in their possession a brass cannon." Not surprisingly, no ar-

rests were made. See Pemberton to Douglas, Victoria, Vancouver Island, 15 May 1859. CO 305/10, 189. NAC, MG 11, reel B-238. The situation was no better on the mainland, for in 1887 Kootenay Chief Isadore, assisted by fifteen or twenty Indians, broke down the door of the jail and rescued Kapla, one of their compatriots. See Powell to Superintendent General of Indian Affairs, Victoria, 13 July 1887, RG 10, v. 3738, f 28013-1. Less spectacular, but no less frightening (for the Europeans) confrontations with Natives in the nineteenth century are discussed in Bruce Colin Stadfeld, "Manifestations of Power: Native Responses to Settlement in Nineteenth Century British Columbia," MA, Simon Fraser University, 1993. Douglas Cole and Ira Chaikin, *An Iron Hand Upon the People* (Vancouver: Douglas and McIntyre, 1990) and my own piece on the law against the potlatch ("Dan Cranmer's Potlatch: Law as Coercion, Symbol, and Rhetoric in British Columbia, 1884-1951," *Canadian Historical Review*, 73 (1992): 125-165) also suggest the difficulties in enforcing a law that Native peoples opposed.

85. The Indians who captured Moise in 1863 received £20. See Hatch, "The British Columbia Police," 89. Also see *R. v. Emia*, CCF.

86. Public Accounts, 1 July 1885 to 30 June 1886. British Columbia Sessional Papers, 1886, 49.

87. Public Accounts, 1 July 1888 to 30 June 1889. British Columbia Sessional Papers, 1889, 34.

88. Public Accounts, 1 July 1889 to 30 June 1890. British Columbia Sessional Papers, 1890, 31.

89. Public Accounts, 1 July 1892 to 30 June 1893. British Columbia Sessional Papers, 1893, 41.

90. Gore to Morrow, C.M.S., Kitkatla, B.C., 23 November 1903. RG 10, v. 4082, f 484536.

91. Morrow to Vowell, Northwest Coast Agency, Metlakatla, 17 December 1903, *ibid.* Similar instances of Native constables enforcing their own customary law against suspected witches occurred in Bella Bella in the 1920s, and the agent was forced to remind the constables that "they have no authority to place anyone in irons without just cause, and that when they place a man in irons he must be brought before the magistrate at the earliest possible moment." See RCMP E Division to the Officer Commanding, Coast Sub-District, Prince Rupert, B.C., Ocean Falls, 12 December 1921, *ibid.*

92. Wood to the Acting Colonial Secretary, Attorney General's Office, 24 November 1864. Colonial Correspondence. BCARS. GR 1372, box 147, file 54/19. Wood considered that without any checks on the reliability of Native testimony "there would be many cases of Judicial Murder from Indians swearing away the lives of their enemies in the Tribes or slaves, whom they would sacrifice, instead of giving up the real Murderer *a thing already believed to be done.*" (emphasis added).

93. For instance, in the case of *R. v. Klatsmick* for the murder of William Bamfield in 1864, the Attorney General reported "his strong suspicion that the tribe desired to get rid of Klatsmick as a dangerous member of the community irrespective of his complicity in the matter." See Wood to the Acting Colonial Secretary, Attorney General's Office, 24 November 1864. Colonial Correspondence. BCARS, GR 1372, box 147, file 54/19. Also see *R. v. Emia*, NAC, RG 10, v. 1427, f 250A; *R. v. Basil*, NAC, RG 10, v. 1457, file 431A; and *R. v. Ernest* Louis, NAC, RG 10, v.

1457, file 430A. In the latter two cases there is no direct evidence of Indians trying to railroad Basil and Louis, but if the testimony of the crown's witnesses was
so consistent and so similar, one wonders. In any case, and somewhat unusually,
there were no petitions on behalf of either of these condemned men from their
communities. This may indicate their outsider status if nothing else.

94. Transcript, R. v. Klemadikdinhuhu, 9 May 1905 before Duff, J. See *R. v. Tom
Klemadikdinhuhu*, CCF, NAC, RG 13, vol. 1449, file 369A. The Crown Attorney,
who also happened to be the province's Attorney-General, tried to recover redi-
recting after the cross-examination, but only succeeded in making his case worse.
This is what transpired on the re-direct of Johnson:

Q: You told my friend that Tom was not popular and was not well liked – why is this?
A: Because he is many times the cause of ill-feeling – general bad feeling amongst his
own people and his own people and relatives there say so.

And when the prosecutor asked Mrs. Peter why his own people didn't wish to be
with them, she simply said "They all say he is a bad man."

95. Burr to Campbell, Ashcroft, BC, 30 December 1912. *R. v. Paul Splintlum*, CCF.

96. Cummiskey to Bowser, Vernon, 4 January 1913, *ibid.*

97. O'Daunt to Campbell, Lillooet, 16 January 1913, *ibid.* O'Daunt was not entirely
correct. The newspapers were not so much filled with the "yarns of glory-hunting
Chief Constables" but with tales of Thomas Cummiskey's exploits. *The Inland
Sentinel* printed Cummiskey's narrative of the capture of the Wild Boys, below
this headline: "Capture of Indian Outlaws: Thrilling Narrative by the Captor –
Tact Triumphs where Force Fails. . ." [31 December 1913]. The Bonaparte reserve,
where Paul and Splintlum surrendered, is in Secwepemc territory. See Duff, *The
Indian History of British Columbia*, 31.

98. Graham to Bowser, Lytton, 4 February 1913. *R. v. Paul Splintlum*, CCF.

99. O'Daunt to Campbell, Lillooet, 16 January 1913, *ibid.*

100. Reid, "Principles of Vengeance."

101. Thomas Stone, "Atomistic Order and Frontier Violence: Miners and Whalemen
in the Nineteenth Century Yukon," *Ethnology*, 22 (1983): 331.

102. Cited in Robin Fisher, *Contact and Conflict: Indian-European Relations in British Columbia, 1774-1890* (Vancouver: UBC Press, 1978), 64.

103. Foster, "The Queen's Law is Better than Yours"; and Jonathan Swainger, "A Distant Edge of Authority: Capital Punishment and the Prerogative of Mercy in British Columbia, 1872-1880," in Hamar Foster and John McLaren, eds., *Essays in the
History of Canadian Law: British Columbia and the Yukon* (Toronto: University of
Toronto Press, with the Osgoode Society, 1995).

104. Cummiskey to Bowser, Vernon, 4 January 1913. *R. v. Paul Splintlum*, CCF.

105. At this point I am unable to say exactly when the policy of providing defence
counsel for Indians accused of serious crimes started. My best guess is the late
nineteenth century. This is based on a series of letters between H.C. Lisle, who
defended four Indians for murder in the Yukon in 1898 and who sought reim-
bursement for his services from the Department of Justice. Justice refused, noting
that "hitherto when it was thought advisable to employ counsel to defend Indians charged with similar offences the Department of Indian Affairs gave the necessary instructions and defrayed the expenses." [Newcombe to Smart, Ottawa,
November 1898. RG 10, v. 3990, f 177,044]. The earliest British Columbia cases

in which there is a discussion about appointing counsel date from the turn-of-the-century [see RG 10, v. 7471 f 19151-2 to v. 7475 f 19165-7]. As well, I have found two circular letters issued to agents – one from the Department of Justice and the other from the Department of Indian Affairs – instructing agents on how they are to proceed in appointing counsel [see Department of Justice. Instructions to Agents, Ottawa, January 1904, RG 10, v. 7474 f 19164-3, pt. 1; and Department of Indian Affairs, Circular letter to all Indian Agents, Ottawa, 15 October 1907].

106. *R. v. Qutlnoh*, CCF, RG 13, v. 1409, file 57A; on Toby see the comments and clippings in *R. v. Jacob*, CCF, RG 13, v. 1416, file 132A; *R. v. Tsimequor*, CCF, RG 13, v. 1425, file 230A; *R. v. Johnny Peters*, CCF, RG 13, v. 1446, file 358A; on the case against Big Alec and Edie, see the RCMP reports in Stikine Agency – murder of Atol or Moccasin, 1923-1927, RG 10 v. 7473 f 19158-3 pt. 1.

107. *R. v. Attoo alias Johnson*, CCF, RG 13, v. 1417, file 137A.

108. See *R. v. Ha-atq (or Aht)*, CCF, RG 13, v. 1421, file 190A. The details of this case are discussed in Foster, "The Queen's Law is Better than Yours," 41-48.

109.

Date	Native Population (%)
1871	70.8
1881	51.9
1891	27.8
1901	16.2
1911	5.1
1921	4.3
1931	3.5

From Barman, *The West Beyond the West*, 363.

110. Beginning in about 1900 the Public Accounts reveal a decline in the numbers of Indians employed as constables and in other aspects of law enforcement, such as transportation and provisioning. This decline was uneven: in the more remote parts of the province Natives continued to be used.

111. See Peter Carstens, *The Queen's People: a Study of Hegemony, Coercion, and Accommodation amont the Okanagan of Canada* (Toronto: University of Toronto Press, 1991), 90; and P. Trefor Smith, ""A Very Respectable Man": John Freemont Smith and the Kamloops Agency, 1912-1923," MA, Simon Fraser University, 1993, 75-78.

112. Smith, ""A Very Respectable Man"," Chapter 7.

113. Chief Pierre Michel was deposed four weeks after he was elected in 1908, ostensibly because of his intemperance, but more likely because "he opposed the authority of [Indian] agent Irwin." Though Isaac Harris, Irwin's favourite, was appointed to replace Michel, the agent was unsuccessful in convincing Natives to vote for him, and in 1909 he was replaced by Baptiste Logan, who was the people's choice. Near the end of his term in 1912, Logan was deposed by B.C. Superintendent Thomas Cummiskey, allegedly because Logan's adultery rendered him unfit for office. The next chief was none other than Pierre Michel, the man who was deposed after just one month in office. This time, Michel remained in office until 1915 or 1918, and was followed by Gaston Louie, and Baptiste Nicholas, both of whom ran afoul of the agent and were deposed in 1919 and 1922 respectively. Carstens, *The Queen's People*, Chapter 7. Also see Thomson, "A History of the Okanagan," 62-77.

114. Smith, ""A Very Respectable Man"," Chapter 7.

115. James Alexander Teit, *The Secwepemc* (Leiden: E.J. Brill, Ltd., 1909), Chapter Ten. Teit notes that the western part of the tribe (a distinct minority) had a social organization that was more hierarchical. Nonetheless, I think the point about the increase in social conflict arising from some Natives' manifesting priestly power for their own benefit can still be made.

116. Cited by Thomson, "A History of the Okanagan," 90.

117. J. W. McKay to A. W. Vowell, Kamloops-Okanagan Agency, Kamloops, B.C., 24 May 1892. RG 10 v. 3875 f 90,667-2; c-10193.

118. Native communities missionized by the Oblates were not the only ones to suffer from factionalization. William Duncan's enormous power and the dependence and division it created among the Tsimshian themselves as well as the Anglican missionary community is the subject of the last two chapters in Usher's *William Duncan of Metlakatla*.

119. Various petitions from Indian bands concerning Indian women residing unlawfully with whitemen, 1872-1891, RG 10, v. 3842 f 71799 as well as those in RG 10, v. 3816 f 57045-1, 1889-1914.

120. On the centrality of gender to the European colonization project among Canada's Native peoples, see Karen Anderson, *Chain Her By One Foot: the Subjugation of Women in Seventeenth-Century New France* (London: Routledge, 1991).

121. On Mountain and Se-in-shoot, see Foster, "The Queen's Law is Better than Yours," 45, 76.

122. See Arthur J. Ray, *Indians and the Fur Trade: their role as hunters, trappers, and middlemen in the lands southwest of Hudson Bay, 1660-1821* (Toronto: University of Toronto Press, 1974), 137-141.

123. Collison to Superintendent General of Indian Affairs, Prince Rupert, 30 September 1925. RG 10 v. 7473 f 19158-3 pt 1.

124. One of Gary Larson's cartoons shows an old Lone Ranger, mask hung on the wall, in his armchair, reading an Indian dictionary. The bubble containing his thoughts reads: "Oh, here it is. . . "Kemosabe: Apache expression for a horse's rear end." What the hey?. . ." The caption is "The Lone Ranger, long since retired, makes an unpleasant discovery." See Gary Larson, *The Prehistory of the Far Side: a Tenth Anniversary Exhibit* (Kansas City, Missouri: Andrews and McMeel, 1989), 205. This is not as unlikely a scenario as it may seem. My colleagues Don and Teresa Kirschner suggest that "Kemosabe" may be a corruption of the Spanish phrase "qui no sabe," or "I don't know." As a noun, it would mean "ignoramus." So the Lone Ranger and Tonto could also be known as "Ignoramus" and "Stupid"!

Clearcutting the British Columbia Coast: Work, Environment and the State, 1880-1930[1]

RICHARD A. RAJALA

West of the Cascade mountains that divide the coastal and interior regions of British Columbia the interaction of heavy precipitation, mild climate and favourable soil conditions produced one of the earth's magnificent temperate rainforests. The pre-eminent species, in terms of both scale and commercial importance, is Douglas fir. Commercial exploitation began in the 1850s, and by 1867 Sewell P. Moody and Edward Stamp had established cargo mills on Burrard Inlet, turning out lumber for Pacific markets.[2]

Lumbermen had little difficulty securing control of timber to supply their plants. The crown stopped granting tracts to interests during the mid-1860s, instead adopting the practice of issuing leases. After the united colonies entered the new Dominion in 1871 all forestland not already alienated became the property of the provincial government. Leases continued to be available on easy terms involving an annual rental and royalty payment on timber when cut. An important exception was the 1884 grant to coal magnate Robert Dunsmuir, who received two million acres of Vancouver

In June 1891, dignitaries on a ready-made platform unveil a monument to commemorate the events at Seven Oaks. Despite the blazing prairie sun, the mood appears sombre and the presence of several uniformed men as well as the formal attire
of others suggest efforts to give the occasion legitimacy and solemnity. (Chapter 1:
THE SEVEN OAKS INCIDENT AND THE CONSTRUCTION OF A HISTORICAL TRADITION, 1816
TO 1970)

Left: "Mrs. Gowanlock 1885." A photograph taken by Malcom T. Miller at Fort Pitt, just after Mrs. Gowanlock's release from the Cree. (This page and facing page: Chapter 2: THE EXPLOITATION AND NARRATION OF THE CAPTIVITY OF THERESA DELANEY AND THERESA GOWANLOCK, 1885)

Below: "A War Dance Near Fort Pit [sic]." This drawing appeared in *Two Months in the Camp of Big Bear* and was intended to show the menacing behaviour experienced by the captives, described in the book.

BOTH: GLENBOW ARCHIVES

A WAR DANCE NEAR FORT PIT.

Right: Mrs. Delaney and Mrs. Gowanlock are found. The Field Force did not dramatically rescue the two women. In fact, they and a large party of Métis men, women and children left the Cree and travelled for several days before police scouts found them. A version of this drawing also appeared in *Two Months in the Camp of Big Bear*, but the seated weeping woman is shown also standing in anticipation.

John Pritchard guarding Mrs. Gowanlock and Mrs Delaney, May 1885, from the *Canadian Pictorial and Illustrated War News*. John Pritchard appears here in a heroic stance, keeping an eye on the Indian camp in the background. This "heroic" image was tarnished in the weeks and months after the captives' release: the Anglo-Canadian public did not view any Métis as heroic.

High-Lead Cold Deck

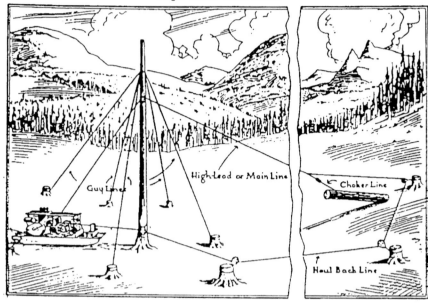

Aerial Interlocking Skidder

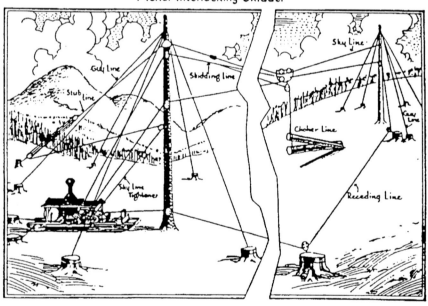

An illustration of two overhead logging systems, from an old equipment supply catalogue. This new method of transporting logs was common by 1915 and reflected the culmination of employers' efforts to reduce both costs and their reliance on skilled labour. (Chapter 4: CLEARCUTTING THE BRITISH COLUMBIA COAST: WORK, ENVIRONMENT AND THE STATE, 1880-1930)

A striking image from a prairie homestead: two men relaxing in front of their sod house, with heaped buffalo bones, recalling the changes wrought by Europeans in the West. The photograph's caption, "The Beginning of Better Things," suggests the optimism of the new settlers. (Chapter 6: "A Bachelor's Paradise": Homesteaders, Hired Hands, and the Construction of Masculinity, 1880-1930)

A farm family in formal pose: the man astride a binder, the woman and children sitting demurely below him in their best clothing. The image reproduces the patriarchal hierarchy that denied equal property rights to farm women. Appropriately, the photograph's caption was "M. Seagert's Farm House." (Chapter 7: The Limitations of the Pioneering Partnership: The Alberta Campaign for Homestead Dower, 1909-1925)

民國四年春多多天加華埠初等第一次小學甲班畢業校長教員學生紀念合

Above: Members of the Chinese Public School's first graduating class pose for a photographer in Victoria, around July 1915. The school was a vital part of the Chinese public sphere in British Columbia. (Chapter 8: SCHOOLING, WHITE SUPREMACY, AND THE FORMATION OF A CHINESE MER-CHANT PUBLIC IN BRITISH COLUMBIA)

Left: James Keelaghan's songs resonate with a sense of place, many reflecting the history of Western Canada. Despite an uncompromising identification with the prairie west, his four albums have reached a wide audience across North America. (Chapter 9: "THE PAST OF MY PLACE": WESTERN CANADIAN ARTISTS AND THE USES OF HISTORY)

Island's richest timberland in exchange for construction of the Esquimalt and Nanaimo railway (E & N).[3]

During the late nineteenth and early twentieth centuries the construction of a transcontinental rail system and changes in the structure of the North American resource economy made private and Crown timber alike an attractive investment for lumber interests. The completion of the Canadian Pacific Railway coincided with the onset of forest depletion in the American midwest and eastern Canada, prompting resource capitalists to look west. The Douglas fir forests of Washington and Oregon drew much of the early attention, but operators also sought access to British Columbia timber, particularly between 1905 and 1907 when the Conservative government's transferable twenty-one year licences resulted in the staking out of over fifteen thousand square miles of public forest. Within the E & N belt the Rockefeller interests and Standard Oil assumed outright ownership of huge tracts.[4]

Competitive capitalism bred a ruthless, destructive approach to forest exploitation. By 1930 the growing expanse of denuded, barren land in some locales within the E & N belt prompted some to predict a future timber famine. Devastation continued for another decade before the state adopted a sustained-yield model, promising to regulate the cut in accordance with the rate of forest growth. The new Tree Farm Licences contributed to a process of consolidation that placed firms such as MacMillan Bloedel, B.C. Forest Products and Crown Zellerbach, the latter two entities recently absorbed by the New Zealand multinational Fletcher Challenge, at the head of the province's forest economy.

Booming construction and wood fibre markets sustained the structure through the immediate post-war decades, producing record cuts and high employment levels that seemed to herald a new era of stability. Over the past two decades, of course, the industry has gone into a decline caused by a host of factors related to the transnational nature of the forest products economy and the onset of what was once unthinkable – the exhaustion of timber supplies.

This essay seeks to shed light on the roots of our present crisis by integrating class, environmental and political analysis, directing attention to the technological and regulatory structures of forest exploitation to 1930. In essence, this amounts to an early history of clearcutting, the industry's primary approach to harvesting after the mechanization of logging in the late nineteenth century. Scholars such as Patricia Marchak, Ken Drushka, Stephen Gray, R. Peter Gillis and Thomas Roach, Mary McRoberts and Jeremy Wilson have begun to lay a foundation of work on policy formation, the timber economy, and single-industry communities. My own approach to the study of deforestation on the west coast, however, rests on a recognition that corporate resource exploitation takes place within the context of, in fact is dependent upon, exploitation of workers. This conceptual framework encourages analysis of the complex interplay of technological, ecological and regulatory processes, rather than their separation.[5]

Recognition that workers constitute a vital intermediary position in capital's relationship to nature suggests the relevance of Marxian concepts to the study of environmental issues.[6] R.J. Johnson, for example, directs attention to "the extent to which environmental practices . . . are largely determined by the capitalist mode of production," which mobilizes land, labour and technology in the process of wealth accumulation. K.J. Walker sees the mode of production as the essential analytic concept in a Marxian theory of human-environmental relationships.[7]

Such a perspective provides a point of entry for a history of the Douglas fir timber industry that probes how changing technologies and government interventions shaped the process of deforestation. Seen in this light, the history of exploitation of natural resources becomes a narrative concerning a changing mode of production, in which corporate leaders are drawn into relations with wage workers, managers, and the state comprised of elected politicians and administrative personnel. In short, it is necessary to comprehend the advantages particular production processes held for business in extracting maximum value from the labour of employees and the bounty provided by nature before one can understand precisely what was at stake in the negotiation of forest regulations.

Part I of this essay is devoted to a class analysis of mechanization, a process which brought a steady increase in the capacity of logging operators to exploit workers. The primary influence on my approach to this subject is Harry Braverman's *Labor and Monopoly Capital* and the outpouring of labour process research this seminal book has inspired. For Braverman, the introduction of machines could be attributed to capital's all-consuming desire to wrest control of the workplace from skilled craft workers. At the heart of his analysis, and indeed all Marxian thinking about the labour process, is the concept of labour power. "What the worker sells and the capitalist buys is not an agreed amount of labour," Braverman writes, "but the power to labour over an agreed period of time." Accordingly, employers have mechanized the workplace to effect the transformation of labour power into work on their terms. Thus machines divested "the mass of workers of their control over their own labour."[8]

Braverman's assessment of capital's overwhelming success in this project has drawn the ire of a second generation of labour process analysts who cite his naive acceptance of managerial ideology, exaggeration of deskilling, and disregard of class consciousness and class struggle. From this perspective the history of work represents less an inevitable "consolidation of untrammelled capitalist power" than a dynamic process exhibiting complexity, counter-tendencies and possible contradictions. The second generation's critique has produced a more richly textured view of workplace relations, but my analysis of corporate timber capital's pursuit of efficiency confirms the general thrust of Braverman's degradation of work thesis.[9]

Industry's concept of efficiency drew heavily on the example of the factory, a model offering operators a high degree of control in their relations with loggers. The fundamental importance of class forces is apparent in the development of extractive technologies which brought a progressive reduction in labour requirements, less reliance on physical and conceptual skills once considered essential to the industry, and a consequent loss of autonomy for loggers who found themselves increasingly subject to the discipline of machine-pacing. True, technological sophistication involved the emergence of highly skilled occupations, but these invariably enhanced capital's control over the collective labour process.

West coast logging's industrial revolution began in the late nineteenth century with the displacement of oxen and horse teams by the steam engine, or "donkey," and achieved real significance with the adoption of overhead logging systems early in the twentieth. Although environmental factors, product and labour markets cannot be discounted in the long-term record of technological progress, operators evaluated innovations primarily in terms of their capacity to contribute to the creation of a factory regime in coastal logging.

Having analyzed the class dimension of the mode of production in coastal logging, the paper proceeds to an environmental/political history of clearcutting to 1930. The intent here is to document the impact of industry practices on the regenerative capacity of the Douglas fir forest, the accumulation of scientific knowledge on this subject, and early relations between industry and governments in the regulation of cutting practice. Even the best scholarship on North American forestry fails to situate the policy-making process adequately in its technological and scientific context. As a result, able work by historians such as Robbins and Nelles provides ample evidence of corporate influence, but falls short of fully elucidating its social and ecological implications.[10]

These analyses are consistent with the corporate liberalism model of business-government relations, an intellectual tradition that emphasizes the capacity of business interests to shape public policies in a manner consistent with the corporate goal of economic stability and order.[11] They also have much in common with the orthodox Marxist depiction of the state in capitalist societies as a simple tool of big business. More recent neo-Marxist thinking questions this instrumentalist assumption, positing that the state, consisting of administrative managers and elected politicians, exhibits a "relative autonomy" in its relationship to the capitalist class. In serving the interests of capitalists as a whole, this theory assumes, state personnel must have the freedom to act in ways that particular business interests may find objectionable.[12] Although application of the relative autonomy model to the study of welfare and collective bargaining reform by national governments has proven insightful, its usefulness in interpreting the workings of regional levels of government seems less certain.

This account depicts the origins of British Columbia's status as a "client state," one sufficiently dependent upon corporate resource revenues that provincial administrations tended to define the public interest in terms of the corporate interest.[13] This essential constraint on the policy-making process, which took shape during the early twentieth century, was particularly noticeable in the 1930s when the Pattullo administration turned back a movement to reform logging practices, or in the 1940s when the Coalition government's Tree Farm Licences met the timber supply needs of dominant firms. Gray has revealed the shared objectives of timbermen and political elites in policies governing protection, log exports, timber allocation and royalties during the earlier period, but it is also evident in the provincial state's reluctance to introduce what was known about the minimum requirements necessary to restock forestland in cutting practice regulations.[14]

Timber is a flow resource, sustainable through the understanding and application of management principles based in natural science. But as radical sociologists of science have observed, such knowledge achieves legal status only when linked to the power of dominant economic and political interests.[15] Analysis of forest science and policy formation during the initial years of forest administration in British Columbia draws attention to the shared preoccupation of these elites with capital accumulation through the efficiencies of the factory regime. It also provides empirical support for John Bellamy Foster's argument that ecological degradation is "an inherent part of the accumulation process that defines capitalist society and its class struggle."[16] Viewing class and ecological exploitation historically through the prism of the factory regime, this paper suggests, provides an intellectual framework for a common critique of timber capital and the state among woodworkers and environmentalists currently battling over the fate of the old-growth forest.

The Forest as Factory

The earliest logging on the west coast required no external power source, as trees could be cut so that they dropped directly into rivers, lakes or inlets which provided ease of transportation. Although the hand logger plied his singular craft along the British Columbia coastline well into the twentieth century, once the timber standing in close proximity to water bodies had been cut logging evolved into a three-stage process. Trees are first felled and bucked into logs, then yarded to a central point or "landing" for the final stage, transportation to a mill for processing into lumber or pulp.

Prior to the 1930s falling and bucking underwent little change. By the 1880s the crosscut saw was in use for both procedures, and hand methods prevailed until the introduction of the motorized chain saw in the 1940s. Innovations in yarding involved the replacement of oxen and horses by the steam engine or "donkey" during the last fifteen years of the nineteenth century, followed by the transition from steam-powered ground-lead yarding to overhead systems of logging in the 1900-1920 period. The final stage, transportation of logs out of the woods, was accomplished first by driving logs down rivers during the winter freshets. During the 1880s the logging railroad appeared on Puget Sound to feed the mills in that locale. The technology was introduced to the British Columbia industry in the next decade. In the mid-1920s seventy-nine logging lines operated in the province, totalling over 700 miles of track.[17]

The epitome of labour process control is the mechanized factory, a model that has inspired the development of exploitation systems in the west coast logging industry. Innovators focused much of their energy on the yarding procedure, the most labour-intensive phase of logging, and the one most dependent upon the physical and conceptual skills of loggers to cope with the variable conditions of the coastal environment. Yarding, remarked one operator, "more than any other part of the organization, makes or mars the work of a day."[18]

Timber capitalists confronted real obstacles in their effort to emulate the factory mode of production. Unlike their counterparts who headed manufacturing enterprises, they had to organize workers and machinery within constraints laid down by nature. Rough terrain, dense timber stands, underbrush, and the need to shift operations constantly contributed to a chaotic productive context that bore little resemblance to the ordered factory setting. "The work of the logger is never the same," observed Washington operator Frank Lamb in 1909,

> each tree grows in a different location, each behaves a little differently in the handling. Fixed rules of procedure are of very little use, every proposition, every location, every camp, every day's work, even every log is a separate engineering proposition.[19]

In this industrial context the "working knowledge" of loggers was paramount, particularly during the pre-mechanized era of bull and horse team logging. Skidroads, carefully constructed to speed the passage of logs, offered some measure of control over the unstable productive setting. But in maneuvering logs to that point operators relied on the ability of the teamster and hooktender to overcome the forest environment. Ten logs, wrote journalist Louise Wall, could be hauled down the road with less effort than was required to move a single log to its head.[20]

Swampers first cleared a path between the log and skidroad, removing windfalls and debris. While axemen bevelled or "sniped" the log's lead end and removed bark and knots from one side the team was "prodded, sworn, and cajoled" into position by the teamster. The hooktender attached a complex block and tackle arrangement to the log and adjacent trees or stumps to increase pulling power and maneuverability. "A considerable amount of rude science," remarked Wall, "is required to accomplish this without accident or waste of time." After several logs had been labouriously yarded to the skidroad they were coupled with chains into a "turn" and hauled to water by the roading team, usually consisting of six or seven yoke of oxen or an equal number of horses.[21]

Along with the hooktender, the teamster controlled the pace of these operations. Coordinating the efforts of up to fourteen oxen to form a cohesive yarding unit necessitated that the bull puncher "know each bull's characteristics" and develop a special accord with the lead oxen so the team would respond to commands in unison. The animals, recalls one British Columbia horse logger, "became . . . part of the man that drove them." The teamster's power over production provided capital with one motivation for adapting the steam donkey to coastal logging.[22]

In 1899 the trend toward steam-powered logging was well under way. The Victoria Lumber and Manufacturing Company likely introduced the donkey to British Columbia around 1892, inaugurating the brief era of ground-lead yarding. Traditionally explained as a response to the longer hauling distances caused by timber depletion, the adoption of steam power offered operators a range of advantages: increased control over terrain; faster yarding at lower cost; and a fractional reduction in their reliance on the skills of loggers.[23]

The essential components of a donkey consisted of a vertical boiler, engine, and winch mechanism mounted on an iron or steel frame, the entire apparatus usually resting on a wooden sled to facilitate moving. In operation, the chokerman, working under the authority of the hooktender and his assistant the rigging slinger, looped a choker around the log and hooked it to the haul-in line. The donkey engineer then engaged the winch, starting the log to the landing. Donkeys also required wood buckers and firemen to fuel the machines, and a spool tender to take the turns of manilla rope, soon replaced by flexible steel cable, off the capstan as the log advanced. When it reached the landing a worker fastened the rope to the line horse and guided the animal to the next log selected for yarding.

Before the turn of the century western machinery manufacturers began turning out increasingly powerful and sophisticated donkeys. The introduction of the horizontal yarding drum displaced the spool tender and accelerated the log's passage. Mechanization advanced further with development of the two-drum donkey, eliminating the line horse. Now when a log reached the landing the engineer simply reeled in the "haulback" line, returning the mainline and rigging through a series of blocks to the crew in the woods.[24]

The arrival of steam power had a significant impact on the nature of loggers' work, but represented only a marginal advance toward the realization of a factory regime. The pace of production still hinged upon the speed at which logs could be yarded from where they lay in the woods to the head of the skidroad, and in this procedure timber capital continued to depend on loggers' abilities to cope with a productive setting that bore no resemblance to the factory floor. Negotiating the log's passage over rough, stump-covered terrain remained a tortuous affair. R.V. Stuart described ground-lead logging as "the most frustrating and irritating business" imaginable, and went on to recall the "turmoil" of early mechanized yarding:

> The yarder would haul a log . . . some 1,500 feet if it had room to do it, but the stumps were so thick on the ground that it probably wouldn't haul it more than fifty feet on the first lap, they had to change the choker and go another fifty feet. There was a lot of jumping back and forward.

Decisions concerning the use of auxiliary rigging to increase power and maneuver the log rested with the hooktender. "Upon his alertness and ability to keep the logs moving without loss of time," wrote one observer, "depends largely the profit in logging."[25]

But if the initial application of steam power to coastal logging failed to achieve the stability of the factory setting, it did initiate a collaboration among machinery manufacturers and operators that edged the industry further along this path. New compound-geared donkeys with larger engine cylinders generated sufficient power to render obsolete some of the rigging expertise formerly needed to overcome minor obstructions. An increase in the diameter of haulback drums accelerated the return of rigging to the woods, a measure intended to "keep the yarding crew constantly on the jump."[26]

Loggers welcomed neither their first experience with machine-pacing nor the new hazards they confronted at the workplace, but the real breakthrough in forest and labour exploitation came with the introduction of overhead logging systems.[27] By passing cables through blocks stationed atop a spar tree the skidder system and less sophisticated high-lead achieved a fundamental advance over the ground yarding method, allowing logs to be pulled to the landing while partially suspended. First employed in Michigan in the mid-1880s, the Lidgerwood skidder system was introduced to the west coast by the Kerry Mill Company at Kerriston, Washington in 1902. The Comox Logging and Railway Company brought the first Lidgerwood to British Columbia in 1910, followed quickly by the Victoria Lumber and Manufacturing Company and Empire Lumber Company. Firms lacking the financial resources to purchase a Lidgerwood or one of the similar systems produced by the region's equipment manufacturers opted for the high-lead, in widespread use by 1915.

The accepted wisdom concerning the transition to overhead logging is that operators were adapting to increasingly difficult terrain as logging progressed inland. But those who related their experience with the new technology at industry gatherings referred almost unanimously to favourable topographic conditions. When timbermen explained the advantages of overhead logging they emphasized increased productivity, the elimination of positions on the yarding crew, and diminished control exercised by skilled workers over the pace of production.[28]

The fundamental superiority of these systems lay in their capacity to restructure timber capital's relationship to the forest environment and workers. So long as operators were confined to ground-leading logs, control of yarding rested with loggers. But by providing log elevation overhead systems brought corporate control to a new level, reflected in a one-third reduction in logging costs. With log preparation no longer necessary firms put swampers, snipers and barkers on an "eternal vacation." Moreover, operators enjoyed a new-found capacity to transform the labour power of loggers into work. R.D. Merrill, with major interests in both Washington and British Columbia, boasted that the Lidgerwood moved logs through the air at two to three times the speed permitted in ground yarding. Rigging returned to the crew at an accelerated rate, speeding up the entire yarding cycle. Machine pacing, the essence of the factory system, had come to coastal logging.[29]

In ground yarding, one operator explained, an experienced crew working on level terrain might bring in an average of thirty logs per day, but only half their time was devoted to yarding. With the overhead system, no time was lost preparing yarding roads and swamping, and "the time consumed in placing and throwing lines in and out of lead blocks and in blocking logs away from obstructions is devoted to hauling logs." The new technique, in short, represented a "solution to the yarding problem," marking the end of the "necessity for an endless shifting of chokers and pulling of lines to permit one, and seldom over two logs to bore a tortuous path through acres of stumps and debris." Companies could now transport up to six logs to the landing at one time, "with seldom a stop after the go-ahead whistle."[30]

Routinization was accompanied by an equally significant deskilling of loggers. Machinery manufacturers and operators may have been prone to exaggeration, but their testimonies reflect an undisguised enthusiasm over a diminished reliance on loggers' skills. The designer of one early apparatus pointed out that his system required only two "high priced men," the donkey engineer and hooktender. The latter, "upon whose caprices hangs the day's output" in ground logging, declared another writer, exercised less control under overhead methods. The recollections of Sid Smith, a veteran British Columbia logging manager, buttress these impressions. According to Smith, the high-lead undermined the hooktender's authority and "took away the necessity of having good chokermen and rigging slingers."[31] The efficiencies provided by overhead systems did generate the occupation of high rigger, whose task was to prepare the spar tree, but companies accepted this skilled position in exchange for a higher level of control over the logging labour process.

By 1930, then, operators had erected a rudimentary factory regime. The oppressive technology that further increased the hazardousness and regimentation of work in the industry held little appeal for loggers. Firms introducing overhead systems experienced higher quit rates, but resistance did not reach sufficient proportions to slow their adoption. While the loggers' individual and collective protest against squalid camp conditions and dawn to dusk work days achieved some reforms, they had no success in resisting the instruments of production that structured their labour.[32]

Although overhead technologies advanced the industry a full step closer to the realization of a factory mode of production loggers continued to exert a collective control over the pace of logging, especially on rough ground where the ability to avoid and overcome "hang-ups" was critical. But if loggers were not utterly subordinated by sophisticated technologies, it would be an error to underestimate the change in workplace relations wrought by the new generation of machinery. Mechanization and related changes in the division of labour reduced timber capital's dependence on the physical and conceptual skills of loggers, confirming the general thrust of Braverman's degradation of work thesis. High-lead logging "isn't exactly an assembly line," wrote Stewart Holbrook in 1938, "but it's all routine." Logging operations had indeed come to resemble "a giant factory without a roof."[33]

Forest Science and Regulation

This paper now shifts from the arena of class conflict to study the ecological implications of industry's factory regime, assessing the foundation of British Columbia's client state. The years to 1930 witnessed the emergence of clearcutting as a technique of forest exploitation, the initiation of research into the impact of logging practices on Douglas fir regeneration, and the establishment of an enduring pattern of cooperative industry-government relations. An awareness of structures laid down during the late nineteenth and early twentieth centuries is vital to an understanding of the current crisis facing the province's coastal timber industry.

Prior to coastal logging's industrial revolution, commercial exploitation was carried out with little negative impact on the forest's regenerative capacity. Small in scale, selective in nature, and conducted at a slow pace, bull and horse team operations extracted only high-quality timber situated close to waterway or sawmill. Mature trees and young growth that did not justify the arduous tasks of falling and removal remained to produce seed, and foresters who studied such selectively logged areas in later decades concluded that team logging left the forest in "good producing condition."[34]

The adoption of the steam donkey to ground-lead logs began the transition from selective logging to clearcutting, increasing the pace, scale, and environmental degradation associated with logging. While not as destructive as the overhead systems that followed, ground yarding with powerful steam donkeys tore up the forest floor, knocked over immature timber, and left an enormous amount of slash that increased the likelihood of fire. Damage was heaviest along the trails over which logs travelled, but logging was confined to relatively small areas open to reseeding from adjacent stands.[35]

Foresters accepted both clearcutting and the technology that fostered the practice when they first contemplated the relationship between mechanized logging and forest renewal. On the Douglas fir stands within the national forests of Washington and Oregon, Burt Kirkland explained in 1911, methods necessary to remove the heavy timber did not "permit the saving of young growth." U.S. Forest Service silviculturalist Thornton Munger agreed that where steam logging was practised, "any other system than clearcutting is practically impossible."[36] Research into the ecological character of Douglas fir had already discovered that the species reproduced best on "open ground," providing foresters with a scientific rationale to embrace the existing mode of production. Knowledge of Douglas fir's shade intolerance lent clearcutting a silvicultural legitimacy that conformed with its cost efficiency. The U.S. Forest Service reserved two or three seed trees per acre to achieve reforestation on timber sale areas, a restocking measure requiring no "decided modification of present logging methods" under the ground-lead system.[37]

In British Columbia, which experienced a timber boom of remarkable proportions after Richard McBride's Conservative government opened the province to speculators and timber capitalists in 1905, knowledge of forest conditions was negligible. By 1909 politicians and lumbermen alike recognized the need for rational administration of the province's disorganized mix of leased, licensed, and Crown-grant land. Hoping for government action to secure perpetuity of tenure, improved fire protection and price stability, industry supported Conservative Premier Richard McBride's appointment of a royal commission under F.J. Fulton to investigate the forestry situation.[38]

Those whose experience in the woods qualified them to submit opinions on cutting regulations to the Fulton Commission generally argued that fire, not logging methods, posed the greatest threat to forest perpetuation. One Department of Lands and Works official conceded that damage to young growth made steam-powered operations "a much greater menace to the forest than team logging," suggesting rules to protect immature timber might be appropriate. More reflective of contemporary thinking, however, were the comments of land surveyor Noel Humphreys, who expressed confidence in nature's capacity to provide a second crop after logging given adequate fire prevention. Provincial Timber Inspector R.J. Skinner, more concerned about economics than conservation, advised against adopting "ill-judged or unnecessary obligations and restrictions" that might impair the profitability of enterprises.[39]

Skinner's reflections on the regulation issue matched those of the B.C. Loggers Association. The province's major operators feared that the "theoretical might predominate over the practical" and prompt the Commissioners to recommend controls damaging to their competitiveness. With lumbering interests having a prominent place on it, there was little chance of the Commission issuing radical proposals, and its report was consistent with the goals of a "continental conservation movement dedicated to the promotion of large-scale corporate enterprise and the application of scientific management." Recommendations included establishing a forestry department to enforce utilization and slash disposal rules, competitive bidding, and placing forestry revenues into a protection fund. An appendix to the report presented a statement of practices followed by the U.S. Forest Service on its public lands but the Commissioners said little about the impact of logging on regeneration. "Effective reafforestation," they concluded, "depends upon effective discouragement of waste."[40]

Passed with the support of lumbermen, the 1912 Forest Act created a Forest Branch within the Department of Lands to collect revenue and administer a Forest Protection Fund jointly supported by government and industry. The new timber sale programme featured contracts specifying uti-

lization standards and slash disposal obligations, but demanded no reservation of seed trees. Unfortunately, the new bureaucracy was given very little
authority over temporary tenures issued prior to 1912. Although operations
on the 1,500 square miles of land under lease and 14,000 square miles of
licensed timber were in theory subject to any regulations issued under the
Act, cutting went largely uncontrolled. On these lands the Branch's major
concern was to prevent illegal cutting of adjacent public timber and to collect rental fees and royalties for the provincial treasury. Completely beyond
the influence of the Forest Branch were 6,000 square miles of timberland
under private ownership. On Crown-grant lands, including the enormous
2 million acre E & N Railway grant on southeastern Vancouver Island, operators had a free hand to exploit the resource without challenge to their
property rights.[41]

The organization of a provincial forest administration coincided with
the transition to overhead methods of timber exploitation. High-lead and
skidder systems necessitated complete clearcutting. While isolated patches
of young growth and defective trees might survive on high-lead settings,
almost total devastation of huge areas accompanied the use of sophisticated
aerial systems. In either case, operators cut timberland clean to permit rapid
shifting of lines and unimpeded passage of logs to the landing. Any small
or unmerchantable timber that escaped the falling crews was knocked over
and uprooted during the yarding operation, a consequence of the high
speeds at which logs and rigging now travelled under the power generated
by enormous skidders.[42]

On the American national forests in the southern part of the Douglas fir
region foresters quickly recognized the need to adjust practices to cope with
the destructive effects of the new technology. After a 1916 inspection R.Y.
Stuart reported that "the use of high lead logging has presented difficulties
in ensuring reservation of individual trees or groups of trees for seed purposes."[43] But the profession voiced no general protest against overhead logging at this time. One major source of complacency was the sheer abundance of the resource; another, the "seed storage" theory propounded by
J.V. Hoffman, director of the U.S. Forest Service's Wind River field station.
Although never accepted wholeheartedly by some foresters and proven to
be without foundation in the 1930s, Hoffman's interpretation of Douglas

fir reproduction legitimated unregulated clearcutting and, by extension, provided coastal operators with a scientific rebuttal against those who favoured government control of cutting practices.[44]

Hoffman's theory had its genesis in 1913, when he discovered young growth on vast areas burned over eleven years earlier during the 1902 fires that swept through southwestern Washington. Though no accurate data on Douglas fir seed flight had been compiled, the presence of what appeared to be even-aged seedlings two or three miles from timber suggested to the silviculturalist that the reproduction originated from seed stored in the forest floor which survived the fire. Hoffman advanced a startling new theory: Douglas fir seed could retain its vitality for long periods, perhaps up to eight years, while stored in the "duff" or layer of organic material coating the forest floor. The seeds germinated, he argued, when exposed to sunlight after logging or fire removed the forest canopy.[45]

The theory found immediate acceptance in British Columbia, where Ontario forester C. D. Howe was making the first scientific investigation of the province's coastal forest resource in 1915 for the Federal government's Commission on Conservation. After conducting regeneration surveys and discussing the issue with Hoffman, Howe accepted the "probability of dense stands of Douglas fir arising from several seed crops accumulated in the soil." As he explained to the B.C. Forest Club, this feature of the species made close attention to seed tree reservation unnecessary. Regeneration could be obtained simply by clearcutting, conducting a light slash burn immediately after logging, and preventing subsequent fires.[46]

Even within his own agency some doubted the veracity of Hoffman's hypothesis. Reluctant to rely exclusively on stored seed as an agent of restocking, the U.S. Forest Service continued to reserve seed trees on timber sales. British Columbia's Forest Branch, "very weak scientifically" in its formative years, took no such precautions. After World War I the agency's George McVickar observed that Howe's 1915 report, "hardly complete or definite enough to form the basis of any action," remained the only source of information on the province's forest resource. Chief Forester Martin Grainger supported McVickar's proposal to conduct further study to provide data for logging regulations, and the latter apparently assessed regeneration on some coastal timber sale areas in 1921.[47]

The following year J. L. Alexander received an assignment to investigate the relationship between logging and reforestation in British Columbia's coastal forests. In 1922 he established a few sample plots to determine the amount and distribution of seedlings after logging and provide an informed estimate on the distance of seed dissemination. Initial results of this work, initiated to ascertain if seed trees should be reserved on timber sales, indicated that the effective range of seeding from a 175-foot Douglas fir approximated 350 feet and raised questions about the wisdom of slash burning to encourage reproduction of this species. American silviculturalists already suspected that while slash burning was essential for fire hazard reduction, it probably served no regenerative function.[48]

By this time a growing number of foresters on both sides of the border attributed the growing expanse of barren land, at least in part, to the extensive clearcutting practised by operators. In a 1922 "Minimum Requirements Report" Thornton Munger urged American operators to adopt U.S. Forest Service methods, but even in the national forests, cutover areas often appeared in an "unsatisfactory silvicultural condition," prompting demands for greater care in timber sale management. British Columbia's Chief Forester P.Z. Caverhill also felt that the relationship between logging methods and the process of forest renewal required attention. "There is a growing feeling," he informed C.D. Howe in 1923, "that the high-lead system of logging is responsible for large areas of cut-over land not restocking." These methods could not be prohibited because of their widespread use and engineering superiority, but the Branch needed to "ascertain the technical measures, necessary and practical, to ensure perpetuation of our timbered areas."[49]

J.L. Alexander's early work suggested that most sites would restock quickly after logging "even where present methods of logging are used," provided that fires were controlled. Another Branch forester went so far as to deny the existence of devastated forestland. "Nature reclothes all," G.E. Stoodley informed P.Z. Caverhill. "It is only a question of the time element." But even optimists knew that the creation of larger contiguous areas of logged-off land would impede natural reforestation. Still confident at the end of 1924, Caverhill assured his Minister of Lands that reproduction after logging was "ample to assure a new forest" at no cost to the government.

Planting, on the other hand, would involve considerable expense. In fact, the Chief Forester's statements to colleagues, elected officials and the public were uniformly reassuring to 1928.[50]

The data that informed such pronouncements in British Columbia was hardly substantial, given the low priority assigned to research within the Department of Lands. Alexander remained the Branch's only silvicultural investigator until 1924, and future Chief Forester E.C. Manning criticized the meagre resources devoted to science. "As it is now," he observed, "everyone has a hand in it whenever we can get a little time off from our routine work." Continuing the present half-hearted effort would carry a high price to be paid in "useless experiments, wrong conclusions based on ignorance or insufficient data . . . resulting in money spent in adhering to regulations which are later found not to be practicable." Percy Barr was assigned to research in 1924, but Caverhill's recommendation that experimental stations be established went unheeded. Progress of a bureaucratic sort was made in 1927 when Barr became director of the Forest Branch's new Research Division.[51]

While British Columbia foresters pressed for a stronger commitment to research, some of their colleagues to the south called for a reassessment of the seed storage theory. Caverhill confessed to *Timberman* editor George Cornwall that foresters in his Branch had "for some years not been fully convinced" of Hoffman's theory. He wanted to proceed with caution, however, at least in part because of his concern over "the effect upon the public mind" of repeated shifts in forestry science and practice. J.L. Alexander shared his Chief's conviction that the issue demanded more study. In October 1925, after examining approximately 1,000 cutover areas in the coastal region he could not yet definitively rule out stored seed as a factor.[52]

U.S. Forest Service silviculturalist Leo Isaac performed the experiments that discredited the seed storage theory. In 1925 he began replicating Hoffman's germination tests. Fresh seed was collected, placed in containers of forest soil, and embedded at various depths in the forest floor. Seeds taken up the first year germinated, a very few the second, but none thereafter. Reluctant to "destroy an established theory if it had, any foundation of fact," Isaac delayed publication until he had repeated the tests. Alexander, performing a similar series of investigations in British Columbia was less hesitant. In 1926 he replied to an American executive's inquiry that stored seed was "relatively unimportant when compared to wind disseminated seed" in reforesting cutovers.[53]

These studies confirmed that no accumulation of Douglas fir seed crops awaited removal of the forest canopy to spring to life. Foresters would have to rely on seed trees or adjacent timber to reforest clearcuts. Experiments to determine the effective range of Douglas fir seed flight indicated that under average conditions one-quarter mile was the maximum distance foresters could expect Douglas fir seed to be disseminated from a bank of timber in sufficient quantity.[54]

This information gave resource agencies new insight into the ecological character of Douglas fir. Better equipped to adjust clearcutting practices to secure natural regeneration, foresters were increasingly aware of the need to do so. Ongoing examination of cutovers pointed to the scale of the reforestation problem and the extent to which unregulated clearcutting was responsible for the growing expanse of land that exhibited no new commercial crop.

Alexander had initiated a history map study of ten major operations on Vancouver Island and the Lower Mainland in 1924, with the intention of making annual examinations of these areas to determine the rate of reforestation. Although the project had lapsed, in 1928 Percy Barr was authorized to update the maps. Defining 1,000 seedlings per acre as satisfactory restocking, Barr and Eric Garman estimated that 60 per cent of the cutover lands failed to meet this standard. Logging and fire, the Forest Branch's 1928 annual report explained, had created extensive denuded areas too far removed from seed sources to restock. The Branch had not yet made an effort to reserve seed trees, even on timber sales where it possessed strong authority. "Personally," Caverhill informed U.S. Forest Service Regional Forester Christopher Grainger in late 1927, "with the high-lead method of logging I can hardly visualize how these trees are protected during the yarding operation, especially if they are left in any regular or systematic manner."[55]

A survey of early sales in the Vancouver Forest District left little doubt that overhead logging techniques were more destructive than earlier methods. Logged between 1915 and 1919, most of these small areas averaged approximately 200 acres, and featured an abundance of seed trees. On the whole, the cutovers exhibited optimal opportunities for natural reforestation, resulting in satisfactory restocking on 75 per cent of the area. This contrasted sharply with the situation Barr discovered on lands logged recently, a difference he attributed to the fact that "on these large operations very few seed trees have been left, and most of these have been destroyed in fires subsequent to logging."[56]

In a 1930 *Forest Chronicle* article Barr and Eric Garman set out in explicit terms what they had learned about the relationship between changes in technology, logging practices and reforestation. In logging selectively, oxen and horse loggers left plenty of seed trees and did little damage to remaining timber and saplings. Slash accumulations were minimal, and, protected by trees and undergrowth, did not become dangerously flammable. Forest reproduction became much less certain with the adoption of the steam donkey. Utilization was more intensive, and greater damage inflicted upon young growth. The amount of debris left behind increased significantly, creating a more favourable environment for fire. Nevertheless, some timber remained to produce seed, and fires were usually restricted to comparatively small areas exposed to reseeding from adjacent stands.

The unrestrained application of high-lead and skyline systems of logging in the years around World War I shattered any residual harmony between the processes of forest exploitation and renewal. Clearcuts became much more extensive, and yarding with high-speed heavy equipment levelled the young growth that had survived earlier methods. A vastly increased amount of slash was left fully exposed to the sun and wind. The intense fires which inevitably swept through such cutovers destroyed both the fresh seed present on the ground, and any remaining timber. Moreover, the two silviculturalists observed, clearcutting on the coast was "conducted on such a large scale and at such high speed that the operations of a single company may cover several hundred acres during a year." Much cutover land was thus "too far removed from marginal stands to receive any seed."[57]

By 1930, then, foresters held the operators' use of sophisticated cable logging systems directly responsible for the slow pace of restocking in British Columbia's Douglas fir region. The Forest Branch opened its Green Timbers that year to produce seedlings for about 50 per cent of the logged coastal lands that required planting. But the cost of artificial reforestation ruled out this technocratic option as a practical solution to restocking problems. Natural methods would secure a new forest at nominal cost to the public if operators adopted slight modifications to their clearcutting practices.[58]

Precisely what needed to be done to transform clearcutting into a sound silvicultural system had been the subject of considerable research. Foresters had dispelled some myths and gained an understanding of the problem, if not its ultimate solution. Establishment of a permanent experimental station at Cowichan Lake in 1929 reflected a growing awareness of the need for accurate scientific data. Knowledge, of course, was a necessary but not sufficient precondition of rational forest management. The province's timbermen had already "succeeded in penetrating the administrative process in order to shape public policy to their private needs," and the accord between political elites and industry held throughout the latter 1930s when Chief Forester E. C. Manning led a campaign for forest practice reforms.[59]

In the meantime, residents of some lumbering communities within Vancouver Island's E & N Railway belt were already criticizing industry's lack of regard for sustainability and pondering the eventual exhaustion of local timber supplies.[60] But as the 1920s ended those at the head of the province's forest bureaucracy had little enthusiasm for intervention to control the conduct of logging. Although the Forest Act gave the state power to regulate exploitation on Crown lands, officials were reluctant to adopt any regulation that might raise logging costs and impair the competitiveness of firms. In any case, 50 per cent of the provincial cut came from the largest enterprises cutting private timber within the E & N belt. Reluctant to place those logging on public lands at a disadvantage with these influential operators, the state allowed unregulated practices on private land to set the provincial standard. "With regard to Crown Grants," Chief Forester Caverhill informed an Ontario colleague in 1929, "public opinion has not yet reached the point where interference with the free use of private lands will be countenanced." Caverhill's reference to public opinion notwithstanding, the accord between the province's lumbermen and ruling politicians dictated that his Branch followed a policy of "education and cooperation rather than a blind and unyielding effort to enforce to the letter the rather wide powers conferred by the Act."[61]

Conclusion

During the late nineteenth and early twentieth centuries west coast logging underwent its industrial revolution, involving an expansion in scale, the arrival of steam technologies, and the development of a more elaborate managerial structure.[62] The steam engine, first used as an energy source in ground-lead logging, then integrated with overhead systems, created a rudimentary factory regime that boosted productivity while placing loggers under more rigid forms of workplace discipline. Although the complex, ever-changing forest environment continued to dictate a central role for loggers' physical and conceptual skills, by 1930 operators had made considerable headway in forging an exploitation process embodying the essential features of mass production factory settings.

Corporations applied the first generation of overhead logging technology with catastrophic ecological results, typically pushing railroads up valley bottoms, clearcutting as they went. This practice denuded vast contiguous areas of seed sources and young growth, at best leaving a few marginal patches of unmerchantable trees with the impossible task of reseeding cutovers. British Columbia appeared to be at the cutting edge of progress in conservation in 1912 when the province adopted a comprehensive Forest Act and established a professional bureaucracy to administer cutting. But, as in other provinces, Crown ownership of the resource and the presence of foresters in the public service generated the appearance rather than reality of effective resource stewardship.[63] The provincial state's half-hearted commitment to conservation held even in the face of mounting scientific evidence of the factory regime's negative impact on the forest's regenerative function.

To be sure, the early twentieth century was not a propitious period for stringent regulation of industry in the wider political economy. During the 1920s in the United States Herbert Hoover's Department of Commerce cooperated with trade associations in an effort to eliminate market competition and inefficiency. Throughout Canada as well, those in government followed a policy of partnership with business interests in promoting economic development.[64] As for British Columbia, the Forest Branch possessed neither the resources nor expertise necessary to introduce an effective programme of silvicultural regulation during the first two decades of its existence. That the province's political elites also lacked the will to challenge timber capital's entrenched tendency to "mine" the Douglas fir forest would become more apparent during the Great Depression. During that decade sentiment favourable to stronger state intervention in social and economic affairs coincided with the emergence of widespread demand for reforms ranging from enforced selective logging to the imposition of "seed tree" regulations. Additional evidence came soon after when the provincial state introduced a sustained-yield policy that granted corporations monopoly control over much of the remaining timber supply without adopting a regulatory apparatus capable of ensuring that cutting on the new Tree Farm Licences met the promised silvicultural standards.

But the fundamental technological, scientific and regulatory structures of resource exploitation on the west coast were erected during an earlier period of the province's forest history. First, no subsequent innovation restricted timber capital's relationship to workers and nature so fundamentally as the steam donkey and overhead logging system. The motorized steel-spar and modern grapple yarder merely sharpened the focus of the factory analogy by bringing further sophistication to the essential principle of overhead-logging.

Second, because steam-driven cable systems did not permit selective logging, foresters began to address the problems of clearcutting. Much of what follows, in policy terms, can be interpreted as an ongoing struggle between corporate interests determined to defend the technique's efficiency in timber liquidation against those who sought regulation to curb its destructive ecological effects. One explanation for industry's success lies in the provincial state's reluctance to forge a rational integration of the scientific and policy-making processes.

Finally, the factory regime's genesis brings into plain view the role of technology in the related processes of natural resource and worker exploitation. Forests and labour power share a status as mere commodities in the calculus of industrial capitalism. The primary appeal of steam technology when utilized in the typical "high-ball" fashion lay in its capacity to extract maximum immediate value from both, regardless of the cost in human and ecological terms. A stronger grasp of this reality on the part of woods unions and environmentalists would serve to focus attention on their shared concern with sustainable forest practice. So long as bickering over the remaining scraps of old-growth continues to divide these interests, governments will remain free to respond to corporate imperatives.

Notes

1. I would like to thank Patricia Roy and Mary McRoberts for commenting on an earlier draft of this paper, and to acknowledge support from the Social Sciences and Humanities Research Council of Canada.
2. Donald MacKay, *Empire of Wood: The MacMillan Bloedel Story* (Vancouver: Douglas & McIntyre, 1982), pp. 1-12.
3. R. Peter Gillis and Thomas R. Roach, *Lost Initiatives: Canada's Forest Industries, Forest Policy and Forest Conservation* (New York: Greenwood Press, 1986), p. 131; C. J. Taylor, *The Heritage of the British Columbia Forest Industry: A Guide for Planning, Selection and Interpretation of Sites* (Ottawa: Environment Canada, 1987), p. 75.
4. G. W. Taylor, *Timber: History of the Forest Industry in B.C.* (Vancouver: J.J. Douglas, 1975), pp. 49-74; Stephen Gray, "The Government's Timber Business: Forest Policy and Administration in British Columbia, 1912-1928," *BC Studies* 81 (Spring 1989), pp. 25-6; Jean Barman, *The West Beyond the West: A History of British Columbia* (Toronto: University of Toronto Press, 1991), pp. 182-3.
5. Patricia Marchak, *Green Gold: The Forest Industry in British Columbia* (Vancouver: University of British Columbia Press, 1983); Ken Drushka, *Stumped: The Forest Industry in Transition* (Vancouver: Douglas & McIntyre, 1985); Gray, "The Government's Timber Business"; Gillis and Roach, *Lost Initiatives*; Mary McRoberts, "When Good Intentions Fail: A Case of Forest Policy in the British Columbia Interior, 1945-1956," *Journal of Forest History* 32 (July 1988), pp. 138-49; Jeremy Wilson, "Forest Conservation in British Columbia, 1935-1985: Reflections on a Barren Political Debate," *BC Studies* 76 (Winter 1987-1988), pp. 3-32. For a thorough elaboration of this theme in relationship to the Canadian and American context, see Richard A. Rajala, "Clearcutting the Pacific Coast: Production, Science and Regulation in the Douglas Fir Forests of Canada and the United States, 1880-1965" (PhD, York University, 1994).
6. See Ted Benton, "Marxism and Natural Limits: An Ecological Critique and Reconstruction," *New Left Review* 178 (1989), pp. 51-86; Michael Clow, "Alienation From Nature: Marx and Environmental Politics," *Alternatives* 10 (Summer 1982), pp. 36-40; James O'Connor, "Socialism and Ecology," *Our Generation* 22 (Fall 1990 – Spring 1991), pp. 75-87.
7. R. J. Johnson, *Environmental Problems: Nature, Economy and the State* (New York: Belhaven Press, 1989), pp. 50 & 75; K. J. Walker, "Ecological Limits and Marxian Thought," *Politics* 14 (May 1979), p. 41; see also H. M. Ezenberger, "A Critique of Political Ecology," *New Left Review* 84 (Mar./Apr. 1974), pp. 3-31; Karl W. Kapp, "Environmental Disruption and Protection," in *Socialism and the Environment*, ed. Ken Coates (Nottingham: Spokesman Books, 1972), pp. 13-24.
8. Harry Braverman, *Labor and Monopoly Capital: The Degradation of Work in the Twentieth Century* (New York: Monthly Review Press, 1974), pp. 54, 193.
9. For a more thorough discussion of these issues, see the author's "The Forest as

Factory: Technological Change and Worker Control in the West Coast Logging Industry, 1880-1930," *Labour/Le Travail* 32 (Fall 1993), pp. 73-104.

10. William Robbins, *Lumberjacks and Legislators: Political Economy of the U.S. Lumber Industry, 1890-1941* (College Station: Texas A & M University Press, 1982); H. V. Nelles, *The Politics of Development: Forests, Mines and Hydro-Electric Power in Ontario, 1891-1941* (Toronto: MacMillan, 1974).

11. See James Weinstein, *The Corporate Ideal in the Liberal State, 1900-1918* (Boston: Beacon Press, 1968); Gabriel Kolko, *The Triumph of Conservatism: A Reinterpretation of American History, 1900-1916* (New York: Free Press, 1963).

12. For discussion of this approach see David A. Gold, Clarence Y.H. Lo and Eric Olin Wright, "Recent Developments in Marxist Theories of the Capitalist State," *Monthly Review* 27 (1975), No. 5, pp. 29-43, & No. 6, pp. 35-51; Theda Skocpol, "Bringing the State Back In: Strategies of Analysis in Current Research," in *Bringing the State Back In*, eds. Peter B. Evans, Dietrich Rueschmeyer and Skocpol (Cambridge: Cambridge University Press, 1985), pp. 3-37; Gregory Albo and Jane Jensen, "A Contested Concept: The Relative Autonomy of the State," in *The New Canadian Political Economy*, eds. Wallace Clement and Glen Williams (Montreal: McGill-Queen's University Press 1989), pp. 180-211.

13. See L. Anders Sandberg, "Introduction," *Trouble in the Woods: Forest Policy and Social Conflict in Nova Scotia and New Brunswick* (Fredricton: Acadiensis Press, 1992), p. 2.

14. See Gray, "The Government's Timber Business."

15. Stanley Aronowitz, *Science as Power: Discourse and Ideology in Modern Society* (Minneapolis: University of Minnesota Press, 1988), p. 293; see also David Dickson, *The New Politics of Science* (New York: Pantheon Books, 1984), p. 314.

16. John Bellamy Foster, "The Limits of Environmentalism Without Class: Lessons from the Ancient Forest Struggle in the Pacific Northwest," *Capitalism, Nature, Socialism* 13 (March 1993), p. 12.

17. Robert D. Turner, *Logging By Rail: The British Columbia Story* (Victoria: Sono Nis Press, 1990), p. 48.

18. J. J. Donovan to N. L. Wright, 27 May 1913, Box 1, University of Washington College of Forest Resources Records, Acc. 70-1, University of Washington Libraries; see also Clarence Ross Garvey, "Overhead Systems of Logging in the Northwest," (M.Sc. in Forestry thesis, University of Washington, 1914), p. 1.

19. Frank H. Lamb, "Logging Engineering Requires Skill and Experience for Success," *Timberman* 10 (Aug. 1909), p. 32. (hereafter *TMN*).

20. Louise H. Wall, "Hauling Logs in Washington," *Northwest Magazine* (Apr. 1893), p. 21.

21. Wall, "Hauling Logs," p. 20; Lloyd C. Rogers, interviewed by C. D. Orchard, Box 3, C. D. Orchard Collection, British Columbia Archives and Record Service (hereafter BCARS); see also Wallace Baikie, "Early Logging Days on Denman Island," *British Columbia Forest History Newsletter* 5 (Apr. 1983), p. 3.

22. George P. Abdill, "Bull Team Logger," *True West* 21 (July-Aug. 1974), p. 28; Albert Drinkwater, interviewed by Imbert Orchard, BCARS; see also W. Baikie, "Logging with Bulls," *British Columbia Forest History Newsletter* 8 (Apr. 1984), p. 3.

23. "Pacific Coast Logging Methods," *Pacific Lumber Trade Journal* 5 (Aug. 1899), p. 10; McKay, *Empire of Wood*, p. 16; Rajala, "The Forest As Factory," pp. 84-6.

24. "Logging Methods in British Columbia," *Canada Lumberman* 22 (Nov. 1902), p. 8; "The Development of the Logging Engine," *West Coast and Puget Sound*

Lumberman 13 (Jan. 1906), p. 167; G. A. Walkem, "Evolution of the British Columbia Logging Industry," *British Columbia Lumberman* 10 (Aug. 1926), p. 97; H. R. Christie, "Logging Methods on Vancouver Island," *Canada Lumberman and Woodworker* 36 (1 Sept. 1916), pp. 78-80; "Recent Progress in Power Logging Equipment," *Western Lumberman* 8 (Aug. 1921), p. 76.

25. R. V. Stuart, interviewed by C. D. Orchard, p. 10, C. D. Orchard Collection, BCARS; Richard H. Kennedy, "Logging Our Great Forests," *Pacific Monthly* 13 (Jan. 1905), p. 28.

26. James O'Hearne, "How Shall We Teach Logging Engineering," *Proceedings of the Pacific Logging Congress* (Spokane, 1913), p. 21 (hereafter *PPLC*); L. T. Murray, "Changes in Type of Donkey Engine," *Western Lumberman* 11 (Nov. 1922), p. 56; W. H. Corbett, "The Larger Yarding Engine," *TMN* 7 (Apr. 1906), p. 33; W. H. Corbett, "The Era of the Big Drum Yarder," *TMN* 6 (Apr. 1905), p. 320.

27. Andrew Mason Prouty, *More Deadly Than War: Pacific Coast Logging, 1827-1981* (New York: Garland Publishing, 1985), p. 62; Francis Frink, interviewed by Elwood R. Maunder, 1958, Forest History Foundation, p. 3; E. S. Grammer, "Evolution of the Logging Donkey," *PPLC* (San Francisco, 1921), p. 32; *BCL* 26 (Dec. 1942), p. 44.

28. Rajala, "The Forest as Factory," pp. 90-4.

29. R. D. Merrill, "Utilization of the Lidgerwood System of Logging, *PPLC* (Vancouver, 1911), p. 55; "The Lamb Cableway System," *Columbia River and Oregon Timberman* 4 (Aug. 1904), p. 47.

30. "The Lamb Cableway System," p. 47; R. W. Vinnedge, "A Composite Flying Machine," *PPLC* (Spokane, 1913), p. 9; see also Victor Stevens, *The Powers Story* (North Bend: Wegford Publications, 1979), p. 69; R. J. O'Farrell, "The Evolution of Logging – Some Personal Glimpses," *University of Washington Forest Club Quarterly* 8 (Autumn 1929), p. 15.

31. "The Lamb Cableway System," p. 47; "The Evolution of Coast Logging," p. 22; S. G. Smith, interviewed by C. D. Orchard, Orchard Collection, p. 8, BCARS.

32. Rajala, "The Forest as Factory," pp. 101-2; see also Richard A. Rajala, "Bill and the Boss: Labour Protest, Technological Change, and the Transformation of the West Coast Logging Camp, 1890-1930," *Journal of Forest History* 33 (Oct. 1989), pp. 168-79.

33. Stewart H. Holbrook, *Holy Old Mackinaw: A Natural History of the American Lumberjack* (New York: MacMillan, 1945), p. 184.

34. Axel J. F. Brandstrom, *Analysis of Logging Costs and Operating Methods in the Douglas Fir Region* (Seattle: Charles Lathrop Pack Forestry Foundation, 1933), p. 7; Leo A. Isaac, *Reproductive Habits of Douglas Fir* (Washington, D.C.: Charles Lathrop Pack Forestry Foundation, 1943), p. 10; Richard White, *Land Use, Environment, and Social Change: The Shaping of Island County, Washington* (Seattle: University of Washington Press, 1992), pp. 88-91; William G. Robbins, "The Luxuriant Landscape: "The Great Douglas Fir Bioregion"," *Oregon Humanities* (Winter 1990), p. 4.

35. E. H. Garman and P. M. Barr, "A History Map Study in British Columbia," *Forest Chronicle* 6 (Dec. 1930), pp. 14-15; see also Robert Bunting, "Abundance and the Forests of the Douglas-Fir Bioregion, 1840-1920," *Environmental History Review* 18 (Winter 1994), p. 49.

36. Burt P. Kirkland, "The Need of a Vigorous Policy of Encouraging Cutting on the National Forests of the Pacific Coast," *Forestry Quarterly* 9 (Sept. 1911), p. 376;

Thornton T. Munger, "Lectures Delivered at the University of Washington on Silvics, Planting and Reconnaissance," pp. 13-20, Feb. 1911, p. 22, University of Washington College of Forest Resources Library.

37. E. T. Allen, "A Study of the Red Fir," 1903, p. 77, U.S. Forest Service, Timber Management Files, RG 095-54A-0111, Box 59862, U.S. National Archives and Records Service, Pacific Northwest Region; Munger, "Lectures Delivered at the University of Washington," pp. 21-3; Amelia R. Fry, *Thornton T. Munger: Forest Research in the Pacific Northwest, An Interview Conducted by Amelia R. Fry* (Berkeley: University of California Regional Oral History Office, 1967), p. 66.

38. Jamie Swift, *Cut and Run: The Assault on Canada's Forests* (Toronto: Between the Lines, 1983), pp. 58-9; Taylor, *The Heritage*, p. 100.

39. A. Haslam to F. J. Fulton, 31 July 1909; N. Humphreys to R. E. Gosnell, 27 Sept. 1909; R. J. Skinner to Fulton, 31 Aug. 1909, Box 1, B.C., Records of the Royal Commission on Timber and Forestry, 1909-1910, GR 271, BCARS.

40. W. I. Patterson to P. Ellison, 7 Jan. 1910, ibid.; *Final Report of the Royal Commission of Inquiry on Timber and Forestry* (Victoria, 1910), pp. 58-65; Gray, "The Government's Timber Business," pp. 27-8; see also Samuel P. Hays, *Conservation and the Gospel of Efficiency: The Progressive Conservation Movement, 1880-1920* (Cambridge: Harvard University Press, 1959); MacKay, *Empire of Wood*, pp. 33-5; Gillis and Roach, *Lost Initiatives*, pp. 146-50. For discussion of the McBride administration, see Barman, *The West Beyond the West*, pp. 177-81; Martin Robin, *The Rush for Spoils: The Company Province, 1871-1933* (Toronto: McClelland and Stewart, 1972), pp. 87-98.

41. H. R. MacMillan, "Present Condition of Applied Forestry in Canada," *Proceedings of the Society of American Foresters* 10 (Apr. 1915), pp. 126-28; Overton W. Price, "Progress in British Columbia," *American Forestry* 20 (1914), p. 273.

42. Thornton T. Munger, "Minimum Requirements Report: Provisional Draft Submitted for Criticism of Cooperators," 5 Dec. 1922, p. 16, University of Washington College of Forest Resources Library; Peter A. Twight, *Ecological Forestry for the Douglas Fir Region* (Washington, D.C.: National Parks and Conservation Association, 1973), p. 4.

43. R. Y. Stuart, "Memorandum for the Chief Forester," 12 Aug. 1916, Box 14, U.S. Forest Service, District Historical Files, RG 95, U.S. National Archives and Records Service, Pacific Northwest Region (hereafter DHF, NARS-PNW).

44. David M. Smith, "Even-Age Management: Concept and Historical Development," in *Even-Age Management, Proceedings of a Symposium Held August 1, 1922*, eds. Richard K. Hermann and Denis P. Lavender (Corvalis: Oregon State University, School of Forestry, 1973), p. 9.

45. Western white pine was known to have the capacity for delayed germination at this time; see Isaac, *Reproductive Habits of Douglas Fir*, p. 25; J. V. Hoffman, "The Establishment of a Douglas Fir Forest," *Ecology* 1 (1920), p. 51; see also J. V. Hoffman, "How to Obtain a Second Crop of Douglas Fir," *TMN* 23 (Mar. 1921), pp. 90-1; "Forest Perpetuation Through Natural Agencies," *TMN* 23 (Dec. 1921), pp. 34-5; J. V. Hoffman, *Natural Regeneration of Douglas Fir in the Pacific Northwest* (Washington, D.C.: U.S. Department of Agriculture, 1924).

46. C. D. Howe, *The Reproduction of Commercial Species in the Southern Coastal Forests of British Columbia* (Ottawa: Commission on Conservation, 1915), p. 117; C. D. Howe, "Address Delivered Before B.C. Forest Club," *Proceedings of the British*

Columbia Forest Club 2 (1916), p. 86; "Summary of Report of C. D. Howe on the Condition of Reproduction of Commercial Species in the Coastal Region of British Columbia," B.C. Ministry of Lands and Parks Records, Reel 442, File 065342, Ministry of Lands and Parks, Lands Management Branch (hereafter BCMLPR).

47. MacMillan, "Present Condition of Applied Forestry," p. 128; M. A. Grainger to E. H. Clapp, 16 May 1919, BCMLPR, Reel 1213, File 09579; G. M. McVickar, "Memorandum to the Chief Forester," 10 Apr. 1919, B.C. Department of Lands and Forestry Records, Reel B3230, File 04170, BCARS, (Hereafter GR 1441); P. M. Barr, "Summary of Forest Research in British Columbia, 1921-1927," Sept. 1927, *ibid.*

48. "Reforestation in British Columbia," *TMN* 23 (Jan. 1922), p. 53; P. Z. Caverhill, "Forestry Problems in British Columbia," *Journal of Forestry* 20 (Jan. 1922), p. 50; B.C., *Report of the Forest Branch of the Department of Lands* (Victoria, 1923), p. 16; R. C. St. Clair to F. Ames, 18 Oct. 1923, GR 1441, Reel B3531, File 051596, BCARS.

49. T. T. Munger, "Memo for Mr. Ames, Silvicultural Condition of Cut-Over Areas," 19 Sept. 1972, Box 15, RG 95, DHF, NARS-PNW; P. Z. Caverhill to C. D. Howe, 26 Mar. 1923, GR 1441, Reel B3230, File 04170, BCARS; see also B.C., *Report of the Forest Branch of the Department of Lands* (Victoria, 1924), p. 10.

50. B.C., *Report of the Forest Branch of the Department of Lands* (Victoria, 1924), p. 10; Chief Forester, "Memorandum to the Minister of Lands," 12 Nov. 1924, BCMLPR, Reel 442, File 065342; J. L. Alexander, "Government Forest Research in British Columbia," 1924, GR 1441, Reel 3531, File 051596, BCARS; G.E. Stoodley to Chief Forester, 26 Oct. 1925, *ibid.*; P. Z. Caverhill to E. H. Finlayson, 21 Apr. 1925, *ibid.*; P. Z. Caverhill, "B.C. Forest Administration," *TMN* 28 (Feb. 1927), p. 161.

51. E. C. Manning to P. Z. Caverhill, 13 Mar. 1924, GR 1441, Reel B3532, File 051597; Chief Forester to the Minister of Lands, 8 Oct. 1923, *ibid.*, Reel B3531, File 051596; P. M. Barr to A. H. Richardson, 1 Sept. 1927, *ibid.*, Reel B3230, File 04170, BCARS.

52. "T. T. Munger Gives Official Views," *Proceedings of the Western Forestry and Conservation Association* (1925), p. 10; T. T. Munger, "Recent Evidence Affecting Reforestation Theories: Paper for Annual Meeting of the West Coast Forestry Association at Victoria, B.C., Dec. 10, 1925," p. 2, GR 1441, Reel B3531, File 051596, BCARS; P. Z. Caverhill to G. M. Cornwall, 29 Apr. 1925, *ibid.*; J. L. Alexander to E. T. Allen, 27 Oct. 1925, *ibid.* Sociologists have noted that internal controversy over scientific findings is often masked when presented to the public. See Andrew Webster, *Science, Technology and Society: New Directions* (New Brunswick: Rutgers University Press, 1991), p. 25.

53. Amelia R. Fry, *Leo A. Isaac: Douglas Fir Research in the Pacific Northwest, 1920-1956* (Berkeley: University of California Regional Oral History Office, 1967), pp. 66-7; Leo A. Isaac, "Life of Douglas Fir Seed in the Forest Floor," *Journal of Forestry* 33 (1935), p. 62; J. L. Alexander, "Silvicultural Investigation in B.C., Paper Read at the Meeting of the Canadian Society of Forest Engineers, Vancouver, 27 Oct. 1926," p. 4, B.C. Ministry of Forests Library; C. K. Flemming to J. K. Alexander, 28 Feb. 1927; Alexander to Flemming, 8 Mar. 1927, GR 1441, Reel B3531, File 051596, BCARS.

54. Fry, *Leo A. Isaac*, p. 69; Leo A. Isaac, "Seed Flight in the Douglas Fir Region," *Jour-*

nal of Forestry 28 (1930), pp. 492-99; A. E. Pickford, "Studies of Seed Dissemination in British Columbia," *Forest Chronicle* 5 (1929), pp. 8-16.

55. G. P. Melrose to Lands Department, Esquimalt and Nanaimo Railway Co., 22 May 1924, GR 1441, Reel B3531, File 051596; P. M. Barr to P. Z. Caverhill, 26 Feb. 1928, ibid., Reel B3230, File 04170, BCARS; P. M. Barr, "An Outline of the Work of the Research Division of the British Columbia Forest Service During 1928," ibid.; B.C., *Report of the Forest Branch of the Department of Lands* (Victoria, 1929), p. 12; P. Z. Caverhill to C. M. Grainger, 19 Sept. 1927, GR 1441, Reel B3515, File 048525, BCARS.

56. K. Carlisle, "Report on Early Timber Sales in Vancouver District," 17 Sept. 1928, B.C. Ministry of Forests Records, Victoria, File 077546 (hereafter BCMFR); P. M. Barr to R. C. St. Clair, 24 Oct. 1928, BCMLPR, Reel 442, File 065342; see also Barr to P. Z. Caverhill, 17 Jan. 1929, GR 1441, Reel B3230, File 04170, BCARS.

57. Barr and Garman, "A History Map Study," pp. 14-22; see also P. M. Barr, "Forest Research in British Columbia," *British Columbia Lumberman* 14 (Feb. 1930), p. 72.

58. F. S. McKinnon and T. Wells, *The Green Timbers Forestry Station and Forest Tree Nursery: A Brief Review of its Purpose and Development* (Victoria: King's Printer, 1943), p. 4; P. M. Barr to J. M. Gibson, 10 Jan. 1930, GR 1441, Reel B3230, File, 04170, BCARS.

59. Ralph Schmidt, *The History of Cowichan Lake Research Station* (Victoria: B.C. Ministry of Forests, 1992), pp. 4-5; Gray, "The Government's Timber Business," p. 24; Richard A. Rajala, *The Legacy and the Challenge: A Century of the Forest Industry at Cowichan Lake* (Lake Cowichan: Lake Cowichan Heritage Advisory Committee, 1993), pp. 54-83.

60. See Rajala, *The Legacy and the Challenge*, p. 49; Richard A. Rajala, "The Receding Timber Line: Forest Practice, State Regulation, and the Decline of the Cowichan Lake Timber Industry, 1880-1992," in Peter Baskerville, ed., *Canadian Papers in Business History* 2 (1993), pp. 179-209.

61. P. Z. Caverhill to J. R. Dickson, 17 Oct. 1929, File 306313-2, BCMFR; Caverhill to H. I. Stevenson, 27 Jan. 1934, BCMFR, Victoria, File 06313-2.

62. For discussion of managerial change see Richard A. Rajala, "Managerial Crisis: The Emergence and Role of the West Coast Logging Engineer, 1890-1930," in Peter Baskerville, ed., *Canadian Papers in Business History* 1 (1989), pp. 101-28.

63. Nelles, *The Politics of Development*, pp. 491-92; L. Anders Sandberg, ed., *Trouble in the Woods: Forest Policy and Social Conflict in Nova Scotia and New Brunswick* (Fredericton: Acadiensis Press, 1992).

64. On the American context see Ellis Hawley, "Herbert Hoover, the Commerce Secretariat, and the Vision of an Associative State," *Journal of American History* 61 (June 1974), pp. 116-40; Ellis Hawley, "Three Facets of Hooverian Associationalism: Lumber, Aviation, and Movies, 1921-1930," in *Regulation in Perspective: Historical Essays*, ed. Thomas K. McCraw, (Cambridge: Harvard University Press, 1981), pp. 95-123; Grant McConnell, *Private Power and American Democracy* (New York: Alfred A. Knopf, 1966), pp. 64-9. On the Canadian pattern of business-government relations during the 1920s, see John Herd Thompson and Allen Seager, *Canada, 1922-1939: Decades of Discord* (Toronto: University of Toronto Press, 1985), pp. 76-103; Tom Traves, *The State and Enterprise: Canadian Manufacturers and the Federal Government, 1917-1931* (Toronto: McClelland and Stewart, 1979).

5

Workers and Intellectuals:

The Theory of the New Class

and Early Canadian Socialism

MARK LEIER[1]

onflicts between socialists and more conservative trade union leaders in Canada during the late nineteenth and early twentieth centuries have been well documented. In British Columbia, the two groups clashed in the Vancouver Trades and Labour Council from about 1899 to 1905, at the founding convention of the Provincial Progressive Party in 1902, and in the pages of their newspapers. Though the battles were not so heated, socialists and labourists in Winnipeg were often at odds, while a similar left-right split prevented the Toronto District Labour Council from agreeing on the direction its political action would take between 1900 and 1921. And even in the Maritimes, where socialists rarely adopted the "impossiblism" long associated with the B.C. wing of the Socialist Party of Canada (SPC), unity between unionists and socialists was not consistent.[2]

Canadian historians have outlined the material base for more conservative trade unionism. Rooted in artisanal traditions, often working in small shops rather than large impersonal factories, relying on their skills and union organization to create an artificial labour scarcity and thus higher wages, and often able to become contractors and proprietors in their calling, early trade unionists did not tend to see their own employer as the class enemy. More able to succeed in the emerging capitalist society, these trades-men, particularly in the building trades, the running trades of the railways, the printing industry, and the metal trades in this period, seldom believed that their interests could be better served by socialism.[3]

What has been less commonly explored is the material base of socialist leaders in this period.[4] More common has been the assumption that social-ists represented a kind of advance army of the labour movement, that their particular politics pointed the way forward for workers who were far-sighted enough to see it. Certainly socialists of the day made such a claim. Thus, in a thoughtful and interesting reassessment of William Pritchard and the So-cialist Party of Canada, Peter Campbell concludes, along with Pritchard, that "the role of the Marxian socialist was to lift the veil of deception im-posed on the workers by the capitalist state and its institutions."[5] But it may be that socialists too were structured into their beliefs by their class position as well as their analysis of capitalism, and that the ideological battles stemmed, in part, from the different class positions and class experience of the socialist thinkers and trade union leaders. This paper will outline con-temporary theoretical arguments that suggest that socialist intellectuals had different class interests from workers, and that socialism itself reflected the interests of a section of the middle class rather than the working class.[6] It will then explore the utility of this theoretical position for providing a ma-terialist explanation for the factional disputes in Canadian left, labour, and reform movements in the late nineteenth and early twentieth centuries.

Efforts to understand the ideology of socialists by reference to their class position has not often been taken up in the Canadian historiography. The first issue that must be resolved is, what class did socialist thinkers belong to? The theoretical work of Marx, Michael Bakunin, and the Polish revolu-tionary Jan Waclaw Machajski is a useful place to seek the answer. By exam-ining the work of these contemporary critics, we can avoid the dangers of "presentism," that is, of judging the past within a framework that has been constructed in the last years of the twentieth century. This work identifies, at the level of theory, the different class positions and ideologies of the ad-versaries, and is a useful starting point for empirical work.

It has been argued that socialist intellectuals are not members of the petit-bourgeoisie and that they have roughly the same relationship to capital as do workers. It is often suggested, for example, that socialist intellectuals ranging from Marx to Socialist Party of Canada (SPC) editor Phillips Thompson are best described as "brain-workers," a sub-set of the class that also contains manual workers.[7] Such a position is difficult to sustain, however. Clearly Marx was never a member of the working class. His father was an attorney, and was able to give his son a first-class university education. In turn, this education allowed Marx to eke out a living as a writer, editor, and lecturer. Though this income was meagre, it still afforded a bourgeois existence with maids, piano lessons for his children, and ample time to devote to study. For a materialist viewpoint suggests that it is not income that defines class. Rather, it is one's relationship to the means of production. Marx's class position as an intellectual was neither that of employer nor employee, but that of a relatively independent petit-bourgeois. Even if intellectuals often sell their labour power to universities, businesses, corporations, and publishers, this is not a sufficient condition to place them in the working class. After all, presidents and managers of corporations also sell their labour power. Class must be distinguished by two other factors: control over the labour of others in the labour process, and control over one's own labour. If the standard of living of socialist intellectuals resembled that of the working class, the editors, functionaries, and organizers had no boss controlling their work. Their work life was theirs to control to a great extent.[8]

But if intellectuals are of the middle class, not the working class, how are they able to attain the correct consciousness of and for workers? Marx and Engels argued that intellectuals, as people who deal in the coin of ideas, are able to choose to move beyond their own narrow class consciousness. For example, in his article "On the History of the Communist League," Engels held that the artisans operated primarily on the level of "instinct." In contrast to himself and Marx, there was not "a single man in the whole League at that time who had ever read a book on political economy." Thus, according to Engels, those who had the training and leisure to read and write books could go beyond "instinct" and class experience to understand the position of other classes even better than members of those classes themselves. So too did Marx maintain that intellectuals could interpret the world objectively and without the interference of their own class background.

"The critic," he wrote, can "start out by taking any form of theoretical and practical consciousness and develop from the unique forms of existing reality the *true reality* as its norm and final goal." This allowed intellectuals to "take our criticism to the criticism of politics and to a definite party position in politics, and hence from identifying our criticism with real struggles." The role of the intellectual was to "show the world what it is fighting for," as "the reform of consciousness consists . . . in enabling the world to clarify its consciousness, in waking it from its dream about itself, in explaining to it the meaning of its own actions." If workers had the real world hidden from them by their class position, intellectuals had to undertake the "reform of consciousness . . . through analysing the mystical consciousness, the consciousness which is unclear to itself, whether it appears in religious or political form."[9]

This alleged ability of intellectuals to transcend their class position was put more explicitly in *The Communist Manifesto*, where Marx and Engels held that

> when the class struggle nears the decisive hour . . . a small section of the ruling class cuts itself adrift, and joins the revolutionary class. . . . Just as, therefore, at an earlier period, a section of the nobility goes over to the proletariat, so now a portion of the bourgeoisie goes over to the proletariat.

Thus according to Marx and Engels, intellectuals such as themselves are not to be considered part of the working class. They are, however, still able to articulate the demands of the working class, because these "bourgeois ideologists . . . have raised themselves to the level of comprehending theoretically the historical movement as a whole."[10] Marx and Engels here suggest that intellectuals, by dint of their own effort and training, are able to understand the path of history and thus can choose to abandon their class and the class consciousness formed by their experience in the petit-bourgeoisie. In *The German Ideology*, they again make the argument that "the communist consciousness . . . may, of course, arise among the other classes too through the contemplation of the situation of this class."[11]

But the suggestion that "contemplation" is sufficient for a radical change in consciousness is an idealist, not a materialist, one. With their insistence that intellectuals were uniquely able to understand the world and to escape the experience of their class, Marx and Engels have exempted them from the forces of historical materialism. But this is little more than special pleading for their own class, and it is not persuasive. There is no good reason why intellectuals should not be shaped by their class position and their material interest, and no special reason why they alone can change their class position and consciousness by an exercise of thought. If historical materialism is a useful tool, it must be applied even to its creators and their followers.

If it is assumed that the consciousness of intellectuals is shaped by their class position, it follows that their ideology reflects this position. Thus the socialism that they advance must be seen as the creation of intellectuals for intellectuals, whether they realize it or not. Naturally, as Marx suggested in another context, they put forward their particular ideology as "the common interest of all the members of society."[12] This is not to argue that working people would not be attracted to socialism, or that it held no hope of improvement for them. The point is that the socialism put forward by intellectuals was designed to place them in positions of power, award them special privileges, and give them, not capitalists or workers, control of the economy and the state.

Such at least was the judgement of Marx's contemporary and critic, Michael Bakunin. In its express ideology and the philosophical underpinnings, he argued, Marxism sought to empower intellectuals. Both the Hegelian idealism and the positivism that ran through Marxism provided a rationale for the rule of intellectuals. Marxist idealism was found primarily in the use of the dialectic to explain and predict the course of history. But the dialectic could not be verified by evidence; it could only be asserted. Belief in the dialectic was not based on observation and correlation with external reality, but on preconceived abstraction. In making it a crucial element of socialist ideology, Marx laid the groundwork for rule by intellectuals, for only they had the knowledge to understand and predict the unfolding of the dialectic. Similarly, positivism justified the belief that "abstract theory precedes social practice, and that sociology must therefore be the point of departure for social upheavals and reconstructions."[13]

Since intellectuals were a minority, they sought to use the countervailing power of the state against the capitalist to catapult themselves into positions of authority. To do this, they needed the help of the working class at the ballot box or the barricades to end the dominance of the capitalist class. But since the Marxist intellectuals needed the state to maintain their own privilege and power, they called upon workers to overthrow only capital, not the supporting state apparatus. Far from being opposed to the state, Marxists would soon become its "most ardent defenders." They were "enemies only of existing political institutions because these preclude the possibility of their own dictatorship." Ultimately, there was no fundamental difference between the statists of the left and right, for both represented "the same government of the majority by a minority in the name of the presumed stupidity of the one and the presumed intelligence of the other."[14] Though the socialist call for the intervention of the state was supposed to empower all workers, in fact it would empower "a new political class, the representatives of the domination of the state." Since running the socialist state would require more knowledge and control than the less intrusive capitalist state, the result would be "a new class, a new hierarchy of real and fictitious savants, and the world will be divided into a minority ruling in the name of science, and an immense ignorant majority." The success of the Marxists would only continue the political and economic slavery of the masses.[15]

Thus Bakunin resolved the seeming paradox between the socialists' petit-bourgeois origins and their alleged ability to speak for the working class by arguing that their ideology did not address the interests of workers. It did, however, reflect the particular class position of intellectuals. Unlike workers, the class of intellectuals was organically linked to the capitalist class by its "economic and political interests and by all its habits of life, its ambition, its vanity, and its prejudices. How, then, can it have any desire to use the power it has won for the benefit of the people. . .?" Marxist socialism was a creation of the intellectuals, by the intellectuals, and for the intellectuals.[16]

Bakunin's polemics were given a stronger foundation by the Polish revolutionary Jan Waclaw Machajski at the turn of the nineteenth century. Trying to explain why the Social Democratic parties of Russia and Germany were increasingly turning to reformism and revisionism, Machajski picked up where Bakunin had left off. Machajski started by agreeing with Karl Kautsky's observation that a new middle class was growing in industrial, European nations. This new class was increasingly comprised of the "intelligentsia, which makes its living from the sale of its special knowledge and talents."[17] Contrary to some critics, Kautsky's observation of the growth of the middle class was not a break with Marxist orthodoxy. Marx himself had suggested that one feature of late capitalist society was the swelling of the middle class, of those between the workers and the capitalists who were neither employers or employees in the traditional sense.[18] Kautsky suggested that the middle classes were changing. Independent artisans and tradesmen were increasingly replaced by the "paid skilled workers, who sell their services either piecemeal like doctors, lawyers, artists – or in return for a salary, like [government] officials everywhere." Kautsky was quick to point out that though these members of the intelligentsia were wage earners, they could not be considered part of the proletariat. Like Bakunin, Kautsky noted that this new class had emerged from the bourgeoisie, and had familial and social ties to it. Some of the professions taken up by this new class, such as journalism, law, and the priesthood, required a political stance that was opposed to workers and their interests. More importantly, the intelligentsia stood in opposition to the proletariat because its access to higher education made it a privileged class.[19] But while he gave the intelligentsia a specific, objective class location, Kautsky denied that it had a unified class interest. Though the different professions clearly shared a desire to limit access to their ranks to restrict competition and maintain their high status, the intelligentsia did not, according to Kautsky, exploit the working class. Furthermore, as higher education became more universal, the professions would become swamped and devalued. As the intelligentsia became proletarianized, they would "discover their proletarian heart, gain interest in the proletarian class struggle, and eventually participate in it."[20]

Machajski, however, insisted that Kautsky had shied away from the logical conclusion of his observations. The intelligentsia was a class, and it had a class interest. The privileges of the intellectuals, no less than the bourgeoisie, depended on the continual existence and exploitation of the working class. Like the bourgeoisie, these members of the educated middle class were "white-hands" who were freed from manual labour. Some, such as engineers, managers, and directors were virtually indistinguishable from capitalist owners. More importantly, the capital of all intellectuals, higher education, existed because surplus value was expropriated from the working class. It was, after all, the working class that produced the necessities of life and created the surplus that allowed some the leisure to go to school. Therefore intellectuals stood in opposition to workers, for they had a class interest that bound them together and required the continued exploitation of the proletariat. Furthermore, their class was continually reproduced. Intellectuals demanded a higher income based on the claim that its labour was of greater value and skill than that of the working class. This higher income was then used to educate the next generation of intellectuals and ensure that "the greatest riches of mankind – knowledge, science – become the hereditary monopoly of a privileged minority."[21]

Thus because of their class position, socialist intellectuals had no genuine interest in ending the exploitation of workers. Indeed, their continued existence in the middle class depended on maintaining the division of society into workers and managers. By making knowledge, not capital, the justification of authority and power, socialists sought to replace capitalists with intellectuals. They sought to take their place in government and called for increasing the power and jurisdiction of the state because only the state could muster the power they needed to usurp capital. Despite their radical posturing, socialist intellectuals were committed only to furthering their own narrow class interests. Machajski's early disciple, Max Nomad, put the matter more pithily when he suggested that the slogan "all power to the workers" in practice meant "all good jobs to our party members."[22]

Does this contemporary theory of the new class hold any explanatory value for Canadian history of the late nineteenth and early twentieth centuries? I believe it does, for it points the way towards a materialist explanation for a number of historical events that have been portrayed as intellectual disputes over ideology and ideas. In particular, the theory that socialist leaders and union leaders had significantly different class positions and interests may help explain why the Socialist Party of Canada was not very successful in its attempts to become a working class party. The theory is no less relevant to the Canadian labour and socialist movement than the German or Russian.

Preliminary research strongly suggests that the upper echelons of the socialist movement in Canada were staffed not by workers but by the petit-bourgeoisie. Phillips Thompson, probably the preeminent Canadian socialist thinker of the nineteenth century, studied and practised law before becoming a newspaper editor and publisher. George and George Weston Wrigley, who ran several socialist newspapers, were not printers but middle class publishers and editors. Indeed, early in his career as a left-wing publisher, the elder Wrigley came under attack for using "boilerplate," that is, pre-set pages of type, in his newspaper. Boilerplate was usually set by underpaid, non-union workers and supplied to publishers by advertisers and agencies in an attempt to save money by cutting wages and weakening union printers. Wrigley's use of it illustrates his own position between labour and capital.[23]

On the west coast, another stalwart Socialist Party member, candidate, and ideologue, Parmeter Pettipiece, was also better categorized as a member of the petit-bourgeoisie than the working class. Pettipiece started a number of small town newspapers in Alberta and B.C. until he joined with the Wrigleys in 1902 to found the *Canadian Socialist*, which would become the SPC's organ, the *Western Clarion*.[24] Perhaps the most influential SPC theorist was E. T. Kingsley, a former worker who became a fish merchant and then print shop proprietor and publisher after an industrial accident. As an employer, Kingsley may have left much to be desired. One employee found him "selfish, always collecting a generous salary every week, before paying anyone else."[25] William Pritchard went to the Manchester School of Technology and the Royal Institute of Technology, and worked as a clerk and an accountant before becoming editor of the *Western Clarion* in 1914.[26] Other SPC members who held positions in the party tended to come from the petit-bourgeoisie. Ernest Burns and John Cameron were merchants, who ran a second-hand store and a tobacco shop, respectively. Thomas Mathews, another early SPC stalwart, was a real estate and stock broker, while James Boult ran a newsstand before becoming a real estate agent. Fred Ogle, an SPC candidate in the B.C. election of 1903, was a salesman and then a paid organizer for the SPC.[27] James Hawthornthwaite, Socialist MLA from 1901 to 1912, and again from 1918 to 1921, was a university graduate who worked as a real estate agent, mining promoter, and U.S. consular officer before embarking on his political career. Similarly, Wallis Lefeaux, who held several positions in the SPC, was a bookkeeper and clerk, then ran a clothing store and sold real estate before becoming an attorney. In the Mari-

times as well, many early socialists were professionals and small business-
men, not workers.[28]

Even presumed working class activists such as Helena Gutteridge may,
upon closer examination, be better typified as members of the new class.
Born in London in 1879, Gutteridge was active in the B.C. labour and socialist movements from about 1912 until her death in 1960. Like many of
the socialists and reformers of the day, Gutteridge was not a member of the
proletariat so much as she was a moderately educated professional who
eked out a living in the niches of the left and labour movements. President
of the tailors' union, she edited the women's column for the labour paper
the *B.C. Federationist,* and by 1917 was an ill-paid functionary in the Vancouver Trades and Labour Council. Unlike most women who worked in
Vancouver, Gutteridge was not a domestic servant or textile worker. She had
earned a teaching certificate and other certificates in hygiene and sanitary
science in England. Though she often had to augment her meagre income
with work as a tailor, Gutteridge was ultimately able to run for and hold
political office. She was also a member of the Co-Masons, an off-shoot of
Freemasonry that admitted women. Transferring from a lodge in England,
she joined Vancouver Freemasons' Lodge 399, the Inner Light, in 1912.
There she met with real estate brokers, shop owners, insurance vendors,
teachers, and the like. Though her life was often marked with poverty and
hard labour, this was because her class experience was mediated by her gender at a time when opportunities for women of all classes were meagre.
Nonetheless, contrasting her life with those of working class women,
Gutteridge was in her culture, education, and often employment, more like
a member of the petit-bourgeoisie.[29]

The petit-bourgeoisie in the SPC was so prominent that its leaders felt
compelled to defend the middle class as carriers of the socialist message.
Many socialist theorists were "extensive capitalists," Phillips Thompson admitted, but they were "none the less trusted on that account. . . . No socialist ever dreamed of reading such men out of the party." But labour activists
were quick to denounce the middle class intellectuals who presumed to
speak for them. One complained about the "self-styled socialist leaders who
neither toil nor spin for their living, yet they would have you think that
they were being robbed." Other letters and articles in the labour press made

similar remarks that suggest that union leaders believed that the socialists who attacked business unionism were not representative of the working class. Some went even further to argue that socialism itself was not an ideology of particular relevance to the working class. "Socialism is a political institution," wrote one unionist. Therefore,

> It seeks to reform governments by levelling down and levelling up the social inequalities. Socialism bears the same relation to the student and philosopher that it does to the workingman. In fact teachers of socialism have not usually come from the working class.[30]

It is true that like Marx, many of these Canadian socialists did not receive high incomes. SPC organizers were paid $2.00 a day, about the same rate as labourers. As late as 1911, the secretary and editor of the party were paid roughly $60 a month. And the SPC newspaper, the *Western Clarion*, announced in 1903 that Parm Pettipiece had sunk his life savings of $1,600 into the paper.[31]

As argued previously, income is not the determinant of class position. As intellectuals, these socialists were not workers, and in some cases, such as Pettipiece and Kingsley, they even owned the means of production and hired others. Clearly they cannot be included in the same class as the labourers on the Canadian Pacific Railway or even the typesetters at the Vancouver *Daily News-Advertiser* who daily faced the tyranny of the employers' time clock.

What did this mean at the level of politics and ideology? Because of their different class positions and interests, socialist intellectuals and trade unionists tended to be structured into different kinds of struggles. Many of the interests of trade unionists could only be served by economic struggles with employers. This tended to focus their efforts on wages, hours and conditions of work and on better union organization and solidarity. As craft unionists, they depended on an artificial labour scarcity to keep up their wages, and many of their struggles were dedicated to this end. Thus labourists were active in union label campaigns; they battled municipalities to put an end to contracting out for civic works; they opposed attempts to consolidate their craft unions into larger units, for craft jurisdictions in the work place protected the jobs of individual union members. Though they often turned to political action, it was not to overthrow capitalism, but to protect and extend trade union interests. The skilled workers in trade unions were in favour of limited political action: running independent labour candidates or supporting Liberal-Labour politicians such as Ralph Smith, Arthur Puttee, Fred Dixon, and George Maxwell. Unionists tended to fight on the political front for the nine and eight hour day, workers' compensation, labour bureaus to collect employment statistics, the creation of public, not private, utilities, and mediation and arbitration boards. As workers with an artisanal tradition in their crafts and unions, trade unionists often believed that the real class enemy was not their employer, who might well have worked his way up from apprentice to journeyman to master as they had and hoped to. Instead, their class analysis tended to divide the world into producers and non-producers. The real parasites, the real exploiters were not employers as such but huge corporations, trusts, and monopolies. These needed to be fought on the political front, but did not make necessary the complete takeover of the state by workers and the abolition of capitalism. In the ideal world of the labourist and skilled worker, capital would still exist, but it would be small, personalized capital that would allow an honest day's pay for an honest day's work and would offer ample opportunity for employees to become masters themselves. None of this required revolution or capturing the state apparatus. Indeed, the state itself was viewed as necessary but essentially parasitic, and labourists usually wanted to shrink the state to reduce its expenditures, which after all were paid for by productive workers.[32]

Intellectuals, however, would gain nothing from the labourist program. Since they did not have employers in the same way that workers did, fighting for wages and hours of work was irrelevant. Collective bargaining and reforms to ease relations between employers and employees was equally irrelevant to them. What was crucial to the class interests of intellectuals was a range of political measures. Active involvement in political action – running for office, organizing campaigns, calling for action on the political, not economic, front – gave socialist intellectuals their reason for existing. In a period of reduced employment opportunities for Christian clergy and university professors, politics was a logical occupation for intellectuals of all stripes. The call of the SPC for workers "to become the state" may well have been sincere, but it also reflected the fact that the SPC in British Columbia had more professional politicians in its ranks than any other political organization outside of the ruling Tory party between 1903 and 1912. In this context, the call for the takeover of the state through the ballot was also an implicit call to provide intellectuals employment at work that would make use of their particular capital of knowledge. The socialist demand for increasing the intervention and jurisdiction of the state can also be seen as a way to give the intellectuals who would staff it the political power that was in the hands of capital and politicians linked to business. As intellectuals, these early socialists could not expect much under the existing social and political structures. If artisans could at least hope to become masters and proprietors in this period, intellectuals had no similar career path and expectations. They tended to look to the state for hope, and thus tended to be structured into political action rather than economic action.[33]

But to be successful, intellectuals had to rely on the working class to propel them into power. This had several effects on labour and socialist politics of the day. First, it meant that if socialists were to become the political spokesmen for workers, they had to displace the already present cadre of labourist leaders. And to do that, socialist intellectuals had to argue that ideas and facility with words, not class experience, were the attributes that working class leaders should have. Thus early socialists such as Kingsley, Alex Lang, Pritchard, and even Pettipiece insisted that theory was crucial to the party and the labour movement. By insisting that workers would have to become educated in socialist principles before they could recognize their own real interests, and that socialists were themselves the vanguard of the working class, such socialist intellectuals were trying to establish knowledge as the prerequisite for leadership. Within and behind these debates concerning the role of socialist theory in the labour movement, we see the attempt by the socialist intellectuals to change the criteria for choosing the leadership of the labour movement and to substitute themselves for the labourists who had risen through the ranks of trade unionism.[34]

Working class unity was also a higher priority for socialists. Trade unionists had to fight many of their battles against employers, and craft unions, with their tight rules over jurisdiction, had proved more or less equal to the task. But if political power were the goal, it was necessary to bring workers closer together, to insist that they act as a single unit at the polling booth, regardless of craft and trade. Thus it was the left, not the right, that sought to create broader federations that were controlled by a central executive; labourists preferred looser federations that would respect craft boundaries.[35]

Despite these structural differences, unity between labourist trade unionists and socialist intellectuals was of course possible. But reconciliation often meant that socialists had either changed their class position or changed their ideology to fit the needs of the moment. Thus when Pettipiece became a member of the ITU and a printer for a Vancouver daily, he became interested in trade union issues and preached unity where he had previously insisted on theoretical rigidity. When socialists such as James McVety became prominent members of the Vancouver Trades and Labour Council, their socialism became reformist, virtually indistinguishable from the demands of labourists. And if the ascent of socialists to labour councils and federations might be interpreted to mean that labour was increasingly radicalized, it may also suggest that socialists were increasingly conservative and prepared to compromise in order to win working class support for elections and paid positions in the labour movement itself. The failure to deliver something to the workers who had elected them would spell disaster at the next election. Thus as intellectuals turned to the labour movement for electoral support and even paid employment, there was a tendency for them to abandon rigid socialism for reformism.[36]

The theory of the new class holds some other implications as well. Most Canadian accounts of the social gospel movement of the late nineteenth and early twentieth centuries portray the evolution of reform thought as the result of the tension between science and religion. Thus Ramsay Cook, in his justly praised book *The Regenerators*, credits the "rise of social criticism" to "the religious crisis provoked by Darwinian science and historical criticism of the Bible." In *The Social Passion*, Richard Allen argues that the social gospel can only be "fully appreciated" as "a religious experience," while "the heart of the crisis of the social gospel" lay in humanity's need for "eternal significance." Accounts of social reform have also stressed the importance of ideas. Allen Mills, in *Fool for Christ*, does an admirable job of tracing the political thought of J.S. Woodsworth, but sees his ideology as an individual's intellectual evolution with no reference to the utility of socialist thought to the middle class.[37]

Yet surely these movements and individuals were shaped as much by their class position as by the idealistic development of reform thought. Part of the crisis of faith that led to the social gospel was prompted by the over-production of ministers and priests, that is, of an educated elite. As Canada industrialized, it became an urban society, and the number of parishes declined rapidly. Unable to take up their desired profession, these well-educated and visionary young men often had to seek, and to justify, secular employment. In particular, Woodsworth may be seen as an archetypal member of the Canadian new class of intellectuals. Trained in the seminary – the most accessible form of higher education for middle class Canadians at that time – he could not find a parish. Woodsworth instead used his knowledge to become first a journalist in the socialist and labour movements and then a politician. His ideology was an accurate and consistent reflection of his class position. Like the intelligentsia Bakunin and Machajski examined, Woodsworth called for the increased development and intervention of the state into all spheres of modern life. He did not call for the working class to control industry or to dismantle the state apparatus; he called for the state to regulate, control, and correct abuses. In this way, Woodsworth and other middle class reformers created a political agenda that made the state the employer of choice for a generation of intellectuals. If their work resulted in some reforms of benefit to the working classes, the fact remains that their political program was based on priorities, class positions, and class interests very different from those of the workers represented by the labour movement. Though it would be a mistake to deny the power of ideas in these movements, surely it is an equal mistake to ignore the particular class interests and objectives of those involved. Certainly it is "reductionist" to insist that ideology can be easily read off class positions and self-interest, but it is naive to argue that the politics and desire for state control was the result of pure, crystal-clear logic and contemplation. By maintaining that the outside world played no part in the evolution of socialist and reform thought, we attribute to the new class an altruism and omniscience that it did not possess. Their own petit-bourgeois class position led them to hope that the state could be captured for their own purposes and advancement, whether they consciously drew these conclusions from their ideas and actions or not. It should come as no surprise that

Canadian social reformers and socialists were content to hold political office and to work for reforms that might improve life for the working class but would also continue the exploitation that supported the state and the reformers themselves in positions of relative privilege.

None of this implies that somehow reformers and socialists should be vilified for their class origins and their ideology. Nor does it imply that their ideas were necessarily wrong or that their motives were baser than others. It does suggest reasons why "All power to the workers" was not, and could not be, a slogan for the socialist intellectuals of the day. Just as the artisans of the VTLC were constrained by their class and experience, so too were the socialists and like-minded reformers. The observation that a new class did develop in the late nineteenth century and that it did have some specific class interests allows us to understand the ideas and conflicts of socialists and reformers in a more realistic and useful way. It also suggests why workers and union leaders were, for the most part, unlikely and unwilling to take up the cause of revolutionary socialism. The ideology of the new class, whatever its promises for reforms, was foreign to the experience of workers and especially those working class leaders who had risen through the ranks of labour. Splits in the left and labour movements were more than disputes over doctrine and ideas; they reflected the different class position and culture of the combatants as they competed to put their own class interests in the forefront of Canadian political life. That the new intellectuals were, and are, more successful than the working class reflects the relative privilege and power of the middle class. It also demonstrates the ability of the intellectuals to ally themselves with the state and even to reach an understanding with capital. But as Bakunin and Machajski predicted, intellectuals may be no more likely to work for the emancipation of the working class than the bourgeoisie.

Notes

1. Thanks are due to the Social Sciences and Humanities Research Council for the doctoral and post-doctoral funding that made this work possible. I would also like to thank Annette DeFaveri, G. S. Kealey, Linda Kealey, A. A. den Otter, Sean Cadigan, and the anonymous readers of the *Journal of History and Politics/Revue d'Histoire et de Politique* for their helpful comments.
2. A. Ross McCormack has provided the standard account of division in the western

left and labour movements in *Reformers, Rebels, and Revolutionaries: The Western Canadian Radical Movement, 1899-1919*, Toronto: University of Toronto Press, 1979. See Martin Robin, *Radical Politics and Canadian Labour, 1880-1930*, Kingston: Industrial Relations Centre, Queen's University, 1968, for an examination of factionalism in western and central Canada at the municipal, provincial, and national levels. Michael Piva addresses the issue of factionalism in "The Toronto District Labour Council and Independent Political Action: Factionalism and Frustration, 1900-1921," *Labour/Le Travailleur*, 4, 1979, pp. 115-130, while David Frank and Nolan Reilly make reference to some conflicts between left and right in the Maritimes, in "The Emergence of the Socialist Movement in the Maritimes, 1899-1916," *Labour/Le Travailleur* 4 (1979), pp. 85-114. See also Robert Babcock, *Gompers in Canada: A Study in American Continentalism before the First World War*, Toronto: University of Toronto Press, 1974. Such disputes, of course, were not limited to Canada. For overviews of left-right fights in the United States, see David Montgomery, *The Fall of the House of Labor: The Workplace, the State, and American Labor Activism, 1865-1925*, Cambridge: Cambridge University Press, 1987, and his *Workers' Control in America: Studies in the History of Work, Technology, and Labor Struggles*, Cambridge: Cambridge University Press, 1980, especially Chapter 3, "Machinists, the Civic Federation, and the Socialist Party"; Philip Foner, *History of the Labor Movement of the United States*, Volume 2, *From the Founding of the AF of L to the Emergence of American Imperialism*, New York: International Publishers, 1975, pp. 388-403. Two local studies that demonstrate fragmentation in the left and labour movements are Michael Kazin, *Barons of Labor: The San Francisco Building Trades and Union Power in the Progressive Era*, Urbana: University of Illinois Press, 1989, and Richard Jules Oestreicher, *Solidarity and Fragmentation: Working People and Class Consciousness in Detroit, 1875-1900*, Urbana: University of Illinois Press, 1989.

3. See, for example, Craig Heron, "Labourism and the Canadian Working Class," *Labour/Le Travail* 13 (Spring 1984), pp. 45-75. Robert McDonald makes a similar argument for Vancouver workers in "Working Class Vancouver, 1886-1914 – Urbanism and Class in British Columbia," *B.C. Studies* 69-70, (Spring-Summer 1986), pp. 33-69. Though the conclusions he draws from the data are, I believe, wholly inappropriate and unwarranted, Peter Ward does show that support for socialism, at least as expressed at the polling booth, was limited, in "Class and Race in the Social Structure of British Columbia, 1870-1939," *B.C. Studies* 45 (Spring 1980), pp. 17-35. The connection between labourism and the class position of trade unionists is also made in Alvin Finkel, "The Rise and Fall of the Labour Party in Alberta, 1917-1942," *Labour/Le Travail* 16 (Fall 1985), pp. 61-96; Glen Makahonuk, "Class Conflict in a Prairie City: The Saskatoon Working Class Response to Prairie Capitalism, 1906-1919," *Labour/Le Travail* 19 (Spring 1987), pp. 89-124; and Piva. This too was the appraisal of Marx and Engels of the artisanal workers. See, for example, Engels, "On the History of the Communist League, in Marx and Engels, *Selected Works*, Volume 3, Moscow: Progress Publishers, 1977, pp. 177-8, where he maintains that the reformist ideology of Wilhelm Weitling was due to his class position as an artisanal tailor, exploited not by large capitalists but by small masters who had themselves been journeymen, and to whose position other journeymen could reasonably aspire. Marx too would denounce Weitling's ideas as a "dogmatic abstraction" that was still "infected" by his

attachment to "private being," that is, private property. Marx, "For a Ruthless Criticism of Everything Existing," in *The Marx-Engels Reader*, Robert C. Tucker, ed., second edition, New York: W.W. Norton, 1978, pp. 13-15.

4. Nothing in my argument should be taken to imply that trade unionists could not become socialists, or that socialism was absolutely inappropriate to their class position. Nor do I mean to imply that even conservative trade unionists were not class conscious to a high degree. Indeed, we have many examples of skilled workers leading working class revolt. Bryan D. Palmer makes this case, and outlines the literature ably, in *Working Class Experience: Rethinking the History of Canadian Labour, 1800-1991*, second edition, Toronto: McClelland and Stewart, 1992, especially chapters 2-4. My point is that in some periods, skilled workers did not believe that socialism reflected their interests and that they disagreed with socialists who believed that all workers should progress and evolve into socialists.

5. Peter Campbell, ""Making Socialists": Bill Pritchard, the Socialist Party of Canada, and the Third International," *Labour/Le Travail* 30 (Fall 1992), pp. 45-63.

6. I follow Robert J. Brym's definition of "intellectuals" as those "persons who, occupationally, are involved chiefly in the production of ideas (scholars, artists, reporters, performers in the arts, scientists, etc.)" *Intellectuals and Politics*, London: George Allen and Unwin, 1980, p. 12. See also Gyorgy Konrad and Ivan Szeleny, "The Intelligentsia and Social Structure," *Telos*, 38 (Winter 1978-9), p. 48, where they define intellectuals as "people whose knowledge is accepted by society as intellectual knowledge, who are monopolistic possessors of knowledge having cross-contextual validity, and who regard that as their sufficient warrant for receiving social authority and reward." Joseph Schumpeter defines intellectuals as "people who wield the power of the spoken and written word," in *Capitalism, Socialism, and Democracy*, London: George Allen and Unwin, 1976, p. 147. He also makes the point that the difficulty in defining intellectuals is great, and, more facetiously, that such difficulty "is in fact symptomatic of the character of the species," p. 146.

7. On Thompson and other early Canadian socialist thinkers, see Russell Hann, "Brainworkers and the Knights of Labor: E. E. Sheppard, Phillips Thompson, and the *Toronto News*, 1883-1887," in *Essays in Canadian Working Class History*, Gregory S. Kealey and Peter Warrian, eds., Toronto: McClelland and Stewart, 1976, pp. 35-57.

8. Alvin Gouldner defines Marx and Engels as petit-bourgeois in *Against Fragmentation: The Origins of Marxism and the Sociology of Intellectuals*, Oxford: Oxford University Press, 1985, pp. 3-6. Erik Olin Wright has demonstrated that most intellectuals do not fall into the working class in "Intellectuals and the Class Structure of Capitalist Society," in *Between Labor and Capital*, Pat Walker, ed., Montreal: Black Rose Books, 1978, pp. 193-4. Gouldner also argues that they do not belong in the working class in *The Future of Intellectuals and the Rise of the New Class*, New York: Oxford University Press, 1979, p. 8. For a comprehensive overview of the literature defining the working class, see Reeve Vanneman and Lynn Weber Cannon, *The American Perception of Class*, Philadelphia: Temple University Press, 1987, chapter 4, "Who is Working Class?"

9. Engels, "On the History of the Communist League," pp. 177-8. Marx, "For a Ruthless Criticism of Everything Existing," pp. 13-15. Emphasis added. My argument

here follows Gouldner, *Against Fragmentation*, chapter 1.

10. Marx and Engels, "The Communist Manifesto," *Selected Works*, Volume 1, p. 117.

11. Marx and Engels, *The German Ideology*, Moscow: Progress Publishers, 1976, p. 60.

12. Marx and Engels, *The German Ideology*, p. 68-9. In discussing intellectuals here I am referring only to those who advocated socialism, just as Engels applied the principles of historical materialism not to all artisans but only those who held the ideas of the Communist League when he outlined the relationship between their specific class location and their ideology.

13. Michael Bakunin, *Statism and Anarchy*, Marshall Shatz, ed., Cambridge: Cambridge University Press, 1990, p. 136. Bakunin, "The International and Karl Marx," in *Bakunin on Anarchism*, Sam Dolgoff, ed., Montreal: Black Rose Books, 1980, p. 311. For a discussion of Bakunin's critique of Hegelianism and positivism in Marxism, see Richard B. Saltman, *The Social and Political Thought of Michael Bakunin*, Westport: Greenwood Books, 1983.

14. Bakunin, *Statism and Anarchy*, p. 137.

15. Bakunin, cited in Marshall Shatz, *Jan Waclaw Machajski: A Radical Critic of the Russian Intelligentsia and Socialism*, Pittsburgh: University of Pittsburgh Press, 1989, p. 40.

16. Bakunin, *Statism and Anarchy*, pp. 182-3.

17. Karl Kautsky, "Die Intelligenz und die Sozialdemocratie," cited in Shatz, *Machajski*, pp. 32-3.

18. Marx, *Theories of Surplus Value*, Moscow: Progress Publishers, 1975, Volume 2, p. 573.

19. Kautsky, *Selected Political Writings*, Patrick Goode, ed. and trans., New York: St. Martin's Press, 1983, pp. 18-20.

20. Kautsky, *Selected Political Writings*, p. 21. No less than Marx, Kautsky asserted that intellectuals could, by force of will, transcend their class position. He suggested, for example, that it was only their "lack of character and insight" that kept "poets and painters, scholars and journalists" from becoming socialists. *Selected Writings*, p. 23. It seems that most intellectuals, perhaps like most other human beings, are better able to analyze others than they are to analyze themselves.

21. Machajski, cited in Shatz, *Machajski*, pp. 34-36.

22. Cited in Shatz, *Machajski*, p. 61. Max Nomad, *A Skeptic's Political Dictionary and Handbook for the Disenchanted*, New York: Bookman, 1953, p. 3.

23. For a biographical sketch of Thompson, see Jay Atherton's introduction to *The Politics of Labor*, a reprint of some of Thompson's articles, Toronto: University of Toronto Press, 1975, pp. ix-x. For Wrigley's boilerplate episode, see Ron Verzuh, *Radical Rag: The Pioneer Labour Press in Canada*, Ottawa: Steel Rail Publishing, 1988, p. 69.

24. Una Larsen, nee Pettipiece, recalled that her father took up printing – as opposed to publishing – after the failure of his newspaper, the Lardeau *Eagle* and the unremunerative work of publishing various socialist newspapers in Vancouver between 1900 and 1903. Interview with author, Vancouver, February 1989.

25. The remark about Kingsley was made by SPC member Wallis Lefeaux, whose brother Stan worked in Kingsley's print shop. Angus MacInnis Memorial Collection, Special Collections, University of British Columbia, Box 52, File 6.

26. Campbell, pp. 50-52.

27. *Western Socialist*, 14 February 1902, 14 February 1903; *Canadian Socialist*, 9 August 1902; *Western Clarion*, 17 June 1903.

28. For Hawthornthwaite's careers, see Robin, *Radical Politics*, p. 41, and McCormack, p. 69. For Hawthornthwaite and Lefeaux, see Daisy Webster, *Growth of the NDP in British Columbia, 1900-1970*, n.p., n.d., pp. 41-42, 50-51. For examples of petit-bourgeois socialists in the Maritimes, see Nicholas Fillmore, *Maritime Radical: The Life and Times of Roscoe Fillmore*, Toronto: Between the Lines, 1992, pp. 44-53, and Frank and Reilly, pp. 85-114. Though neither study investigates the impact of the petit-bourgeoisie on the socialist movement in the Maritimes, both list several socialist activists who were merchants, farmers, journalists, and even bank officers.

29. For Gutteridge's life and career, see Irene Howard, *The Struggle for Social Justice in British Columbia: Helena Gutteridge, the Unknown Reformer*, Vancouver: University of British Columbia Press, 1992. This is an excellent study, but it does not consider the possibility that Gutteridge was an exemplary member of the new class rather than a gifted member of the working class. An earlier examination of her life may be found in Susan Wade, "Helena Gutteridge: Votes for Women and Trade Unions," in *In Her Own Right: Selected Essays on Women's History in B.C.*, Barbara Latham and Cathy Kess, eds., Victoria: Camosun College, 1980, pp. 187-203. Gutteridge's membership in the Vancouver Masons – surprisingly not noted in Howard's book – may be found in Vancouver City Archives, Additional Manuscripts 831, Volume 1, File 1, and Volume 2, File 7. The occupations of the other Masons were indicated in city directories.

30. Thompson's quote is from the *Canadian Socialist*, p. 23 August 1902. The *Independent*, official newspaper of the Vancouver Trades and Labour Council from 1900 to 1904, carried numerous letters, articles, and short anecdotes that attacked socialists as middle class interlopers in working class politics. The two quoted here are from the *Independent*, 13 October 1900 and 7 April 1900.

31. That Pettipiece had such money to invest suggests more lucrative employment than that of a manual worker, for the sum represented more than the annual wage of a printer. In 1908, for example, union printers in Vancouver earned about $1200 a year. See the *Western Clarion*, 22 October 1903, for Pettipiece's investment in the paper. The *B.C. Trades Unionist*, March 1908, gives printers' wages. See the *Western Clarion*, 17 July 1903, for an organizer's salary of $2.00 a day, and Ronald Grantham, "Some Aspects of the Socialist Movement in British Columbia, 1898-1933," MA thesis, University of British Columbia, 1942, p. 68, for the $60 monthly salary of the SPC secretary and editor in 1911. For annual earnings of workers for 1911, see McDonald, "Working Class Vancouver," Table 2, p. 38.

32. For the politics of labourism, see Heron, "Labourism"; McDonald, "Working Class Vancouver"; Robin, *Radical Politics*; McCormack, *Rebels*.

33. For the theoretical argument that intellectuals tend to be structured into political struggles and workers into economic ones, see Gouldner, *Against Fragmentation*, pp. 100-140. For the SPC's devotion to political action and "becoming the state," see McCormack, pp. 57-59. The *Western Clarion*, 3 February 1912, advised workers that the best way to defeat capitalism was for them "to get the power. . . . be the state." See also Leier, *Where the Fraser River Flows: The Industrial Workers of the World in British Columbia*, Vancouver: New Star Books, 1990, pp. 90-105. The observa-

tion that the SPC had a large number of professional politicians in its ranks may be found in Ross A. Johnson, "No Compromise – No Political Trading: The Marxian Socialist Tradition in British Columbia," Ph.D dissertation, University of British Columbia, 1975, p. 15.

34. For Lang and Kingsley on theory and the working class, see McCormack, pp. 30-31. See Campbell, throughout, for Pritchard's commitment to education, political action, and theory.

35. For the socialist impetus behind larger unions and more united action in this period, see Paul Phillips, *No Power Greater: A Century of Labour in British Columbia*, Vancouver: Boag Foundation, 1967, pp. 49-51; Robin, *Radical Politics*, chapter 8; James Naylor, *The New Democracy: Challenging the Social Order in Industrial Ontario, 1914-25*, Toronto: University of Toronto Press, 1991; and David Bercuson, *Fools and Wise Men: The Rise and Fall of the One Big Union*. Toronto: McGraw Hill Ryerson, 1978. For the argument that labourists were leery of larger federations and insisted on craft autonomy, see Leier, "Class, Bureaucracy, and Ideology: The Vancouver Trades and Labour Council, 1889-1909," Ph.D. dissertation, Memorial University of Newfoundland, 1991, chapter 3.

36. See Johnson, p. 207, for the need of SPC politicians to push for reform measures to gain re-election. For the tendency of socialists in the Vancouver Trades and Labour Council to become more conservative than those outside the labour movement, see McCormack, pp. 32, 56; and Leier, "Class, Bureaucracy, and Ideology," chapters 8 and 9.

37. Ramsay Cook, *The Regenerators: Social Criticism in Late Victorian English Canada*, Toronto: University of Toronto Press, 1985, p. 4. Richard Allen, *The Social Passion: Religion and Social Reform in Canada, 1914-1928*, Toronto: University of Toronto Press, 1971, pp. 3, 354. Allen Mills, *Fool for Christ: The Political Thought of J.S. Woodsworth*, Toronto: University of Toronto Press, 1991.

"A Bachelor's Paradise":

Homesteaders, Hired Hands,

and the Construction of Masculinity,

1880-1930

CECILIA DANYSK

In the 1880s, a young bachelor named Felix Troughton heeded the call to a new life and headed west to the Canadian prairies. When he recorded his experiences fifty years later, he waxed enthusiastic about the possibilities for agricultural settlers. To him, the pioneer prairie west was *A Bachelor's Paradise.*[1]

But the prairie west is full of contradictions. Troughton's title is intriguing, for both contemporary accounts and current literature indicate that the pioneer prairie west was no paradise for bachelors.[2] Despite his title, Troughton appears to concur. Drawing from an unnamed farm journal, he painted a bleak picture of the lonely and uncared-for bachelor. Alone in his "unswept and dusty house," the bachelor rises from a bed "that has perhaps not been made for weeks." Fretful and anxious, he "prepares a hasty and ill-cooked breakfast," eating from "unwashed dishes" at a table where "a million flies gather to feed in undisturbed peacefulness." It is no wonder that the "unrefreshed bachelor goes to his work lonely, miserable and dyspeptic."[3]

Where was Troughton's paradise? Like so many other prairie promises, it was in the future. "What the bachelor requires in his home" declared Troughton, "is a broad-shouldered, stirring wife, who will keep the house in order, as well as the husband who owns it." Then would happiness and success be assured, and the "dejected and forlorn bachelor . . . be transformed into one of the lords of creation."[4]

The contradiction between present realities and future potentials is a recurring theme in the history of prairie settlement. Throughout the pioneering period, the possibilities appeared endless. Settlement literature described the vast area of prime agricultural land simply waiting for the plough, and foresaw the west as the breadbasket of the world. John Macoun, Canada's consummate publicist, declared in 1883 that agricultural prospects in the North-West were "unsurpassed in any other parts of the world."[5] His refrain was echoed in settlement literature well into the twentieth century.[6] And any man could apparently share this largesse. For a mere ten dollar filing fee and a stint of hard but invigorating work, a homesteader was promised economic independence. Like hundreds of thousands of other "plucky, physically fit, and red-blooded" men, Felix Troughton was lured to the land of the future, to the unlimited potential of the pioneer prairie west.

Yet once they arrived in the west, men found the realities of the present overwhelming, and the potentials receding further and further into an idealized future. For many, the promise never materialized. How did these men respond to the economic realities? How did they reconcile the contradictions? Although the economic situation determined their material conditions, they shaped their responses at least in part to expectations of their roles and images of themselves as men in the developing agricultural economy and community. Any attempt to unravel the contradictions with which the men lived and to which they responded must explore the connection between gender and class, a complex relationship that has been the subject of a number of recent studies.[7]

In the case of prairie men and in relation to class, there is not one masculine identity, but many. This essay examines bachelorhood. In the evolving agricultural community of the prairie west a bachelor identity was constructed and then reconstructed, as men sought validation and self-worth in the work they undertook to build a new west. As this new west moved from pioneer self-sufficiency to a mature agrarian economy and society, it became more deeply enmeshed in capitalist relations of production. Social relations were profoundly affected, and the role of bachelors underwent significant change. As bachelors moulded the contours of their gender identity, then reshaped them, they were responding both to ideology and to material conditions determined by class. These influences reinforced one another, but of the two, the most powerful was class.

I

The agricultural community of the prairie west had been designed and was defined, both economically and socially, as family-oriented, based on small-scale units of production – family farms.[8] This design was clear from the 1860s, when the west was envisioned as a colonial empire of central Canada.[9] Out of a complex interplay of economic and political purposes came a comprehensive plan for western development. An agrarian economy and society was to replace the fur trade. Small-scale family-sized units of production would provide a market large enough to absorb eastern manufactured goods. Single-crop production would provide the volume of grain necessary to establish secure international markets. Small landowners and their families would provide a conservative foundation for a stable population.[10] The agricultural industry designed for the west was to provide the basis not only for the economy but for the society as well. "I look upon the agriculturalist . . . as the backbone of every new country" declared Department of Interior agent Peter Fleming:

> they [sic] are its pioneers, and as they succeed in developing its resources they are benefitting the whole community with whom they have cast their lot, paving the way for other industries to thrive in their midst, and at the same time they are making comfortable homes for themselves [and] giving their families a start in life.[11]

The apparatus to secure a whole prairie full of farm families was the Dominion Lands Act which promised 160 acres to any adult male willing to wager ten dollars that he could bring forty acres under cultivation and put up a building or two within three years.[12] The limitation of homesteads to men and heads of families was only the most obvious effort to encourage settlement by families.[13] Others were the reservation of two sections of land out of each township for schools and immigration propaganda that was filled with promises for the economic improvement and happiness of families. Married men with no capital were encouraged to come ahead of their wives and families, then to send for them as soon as possible. The messages aimed at single men implicitly embodied an understanding that they would marry and raise families. The 1897 Department of the Interior report on emigration distinguished between the recommended economic strategies for married or single men, making it clear that the ultimate aim of the latter was to "settle down":

> Work, it must be remembered, is scarce enough among the farmers and the poor man is not able to leave his family and go a distance to work and earn wages . . .
> I should speak otherwise to a young unmarried man, for such a one could earn good enough wages. . ., make improvements in due course on his land, spend every six months fulfilling his conditions for residence, and go back to earn the necessary money for settling down.[14]

The advantages of a family-oriented society were obvious. Small units of production that could be handled by families, and could provide them with an adequate, if modest, living, ensured that the society created in the prairie west would be agrarian and family-oriented. The economic contribution of families was proportionally much greater than their mere numbers, since the costs of their labour and provisions were hidden in their production. There were political and social benefits as well. The economy provided the infrastructure for the society.[15] Individual farm ownership meant conservative values, and the predominance of families ensured the entrenchment of institutions and fostered social stability.[16] The family farm was seen as the "ideal social unit."[17]

II

Yet despite the clear orientation of policy makers and settlers toward families, there was a well-defined niche for bachelors. The term "bachelor" had a particular connotation in the prairie west. Its basic designation, of course, was an unmarried man. But it also referred to married men who were temporarily without their wives. Elizabeth Mitchell, a careful observer of western Canada before the First World War, gave the following definition:

"Bachelor" has the technical meaning of a man living by himself or with other men, with no woman in the house. A widower or grass-widower "batches," an unmarried man with a sister or housekeeper does not.[18]

Married men often found themselves in this condition. When pioneer Wilfrid Eggleston's family decided to begin farming in 1909, his mother and the three children stayed in Nanton, Alberta, for school while his father took up a homestead. Young Wilfrid observed that the family looked forward to their reunion, but "In the meantime my father would have to rough it and "batch it" on his own."[19] The term "to batch" entered the prairie lexicon with ease, indicating the social acceptability of farm men without women. In some ways this is a little surprising, since both the social and economic progress of men on their own was widely believed to lag far behind those of men who had their wives and families at hand.

Bachelors were perceived to live in squalor and loneliness. Their homes were "wretched establishments,"[20] even by rough pioneering standards. Bachelor shacks were makeshift and cramped, thrown up quickly to provide little more than the barest shelter while the men fulfilled homestead duties. They were untouched by "feminine hands" and "showed the want of tender care."[21] They were unpainted, unfurnished and had no amenities.[22] The sorry life was vividly described in the farm journal cited by Troughton. Meals were dismal. "The bread is generally sour, hard or dry, the butter salty and rancid, the coffee worthless, the meat burned on one side and raw on the other." Cleanliness was not even attempted, and the bachelor's "underclothes, seldom washed, become clogged with perspiration, and his bedclothes are in the same unhealthy condition."[23]

Isolation increased the hardship. The "prairie madness"[24] that afflicted women, took its toll on bachelors, too. In an item on the mental illness of a local homesteader, the *Hanna Herald* observed the general self-neglect that resulted from a solitary existence on an isolated farm. "Many a lonely homesteader puts in his hard day's toil and retires at night on a meal quickly made by his own hands and scant." The problem could be apathy or exhaustion: "after working in the field he has not the inclination to go to the trouble of preparing a better [meal]."[25]

Bachelor homesteader Ebe Koeppen had first-hand experience of the toll of isolated living. He recorded in his diary that he had reached a "very sad point." Life without a wife was "slow suicide. Slow spiritual death." He confined his observations to his diary, explaining "I do not write home about these things" because the "staggering drearyness [sic] of such existence is too difficult to make understandable."[26]

Bachelors lamented their fate, although many tried to make light of it. A popular prairie song, "The Alberta Homesteader," described "Dan Gold, an old bach'lor" who was "keeping old batch on an elegant plan." Prairie bachelors could empathize with his miserable conditions:

> My clothes are all ragged, my language is rough,
> My bread is case-hardened and solid and tough
> My dishes are scattered all over the room
> My floor gets afraid at the sight of a broom.

And with his resolve to throw in the towel:

> So farewell to Alberta, farewell to the west,
> It's backwards I'll go to the girl I love best.
> I'll go back to the east and get me a wife
> And never eat cornbread the rest of my life.[27]

But for bachelor homesteaders who were determined to stay in the west and win their ten-dollar bet with the government, the burden of single life was an everyday reality. "Housekeeping batchelor [sic] style," according to a Weyburn, Saskatchewan pioneer, meant living in a box wagon with a make-shift roof, subsisting on "mush and milk for breakfast, fried mush for dinner, and milk and mush for dinner and supper."[28]

Bachelor farmers suffered economically too. Batching on the prairies was "the most expensive way" to keep house, explained newcomer Edward ffolkes, "because [the bachelor] has no time to make bread often, or even butter, in summer, or puddings, or soups with vegetables, which saves the meat – and meat is expensive."[29] Even more seriously, the bachelor's farm suffered. The overworked bachelor could not plough his fields and tend his house at the same time. Troughton warned of the depredations of hawks which "soar around the forsaken house and catch the chickens in the yard," and of unruly livestock that could not be controlled. A bachelor's pigs would surely root up his garden, and his calves were bound to "get out of the enclosure and suck the cows." Even his house might be "burned down from a spark that may drop from the neglected stove." And with no one to mind his homestead while he went to town for mail and supplies, "cattle get into his grain fields, or pull down his stacks, and there is no one to let the dog loose, so the marauders riot at will."[30] *The Nor'-West Farmer* was only one of many voices to counsel the acquisition of a wife as a necessary condition to economic success. "One man on a farm can hardly make a success in mixed farming," it warned a bachelor who was planning to raise livestock. "Better look out for a female partner, if you can arrange to that effect, and plan at the same time for heifers to come in at between two and three years."[31]

But these very tangible impediments to economic and social progress did not cause bachelors to be shunned. On the contrary, they were viewed with tolerance, concern, and benevolence, and often with bemused affection. Westerners, particularly women, felt a certain responsibility toward them. Part of women's duty in the west, claimed Mitchell, was "being kind to poor bachelors round about who need kindness badly."[32] Bachelors were more to be pitied than scorned, and the sorrier their existence, the greater the solicitude.

The men developed strategies for dealing with their unhappy position, and the local community willingly met their needs. Recalling their first winter on their homesteads, Ebe Koeppen and his homesteading partner Hans admitted "we damn near lived on rolled oats and corn syrup." But they soon became acquainted with the nearest family who were "lovely people. The wife would bake bread for us once a week and we would work it off."[33] This kind of response was common. Bachelor homesteader S. Jickling and his partner Stan were often invited by the women in the district "for a clean bite, as they called it."[34] Clearly, there was a special niche reserved for men without women. "I used to feel so sorry for those boys," recalled one pioneer: "They were so pitiful. My mother, she worried over them and she babied them and they came to her with all their troubles."[35]

Aside from compassion, there were practical reasons for welcoming bachelors into the family-oriented community – they did make tangible economic and social contributions. A simple shortage of population meant that all settlers were eagerly included in all economic and social functions. Welcomed at barn-raising bees and on harvest crews, at dances and at ballgames, prairie bachelors pulled their weight in the developing agrarian community. In 1885 the *Qu'Appelle Vidette* reported a dance hosted by "the bachelors of the northern part of this municipality" for a crowd of about forty. An "excellent repast" began at six, and dancing went on "until daylight warned the delighted but wearied party that it was time to homeward wend." The bachelors had done themselves proud and earned the admiration of the community. The *Vidette* summed it up with the observation that "it is doubtful if anything better could be turned out anywhere in the Northwest, outside of Winnipeg."[36]

Bachelors could also be easily forgiven for their bachelorhood, since the prairie population was still very small, and was also badly skewed in its male-to-female ratio.[37] Settlers were acutely aware that "the missing element in homesteading was always the women."[38] Pioneer David Maginnes of Balwinton, Saskatchewan recalled a dance with only three women to thirty men: "We danced until the women got tired."[39] C. A. Dawson and Eva Younge's close examination of ten survey areas shows that the newly settled areas of Turtleford, Saskatchewan, and Peace River, Alberta, had a rural male:female ratio as high as 202:100 during the first decade of settlement. In older, stable settlements such as Red River, Manitoba, the ratio was 121:100 even at the beginning of the century.[40]

But the major reason bachelors found such a ready acceptance in the family-oriented community was because their condition, like many other pioneer hardships, was perceived as temporary. The solution to the problems plaguing the bachelor farmer was to bring his bachelorhood to a close, to find a wife who would share the burden and the joys of building a farm. The social and economic contributions of a wife caused writers to wax rhapsodic. What every hard-working bachelor farmer needed was

> a wife who will keep the house in order, as well as the husband who owns it, and who will see that clothing and bedding are made clean and kept so; who will serve a well-cooked meal with fresh, sweet bread of her own making; who will see that groceries are good, and that proper value has been received for money expended; who will wash and mend her husband's clothing, and will remove the shingle nails that have been used as substitutes for buttons; one who will look after the hens' nests, see that the dairy is kept in order, and who will place the Bible on the table when the day's work is done.[41]

With such a wife, the new husband's "bearing will be erect, his eyes clear, and his purse full, his garden will have flowers, and his shirt will have buttons."[42] Even more restrained observers such as Mitchell insisted that marriage "means leaving a ghastly loneliness for companionship and help, and squalor for decent comfort."[43] A hard-working, supportive wife could spell the difference between success and failure. "A man who would be a failure alone," declared prairie observer Marjorie Harrison, "will pull through if he has a good wife."[44]

Bachelorhood may have been regarded as a disadvantage, but not a permanent one. Married men were batching only until they could send for their wives and families. Single men were bachelors only until they could provide for a family, or until the shortage of women in the west could be redressed. There were few "confirmed" bachelors on the pioneer prairies, most unmarried men were "eligible" bachelors. And given the rate at which "every girl is pounced on directly she puts her face inside the settlement,"[45] it seems that the eligible bachelors were eager to end this temporary condition. "Us bachelors were all desperate," recalled Ebe Koeppen, "you can use the word "desperate" quite properly here – we were desperate to get a wife one way or the other."[46]

III

Just as bachelorhood was temporary, so the family-oriented economy and society of the west had not yet been realized. The reality of the pioneer years was that the population was overwhelmingly male. "Canada is a man's country," declared the Department of the Interior in 1906, recognizing "that all new countries first attract men, because the labour required for early settlement calls for that of man rather than that of woman."[47] The idea of settlement was so strongly linked to masculine endeavour that the term "bachelor homesteader" came into widespread use.

It was a positive designation, embodying many of the attributes needed on a frontier. Men who could claim the title elicited admiration. Kathleen Strange, writing from the perspective of a "modern" pioneer, described the common view:

The first bachelor homesteaders had come out, most of them, with nothing more substantial than courage and optimism with which to battle against the harsh elements of a new country and a new life.[48]

In the crucible of this new country and new life an identity of bachelorhood was forged, an amalgam of the idealized attributes of bachelor homesteaders.

The identity was incorporated into a broader prairie pioneering ideology, which in turn provided the basis for the dominant culture in the prairie west. "Ideology" here means "the set of ideas which arise from a given set of material interests," a definition derived from Raymond Williams, but further refined below. "Culture" is used here in the Thompsonian sense, to include such broad categories as "traditions, value-systems, ideas and institutional forms."[49] The term "dominant culture" is more restricted, and does not imply hegemony.

Although the varieties of pioneering experience precluded a single universal prairie culture, the values and institutions that emerged from and directed rural society were those that reflected the economic base and social attitudes of the dominant agrarian group, the farmers. During the early stages of prairie settlement, they were engaged in the pioneer struggle to create a new economy and society. But this was to be a temporary stage, and ultimately prairie farmers were directing their energies toward full participation in large-scale commercial agriculture. As new farmers themselves, bachelor homesteaders occupied a special niche. This fusion of bachelor status with the dominant culture of the pioneer prairie ideology enabled bachelorhood to receive a very positive assessment, and gave the identity additional legitimacy and strength.

Bachelorhood was male, which meant that attributes ascribed to it would be considered masculine.[50] At the same time, it would mean that traditional qualities of manliness would be incorporated. But gender identities are fraught with contradictions, and manliness in one context is not necessarily manliness in another.[51] So, although bachelorhood was a masculine identity, it was a particular type of masculinity, one that was attuned to the conditions of the pioneer prairie west.[52] It served the needs of men who were generally young, of limited means, and who were engaged in small-scale pioneer agriculture on a relatively womanless frontier. Each of these elements was incorporated into the identity of the pioneer bachelor, which thus resonated with the ideals of the dominant culture.

Much of the definition had to do with physical prowess. Agriculture was a physically demanding occupation requiring strength, stamina, and dexterity. With a long tradition as affirmations of masculine identity and validations of male self-worth, these characteristics were readily accepted. Farmers measured themselves and each other by "the supreme manly qualities" that were shown when a man "could keep up to two binders."[53] Young men bragged of the hard work in the fields. "I am doing first rate," wrote newcomer John Stokoe to his father, "thriving like a young bullock, and growing out of my clothes."[54] Old-timers reminisced fondly of the "real joy in feeling one could do a man's job in the sunshine and the wind in Manitoba."[55] The needs of agriculture were thus well-served by the physical qualities of the identity of bachelorhood.

On the prairies, it was small-scale agriculture being practised, with individual farmers working individual farms, making decisions and carrying out an endless round of tasks on their own. Individualism was thus an important component of the identity, but it was an individualism of self-reliance rather than of competitiveness.[56] Cooperation rather than competition was the trait that most served the needs of an agricultural community struggling to establish itself.

Pioneering called for a spirit of adventure, for courage and resourcefulness, for the desire to leave behind an old life and to embark on a new one. This life required fortitude in the face of adversity, a will to succeed, adaptability, and a willingness to subordinate present gratifications for future possibilities. Taking pride in craftsmanship and deriving satisfaction from a job well done, commonly expressed characteristics of masculine identity, took on added importance to pioneers who often saw little financial reward for their hard work.

Homesteading, too, helped shape the bachelor identity. It required thrift. The low filing fee meant that men with limited resources could begin farming, but they had to be able to husband their financial resources, demonstrate ingenuity and resourcefulness in enlarging them, and be willing to endure hardships in the present in the expectation of comfort in the future. Immigration propaganda invited men "with no money but muscle and pluck."[57] So long as they had "strong hearts and willing hands," were "steady," "sober and industrious," had "energy and perseverance," and could "make light of discomforts" they could succeed.[58] But they should not expect an easy ride to wealth. Intending immigrants were warned against the "great mistake" of thinking "they need only to stoop down and pick up the lumps of gold lying by the roadside," but were assured that "whosoever is able and willing to work will be well repaid."[59]

There was an acceptance, too, of an aggressive democracy that decreed that to be cash-poor was not dishonourable. Homesteaders prided themselves on refusing to acknowledge social distinctions based on economic position. *The Nor'-West Farmer* summed up the attitude toward farming on the frontier, quoting "one of the social teachers of the century," John Ruskin: ""There is no degradation in the hardest manual or the humblest servile, labor, when it is honest"."[60]

Some parts of the identity were derived in contradistinction to other identities. Bachelor manhood was measured in its dissimilarity from womanhood, and also in its dissimilarity from childhood, but these measurements were not derived in an antagonistic way. Women and children both served an important and highly visible economic role in prairie agriculture. The rigours of the frontier provided pioneer women with the opportunity to challenge their gender-defined roles, but except under unusual circumstances their roles were still complementary to those of men.[61] They posed no threat to the occupations of prairie men.[62] Although bachelorhood was the antithesis of femininity and immaturity, the maleness and the maturity of bachelors were neither defensive nor aggressive traits.[63]

Rather than concentrating on their physical superiority, bachelors defined their contrast to women in their lack of such social niceties as an ability to take care of themselves, to cook, to sew, to keep clean, to converse politely, and to demonstrate other features of a gentle civilization. They defined their contrast to children by steadiness both in physical work and in life commitments, maturity of judgement, and wisdom from experience. All were necessary qualities in agriculture. By and large, bachelor homesteaders found their identity within the dominant ideology. They were expected to live a wholesome frugal life in anticipation of the time they would leave the bachelor state to become full-fledged members of the family-oriented agrarian community. Likewise, their actual economic position mattered less in the social network of the agrarian community than did their preparation for full economic membership within it.

IV

But the pioneer era did not last. Homestead lands filled up, purchased lands were taken, more land came under cultivation, and economic and social institutions were established and matured. Sparsely settled and underdeveloped pioneer areas made the transition to mature agricultural communities. This passage was traversed at different times in different regions, and although the rate of change was very uneven, the pattern was repeated throughout the prairie west.[64] A significant marker of the transition was the increase in the number and proportion of farm families. By 1921, more than fifty-five percent of the rural male population aged fifteen years and older was married, bringing the prairie marriage rate into line with the Canadian average.[65] The ideal of a family-oriented economy and society had become the reality.

With the transition to a fully-developed commercial economy, the social position of bachelors came to be more narrowly defined by their economic status. The new equation between bachelorhood and economic position was a reflection of the penetration of capitalism into agriculture.[66] One result was increasing social stratification.[67] Social distinction based on economic position was a phenomenon that had been denied and deplored during the pioneering years and had been held in check by the sharing of pioneer hardships. But it came to be recognized and even – somewhat sadly and reluctantly – accepted as the price of progress. When pioneer William Pettinger reminisced about the early days he recalled that "in pioneering, for the first few years, it's like one big family." But with increasing prosperity, "certain ones feel they can afford to be a little more independent. Others follow suit, and finally, you have a normal community: individuals, factions, etc."[68]

At the same time, men who had not yet achieved farm ownership faced serious impediments. Homestead lands were available only in remote regions unserviced by railways, prices and mortgage rates for purchased lands soared, and expensive machinery was needed to produce large crops in an increasingly competitive market. Entry into farming was becoming extremely costly, and thus extremely difficult. This did not stop the movement of single men onto the prairies, but it did change their position. Instead of being bachelor homesteaders, they were now bachelor hired hands. The distinction was not always clear-cut. In the early days, nearly all homesteaders and probably most men who had purchased farms had worked out as agricultural labourers, but they had been regarded primarily as farm owners. Now there were many more men who were identified only as farm labourers, and they faced seriously diminished opportunities to become farm owners and heads of farm families. As late as 1931, only fifteen percent of waged farm workers were listed in the census as heads of families.[69]

The family-orientation of prairie agriculture achieved particular importance with the new position of bachelors. Originally, the bachelor identity encompassed attributes that were characteristic of masculinity, of agriculture, of pioneering, and of frontiers, but these attributes were not particularly restrained by class position. Even though the ideology upon which it was based was rooted in material conditions, an individual's actual economic position did not figure highly in whether or not he was accepted into the society. It likewise did not figure highly in the identity of bachelors. Most were not wealthy, but their capital-poor position was expected to be a temporary phenomenon. The link between the economy and the ideology, although very strong, was blurred during the pioneer era and, consequently, in the identity that bachelor homesteaders constructed for themselves. However, the cultural construct of bachelorhood came to have a very different meaning as it became defined within narrower economic boundaries.

The resulting shift in attitudes toward bachelorhood presents an interesting glimpse of a culture in flux. Aspects of the prairie culture that had provided a special place for all bachelors in the rural community became applied primarily to the waged agricultural labour force. Bachelorhood was now more restricted. It became part of the definition of agricultural labourers, in contrast to its earlier definition of a great many newcomers to the agricultural community, whether owners or workers.

The cultural change reflected an important structural condition. Bachelorhood was, and continued to be, a precondition of most agricultural employment. Low wages, job insecurity, a high degree of mobility, and a lack of accommodation for families, all continued to preclude marriage and family from the lives of most farm workers. In 1931, only 13.6 percent of farm workers and farmers' sons were married, compared with 79.8 percent of prairie farmers.[70] According to the federal Department of Immigration and Colonization, "nine out of ten farmers want to have nothing at all to do with a [farm hand's] family." Although some farmers welcomed the services that a farm hand's wife could provide, most saw a labourer's family as trouble and expense. "It is only the one out of ten that will even consider giving employment to a man and his wife, and the number who will take care of man, wife, and several children is much more limited still."[71] One farmer went so far as to refuse to honour his agreement to take on a hired man when he discovered that the man's wife was pregnant.[72] It was a circular process that was reinforced as bachelorhood came to be associated with hired hands. Farmers often recognized the advantage of employing married workers whom they regarded as steadier and more reliable, but by far the majority of them hired single men.[73]

Judgements about bachelorhood began to change.[74] In the early years, bachelor farmers were expected eventually to settle down, own a farm, marry and raise a family. Those who had not yet done so were excused on the grounds that they were still economically unprepared to support a family, or there was a shortage of women. But as the male-to-female imbalance was redressed, and as farmers and whole communities began to make economic progress, these reasons lost their validity. And as bachelorhood came to be more restricted to farm workers, it was perceived as evidence of an unambitious nature. Manitoba's Department of Agriculture began to characterize farm workers as men "who have failed in pretty nearly every walk of life."[75] Advertisements in farm journals contrasted the "ambitious man" with those who were satisfied to pitch hay for $4.00 a day or do chores for $3.50.[76]

Hired hands were often seen as too shiftless to settle down and own farms or raise families. Those who were not making definite plans to take up farming on their own account were dismissed as "drifters."[77] And since they had little opportunity to become farm owners themselves, they were no longer eligible to marry the farmer's daughter and thus solve their dilemma. A contemporary observer explained a common perception that placed the farm hand in a double bind:

As the labourer nears thirty-five years of age, at which period in his life he should have accumulated substantial savings, he approaches a transitional period. This phase is noticeable for his desire to be independent. If the labourer fails to show this characteristic restlessness and settles down to the acceptance of agricultural employment as a life task, he has past [sic] beyond that period of most effective service and has entered the final stage indicative of the stagnatory period.[78]

The status of bachelorhood declined. The earlier bachelor homesteaders had been accepted into the dominant culture because they both appropriated and embodied features of the pioneer prairie ideology for their identity. It was in their interest to do so, since social acceptance was an important component of agricultural success. As well, they embraced the ideology because it coincided with the type of future they sought for themselves. They even had a hand in shaping the ideology – they shared the majority vision of agricultural progress based on sacrifice, hard work and a willingness to endure harsh conditions.

But bachelor hired hands did not seem to adopt this view. Their interests, and those of the pioneer ideology, began to diverge. In part this reflected a transition in the ideology itself. With the transition from a pioneer to a mature agricultural economy, the requisites for survival and success also changed. The dominant ideology was shifting from that of pioneering to that of agrarian capitalism. Successful farmers adopted business-like methods, and sought ways to ensure greater returns for their labour dollar.[79] But in part this divergence was evidence of changed material conditions as well.

The economic contribution of the bachelor hired hand to the agricultural community was measured by different criteria than those used for the bachelor homesteader. Even though a bachelor homesteader made slower progress than did a married one, his work on his own land and his potential for developing his own farm were the benchmarks of his success. But the economic contribution of a bachelor hired hand was measured only in his present ability to help his employer bring in a good crop or otherwise improve his employer's farm. His contribution was indirect, undervalued and suspect. When farmer H.A. Kuhn reported to the CPR that the farm he had purchased from them was not doing well, he was blamed for placing too much reliance on his hired man. "Our experience is that where there are such valuable improvements and equipment as you apparently have on the farm, that it requires somebody who is personally interested in the place, to get the best results out of it."[80]

The perceived social contribution of a bachelor hired hand was likewise altered by his economic position. Again, it was a shift in emphasis from potential to present reality. As a bachelor homesteader, a man was judged on his probable ability to find a wife to provide a higher level of culture, sophistication, and gentleness not only to himself but to the broader community as well. As a bachelor farm hand, however, he was less likely than ever to marry, and was thus less susceptible to the civilizing influence of a wife and family. His social contribution was often measured only in terms of whether he brought harmony or discord into his employer's home.

The behaviour of bachelors was likewise examined, and received harsh judgement. Women played an important role in this assessment, for they were charged with providing the guardianship and discipline necessary for a morally and socially upright future generation. This had been an ongoing task for women since the industrial upheaval of the late-nineteenth century.[81] In the rural prairie west, the task had the added dimension of a mission to bring moral and cultural uplift to a male-dominated society.[82] Women were expected to create a climate of social well-being unlike the rough masculine behaviour that had dominated the frontier.[83] While farm women continued to express special concern for young single men who were incapable of taking care of themselves, they also worried about the moral standards of their families. Social conduct such as drinking, gambling, fighting and visiting houses of ill-repute were much less easily forgiven.[84] This type of behaviour did decline with the advent of families, so its occurrence stood in stark contrast to the behavioral norms of the developing agrarian community.

In the home, personal habits of farm workers were scrutinized. Mothers were instructed to protect the morals and health of their families. "Is the average home sanitary?" asked the women's section of *The Grain Growers' Guide*, deploring the use of the common water dipper. Even trusted neighbours might pass on disease through such a practice, and "Then there are the hired help, about whom you may know nothing. Is it right that they should drink out of the same vessel as you and your children?"[85] Farm

women were becoming increasingly concerned to "observe the little niceties and decencies on the farm where we are making a real home and trying
to bring up the children."[86] Farm hands were rated on cleanliness, manners,
and as an example for the children. Many a bachelor hired hand failed the
test. As "A Mother of Two" cautioned:

> I think if a woman does her duty in the home, in the training of her children,
> she cannot be too particular as to those she admits to the privacy of her
> home, especially on the farm, where the hired help . . . are bound to associ-
> ate with and influence the children to a certain extent.[87]

These changes were taking place within the context of a changing position of agrarian life in the larger Canadian economy and society. As industrialization challenged the economic and political hegemony of agriculture,
as scientific thought and method came to dominate the business world, and
as the bright lights and economic opportunities of cities began to lure
young farm people, rural life came under attack.[88] The most visible effect
was the depletion of the rural population in central Canada where governments, churches and concerned citizens began to discuss the issue.[89] Westerners were also worried. Farm journals expressed the common fear that
people did not recognize agriculture as the "anchor" of the nation, the
"great untroubled reservoir of sanity and common sense."[90] Farm people
grew alarmed that agriculture could not hold onto young people. The finest, who possessed "as much courage and capacity for hard work as their
forbears," were finding that "the game has not been worth the candle" and
were being drawn to the cities by "the spirit of adventure, which is the will
to success."[91]

The agrarian community responded by formulating and advocating a
"Country Life Ideology" that counterposed the land as "the fount of
health, peace, virtue and the Spirit" to the city as "unproductive and parasitic, [the] source of dissipation, sham and unfulfillment."[92] This ideology
took hold during the first two decades of the twentieth century and shaped
the attitudes and actions of farm dwellers throughout the 1920s and beyond. It combined with a growing emphasis on the role of women as homemakers. Women were urged to recognize that their responsibilities toward
their families included emotional, psychological and physical well-being. A

farm woman from rural Saskatchewan acknowledged the task. "We of the farm must recognize the fact that there must be time and strength for social, religious and intellectual interests."[93] The attitude was echoed throughout the rural prairies, as the farm home was expected to be a "haven of safety and healthfulness."[94] A contest run in 1922 by the women's section of the *Grain Growers' Guide* asked farm women: "Do you want your daughter to marry a farmer?"[95] Their answers expressed fulfilment in a life close to nature and free of the social hazards of the city environment. They also expressed desire for an intimate family life that by definition included only members of the family circle.

Bachelors came under fire for failing to live up to the agrarian ideal. Their very bachelorhood served to cut them off from membership in the institution that was extolled as the heart of country life. The nurturing and reformist aspects of the ideology identified the family farm as the source and haven "of lasting democratic values, and the structural basis of . . . egalitarian rural communities."[96] The agrarian defence of these values elevated the importance of the family, which was seen to embody the rural virtues. Outsiders such as hired hands could even pose a moral danger. The Salvation Army's mission to rural youth warned of the dangers of hired men, who were "very likely to be men of low ideals and evil practices."[97] Parents were bluntly urged to guard their sons from temptation into bestiality from "the vile talk of farm hands."[98] In such an ideological climate, there was only a restricted place for bachelor hired hands.

They were very visibly just what city-folk were saying was wrong with the country. Their exclusion from family life made them country bumpkins and their low wages made them poor country cousins. In one study, the farm worker of ten years duration was characterized as "lack[ing] sufficient education or initiative to rise above his present situation or . . . mentally incapable of doing so."[99] Moreover, their vision seemed to be narrowly focused on attaining higher wages, not on becoming more efficient producers. Farmers complained that they must have workers of "a class which will work to the interests of the farmer."[100] Farm hands were not recognized as making a significant economic contribution to their industry, let alone to the Canadian economy.

And given the importance of farm ownership in the agrarian ideology, bachelor hired hands were often seen as economic failures, in sharp contrast to earlier bachelor homesteaders who had been viewed as successes or potential successes. This was an important distinction in an industry that offered no guarantees. In the basic insecurity of prairie agriculture, with the uncertainty of rainfall, frost, and disease, the threat of crop failures and foreclosures, and in the context of a soaring cost-price spiral, farmers in next-year country were haunted by the spectre of sinking into agricultural waged labour.

The bachelor identity came under attack. There were two dimensions to this reassessment and harsher judgement. First, there were real changes in what was perceived by both bachelors and outsiders as constituent elements of the bachelor persona. Most of these changes were brought about by the economic changes of the post-pioneering period and signalled a deterioration in the social and economic position of bachelors. Second, tolerance diminished for what was perceived as typical bachelor behaviour. What was formerly seen as healthy independence was now seen as irresponsibility. What had been an endearing quality of inability to care for oneself was now slovenliness. What had once been tolerated as youthful letting-off-steam was now dissipation. Hired hands were subject to strong judgements: "From what I can learn, any work that Traynor may have lost has been his own fault," declared the CPR's Assistant Superintendent of Colonization about a hired hand. "He comes into town whenever he gets an opportunity, and spends most of his time in one of the beer parlors, gets full up and then becomes nasty."[101]

V

In response to these changes, bachelors began to reconstruct their identity. Just as the bachelor homesteaders had embraced traditional attributes of manliness to support and to validate them in their struggle to establish an economy and society, so too did the bachelor hired hands adopt notions of manliness that supported and validated them as their aims began to diverge from the dominant culture. They focused on different attributes, giving new emphasis to some while discounting others, or they reordered them in consideration of their changing importance, or they used them in different ways.

In this chapter, the concept of ideology has a particular definition in the prairie agrarian context. It is used in conjunction with another concept, ethos, from which it is distinguished in the following way: both embody ideas about standards of behaviour, attitudes, morals, ideals, and so on. But these concepts exist in a two-tier relationship. Ethos is a generalized concept encompassing a very broad range of attitudes and ideals that can even be contradictory. Examples are values such as those of cooperation or individuality, both of which were embraced at different times and under different circumstances by prairie residents. These values are not the exclusive property of any particular group. Ideology is more specific in that it selects certain features of the ethos and appropriates them for its own use, or interprets them in a way that is consistent with its own needs. An example of this is the way such values as cooperation and individuality are perceived and used in different cultures.

With the opportunities for farm ownership so curtailed, bachelor hired hands concentrated on immediate issues. "From the farm labourer's point of view," declared the federal Department of Labour, "he is interested first in a suitable wage, next, in reasonable hours for labour and then in stable employment."[102] Unlike bachelor homesteaders who were often as much, or even more, interested in learning to farm as in accumulating capital[103], bachelor hired hands concentrated on improving their wages and their working and living conditions. In doing so, they called on old attributes of the bachelor identity, which had been shaped by an ideology with which they were now sharply at odds, and they used these attributes in different ways.

The anticipation of marriage, which was so significant in shaping the identity of the bachelor homesteader, was a smaller consideration for the bachelor hired hand.[104] Indeed, remaining a bachelor was a positive asset, since the work required such great mobility and paid such meagre wages. "It is a fact that all will admit (except the farmer)," insisted one hired hand in a letter to the editor of the *Farmers' Advocate*, "that the Canadian married farm laborer is not receiving enough to live on, and has to go into debt to feed and clothe his family."[105] Farmers seldom made any provision for the accommodation of a wife and family. A 1922 United Farm Women of Manitoba survey revealed that only 37 out of the 366 respondents reported a separate house for the hired help.[106] The hired hand who was unencumbered stood a better chance to make a living.

The steadiness that was an important attribute of the homesteader bachelors, the willingness to put off present pleasures for future rewards, was less important, indeed often irrelevant, to bachelor hired hands. When the United States Industrial Commission studied hired hands in 1899, it reported that the breakdown of the agricultural ladder undermined the ambitions of bachelor farm workers. With farm ownership beyond their reach, "there seems to be a decided tendency for the farm laborer, if he is unmarried, to work for money without a very definite object." Any money earned "is likely to be used for what his fancy dictates, most likely for a horse and buggy of his own."[107] A quarter century later, when the agricultural ladder on the Canadian prairies had begun to break down, farm wife Kathleen Strange reported that all hired hands yearned for a car. "Automobile agents reaped a fine harvest out of hired men by selling them second-hand cars," she recalled, "and often took the best part of their wages every month in payment."[108]

Above all, hired hands in turn looked out for their own interests. They were not eager to bear the risks of agriculture for the dubious possibilities of future success. Hired hands would have scoffed at the proposal of the disgruntled farmer who wanted "some system for dividing with the hired man under which the farmer's interest will be protected in case of a deficit."[109] They were unwilling to work for meagre rewards and to tolerate wretched conditions. Farmers were urged to recognize that conditions of labour had changed over the past fifteen to twenty-five years. "Labor looks upon life in an entirely different way now than it did then," insisted *The Nor'-West Farmer* in 1920. "Laboring people . . . insist on more pay, a shorter day and more comfort in life than were customary then. Labor is through being driven to work. In the future it must be led to work."[110] Hired hands were working for their own individual betterment and were not willing to sacrifice their own interests for that of the farms on which they were working, nor of the farmers by whom they were employed nor, it seemed, for the agricultural community of the prairie west.

The most significant changes occurred when the men called on old attributes of their bachelor identity and used them in different ways. A case in point is the characteristic of independence. As earlier indicated, this was an important attribute of agricultural pioneers, and it held a revered place in the prairie pioneer ideology. It is not surprising, then, to see it surface in the identity of bachelor homesteaders, who needed it in liberal doses if they were to carve a farm out of the virgin prairie. And when bachelor homesteaders became bachelor hired hands, the attribute retained its significance, although the reasons for its importance changed and so did its uses. Bachelor hired hands shared with the dominant culture an ethos of individuality, but they appropriated it ideologically in an oppositional manner.

In the early pioneering period, and even later, the ethos of individualism was an important part of the value system of the agricultural community. It was championed by those pioneers who were rugged individualists in the first place, having headed west in the exciting days of hard work and free land and the building of a new society. But it was espoused, too by those who saw individualism as self-reliance, and not necessarily inimical to the cooperation necessary to establish a young community. It was an ethos that was embraced to some degree by all members of the agricultural community, whatever their economic situation.

It was also very practically applied to work on the farm, where individual initiative and judgement and resourcefulness were highly valued, indeed essential components of agricultural success, whether as owner or as worker. Bachelor homesteaders were lauded for possessing these qualities, and employers of bachelor hired hands looked for men who exhibited them. The most valued qualification of a hired hand was independence, the ability to work at a complex array of farm tasks without supervision or instruction. Even a newcomer was required to carry on unsupervised. Newly-arrived hired hand Gaston Giscard was surprised at the rudimentary instruction and degree of independence offered by his employer. After only "one or two rounds to show me how to operate the levers [of a plough], . . . he leaves me, telling me to go on doing the same for the rest of the day."[111] It is no surprise that prairie farm workers were independent.

Individualism was thus very important to both farmers and their hired men, but for different reasons. If hired men were dissatisfied with their employer, their working conditions, or the food on the table, they simply quit. They appropriated the ethos and embodied a particular use of it in their ideology in a way that was consistent with their new economic position. When bachelor homesteaders became bachelor hired hands, they applied their own meaning to the attribute of independence, using it in their own interests, and in a way that was inimical to those of their employers.

Hired hands were notorious for job-jumping, for quitting work at the slightest provocation or for no reason an employer could understand.[112] Independent men like Charles Drury admitted "I was a funny fellow – no odds where I was working." He enjoyed being able to say "Go to it" in the morning and find another job in the afternoon.[113] The independence that job-jumping expressed was an important attribute of bachelorhood, and something that farmers deplored – they agreed that married men were much more reliable than bachelors. From the farmer's point of view, single men were a headache, with a "tendency . . . to wander from place to place."[114] But to the men who were using their independence in this way, it was an effective strategy to discipline bosses, to achieve better working or living conditions, and most importantly, to maximize earnings.

The seasonal nature of agriculture resulted in jobs that were short-term and a workforce that was highly mobile. Hired hands were able to parlay the immediacy of seasonal demands for their labour into high wages. When Sydney Metcalfe left the farm of Robert Stuart, the CPR farm placement officer commiserated. Hired hands "are always looking out for a higher wage," declared James Colley. "Many of them prefer to work for higher wages for short periods and take the chance of being out of work during the winter."[115] Acting independently they were able to demand and receive high wages when the farmer was hard-pressed to bring in his crop and could not afford the time to search for cheaper labour. Farmers were forced to recognize that their hired men might want to "quit forthwith without cause or grievance" when the prospect of higher wages beckoned. "Some men get that way about this season when help is scarce and prospects for higher wages in harvest are good," mused the editor of *The Nor'-West Farmer*, "or [when] somebody offers them a better wage than they are getting."[116]

The nature of farm employment and the organization of the industry gave further impetus to independent action. Most hired hands spent far more time with their employers than with other farm labourers, and their work required individual initiative rather than cooperative effort. The many small employers in this extremely time-pressured business could be more quickly and effectively disciplined by immediate direct action, such as job-jumping, than by the slower method of large strikes, which require planning and central organization, and money, and time. Hired hands used independent strategies because they were successful, both in gaining employment and in exercising some measure of control over the conditions of that employment. To bachelor hired hands, individualism took on a particular meaning, one that was sharply at odds with the pioneer prairie ideology in which it had been nurtured.

VI

The construction and reconstruction of identity is a complex process, a response to the practical needs of the group and to the values of the larger ideology. As capitalism penetrated pioneer prairie agriculture, the economic position of bachelors changed, and their interests and those of the larger agrarian community began to diverge. In response to the changing material conditions, bachelors reconstructed their own version of masculinity. In this process, they carved a new niche for themselves – still within the parameters of the dominant agrarian ideology – but one that reflected their own changing needs, and one that gave them a sense of dignity and worth. They created, and lived and worked in, their own definition of "a bachelor's paradise."

Notes

1. Felix Troughton, *A Bachelor's Paradise or Life on the Canadian Prairie 45 years ago*, London: Arthur A. Stockwell, c1930.
2. See for example, diary of Ebe Koeppen, in Rolf Knight, *Stump Ranch Chronicles and Other Narratives*, Vancouver: New Star Books, 1977; letters from Edward ffolkes, in Ronald A. Wells, ed. and intro, *Letters from a young emigrant in Manitoba*, Winnipeg: University of Manitoba Press, 1981; Paul Voisey, *Vulcan: The Making of a Prairie Community*, Toronto: University of Toronto Press, 1988, p. 93.
3. Troughton, *A Bachelor's Paradise*, p. 5.
4. *Ibid.*, p. 6.
5. John Macoun, *Manitoba and the Great North-West: The Field for Investment, The Home of the Emigrant*, London: Thomas C. Jack, 1883, p. 147. For a few of the many other examples, see Canada Department of the Interior, *Some of the Advantages of Western Canada. Practical Farmers give their experiences*, Ottawa 1889; Canada Department of Agriculture and Immigration, *Manitoba. The Prairie Province. The finest agricultural country in the world*, Winnipeg, 1890.
6. See for example, Canada Department of the Interior, *The Last Best West: Canada in the Twentieth Century. Western Canada. Vast agricultural resources. Homes for mil-*

lions, Ottawa: The Department of the Interior, 1907? (reprinted many times, with variations on the title); Canadian Pacific Railway, *Own a "Selected Farm" to fit your needs along the line of the Canadian National Railways. Read, think, act.* Chicago, 1919, 1925; Alberta Department of Agriculture, *A Land of Opportunity*, Edmonton, 1923; Grande Prairie Board of Trade, *Interesting Facts about Grande Prairie*, Grande Prairie, 1930.

7. See for example, Steven Penfold, ""Have You No Manhood in You?": Gender and Class in the Cape Breton Coal Towns, 1920-1926," *Acadiensis* XXIII:2 (Spring 1994); Christina Burr, ""Defending the Art Preservative": Class and Gender Relations in the Printing Trades Unions, 1850-1914," *Labour/Le Travail* 31 (Spring 1993); Shirley Tillotson, ""We may all soon be first class men": Gender and Skill in Canada's Early Twentieth Century Urban Telegraph Industry," *Labour/Le Travail* 27 (Spring 1991); Thomas W. Dunk, *It's a Working Man's Town: Male Working-class Culture in North West Ontario*, Toronto and Montreal: McGill-Queen's University Press, 1991; Ava Baron, ed., *Work Engendered: Toward a New History of American Labor*, Ithaca: Cornell University Press, 1991; Michael Yarrow, "The Gender-Specific Class Consciousness of Appalachian Coal Miners: Structure and Change," in Scott McNall, Rhonda Levine, and Rick Fantasia, eds., *Bringing Class Back In: Contemporary and Historical Perspectives*, Boulder, Colorado, 1991; Joy Parr, *The Gender of Breadwinners: Women, Men, and Change in Two Industrial Towns, 1880-1950*, Toronto: University of Toronto Press, 1990; Mary Blewett, "Masculinity and Mobility: The Dilemma of Lancashire Weavers and Spinners in Late-Nineteenth-Century Fall River, Massachusetts," in Mark C. Carnes and Clyde Griffen, eds., *Meanings for Manhood: Constructions of Masculinity in Victorian America*, Chicago: University of Chicago Press, 1990; Steven Maynard, "Rough Work and Rugged Men: The Social Construction of Masculinity in Working-Class History," *Labour/Le Travail* 23 Spring 1989; Mark Rosenfeld, ""It Was A Hard Life": Class and Gender in the Work and Family Rhythms of a Railway Town, 1920-1950s," *Historical Papers/Communications historiques*, Windsor, 1988; Stan Gray, "Sharing the Shop Floor," *Canadian Dimension*, 18:2, June 1984; Cynthia Cockburn, *Brothers: Male Dominance and Technological Change*, London: Pluto Press, 1983; Paul Willis, "Shop Floor Culture, Masculinity and the Wage Form," in John Clarke, Chas Critcher and Richard Johnson, eds., *Working Class Culture: Studies in History and Theory*, London: St. Martin's Press, 1979.

8. *The Last Best West* and other immigration pamphlets; Chester Martin, *"Dominion Lands" Policy* (1937), edited by Lewis H. Thomas, Toronto: McClelland and Stewart, 1973, p. 151, and passim; Saskatchewan *Royal Commission on Agriculture and Rural Life*, Regina: Queen's Printer, 1955-7, Report 3, "Land Tenure," p. 119; Doug Francis, *Images of the West: Responses to the Canadian Prairies*, Saskatoon: Western Producer Prairie Books, 1989.

9. Martin, *"Dominion Lands" Policy*, Ch. 2, "The Purposes of the Dominion," esp. pp. 10 ff.; Vernon C. Fowke, *The National Policy and the Wheat Economy*, Toronto: University of Toronto Press, (1957) 1975, Chapter 3, esp. pp. 29 ff.; Donald Swainson, "Canada Annexes the West: Colonial Status Confirmed," R. Douglas Francis and Howard Palmer, eds., *The Prairie West: Historical Readings*, Edmonton: Pica Pica Press, 1985; Doug Owram, *Promise of Eden: The Canadian Expansionist Movement and the Idea of the West, 1856-1900*, Toronto: University of Toronto Press, 1980.

10. Owram, *Promise of Eden*, p. 137.

11. Peter Fleming, Agent in the Lowlands of Scotland, in "Annual Report," Department of the Interior, *Sessional Papers of Canada*, No. 13, 1898, 25 December 1897, p. 40.

12. Martin, *"Dominion Lands" Policy*, pp. 140-42.

13. For a brief discussion of the movement to grant homestead rights to women, see Susan Jackel, "Introduction," Georgina Binnie-Clark, *Wheat and Woman* (1914), Toronto: University of Toronto Press, 1979, pp. xx-xxxii.

14. "Annual Report," Department of the Interior, *Sessional Papers of Canada*, No. 13, 1898.

15. Max Hedley, "Relations of Production of the "Family Farm": Canadian Prairies," *Journal of Peasant Studies*, 9:1 October 1981; Harriet Friedmann, "World Market, State, and Family Farm: Social Bases of Household Production in the Era of Wage Labor," *Comparative Studies in Sociology and History*, v. 20, 1978.

16. Owram, *Promise of Eden*, p. 137.

17. Francis, *Images of the West*, p. 233.

18. Elizabeth B. Mitchell *In Western Canada Before the War: Impressions of Early Twentieth Century Prairie Communities*, Saskatoon: Western Producer Prairie Books, 1981 (1915), p. 150n.

19. Wilfrid Eggleston, "The Old Homestead: Romance and Reality," in *The Settlement of the West*, edited by Howard Palmer, Calgary: University of Calgary, Comprint Publishing Company, p. 117.

20. Mrs. [Marian] Cran, *A Woman in Canada*, Toronto: Musson, c1908.

21. National Archives of Canada (hereafter NAC), MG 30 C16 Saskatchewan Homestead Experiences, "Pioneering in the West," p. 418.

22. Jean Burnet, *Next-Year Country: A study of rural social organization in Alberta*, Toronto: University of Toronto Press, (1951) 1978, p. 21.

23. Troughton, *A Bachelor's Paradise*, p. 5.

24. Mitchell, *In Western Canada Before the War*, p. 150.

25. *Hanna Herald*, 5/6/1913, cited in Burnet, *Next Year Country*, p. 19.

26. Ebe Koeppen, diary, reprinted in Rolf Knight, *Stump Ranch Chronicles and Other Narratives*, Vancouver: New Star Books, 1977, pp. 120, 121, 129.

27. Leonora M. Pauls, "The English Language Folk and Traditional Songs of Alberta: Collection and Analysis for Teaching Purposes," M.Mus., University of Calgary, 1981, p. 144.

28. NAC MG 30 C16, Saskatchewan Homesteading Experiences, Vol. II, "Pioneering in the Canadian West," pp. 368, 369, 370.

29. Edward ffolkes to Mother, 15/12/1881, in Wells, ed., *Letters from a young emigrant in Manitoba*, p. 100. For a brief biography of ffolkes, see Patrick A. Dunae, *Gentlemen Emigrants: From the British Public Schools to the Canadian Frontier*, Vancouver: Douglas & McIntyre, 1981, pp. 82-4.

30. Troughton, *A Bachelor's Paradise*, pp. 5-6.

31. "Bachelor Stock Raising," *Nor'-West Farmer*, 6/2/1899, p. 94.

32. Mitchell, *In Western Canada Before the War*, p. 47.

33. Koeppen in Knight, *Stump Ranch Chronicles*, p. 58.

34. NAC MG 31 H15, S. Jickling Papers, unpublished manuscript, "Hoosier Valley," 29/6/1963, p. 78.

35. Cited in Barry Broadfoot, *The Pioneer Years, 1895-1914: Memories of Settlers Who Opened the West*, Toronto: Doubleday, 1976, p. 138.

36. *Qu'Appelle Vidette*, 14/1885, p. 3.

37. In 1911, adult males (21 years and over) outnumbered females 137.7 to 100 in Manitoba, 181.2 to 100 in Saskatchewan, and 184.3 to 100 in Alberta. *Census of Canada, 1921*, Vol. II, Table 26, p. 124.

38. NAC MG 30 C87, John Grossman Papers, unpublished manuscript, "Why I left Germany," nd, p. 28.

39. Saskatchewan Archives Board (hereafter SAB), X2, Pioneer Questionnaires, #5 Recreation and Social Life, David H. Maginnes.

40. C. A. Dawson and Eva R. Younge, *Pioneering in the Prairie Provinces: The Social Side of the Settlement Process*, Toronto: Macmillan, 1940, p. 310.

41. Troughton, *A Bachelor's Paradise*, pp. 4, 6.

42. *Ibid.*, p. 6.

43. Mitchell, *In Western Canada Before the War*, p. 46.

44. Marjorie Harrison, *Go West – Go Wise! A Canadian Revelation*, London: Edward Arnold, 1930, p. 134.

45. ffolkes to Mother, 15/12/1881, in Wells, ed., *Letters from a young emigrant*, p. 100.

46. Koeppen in Knight, *Stump Ranch Chronicles*, p. 66.

47. Canada Department of the Interior, *Twentieth Century Canada*, 1906. But for much evidence to the contrary, see accounts of pioneer women such as Binnie-Clark, *Wheat and Woman*; Cran, *A Woman in Canada*; Susan Jackel, ed., *A Flannel Shirt and Liberty: British Emigrant Gentlewomen in the Canadian West, 1880-1914*, Vancouver: University of British Columbia Press, 1982; and see Marilyn Barber, ""The Empire is Women's Sphere": British Female Immigration to Canada, 1884-1914," Paper presented to the *Imperial Canada, 1867-1917* Conference, Centre of Canadian Studies, Edinburgh, Scotland, 1995.

48. Kathleen Strange, *With the West in Her Eyes: The Story of a Modern Pioneer*, Toronto: George J. McLeod, 1937, p. vii.

49. Raymond Williams, *Keywords: A Vocabulary of Culture and Society*, New York: Oxford University Press, 1976, p. 129; E. P. Thompson, *The Making of the English Working Class*, New York: Penguin Books, (1963) 1982, p. 9.

50. Women could "batch," but they could only homestead if they were heads of households, thus they could not be bachelor homesteaders.

51. For some of the elements of late nineteenth and early twentieth century Canadian manliness, see Gerald Redmond, ""Muscular Christianity" in Colonial Canada, 1830-1912," unpublished paper presented to the American Historical Association Annual Meeting, Los Angeles, 28-30 December 1981; Morris Mott, "The British Protestant Pioneers and the Establishment of Manly Sports in Manitoba, 1870-1886," *Journal of Sport History*, 7:3, Winter 1990; J. A. Mangan and J. Wolvin, eds., *Manliness and Morality: Middle-Class Masculinity in Britain and America, 1800-1940*, Manchester: Manchester University Press, 1987; Mark C. Carnes and Clyde Griffen, eds., *Meanings for Manhood: Constructions of Masculinity in Victorian America*, Chicago: University of Chicago Press, 1990.

52. See for example Richard Allen, ed., *A Region of the Mind: Interpreting the Western Canadian Plains*, Regina: Canadian Plains Research Centre, University of Regina, 1973; John W. Bennett and Seena B. Kohl, "Characterological, Strategic, and In-

stitutional Interpretations of Prairie Settlement," in A. W. Rasporich, ed., *Western Canada: Past and Present*, Calgary: McClelland and Stewart West, 1975.

53. Harold Baldwin, *A Farm For Two Pounds: Being the Odyssey of an Emigrant*, London: John Murray, nd [c1910], p. 45.

54. Glenbow-Alberta Institute (hereafter GAI), A.5874/1, John Stokoe Papers, Stokoe to Father, 9/8/1903.

55. S. J. Ferns and H. S. Ferns, *Eighty Five Years in Canada*, Winnipeg: Queenston House, 1978, p. 53.

56. Kohl, *Working Together*, p. 31.

57. G. A. Cameron, cited in [Alexander Begg], *Plain Facts from Farmers in the Canadian North-west*, London: CPR, 1885, p. 48.

58. W. M. Champion, cited in [Alexander Begg], *Practical Hints from Farmers in the Canadian North-West*, London: Canadian Pacific Railway, 1885, p. 9; Robert Christy Miller, *Manitoba described: Being a Series of General Observations upon the Farming, Climate, Sport, Natural History, and future Prospects of the Country*, London: Wyman and Sons, 1885, p. 105; W. Henry Barneby, *Life and Labour in the Far, Far West: Being Notes of a Tour in the Western States, British Columbia, Manitoba, and the North-West Territory*, London: Cassell and Company, 1884, p. 338.

59. F. Woodcutter, "What Rev. F. Woodcutter, Parish Priest, has to say about his experiences in Canada, and especially about the Esterhaz colony, Kaposvar Post Office, Assiniboia, Canada, July, 1902," in [Paul Oscar Esterhazy], *The Hungarian Colony of Esterhaz, Assiniboia, North-west Territories, Canada*, reprinted in Martin Louis Kovacs, *Esterhazy and Early Hungarian Immigration to Canada: A Study Based Upon the Esterhazy Immigration Pamphlet*, Regina: Canadian Plains Studies, 1974, p. 78.

60. "Ruskin on Labor," *Nor'-West Farmer*, 6/2/1899, p. 100.

61. For examples of the loosening of sex-typed roles on the prairie frontier, see the many reminiscences by prairie women in manuscript collections of the prairie archives. For an accessible collection, see Eliane Leslau Silverman *Women on the Alberta Frontier 1880-1930*, Montreal: Eden Press, 1984. See also Seena B. Kohl, *Working Together: Women and Family in Southwestern Saskatchewan*, Toronto: Holt, Rinehart and Winston, 1976, p. 33.

62. Compare, for example, with the response by male typographical workers to the threatened encroachment into their trade by female workers, in Cockburn, *Brothers*.

63. For a discussion of the muting of gender antagonisms through mutually supportive gender-distinguished work roles, see Ella Johansson, "Beautiful Men, Fine Women and Good Work People: Gender and Skill in Northern Sweden, 1850-1950," *Gender and History*, 1:2, Summer 1989.

64. Dawson and Young, *Pioneering in the Prairie Provinces*, Chapter II, "The Settlement Cycle in the Prairie Region," pp. 11-25.

65. Author's calculations, from *Census of Canada, 1921*, Vol. II, Table 28, pp. 128-9, 154-7.

66. For comparative studies, see Steven Hahn and Jonathan Prude, eds., *The Countryside in the Age of Capitalist Transformation: Essays in the Social History of Rural America*, Chapel Hill: University of North Carolina Press, 1985; Christopher Clark "Household Economy, Market Exchange, and the Rise of Capitalism in the Connecticut Valley, 1800-1860," *Journal of Social History*, 13:2, 1979; John Shover,

First Majority – Last Minority: The Transformation of Rural Life in America, Northern Illinois University Press: DeKalb, Illinois, 1976.

67. Allan Kulikoff, "The Transition to Capitalism in Rural America," *William and Mary Quarterly*, 3rd Series, XLVI, January 1989, pp. 141-144. Kulikoff finds that "Yeomen were embedded in capitalist world markets and yet alienated from capitalist social and economic relations." (p. 144.) In the prairie west, this applies to a much greater extent in theory than in practice, as evidenced by the disjuncture between ideology and reality. Conflicting attitudes were often held at the same time.

68. William Pettinger, *A Prairie Letter*, Berwick, 1969, p. 14.

69. Author's calculations; 12,669 farm workers were listed as heads of families. *Census*, 1931, Vol. V, Table 45, pp. 786, 796, 802.

70. Author's calculations; there were 150,038 single and 23,632 married farm workers and farmers' sons, and 51,549 single and 195,822 married farmers. *Census*, 1931, Vol. VII, Table 54, pp. 644-5.

71. NAC RG 76, Immigration Branch Records, Vol. 234, File 135755, part 5, John Barnett to W. J. Egan, 2/4/1927. See other letters in this file. See also GAI, BN .C212 G, Canadian Pacific Railway (hereafter CPR) Papers, James Colley Correspondence; P. L. Naismith Correspondence.

72. *Ibid.*, part 6, C. W. Vernon to Barnett, 20/5/1927.

73. For example, the CPR's Colonization Department, involved in farm labour placement, reported in 1926 that the local colonization boards placed orders for only 53 married couples and 98 families, but 13,494 single men. This was typical of placements throughout the decade. GAI BN.C212 G, CPR Papers, Advisory Committee Papers, "The Departmental Organization in Western Canada," [1926].

74. See for example NAC RG 76, Immigration Branch Records, Volume 234, File 13577, part 5, John Barnett to W. J. Egan, 2/4/1927, and other letters in the file.

75. Manitoba Department of Agriculture, *Annual Report*, 1920, p. 12.

76. "What your Ambitious Friends are doing," *The Farm and Ranch Review*, 5/11/1920, p. 6.

77. Duncan Marshall, *Farm Management*, Canada: Imperial Oil, 1931, p. 65.

78. Maurice Fitzgerald, *The Status of Farm Labour in Saskatchewan*, MA, McMaster University, 1926, p. 35. This thesis contains much personal observation and is useful as a primary source.

79. Cecilia Danysk, "Against the Grain: Accommodation to Conflict in Labour-Capital Relations in Prairie Agriculture, 1880-1930," PhD, McGill University, 1991, pp. 303-36; Ian MacPherson and John Herd Thompson, "The Business of Agriculture: Farmers and the Adoption of "Business Methods," 1880-1950," in Peter Baskerville, ed., *Canadian Papers in Business History*, Vol. I, Victoria: Public History Group, University of Victoria, 1989.

80. GAI BN .C212 G, CPR Papers, P. L. Naismith Correspondence, File 189, P. L. Naismith to H. A. Kuhn, 25/2/1925.

81. For discussion of the moral and social reform campaigns primarily in central Canada, see for example Linda Kealey, ed., *A Not Unreasonable Claim: Women and Reform in Canada, 1880s-1920s*, Toronto: Women's Educational Press, 1979; Mariana Valverde, *The Age of Light, Soap and Water: Moral Reform in English Canada, 1885-1925*, Toronto: McClelland and Stewart, 1991.

82. See for example, Cran, *A Woman in Canada*, pp. 108-110; Jackel, ed., *A Flannel Shirt and Liberty*; Voisey, *Vulcan*, p. 213; Burnet, *Next-Year Country*, p. 69. For the American experience, see Julie Roy Jeffrey, *Frontier Women: The Trans-Mississippi West, 1840-1880*, New York: Hill and Wang, 1979; Sandra Myers, *Westering Women and the Frontier Experience, 1800-1915*, Albuquerque: University of New Mexico Press, 1982; Glenda Riley, *Frontierswomen: The Iowa Experience*, Ames: Iowa University State Press, 1981.

83. Mark Rosenfeld has found that even in a non-frontier area, men who were temporarily without their wives engaged in a "bachelor culture of recreation." Rosenfeld, ""It was a hard life"," pp. 262-3. See also Kohl, *Working Together*, pp. 34-6.

84. Compare with similar attitudes toward other groups of single men: Robert Harney, "Men Without Women: Italian Migrants in Canada, 1885-1930," in Betty Boyd Caroli, Robert F. Harney and Lydia F. Tomasi, eds., *The Italian Immigrant Woman in North America*, Toronto: The Multicultural History Society of Ontario 1978; Karen Dubinsky, *Improper Advances: Rape and Heterosexual Conflict in Ontario, 1880-1929*, Chicago: University of Chicago Press, 1993.

85. "Is the Average Home Sanitary?" *Grain Growers' Guide*, 13/9/1922, p. 13.

86. *Grain Growers' Guide*, 23/9/1925, p. 18.

87. "A Mother of Two" to editor of "Sunshine" column, *Grain Growers' Guide*, 16/10/1912.

88. James Forbes Newman, "The Impact of Technology upon Rural Southwestern Manitoba, 1920-1930," MA, Queen's University, 1971.

89. See for example John MacDougall, *Rural Life in Canada, Its Trends and Tasks*, Toronto: University of Toronto Press, (1913) 1973.

90. *Farmer's Advocate*, 16/6/1920, p. 1028; 17/11/1920, p. 1854.

91. Harrison, *Go West – Go Wise!*, p. 131.

92. David C. Jones, ""There is Some Power About the Land" – The Western Agrarian Press and Country Life Ideology," *Journal of Canadian Studies*, 17:3, Fall 1982, p. 96.

93. *Grain Growers' Guide*, 1/4/1926, p. 31.

94. *Canadian Power Farmer*, June 1923, p. 4.

95. "Do You Want Your Daughter to Marry a Farmer?" *Grain Growers' Guide*, 8 March 1922, p. 15. For an assessment of the letter as a reflection of farm womens' unpaid labour, see Mary Kinnear, ""Do You Want Your Daughter to Marry a Farmer?": Women's Work on the Farm, 1922," in Donald H. Akenson, ed., *Canadian Papers in Rural History*, Vol. VI, Gananoque, Ontario: Langdale Press, 1988.

96. Hedley, "Relations of Production of the "Family Farm"," p. 78.

97. Winfield S. Hall, "Sex Instruction for the Country Boy," *Rural Manhood*, 1:4, April 1910, p. 9.

98. D. Vandercook, "Rural Delinquency," *Rural Manhood*, 4:5, May 1913, p. 151.

99. Fitzgerald, *Status of Farm Labour*.

100. Provincial Archives of Alberta (hereafter PAA), 69.289, Premier's Papers, Employment Bureau, File 508, F. W. Crandall to Greenfield, 5/7/1923.

101. GAI BN .C212 G, CPR Papers, James Colley Correspondence, Memorandum James Colley to Van Scoy, 10/10/1928.

102. *Labour Gazette*, 1929, p. 496.

103. Danysk, "Against the Grain," pp. 111-155.

104. Nancy Forestall has discovered a "homosocial bachelor culture" in a predominantly-

male mining community in Northern Ontario, in which the ideology of the family was largely absent and emphasis was placed on the "rough" rather than the "respectable" elements of masculinity. Nancy Forestall, "The Rough and Respectable: Gender Construction in the Porcupine Mining Camp, 1909-1920," paper presented at the Canadian Historical Association Annual Meeting, Kingston, 1991.

105. "Farm Laborer's Point of View," *Farmers' Advocate*, 23/4/1925, p. 636.

106. Provincial Archives of Manitoba (hereafter PAM), MG10/E1, United Farmers of Manitoba Papers, Box 12, United Farm Women of Manitoba, Survey of Farm Homes, Questionnaire, 1922.

107. Dean Davenport to the *Industrial Commission*, 1899, cited in Paul Taylor, "The American Hired Hand: His Rise and Decline," *Land Policy Review*, VI:1, Spring 1943, p. 12.

108. Kathleen Strange, *With the West in Her Eyes: The Story of a Modern Pioneer*, Toronto: George J. McLeod, 1937, p. 253. See also, for example, Barons History Book Club, *Wheat Heart of the West*, Barons, Alberta: Barons History Book Club, 1972, p. 246.

109. "Wants Farmer Protected," letter from Farmer, Saskatchewan to Editor, *Nor'-West Farmer*, 20/2/1920, p. 230.

110. "Labor for Live Stock," *Nor'-West Farmer*, 20/7/1920, p. 1057.

111. Gaston Giscard, *Dans La Prairie Canadienne*, trans. by Lloyd Person, ed. by George E. Durocher, Regina: Canadian Plains Research Centre, 1982, p. 13.

112. This strategy is examined more fully in Cecilia Danysk, *Hired Hands: Labour and the Development of Prairie Agriculture, 1880-1930*, Toronto: McClelland and Stewart, 1995, Chapter 8.

113. PAM MG 8/B9, Charles Drury Papers, pp. 22, 24.

114. GAI BN .C212 G, CPR Papers, James Colley Correspondence, File 692, James Colley to Vanscoy, 7/4/1926.

115. *Ibid.*, File 1484, James Colley to Robert Stuart, 25/10/1925.

116. "Hired Men Want to Quit," *Nor'-West Farmer*, 20/7/1920, p. 1052.

The Limitations of

the Pioneering Partnership:

The Alberta Campaign

for Homestead Dower, 1909-1925

CATHERINE CAVANAUGH

U ntil recently, scholarly investigation of "first wave" feminism in Canada has focused on the campaign to win votes for women.[1] This emphasis on the suffrage question has led to a narrow interpretation of women's political aims and obscured the significance of regional differences in the evolution of women's organized reform activities in Canada. Thus, the relative success of the votes for women campaign in the three prairie provinces has led to a view of the early women's movement in Western Canada as peaceful, popular and short. According to Catherine L. Cleverdon, *The Woman Suffrage Movement In Canada* (1950), in Alberta and Saskatchewan "it was only necessary to arouse enough general interest in the issue to ask for and receive the franchise."[2]

Cleverdon's interpretation is based on assumptions about frontier democracy and the pioneering partnership of men and women who worked side by side in settling the West. She argues that democracy triumphed on the Canadian prairies, as it did on the American frontier, because men were quick to recognize women's contribution to Western settlement.[3] As a result, men in Western Canada were more willing than their Eastern counterparts to grant women a greater share of political power. This view of frontier-as-equalizer persists in the literature. In his introduction to the 1974 reissue of Cleverdon's book, Ramsay Cook argues that in the fight to win the vote Western women enjoyed an advantage as "equal partner in pioneering conditions" which made it difficult for their husbands to "fall back on the argument of the different spheres."[4] Subsequently, Carol Bacchi has extended the pioneering partnership argument to include shared social, economic, and moral reform objectives. She maintains that class solidarity and agrarian radicalism formed the basis of co-operation between prairie feminists and Western progressives.[5]

This analysis founders when applied to the struggle for "homestead" dower in Alberta, a campaign whose main objective was shared ownership in the proceeds of the pioneering partnership.[6] Beginning in 1909, provincial women called for legislation guaranteeing the married woman an interest in the matrimonial home. Their efforts culminated, in 1925, in a failed bid to establish the wife's equal right to family property. The fight for dower legislation was a direct assault on arbitrary male privilege which guaranteed sole possession of family assets to the husband. An examination of the Alberta campaign calls into question prevailing notions about frontier democracy in the Canadian West, and raises fundamental questions concerning family relations to reveal patriarchy preserved on the prairies.

The first stirring of an organized woman's rights movement began in Alberta in 1909 with a campaign to secure property rights for women. Two main objectives were at stake: equal rights with men to the "free" homesteads being distributed by federal authorities and provincial legislation guaranteeing the married woman a dower interest in her husband's estate. By 1913, the intense campaign for equal homesteading privileges for women being waged in all three prairie provinces had met with little success and became bogged down in the question of federal-provincial jurisdiction over natural resources.[7] It continued sporadically until 1930 when Ottawa finally granted Alberta and Saskatchewan control over natural resources and crown lands.[8] Although the Alberta legislation was immediately amended to allow any "person" over the age of eighteen to qualify for a homestead, this victory came too late to benefit many women. Western immigration had long since peaked and prime agricultural land was already largely settled. A few women were able to claim homesteads, chiefly in Alberta's Peace River district. In Saskatchewan and Manitoba, homesteading privileges were abolished altogether.

The struggle for married women's dower rights, on the other hand, gained momentum. In part, it benefited from the fight for woman suffrage, which became the central focus of the provincial women's movement from 1913 to 1917, and from an acceleration of the women's club movement during the period of the Great War. Both in its organization and its leadership, the dower campaign was dominated by middle class women with an obvious interest in property rights. However, in a predominantly rural and agricultural province, property laws directly affected the overwhelming majority of women. The campaign was launched by the Women's Christian Temperance Union (WCTU) and the local National Council of Women of Canada (NCWC). While the WCTU and the NCWC continued to play a leading role in the campaign, other women's clubs and organizations were quick to join their voices to the call for legislation guaranteeing the married woman a right in family property. This dynamic coalition varied over time and included provincial suffrage associations, the Women's Canadian Club, the Canadian Women's Press Clubs, the Women's University Club of Edmonton and women's patriotic clubs such as the Next-of-Kin Association and the War Widows Association. In rural areas the campaign was supported by the Women's Institute (WI) and the United Farm Women of Alberta (UFWA). From 1916, when it won independence from its parent organization, the United Farmers of Alberta (UFA), the UFWA dominated the struggle to secure property rights to the married woman. Supported by farm and labour women, the UFWA was instrumental in introducing the concept of matrimonial property, or the equal division of family assets between wife and husband, into the dower debate.[9]

The Alberta campaign also benefited from the skill, energy and sheer persistence of individual women, most notably, the so-called "Famous Five" Alberta women associated with the Persons Case of 1928-29.[10] As provincial president of the WCTU, Louise Crummy McKinney was a driving force behind the early petitions and considered the achievement of dower legislation among her proudest accomplishments. Henrietta Muir Edwards,

McKinney's counterpart in the NCWC and long-time convenor of the Council's Committee on Laws, provided critical legal expertise. Edwards' pioneering work on the legal status of women in Canada and Alberta helped to draw attention to legal discrimination against women and the urgent need for legislative reform. Emily Murphy quickly established herself as an outspoken advocate of the rights of the married woman following her arrival in Edmonton in 1907. She spoke and wrote widely on the dower issue and was a major contributor to early draft legislation. Murphy's appointment as the first woman magistrate in the British Empire in 1917 was a significant victory for the reform movement and gave added authority to her criticism of sex-based legal discrimination. Nellie McClung, popular writer, feminist, politician, and social activist, was equally critical of male power and privilege. McClung's celebrity assured her a wide audience which she used effectively to advance the cause of women. In her novel, *Purple Springs*, published in 1921, McClung provided one of the most scathing indictments of man-made laws to come out of the campaign.[11] As President of the UFWA and Minister Without Portfolio in the United Farmers' government, Irene Parlby presided over the campaign in rural Alberta. Parlby was widely seen as women's representative; however, as the lone woman in cabinet, she faced an up-hill battle in her attempts to persuade her male colleagues to take action on property rights for married women. With the support of farm women, she did introduce a matrimonial property bill in the legislature in 1925 aimed at guaranteeing the wife an equal share in family assets, and headed a provincial enquiry into the law as it affected women's property rights during marriage.

Women's claim to an interest in family property took two forms. On the one hand, they demanded equal rights with their husband to property they had helped to acquire and maintain through their joint labour. On the other hand, they sought special protection for the wife in the event of her husband's death or desertion, or following marriage breakdown. These two arguments, one based on "sameness," the other on "difference," appear to be logically contradictory. In fact, they accurately reflected women's material circumstances. Women's simultaneous claim to the same property rights as men as well as special protections for the wife was motivated by recognition of the injustice of laws that discriminated against women on the basis of sex alone, an uncomplicated resentment of arbitrary male power and privilege, and a cognizance of women's unique social value as wives and mothers. One author has explained this paradox in nineteenth and early twentieth century feminism by pointing out that "'women's sphere' was both the point of oppression and the point of departure."[12] This contradiction in women's lives led critics in Alberta to see the married woman's relationship to family property as both the locus and the symbol of her subordination. In her attack on laws that perpetuated the economic dependence of the married woman, Emily Murphy called for the full recognition of women's domestic labour, stating that "the work of a wife who rears a family; who contributes to the upbuilding of a home; who aids and comforts her husband is worthy of the most valuable consideration. . . . Yet, by law, she has no pay, no property, no possessions and is even dependent for her food and clothing." According to Murphy "the thing sought is that the wife shall no longer be considered as a 'kept' or 'supported' person."[13] Lillie Young McKinney (no relation to Louise McKinney), a member of the Calgary UFWA, also saw the question of property rights as central to women's equality, arguing that while "some authorities (see) the status of the married woman . . . settled by the franchise, . . . in our present plan of life it might be questioned whether a truer test is not the standing of the married woman regarding property rights."[14]

The legal disabilities imposed on married women were firmly established in the laws of England received into Alberta on September 1, 1905.[15] Under English law a married woman controlled her separate property; however, she had no right to the matrimonial home usually held in her husband's name or to property or income acquired by joint labour with her husband. Following from the ancient doctrine of coverture, the husband's proprietary right to his wife's services prevented a married woman from claiming any direct compensation for her domestic labour.[16] Thus, the pioneering woman who worked with her husband in building family assets was entirely dependent on him for her economic well-being. Furthermore, in the event of her husband's death, a woman had almost no protection against the loss of her home. In the case of farm women, this meant the loss of her very livelihood. Although a widow could ask the court to grant her a portion of her husband's property if he died without a will, the married man had an absolute right to dispose of part or all of his property before his death or by will, thus defeating his wife's right to an interest in his estate.[17]

The widow's interest was well established in England before the Norman conquest and was recognized in the Magna Carta.[18] In its final evolved form, common law dower was reduced from an absolute right to a portion of her deceased husband's property to a life interest in one-third of the free-hold estates which he had held at any time during the marriage. This dower interest arose at the time of marriage, existing as an inchoate right which was consummated following the death of the husband. It attached to land and thus could not be defeated by sale or disposition by will without the wife's consent. The extent of the wife's dower right was greatly eroded in English law in 1833, allowing the husband to dispose of his property as he saw fit during his lifetime or by will, thereby defeating his wife's dower.[19] Under these provisions dower became an illusory protection since it was made contingent upon the husband not depleting the estate. Dower was abolished in the Canadian West by the Territories *Real Property Act* of 1886.[20] Part of the Dominion Government's settlement policy for the Northwest Territories, the Act introduced a Torrens system of land registration.[21] Since common law dower created an invisible encumbrance on the title, it was held to be inconsistent with this attempt to rationalize land registration on the prairies and was eliminated.

The combined effect of federal and territorial law was to ensure that, in the newest of the provinces, land, and therefore wealth, was to be overwhelmingly owned and controlled by men, thus reinforcing a traditional patriarchal social order that dictated a dependent womanhood. While the lure of the frontier lay in the promise of opportunity in the form of "free" land, the vast majority of women were excluded by regulations from access to homesteads available to any man over eighteen.[22] Only if she were head of a household could a woman earn title to a quarter section of land by farming it. Under the terms of the *Dominion Lands Act* of 1872, homesteads could only be granted to women who were widows, divorcees, separated or deserted wives, provided that they had children under the age of eighteen dependent on them for support. Each application was carefully scrutinized, and where there was doubt as to a woman's status as the sole head of a family, the Act gave full discretion to the minister to approve or reject it.[23] In

1910, Frank Oliver, Minister of the Interior, gave clear proof of the kind of consideration women could expect when he was asked to rule in the case of Mrs. Oxilia Grant, a widow whose daughter, although an adult, was an invalid and totally dependent on her mother for support. Despite the Act's provision for "a widow who has a daughter over 21 years of age . . . [who] through physical infirmity is dependent for support upon the widowed mother," Grant's application was refused and returned along with Oliver's hastily scrawled reply, "Not eligible. Daughter is not a minor."[24]

The prohibitions against women as homesteaders severely restricted women's participation in the chief economic opportunity offered by the frontier. According to one informal survey conducted by the woman's editor of a popular farm journal, in 1916 only twenty-one women were operating farms independently in Alberta.[25] A number of these women were widows but it is not clear how many had qualified under homestead legislation. Women could, of course, purchase land, provided they had adequate funds or could convince their local banker to provide the necessary financing. The autobiography of Georgina Binnie-Clark, English gentlewoman turned Saskatchewan grain grower, reveals the prejudice of western lending institutions as only one of the many obstacles encountered by women who chose to defy convention and pursue farming as an occupation.[26] The success of Binnie-Clark and others like her should have been ample evidence that the "fair sex" could "prove up" on homesteads as well as men but conventional wisdom insisted that work on the land was "men's work."[27] Frank Oliver, Laurier's Minister of the Interior, defended government policy as "in the best interests of the west" since "the object of giving homesteads is to make the land productive, and this would not be the case if held by women."[28] In private Oliver apparently went further, arguing to Cora Hind that "to admit [women] to the opportunities of the land-grant would be to make them [sic] independent of marriage."[29]

Denied a right to family property and to an interest in her husband's estate, a married woman and her dependent children in pre-World War I Western Canada were threatened with extreme hardship and even destitution in the event of her husband's prolonged absence or death. At the turn of the century, Alberta was a predominantly rural, agricultural society which offered few economic opportunities outside of farming.[30] It is true that as the population increased, urban development opened jobs to women in what have since come to be seen as traditional areas of female employment. Women worked as teachers, nurses, and in a variety of public and private sector service industries as clerks, bookkeepers, secretaries, telephone and telegraph operators.[31] Women were in high demand as domestic servants and skilled milliners and dressmakers. Some women found employment in factories like Great Western Garment of Edmonton, and a few carved out successful careers in the professions as doctors, lawyers, writers and newspaper editors. Still others operated their own shops, boarding houses, and maternity homes.

Although women could and did support themselves in such occupations, limited opportunity, low wages and harsh working conditions militated against women remaining in the paid labour force following marriage. Statistics show that during the early decades of the twentieth century the vast majority of adult women living in Alberta were married.[32] While there is little reliable information on the number of married women in the paid work-force, census figures show that in 1911 of the total number of people "gainfully employed" in Edmonton and Calgary only 7.3% were women.[33] Ten years later, slightly more than a quarter of this work-force was female. Although women worked more hours than men, women's income accounted for only 16.5% of total yearly earnings.[34] Restricted opportunities, domestic responsibilities and social disapproval of working mothers meant that few women continued to work for wages outside the home following marriage. As a result, the overwhelming majority of women were wholly or largely dependent on their husband for their economic well-being.

While most married men presumably provided for their families as their means allowed, a significant minority did not. Scattered and incomplete records make it difficult to ascertain with any accuracy the extent to which married women suffered as a result of disinheritance, desertion or their husband's penury. The evidence that does exist, however, suggests that abandonment, neglect and violence against women and children were serious social problems encountered on the frontier.[35] When violence and neglect did occur, the economic consequences were exacerbated by severe climatic conditions, isolation and the absence of kin who might have provided protection against hardship.

As police magistrate, Emily Murphy received a number of appeals for assistance from destitute women. One young Edmonton mother with four children under the age of seven years, and "no mother nor anyone" to turn to, confided that her husband had refused to provide for their eldest child to attend school and the previous winter she and her children had "nearly froze and starved to death . . . going without winter underwear or shoes part of the time . . . [they] had no blankets . . . and had to sleep with [their] clothing on . . . the little ones going many a night without food."[36] Unable to provide for herself and her children, she was afraid that if she remained with her husband "yet another little one will be brought into the world."[37]

The evidence suggests that husbands who deserted frequently did so in the early autumn.[38] When they took the receipts from the year's harvest, their wives and children were left without sufficient funds or supplies to see them through the long Alberta winter. In the fall of 1916, Fred C. Clark of Dewberry left his family to face the winter with only three dollars and ninety cents.[39] That same year, C. M. Howe of Radway Centre took a four hundred dollar mortgage on the family farm before leaving his wife and three children "without food or clothing . . . and cold weather at hand."[40]

Desertion by their husband frequently meant that women were forced to seek paid employment. Finding few alternatives, many turned to domestic labour in other people's homes. During a ten year period of separation from her husband, a "female member" of Reverend George Hopkin's congregation in Bashaw was barely able to support herself on the thirty-five or forty dollars a month she earned "doing scrubbing and washing for a living."[41] Other women were even less fortunate. Mrs. Tetreault, for example, whose husband left her in the spring of 1918 after "renting all of the cultivating land to his neighbour," had "no way of making a support [as] she [was] old."[42] Any woman unable to find work outside her home would have little choice but to return to a violent and abusive husband. Such was the case of a woman in Hays who reported that with no means of support she was compelled to return to her husband who "licked her with a club."[43]

Accounts of physical abuse are a common feature of the many appeals for assistance from deserted wives. A letter from Mrs. McAlpine of Walsh is typical. In 1916 McAlpine wrote to the provincial Attorney General stating that she had suffered from her husband's "beatings" for sixteen years.[44] Recently, he had "threatened to stick [her] with a butcher knife" before selling his property, including several cows and sheep belonging to his wife, and leaving "for four months."[45] Jessie O. Scott of Spokane, Washington sought assistance on behalf of her sister, Mrs. John M. Spurling of Elnora, who was "hovering between life and death" as a result of "cruelty and abuse at the hands of her husband."[46] Scott reported that Spurling had forced his wife "to do a man's work in the fields, driven her about with a horsewhip, drawn a gun on her and threatened to kill her if she tried to leave him."[47] Spurling was planning to sell the family farm and return to England, leaving his wife of fourteen years with nothing. Scott asked what legal protections were available to her sister. There were none.

The law granted the married woman control and management of her separate property but offered little protection to non-wage earning women or farm wives whose labour was deemed to be a wifely duty for which they were not entitled to compensation. A married couple could hold land jointly, but few did. Title was usually registered in the name of the husband who was free to use or dispose of it as he wished. Although a married woman had no legal right to family property, her husband's home was deemed to be her home. She was guilty of desertion if he moved and she refused to move with him.[48] Forced resettlement under pioneering conditions imposed additional hardships on aging women like Mrs. Bery Murray of Murrayville, whose husband was "unsettled and like[d] to move around."[49] In law, she was compelled to follow him although she was "getting old and [did] not care to move anymore."[50] While Government officials were often sympathetic, they could only advise that married women had no remedies: "in Alberta the husband [had] a perfect right to do with his property as he please[d]."[51]

This injustice was particularly offensive when it involved a homesteader's wife like Jessie Swan of Chauvin who had laboured for twenty years, making herself "old before [her] time," only to find that her husband could "sell out" and leave her "in the lurch."[52] Another "Western Canadian Wife" with seven children confided the bitter details of her homesteading experience in an undated letter to Emily Murphy in which she states: "I left all my friends and comforts and society and came to this new country and had many trying times, endured many hardships including hunger and cold. . .

I had to do all kinds of work out doors in all kinds of weather, chop wood, carry water, milk cows, feed horses, cattle [and] pigs. . . I help in the haying and harvest . . . besides all the baking, cooking, washing . . . make my children's clothes . . . besides most of my own and my husband's. . . I am seldom from home, never get to church or parties. . . I raise lots of chickens, ducks and turkeys . . . the profits of which I never get."[53]

In response to this clear inequity in the law, women across the West began to organize. Initially, they sought to protect the widow by restricting the right of married persons to alienate their property by will, extending to all women the benefit enjoyed by widows whose husband died intestate. By 1910 their demands had escalated. That year Emily Murphy enlisted the support of a young Calgarian and member of the opposition, R.B. Bennett, to help draft a bill which would provide a married woman with a right to family property during her husband's life-time. The result of their collaboration, *An Act Respecting the Married Woman's Property Act*, was introduced in the Legislature on December 6 and received second reading later in the month.[54] In the meantime, Premier Rutherford's government had prepared its own legislation. Lacking majority support, Murphy's bill quickly died in committee but within days the Liberals passed their own *Married Woman's Relief Act*.[55] The new Act fell far short of Murphy's vision of a positive right to the wife in family property and even failed to meet the limited objective of the original petition to provide an automatic protection to the widow. Indeed, it reinforced notions of the wife's dependence since it merely granted a married woman the right to apply to the courts for relief where by the terms of her husband's will she received less of his estate than she would have if he had died intestate.[56]

Murphy must have been severely disappointed. Her bill had been defeated and her closest ally in the legislature, Bennett, dismissed as "a susceptible young man affected by the pleadings of the ladies."[57] Convinced of the urgent need for home protection and the simple justice of women's claim, Murphy took her campaign to the province's club women. Addressing the Edmonton Council of Women in October, 1911, she warned that women's reform agenda was doomed without the franchise since "their going to the Legislature was not taken seriously."[58] Indeed, in response to yet another delegation of provincial women, Alberta's Attorney General, Charles W.

Cross, dismissed any change to the existing property law as amounting to an encouragement to the wife to interfere with her husband's property during his lifetime; "Time enough after he's dead," he opined.[59]

There is no evidence that the Farmers Anti-Dower Law Association of Saskatchewan was active in Alberta; however, the legislation was widely criticized as unnecessary government interference in private family matters. Even where opinion was sympathetic to the wife, the dower remedy was seen to be worse than the "ill it [was] intended to cure" and bound to create other "injustices, tyranny and home dissensions."[60] The big obstacle to a dower law was the "Torrens title."[61] Harkening back to the original arguments for the abolition of dower in 1886, opponents feared that it would impede land sales. They argued that "in a country where land [was] transferred as frequently as it [was in Alberta], [dower] would hamper proceedings terribly if a man were compelled to always get his wife's signature when selling a piece of property."[62] According to one contemporary observer, fear that dower would place a check on Western expansion was so widespread that the "average legislator" believed he had "offered the final word on the subject, when he [sic] uttered that one word: 'Torrens'."[63]

Concern for the unfettered exchange of property would certainly have loomed large in the minds of those Albertans who stood to benefit from escalating prices as a result of the land boom that accompanied Alberta's rapid population growth during the pre-war period. Accelerated property sales must also have contributed to the sense of urgency expressed by those interested in the security of the home. Newspaper headlines told of "Women and Children Left Homeless On The Prairies" as homesteaders sold out to the highest bidder and destitute families were forced to turn to the community for support.[64] Although women in Calgary and Edmonton had some access to public relief, fledgling frontier towns were ill-equipped to respond to such emergencies and town fathers looked to the provincial government for assistance. When the town council of Hays was faced with the problem of having to assist "the wife of one of [their] ratepayers," the Secretary-Treasurer candidly admitted to the Attorney-General that they did not "wish to have her on [their] hands."[65]

The *Married Woman's Relief Act* was clearly inadequate to the mounting numbers and urgent needs of destitute women and children. Under increased pressure to provide some guarantee of protection to the family home, Arthur Sifton's newly elected Liberals passed *The Married Woman's Home Protection Act* in the spring of 1915.[66] Once again, however, legislators failed to come to grips with the question of the wife's right in family assets. The Act merely reiterated the wife's traditional right to an interest in her husband's estate by allowing her to file a caveat against the homestead. As long as the caveat remained in place, the homestead – defined as the house and buildings occupied by the wife as her home – could not be transferred, mortgaged, leased or in any way encumbered. Even supporters of the Act admitted that the caveat provision was a less than satisfactory compromise but they argued that it granted the wife "all the protection of a dower law with the objectionable feature of interference with the title eliminated."[67]

Provincial women dismissed the new legislation as a "delusion and a hoax."[68] They criticized the government for not going far enough in protecting the home against foreclosure or "where the family might own from one house upwards but [lived] in rented property."[69] The Calgary Council of Women immediately called for an amendment which would prevent a married man from encumbering or disposing of any of his property without his wife's consent. They charged that the Act was impractical and discriminatory since it required time, money and a knowledge of the law to implement.[70] More to the point, as the provincial Registrar acknowledged, filing a caveat could be interpreted by the husband as a hostile or disloyal act. After receiving a number of letters from women who feared that their husbands were preparing to dispose of their homesteads, the Registrar wrote to the new Attorney General, J. R. Boyle, stating that he could "only imagine that when a farmer's wife puts on her bonnet and spends a day in town at some law office on a mysterious mission, there is liable to be trouble at home."[71] Farmer's wives did indeed put on their bonnets but when they went to town it was to organize on their own behalf.

In 1916 the dower campaign received a much needed boost when it was joined by the United Farm Women of Alberta. Meeting in convention that year, farm women fought for and won autonomy from the United Farmers of Alberta.[72] In addition to expanding the ranks of the women's coalition, the UFWA was instrumental in shifting the emphasis in the debate away from the notion of relief to the wife, to a shared interest in property she helped to acquire and maintain.[73] In part, this was due to their newly won status as a separate, autonomous voice for farm women. Having rejected their former auxiliary status, the women could more effectively set their own agenda and pursue free and open discussions on a full range of issues which might otherwise have been directly or indirectly suppressed by the men.[74]

Historians have argued that the pioneering partnership of men and women in Western Canada lay behind the early UFA endorsement of woman suffrage, yet the organization was conspicuously silent on the issue of married women's property rights. The question of ownership of family assets seems to have been a much more thorny issue for the men. For farm women, on the other hand, the existing legal bar to ownership in family assets they had helped to acquire was a clear injustice. From the outset farm women based their claim on earned entitlement and protection against their husband's sole power to dispose of or encumber family property. In January, 1917, the UFWA passed a resolution calling for a "Dower Law" protecting women against the loss of "property for which they have toiled mightily."[75] The resolution labelled existing legislation a "great injustice" which deprived the wife of her home as well as her livelihood and demanded that all family property be protected against the "caprice" of the husband.[76] As approved by convention, the resolution applied to only one-third of family property.[77]

The entry of organized farm women into the dower debate coincided with the emergence of the UFA as the main opposition to the provincial Liberal government, and the achievement of woman suffrage in Alberta in 1916. Their links to the farm movement coupled with their newly won franchise gave farm women a powerful voice in provincial politics. If they did not directly influence the government in its decision to introduce "homestead" dower in 1917, they were a force that could not be easily ignored.

The Alberta *Dower Act* came into effect on May 1, 1917, eight years after provincial women had first called for legislation.[78] The new Act relied heavily on similar homestead laws granting the wife extensive rights in family property which were common in the American West.[79] American "homestead" or legislative dower, first introduced by the Republic of Texas in 1839, stemmed from a broad public policy that deemed the preservation of the home and security of the community of paramount importance in attracting settlers to the frontier. The substantial difference between "homestead" dower and common law dower arose out of this overriding concern for community stability and security of the home even against "just demands." As a result, it granted the wife legal rights over and above those traditionally associated with dower. The intent of common law dower was to provide a form of maintenance to the widow as a guard against economic hardship due to her husband's death. Under homestead legislation, the wife's historical claim was preserved in the form of her guaranteed use of family property after her husband's death. In addition, it established an interest in the wife that arose during her husband's lifetime. Under homestead dower, the wife's interest in family property was not contingent on her surviving her husband. It protected family property against certain kinds of creditors and limited the owner's freedom of disposition since the consent of the wife, the non-owning spouse, was required for a conveyance or encumbrance of the property.

Alberta's *Dower Act* was really a homestead act although it did not include protection against general creditors, as these provisions were already available under separate legislation.[80] Following the American example, the Act granted a married woman a life estate in the homestead arising on the death of her husband and provided that any disposition of the homestead made by a married man without his wife's written consent would be "null and void."[81] It further stated that "the domicile of the married man shall not be deemed for the purpose of this Act, to have changed unless such change of domicile is consented to in writing by the wife of such married man."[82]

The Act required consent in the form of a certificate of acknowledgement signed by the wife "apart from her husband."[83] A homestead was defined in the Act as "the dwelling house and the land on which it was situated," that is, "not more than four [city] lots" or "one quarter section."[84]

The new Act was heralded by the local press as marking the completion of the emancipation of Alberta women. In an attempt to appeal to the new woman voter, the pro-government Edmonton *Bulletin* provided a complete review of legislative reforms concerning women and concluded that "this act, coupled with all the beneficent legislation that the Sifton government [had] already passed in the interests of women, place[d] the fair sex of Alberta on a very high plane indeed . . . making legislation for women one of the outstanding features of the Sifton regime."[85] Quoting almost verbatim from the government's own press release, the paper declared that, together with the recently enacted equal suffrage bill, the new *Dower Act* placed Alberta women in a more favoured legal position than women in most countries around the world.

Reaction from organized women, while generally positive, was more mixed. Although Henrietta Muir Edwards praised the Premier and members of his cabinet for their "courteous and sympathetic understanding" of women's concerns, she also noted that the question of equal parental rights remained to be resolved.[86] The Alberta Council criticized the Act for its failure to protect the wife's livelihood, pointing out that legislators had given the widow "a home, but only the use for life of an empty house and accompanying land without any provision for furniture in the home or means of working the land."[87] Rural women were particularly outraged by the government's failure to recognize the property right of the wife. The UFWA responded to the government's legislation by calling for laws guaranteeing the married woman an equal share in family property. It demanded that dower be abolished and replaced with the statutory recognition of "the principle of community (of) interests of husband and wife with regard to property acquired as a result of their common labour and effort."[88] Premier Sifton firmly refused this new demand. He claimed that his government had already granted provincial women legal rights "in advance of any of the Western Provinces" and he contemplated "no change in the existing laws."[89]

Although homestead dower had gone further than any previous legislation in guaranteeing the married woman's interest in the family home, Alberta women were quick to point out its serious shortcomings. The Act had not created a property right in the wife that she could deal with in her own name. It merely provided a life interest to the widow in her husband's homestead. That is, upon the death of her husband, a married woman was assured the use of the family home and the land upon which it was situated for her lifetime. She could not sell or dispose of the homestead by will nor could she mortgage it or in any way encumber it. Furthermore, homestead dower did not include chattels or movables. It did not provide the wife with the use of home furnishings, farm equipment, livestock, seed or the like.

Nor could she use the homestead as collateral to raise money for business or any other purpose. As Henrietta Muir Edwards stated, dower provided that the wife "may be left the bare home or homestead, but without the wherewithal of making a living."[90]

The more significant provision of the new legislation was the prohibition against disposition of the homestead without the wife's written consent. Unlike the wife's right to a life interest in her husband's estate, section 3 of the Act did not depend upon the wife surviving her husband but, as described by Mr. Justice Ives, of the Alberta court, "secured the home to the wife during her husband's life."[91] Yet serious doubt was cast over this very right barely a year after the Act was passed.

In May of 1918 Kasko Choma and her husband, Petro, brought an action under the new Dower legislation, contesting the sale of land, including their homestead, to the defendant, Mr. Chmelyk.[92] Initially, all appears to have gone well following the agreement of sale which the parties had entered into the previous year. Chmelyk had made a $1,000.00 down payment and agreed to pay the remaining $2,650.00 in annual instalments over a seven year period. He proceeded to farm the land and the Chomas remained in the "dwelling house" as agreed. Sometime during 1917 the Chomas must have had second thoughts about the agreement they had made with Chmelyk. During the trial they claimed that "the purchase price was grossly inadequate" and that Chmelyk had forced Petro Choma to agree to it against his will. They further charged that "the agreement for sale was entered into without the consent in writing" of Kasko Choma and that it was therefore "null and void" under section 3 of the *Dower Act*.

In his judgement Mr. Justice Scott seems to have been unaware of American homestead precedents. Instead, he referred to "Webster's Dictionary" and William Blackstone's *Commentaries on the Law of England*, published in 1765-69, for direction as to the meaning of dower and he found that "the right to dower is merely an inchoate right dependent upon the wife surviving her husband. Neither at common law nor under any English statue did it give her any rights to any interest in his lands during his lifetime."[93] Once Scott had determined that there was no significant difference between homestead dower and common law dower, it was a relatively simple step for him to completely undermine the legislation. This was the effect of his finding that "the sole intention of the Legislation was to restore the wife's right to dower [which had been abolished by the *Territories Real Property Act* in 1886] in respect to her husband's homestead . . . [and] it was not the intention [of the legislature] to extend the wife's interest in the homestead beyond that which she would have possessed had the common-law right to dower existed."[94] Having thus restricted the aim of legislative dower, Scott further limited the wife's interest when he added that "[any disposition] of his homestead by a married man without his wife's consent in writing shall be null and void *only in so far as it may prejudice or affect her estate in dower therein*."[95]

It is difficult to comprehend Scott's intention in imposing these restrictions on the wife's dower right under the legislation. He may have believed that the Chomas were attempting to use the new Act in order to withdraw from the original agreement for sale, thinking that they could obtain a higher price for their land. If, for this reason, he wanted to find in Chmelyk's favour, he might have done so in a number of ways without redefining the Act so that the wife's interest during her husband's life was all but eliminated on the erroneous grounds that it was contingent.[96]

Scott's decision became law in 1919 when the *Dower Act* was amended to say that disposition without consent was "null and void only insofar as it may affect the interest of the said wife."[97] As to the precise nature of the wife's interest, the court was divided. One year later, in *Overland* v. *Himmelford*, a husband and wife sought to evade the lease of their home charging that although the wife had signed it as though she were the lessor, she had not acknowledged her consent in writing as required under the *Dower Act*.[98] In their decisions justices Beck and Harvey held that the lease was valid, agreeing with Scott in *Choma* v. *Chmelyk* that the wife's only interest in the homestead was a life estate "which she has contingent on her surviving her husband."[99] Ironically, Beck added that the wife had a right to dispose of her dower interest since "to hold otherwise would be to put a check upon the whole present day current of legislation in favour of the equality of the sexes in regard to property and civil rights."[100] Justices Stuart and Ives were of the contrary opinion. They stated that the lease was invalid as it interfered with the clear intention of the Act "as it stood in 1918" which was "to create a right in the wife to occupy and reside in the homestead even while the husband lived and in addition to that to give her a life estate after his death."[101]

Critical of Scott's decision in *Choma* v. *Chmelyk*, Stuart went on to say that the "meaning of this new legislation . . . whether we agree with its policy or not . . . [was] to remove what was doubtless considered by the Legislature some injustice in the position of married women with respect to their homes and to give them the power to restrain the husband from alienating them."[102] "I think," he said, "the amendment of 1919 did not declare the law but altered it to the detriment of the wife."[103]

When the dower question was again brought before Stuart in 1922 in *Johnsen* v. *Johnsen*, he changed his mind. In that case the wife challenged the forced sale of the homestead to satisfy her husband's judgement debt, claiming that she had a dower interest in the land and that it could not be sold without her consent.[104] Stuart upheld the sale and in so doing contradicted his own earlier decision, stating that "whatever I may have said in Overland v Himmelford . . . [my] present opinion [is] that The Dower Act gives the wife an interest in the homestead in the nature of a life estate which vests upon the husband's death."[105]

In the meantime, in *Rigby* v. *Rigby*, the court had been asked to further define the wife's dower right. In that case the wife, living in California at the time, had placed a caveat on the homestead lands to prevent their disposition without her consent.[106] The husband having made a will leaving the land to his brother and sister applied for an order dispensing with his wife's consent to the intended testamentary disposition. The court refused to grant the order, finding that the wife had "such an interest in the homestead [the home] of her husband as to entitle her to file a caveat . . . to protect her interest" and that this was a vested interest, there being no express provision in the Act to permit a court to dispense with wife's interest in these circumstances, as there was in the case of an intestacy.[107] This decision of the court would appear to have given the wife a present vested interest in her husband's homestead during his lifetime but the Court of Appeal refused to define the wife's interest beyond the right to file a caveat since it was not asked to do so. Thus, it left the question open to interpretation and the rights of the married woman under the Act remained uncertain if not clearly diminished.

Faced with these conflicting opinions, Mr. Lorne N. Laidlaw, solicitor for Lucinda F. Nicholson of Bowmanton, Alberta, wrote to the Deputy Attorney General for clarification of the law. Nicholson had applied to the court to have her husband's lease to James Collipriest set aside on the grounds that the lands being leased included her homestead and she had not given her consent.[108] In her affidavit she stated that she had worked hard "in helping to build up . . . a comfortable home."[109] She was sixty-four years old, had "developed an affection for [her] present residence and desire[d] to spend the remainder of [her] life in it."[110] In his decision, Mr. Justice Ives stated that except for *Johnsen* v. *Johnsen*, he "would have been prepared to hold [her husband's lease] a nullity" but that decision of the Appellate court applied in this case and "the wife's application must be refused."[111] Laidlaw's client did not have the "means" to pursue the matter further in spite of the fact that the court's refusal to grant her application "appeared to violate the clear intention of the Dower Act."[112] Hence, he was seeking guidance from the Department. In a complete retreat from the spirit and intention of homestead legislation, government lawyers agreed with Ives and wondered how the courts "could ever uphold anything in contradiction of their present attitude in *Johnsen v. Johnsen*."[113] There is no evidence that Nicholson pursued her case in the courts. We can only assume that she was forced to settle for the "dwelling house and garden patch" her husband had agreed to provide for her.[114]

The thrust of the dower campaign was to establish a married woman's separate interest in family property. Women who had fought for nearly two decades for the wife's right were outraged by the courts' narrow interpretation of the *Dower Act*. Their repeated calls for amendments were refused. In 1926, Henrietta Muir Edwards charged that the court's ruling in *Johnsen v. Johnsen* was a clear violation of the original intention of the legislature. Angered by this betrayal, she attacked the government for its failure to remedy the situation. In her submission to George Hoadley, Minister of Agriculture, she protested that "99 out of 100 women have thought that the use of her home was protected. . . We had no idea women could be turned out. Every year we have been coming up asking for amendments to the Act . . . . [but] we have not got what we thought we had . . . we know now we are not protected."[115]

In the wake of the courts' decisions, the UFWA had called for the restoration of section 3 of the *Dower Act* as early as 1919. They sought an amendment that would not only clearly prevent disposition without the wife's consent but would also extend dower to include the "furnishings of the home . . . and in the case of farm women . . . the necessary supplies for the carrying on of making a living from the farm."[116] However, when a delegation of provincial women met with members of the Liberal government to discuss the proposed amendment they were turned down. Premier Stewart was "strongly opposed to anything in the way of exemptions" since, in his opinion, they tended "to work great hardship" to the creditor. However, he did offer to find some other solution so that "justice would be done the widow."[117]

Stewart's concern for the welfare of the widow came too late. It fell to the United Farmers' government to provide justice to the wife. Women across the province, particularly rural women, were encouraged by the overwhelming victory that swept the UFA into office in 1921. With two leading feminists elected to the legislature, Nellie McClung as a member of the Liberal opposition and Irene Parlby as a member of the government and Cabinet minister, they anticipated greater cooperation in realizing their reform objectives.[118] Marion L. Sears, Parlby's successor as President of the UFWA, expressed confidence that under the United Farmers' women in Alberta would be spared the "long and bitter" struggles for "just laws" waged in "older more settled regions" of the country.[119] Invoking the pioneering partnership, Sears claimed that their joint labour gave men and women in the West "a mutual regard for the rights and privileges of one another."[120]

Sear's optimism was ultimately rewarded although only in part and not until 1926. That year the UFA government restored section 3 of the *Dower Act* to its original form by striking out the objectionable wording added in 1919.[121] The new provisions also strengthened consent in some cases. As it was possible to mortgage property without documentation and thereby circumvent the consent provision, the amending legislation specifically stated that the wife's written consent was required for "every mortgage by deposit of certificate of title or other mortgage not requiring the execution of any documents."[122] In addition, the wife's dower was extended to include "the personal property of the deceased husband," but the court was granted discretionary powers to determine the extent of the personal property "in the event of any dispute arising."[123] Given earlier judgments, Alberta women had little reason to be encouraged.

Although the government's action was applauded by some women as a "great boon to many a wife whether she lives in an urban or rural municipality," others had become disillusioned with homestead dower altogether, seeing it as far too limited in principle.[124] By 1926, Emily Murphy had arrived at the conclusion that dower was one of the many "stumbling blocks" to equality in marriage since it perpetuated the economic dependence of the wife.[125] Women were no longer content with the "mere re-shuffling of the matrimonial cards," she argued, "the time had come [for] adjusting the rights and responsibilities of the marriage contract."[126] Lillie Young McKinney agreed, declaring that women had "passed the stage where they [were] asking for a "life interest" in a little corner of the "joint estate" they had helped to build."[127] She dismissed the "Little bits of favoritism in legislation" women had received thus far as insufficient if the "interests of the two home builders" were to be fully recognized in law.[128] In the course of their struggle to protect the interest of the wife, women had come to recognize the limitations of the "relief provisions" of dower as a complete solution to their continued legal subordination to the power of the husband to control family property. They had also gained confidence in their rightful claim to a share in the property they had worked to acquire and maintain. Nothing short of the recognition of "community of interest," what today is known as matrimonial property, would provide the justice they sought. According to Murphy, "Western women" were "desirous of abolishing the whole system of coverture, and of conferring equal rights and responsibilities" on both spouses.[129] Lillie Young McKinney put it more succinctly when she wrote that the wife was no longer content to "eat bread because she was her husband's wife," but rather, because "she has earned it."[130] Only under the community of interest "plan" would the old "vassalship of the wife" be abolished and her labour recognized in law.[131]

The main impetus for community of property came from organized farm women. On behalf of the UFWA, Irene Parlby introduced "An Act Establishing Community of Property As Between Husband And Wife" to the legislature in 1925.[132] Despite expressions of sympathy for women's demands, the bill was defeated and a government committee struck to investigate married women's property rights in Alberta. Parlby was named as head of the committee which included Nellie McClung, Emily Murphy, and Henrietta Muir Edwards. Following a lengthy enquiry, the committee recommended against the adoption of community of property. Notwithstanding the pioneering partnership, public opinion was against it. In the absence of widespread support, the Farmers' government was unprepared to extend to the wife the same ownership rights as her husband enjoyed in the proceeds of their joint labour. Besides, an earlier government investigation into the question had concluded that despite existing "inequalities" and "apparent injustice" in the law as it concerned married women, any solution would require "community practically on the basis of partnership."[133] In the opinion of the authors, such a remedy would do "more harm . . . than [was] realized."[134] Since the position of the married woman in Alberta was already "more favourable than in any other Province or in England," they recommended against any further reform "to attain the result of general joint ownership."[135] They anticipated that any such change would be too costly, too radical, inconvenient, unjustifiable, as well as generally too disruptive to the economy and therefore bad for business.

In the face of this opposition, and lacking government support, the failure of community of property is not surprising. Still, the proposed legislation represented a considerable achievement for Alberta women. In their struggle for justice, they had taken on centuries-old rules of law that preserved and protected the husband's authority in marriage, law which perpetuated what Jo Freeman has described as "the oldest most firmly entrenched caste system known to Western Civilization."[136] They had won significant concessions for the wife and in the process raised public awareness of the disabilities imposed on married women. Their persistent attack on oppressive, sexually-discriminating property laws had forced a public debate on the condition of women in marriage. Indeed, by exposing the limitations of the pioneering partnership as a domestic ideal, the dower campaign threatened the business of Western settlement, if only temporarily. The way out for the male-dominated political and legal establishment was to extend the wife's protection under dower, while preserving the husband's ownership in private property.

Alberta women would wait another half century for the law to recognize their right to an equal share in family property. This equality came only after yet another farm woman, Iris Murdock, failed in her claim to share in the value of the farm which she had helped to build. In *Murdock v. Murdock* the court found that the work Murdock had contributed to the family farm was "just about what the ordinary rancher's wife does" and did not entitle her to a share in it.[137] Galvanised by the court's decision, women's groups across the country fought for and won matrimonial property legislation based on the principle of joint ownership. This legislation came into effect in Alberta on January 1, 1979.[138]

Notes

1. An earlier version of this article appeared as part of my M.A. Thesis, "The Women's Movement In Alberta As Seen Through The Campaign For Dower Rights 1909–1928," (University of Alberta, 1986). I am grateful to David Jones, Nanci Langford, and Randi Warne for their support and thoughtful criticisms which were particularly helpful in the preparation of this paper.
2. Catherine L. Cleverdon, *The Woman Suffrage Movement in Canada* (1950; new ed. intro. by Ramsay Cook, Toronto, 1974: University of Toronto Press), 46.
3. Cleverdon's interpretation owes much to the "frontier thesis" of Frederick Jackson Turner, whose influential essay, "The Significance of the Frontier in American History," was first printed in the Proceedings of the State Historical Society of Wisconsin, December 14, 1893. For a discussion of the limitations of the frontier thesis as a complete explanation of the position of women in the Canadian West see Deborah Gorham, "Singing Up The Hill," *Canadian Dimension*, 10, 8 1975, 26-38.
4. Ramsay Cook, Intro., *The Woman Suffrage Movement in Canada*, Catherine Cleverdon (1950: new ed. Toronto, 1974: University of Toronto Press), xvi.
5. Carol Bacchi, "Divided Allegiances: The Response of Farm and Labour Women to Suffrage," in Linda Kealey, ed., *A Not Unreasonable Claim* (Toronto, 1979: The Women's Press), 89-107.
6. While the Alberta campaign is the focus of this paper similar campaigns were waged simultaneously by women in Manitoba and Saskatchewan.
7. The homesteads for women movement is discussed by Susan Jackel, Introd., *Wheat and Woman*, Georgina Binnie-Clark (1914; new ed., Toronto, 1979: University of Toronto Press), xx-xxxi.
8. Statutes of Alberta, 1931, 21 Geo. V, c43, s15 (1).
9. The influence of labour women on the dower campaign seems to have been largely indirect and through their association with farm women. For a discussion of this relationship see Patricia Roome, "Amelia Turner and Calgary Labour Women," in Linda Kealey and Joan Sangster, eds., *Beyond the Vote* (Toronto, 1989: University of Toronto Press), 89-117 and Bacchi, "Divided Allegiances."
10. The Persons Case refers to the Privy Council decision of October 18, 1929 which found that women were included as "persons" under Section 24 of the BNA Act

and therefore eligible for appointment to the Canadian Senate.

11. In her criticism of legal discrimination against the married woman, McClung has her character, Mrs. Pain, "The Woman With a Sore Thought," declare that she has lost all faith in male authority. "Men," Pain charges, "have made the world and they've made it to suit themselves." Nellie L. McClung, *Purple Springs* (Toronto, 1921: Thomas Allen), 126-27.

12. Nancy F. Cott, "Feminist Theory and Feminist Movements: The Past Before Us," in Juliet Mitchell and Ann Oakley, eds., *What is Feminism?* (New York, 1986: Pantheon), 51.

13. City of Edmonton Archives (CEA), Emily Murphy Papers, file 50, Janey Canuck, "Partnership in Marriage."

14. Provincial Archives of Alberta (PAA), Attorney General Papers, item 1107a.

15. Statutes of Canada, 1905, 4 Edw. VII, c. 3.

16. The husband's right to his wife's services arose from the feudal doctrine of coverture which rested on the principle of unity of person in husband and wife. Coverture established the husband as his wife's guardian and resulted in her loss of legal personality during marriage. The notion of the husband's legal primacy was given full expression by the English jurist, William Blackstone, *Commentaries on the Laws of England*, (1765-1769; George Tucker, ed., new ed., Philadelphia, 1803: Young Birch and Small). A twentieth century American jurist described coverture as resting on the "old common law fiction that the husband and wife are one. . . (which) has worked out in reality to mean . . . the one is the husband." Leo Kanowitz, *Women And The Law: The Unfinished Revolution* (Albuquerque, 1968: University of New Mexico Press), 36.

17. *An Act Respecting the Transfer And Decent of Land*, S. A. 1906 , 6 Edw. VII, c19 and *An Act Respecting The Devolution of Estates*, O.N.W.T., 1901, 1 Edw. VII, c3.

18. George L. Haskins, "The Development of Common Law Dower," *Harvard Law Review*, 62, 1948-49, 42-55.

19. *Statutes*, 3 & 4 Will. IV, c105.

20. *Territories Real Property Act*, S.C. 1886, c.26. For a discussion of the affect of this Act on dower see Wilbur F. Bowker, "Reform Of The Law Of Dower In Alberta," *Alberta Law Review*, 1, 1961, 501-515.

21. The Torrens system registered land rather than ownership. It originated in Australia and simplified land law which under the registry system required legal expertise. James Edward Hogg, "Australian Torrens System (1905)," *Alberta Law Review*, 1, 1955-1956, 193-218.

22. *Statutes of Canada*, 1872, 35 Vict., c23.

23. *Ibid.*, s33.

24. Quoted in Jackel, Intro., *Wheat and Woman*, xxv – xxvi.

25. The Canadian Census shows that in 1911 approximately 1.5% of the total number of people employed in agriculture in Alberta were women. Of those who described themselves as farmers or farm labourers in 1921 approximately 1.4% were women. During this same period, American Census figures indicate that two to three times that percentage of women were gainfully employed on farms in the Western United States where homestead legislation did not discriminate against women. According to one contemporary observer quoted by Sandra Myers, *Westering Women and the Frontier Experience 1800 – 1915* (Albuquerque, New Mexico,

1982: University of New Mexico Press), ff 2, 258, homesteading was so popular among young women on the American frontier that by the turn of the century one-third of the land in the Dakotas was held by women.

26. Although Binnie-Clark's Union Jack Farm Settlement on the outskirts of Fort Qu'Appelle, Saskatchewan was largely financed by her father, concern over operating costs is a recurring theme in this account of her first three years in the Canadian West.

27. Even the usually tolerant Roddy McMahon, Binnie-Clark's hired man, took exception when his employer decided to help "stone" the land, claiming "it ain't no work for a woman." Binnie-Clark, *Wheat and Woman*, 146.

28. Quoted in Jackel, Intro. *Wheat and Woman*, xxvi.

29. Binnie-Clark, *Wheat and Woman*, 308.

30. 54,000 Albertans lived in rural areas in 1901 while only 19,000 described themselves as urban. The rural/urban balance revealed a similar distribution ten years later when 366,000 people were living in the country and 223,000 occupied towns and cities. By 1931 over 60% of the province's population was still rural. Paul Voisey, "Urbanization of the Canadian Prairies, 1871-1916," *The Prairie West*, eds. R. Douglas Francis and Howard Palmer (Edmonton, 1985), 383-407.

31. For a further discussion of women and work in turn-of-the-century Alberta see, *The Last Best West*, Elaine Leslau Silverman, ed. (Montreal, 1984) and *A Flannel Shirt & Liberty*, intro. by Susan Jackel (Vancouver, 1982).

32. In 1911 of all women over the age of 25 years 87.4% were married. In 1921 87.6% were married and 90.7% of all women between the ages of 30 and 39 years were married. *Census of Canada*, 1911 and 1921.

33. *Ibid.*, 1911.

34. *Ibid.*, 1921.

35. In her study of wife beating in Alberta, 1905-1920 ("Til Death do us Part," *Alberta History*, 36, 4, Autumn, 1988, 13-22), Terry L. Chapman found that the provincial justice system was reluctant to enforce the law in cases of domestic violence and the court was relatively lenient when sentencing a husband found guilty of beating his wife.

36. CEA, Emily Murphy Papers, file 8.

37. *Ibid.*

38. Husbands deserting to the United States was apparently so common that in 1922 the UFA government considered extradition as a means of forcing their return but no action was taken.

39. PAA, Attorney General Papers, item 1256b.

40. *Ibid.*

41. *Ibid.*, item 1107a.

42. *Ibid.*

43. *Ibid.*

44. *Ibid.*, item 1256b.

45. *Ibid.*

46. *Ibid.*

47. *Ibid.*

48. The common law principle of the unity of domicile followed from coverture and the notion that a married woman had no legal existence apart from her husband.

49. PAA, Attorney General Papers, item 1256a.
50. *Ibid.*
51. *Ibid.*, item 1106.
52. *Ibid.*, item 1256a.
53. CEA, Emily Murphy Papers, file 8.
54. *Journals of the Legislative Assembly*, Vol. 6, 49 and 72. There does not appear to be a copy of this bill in existence; however, as it clearly anticipated changes to the Married Woman's Property Act, it seems likely that its main thrust was to provide a positive right to the wife in family property.
55. *Statutes of Alberta*, 1910, 1 Geo. V, c18.
56. As mentioned, provincial statute provided that where a man died without a will and there were no children his widow received his entire estate.
57. Bryne Hope Sanders, *Emily Murphy Crusader* (Toronto, 1945: MacMillan), 122.
58. Edmonton *Bulletin*, 27 January 1912.
59. Sanders, *Emily Murphy Crusader*, 121.
60. Reproduced in *A Harvest Yet To Reap*, Linda Rasmussen *et. al.*, eds. (Toronto 1976), 162.
61. *Ibid.*
62. *Ibid.*
63. *Ibid.*
64. CEA, Emily Murphy Papers, scrapbook 4, 21.
65. PAA, Attorney General Papers, item 1256b.
66. *Statutes of Alberta*, 1915, 5 Geo. V, c14.
67. CEA, Emily Murphy Papers, scrapbook 4, 21.
68. *Edmonton Journal*, 22 April 1915.
69. *Ibid.*
70. *Woman's Century*, 3, 6 December 1915.
71. PAA, Attorney General Papers, item 1106.
72. A more detailed history of the UFWA can be found in Leslie May Robinson, "Agrarian Reformers: Women And The Farm Movement In Alberta 1909-1925" (M.A. thesis, University of Calgary, 1979). A separate women's auxiliary to the UFA was formed in 1915; however, according the Irene Parlby, farm women sought full status as an integral part of the farm movement, rather than as an adjunct to it. Parlby recalled that the women's bid for autonomy was by no means a "natural sequence of events" but one that "required a great deal of persistence and patience on the part of the Auxiliary before the men realized the value of accepting the women's branch as an integral part of their organization with equal privileges." *Ibid.*, 51.
73. In 1921, at the height of the farm movement in Alberta, there were 4536 UFWA members in 309 locals. *Ibid.*, 58.
74. Constitutionally the UFWA was free to meet apart from the UFA; however, in practice the two groups met in simultaneous but separate conventions and UFWA resolutions were routinely submitted to the general convention for approval. In 1920, the UFA executive (which included the President of the UFWA) was asked to rule on the relationship between the two groups and it concluded that the UFWA was "regarded as a committee or Section of UFA proper." Glenbow Museum Archives, UFA Executive Minutes, June 1920.
75. UFA *Annual Report*, 1917, 316.

76. *Ibid.*
77. *Ibid.*, 215.
78. *Statutes of Alberta*, 1917, 7 Geo. V, c14. Alberta was the second of the three prairie provinces to introduce homestead dower. Saskatchewan had passed its *Homesteads Act* two years earlier and Manitoba followed Alberta with a *Dower Act* in 1918.
79. This interpretation of homestead dower relies heavily on the Manitoba Law Reform Commission, "Report On An Examination Of "The Dower Act"" (1984).
80. In Alberta the family home was protected against seizure under the *Exemptions Act, Revised Statutes of Alberta*, 1922, c95, which repealed *Consolidated Ordinances of the North West Territories*, 1898, 61 Vic., c27. This provision dated back to a Territorial Ordinance of 1884.
81. *Statutes of Alberta*, 1917, 7 Geo. V, c14, s3. These provisions did not extend to the husband but existed solely for the protection of the wife. The Act was revised in 1948 to read "spouse."
82. *Ibid.*, c7, s5.
83. *Ibid.*, s7. An amendment in 1919 provided that an affidavit by the husband to the effect that he was unmarried could be substituted for the wife's certificate of acknowledgement. See, *Statutes of Alberta*, 9 Geo. V, c40, s3. Section 9b of this amendment stated that the wife's signed certificate of acknowledgement constituted consent to disposition under the Act. By an earlier amendment the wife forfeited her rights under the Act when she was living apart from her husband "under circumstances disentitling her to alimony." *Statutes of Alberta*, 1918, 8 Geo. V, c4, s4.
84. *Statutes of Alberta*, 1917, 7 Geo. V, c14, s2(a) & (b).
85. PAA, *Scrapbook Hansard* (1927), 57.
86. Henrietta Muir Edwards, preface, *Legal Status of Women in Alberta* (National Council of Women of Canada, 1917).
87. PAA, Attorney General Papers, item 1106.
88. PAA, Premier Papers, items 168 -170B.
89. UFA *Annual Report* (1918), 25.
90. *Woman's Century*, 7 , 2, Feb. 1920, 10. According to the Attorney General's department, the wife had a right to dower as well as the right to husband's entire estate, where there were no children and her husband had died without a will. In practice the widow was forced to choose.
91. *Overland* v. *Himmelford* (1920) 2 *Western Weekly Report* (W.W.R.), 481-490.
92. The facts of the case presented here are taken from *Choma* v. *Chmelyk* (1918) 2 W.W.R. 382-386.
93. *Ibid.*, p. 384.
94. *Ibid.*
95. *Ibid.* Italics have been added for emphasis.
96. Professor D. P. Jones has pointed out the following possibilities. In the first place, a declaration such as was sought by the Chomas is a discretionary remedy, and the court could have declined to grant the vendor such a declaration to set aside the transfer on the grounds that he was not coming to the court "with clean hands." Secondly, this was a perfect case for equity to issue an injunction in favour of the purchaser to prevent the vendor from bringing his action under the statute to have the sale declared null and void. Finally, the court could perhaps have interpreted the Act merely to require consent by the dower spouse in fact and not the

completion of a particular form, thus, anticipating the Supreme Court of Canada's decision some sixty years later in *Sensted* v. *Makus*, (1977) W.W.R., 5, 731-745.

97. *Statutes of Alberta*, 1919, 9 Geo. V, c40, s2.

98. The facts of the case presented here are from (1920) 2 W.W.R. 481-491.

99. *Ibid.*, 489.

100. *Ibid.*, 490.

101. *Ibid.*

102. *Ibid.*, 488.

103. *Ibid.*

104. The facts of the case presented here are from (1922) 2 W.W.R., 272-278.

105. *Ibid.*, 274.

106. The facts of the case presented here are from (1922) 1 W.W.R., 397-401.

107. *Ibid.*, 397.

108. PAA, Attorney General Papers, item 1107a.

109. *Ibid.*

110. *Ibid.*

111. *Ibid.*

112. *Ibid.*

113. *Ibid.*

114. *Ibid.*

115. PAA, Attorney General Papers, item 692.89.

116. UFA, *Annual Report* (1919), 123.

117. *Ibid.*

118. Parlby was the second woman in the British Empire to achieve cabinet rank. She was preceded by a few months by Mary Ellen Smith of British Columbia.

119. UFA, *Annual Report* (1923), 7.

120. *Ibid.*

121. *Statutes of Alberta*, 1926, 16-17 Geo. V, c9.

122. *Ibid.*, s2.

123. *Ibid.*, s4.

124. National Council of Women of Canada *Year Book*, 1926-27, 68.

125. Emily Murphy, "Partnership in Marriage," CEA, Murphy Papers, manuscript, file 50.

126. Emily Murphy, "About Marriage Settlements," CEA, Murphy Papers, manuscript, 5, file 33.

127. Lillie Young McKinney, "Round Table Regarding Laws," *Women's Century*, May, 1921, 24.

128. *Ibid.*

129. Murphy, "Partnership in Marriage."

130. PAA, Attorney General Papers, item 1107a.

131. *Ibid.*

132. *Journals of the Legislative Assembly of the Province of Alberta*, 22 (1925) 7.

133. PAA, Attorney General Papers, item 1108.

134. *Ibid.*

135. *Ibid.*

136. Freeman, "The Legal Bases of the Sexual Caste System," 208.

137. *Reports of Family Law*, 13 (1974): 185-209.

138. *Matrimonial Property Act*, S.A. 1978, 27 Eliz. II, c22.

Schooling, White Supremacy,

and the Formation of a

Chinese Merchant Public

in British Columbia[1]

TIMOTHY J. STANLEY

On 9 July, 1919, two hundred people, including one hundred students, participated in the First Annual Picnic of the Victoria Chinese Public School (CPS) [Weibu Huaqiao Gongli Xuexiao]. While this event may not have been remarkable in itself, it is significant that it was reported in *Tai-hon Kung-po* [*Dahan Gongbao*] or *The Chinese Times*,[2] a paper published by the Chee Kung Tong (CKT) [Zhigongtang] or "Chinese Free Masons," in Vancouver.[3]

The Chinese Times had a number of reasons for reporting the picnic. Victoria, as the second largest and oldest Chinese community in Canada, was an essential part of the newspaper's market. In addition, Victoria was the location of the CKT's Canadian headquarters, and the organization was actively involved in local politics and community organizations.[4] These factors no doubt encouraged the newspaper to follow events in Victoria with great interest, as indeed it did.[5]

The CPS picnic did not attract the interest of Victoria's English-language daily newspapers even though these papers did report regularly on the social activities of various groups in and around Victoria. Indeed during the same week as the CPS event, the *Victoria Daily Colonist* and the *Victoria Daily Times* reported on the picnics of groups as diverse as the Corner Club, the St. Jude's Junior Women's Auxiliary, and the Board of Trade.[6] These papers tended to be interested in Chinese events only insofar as they directly affected whites, provided local colour, or offered a further opportunity to paint the Chinese as intrinsically different from whites.[7] By World War I, the "social distance" between Chinese and whites was such that most whites were unaware of Chinese activities like the CPS picnic.[8]

Whatever else this state of affairs implies, it points to the existence of a Chinese "public" largely separate from that of British Columbia's Anglo-Canadian society. Historians have tended to use the concept of "public" uncritically, referring to such things as "public opinion," "public policy," or "public life," as if they were monolithic.[9] But as Jürgen Habermas has pointed out, the concept really involves "a multiplicity of concurrent meanings." According to Habermas, in bourgeois societies these meanings have built up over time into a single category so that the various meanings "fuse into a clouded amalgam."[10] Thus, although the distinct Chinese "public" of British Columbia encompassed a significant number of people whose activities within a complex network of institutions were beyond the ken of the Anglo-Canadian society, it can best be understood as comprising a number of overlapping phenomena.

The coverage afforded by *The Chinese Times* to the annual picnics of the Victoria CPS, and to similar events in the Chinese communities of British Columbia, points to the existence of a Chinese "public" in at least three different senses of the term. First, it documents a network of "public" institutions within B.C.'s Chinese communities. The Chinese Public School itself was part of this network, under the direct control of, and funded by, what for most Chinese was a "public" institution: the Chinese Consolidated Benevolent Association (CCBA) [Zhonghua Huiguan]. For the Chinese, the CCBA, and the Chinese Benevolent Associations (CBAs) [Zhonghua Huiguan][11] of other cities performed key local governmental functions including organizing self-defence, social control, and welfare. These organizations were accountable in their actions to other Chinese, in particular adult male members of the merchant class. Thus, for the Chinese, the Victoria CPS was a "public" institution in much the same way that B.C.'s provincially controlled public schools were for members of the dominant society. Second, the Chinese "public" extended beyond the leadership of these institutions. As the CPS picnic illustrates, the students and teachers of the Chinese schools[12] were part of a broader group of people whose activities were open to the view of others. Third, the schools themselves were actively involved in creating and recreating a "public" or audience for Chinese institutions.[13] This involved instilling an identity as Chinese in students and continuing such acts of "public representation"[14] as the annual celebrations of Confucius' birthday. By maintaining and extending the group of people literate in Chinese, language instruction in itself formed a Chinese "reading public" which was an additional way of creating this Chinese public.[15] As the Chinese schools illustrate, various aspects of this separate Chinese public had complex relationships with the institutions, ideology, and officials belonging to the Chinese "state."[16]

While not all individuals involved in the Chinese public in each of the above senses belonged to it in every sense, most were involved in it in more than one sense. For example, not all those literate in Chinese belonged to the audience for such practices as honouring Confucius' birthday or could claim Chinese public institutions as their own. A few non-Chinese were literate in Chinese as indeed were some Chinese women. However, men were overwhelmingly the predominant actors within Chinese public institutions. By the same token, although male Chinese workers were often the intended clients of the programs organized by CBAs, such as public welfare undertakings like Chinese hospitals, the CBAs themselves as a terrain of action primarily belonged to upper-class male merchants. These considerations point to the class and gendered nature of the Chinese public sphere. As a sphere controlled by merchants, it was an important element in the class relations of Chinese communities. As an sphere controlled by men, it played an important role in the social construction of gender within these same communities.[17]

The fragmentation of the public realm that the existence of this separate Chinese public indicates has been an important element in the social structure of racism in British Columbia. As will be argued below, it was occasioned in the first place by the racist measures adopted in British Columbia following Confederation and the resulting need for Chinese merchants to create their own institutions to further their class interests. Like their Anglo-Canadian counterparts, Chinese British Columbians drew upon those cultural practices with which they were already familiar – i.e. those of their homeland – to create their institutions and to define their interests.

Once this separation between Chinese and Anglo-Canadian publics was effected, it also helped to perpetuate racism by insulating whites from the consequences of anti-Chinese racism, while allowing these consequences to be only too real for Chinese British Columbians. The large English daily newspapers, for example, not only failed to report school picnics, they also failed to notice recurring anti-Chinese violence as well, a matter actively followed in the Chinese press.[18] In other words, the consequences of anti-Chinese racism were private as far as members of the dominant society were concerned and only too public as far as the Chinese were concerned.[19]

It should be noted that this fragmentation of the public realm has often led historians of British Columbia's "race relations" to underplay the significance of racism in shaping the lives of the members of affected groups such as the Chinese. In focusing almost exclusively on white attitudes and activities, they have most often fallen into one of two perspectives on the Chinese themselves. Either historians have pointed to the separate institutional life of the Chinese as evidence of an unwillingness to assimilate – i.e. as a cause of the alleged "alienness" which bred anti-Chinese racism – or they have tended to represent the Chinese as the hapless victims of white racism, objects of, rather than actors within, the province's history.[20] Both perspectives arise from the sources that these historians have used for their studies, sources which have themselves been shaped by racism. Insofar as Anglo-Canadians were insulated from the consequences of racism, their historical records are silent on the issue. It is only by recognizing that Chinese language sources are also part of British Columbia's historical record that a fuller view of Chinese British Columbia and of racism becomes possible. This view sees the Chinese as actors in the province's history in their own right and sees racism as a structuring of relations between white and Chinese British Columbias. Thus, although white attitudes and exclusionary measures have been thoroughly documented, it is still necessary to outline them in order to delineate some of their consequences for the creators of the Chinese public, the men of the merchant class.

* * *

Following British Columbia's entry into Confederation, the laws and procedures established during the colonial period were remade to better fit the
needs of British and Anglo-Canadian "settlers," the institutions of the new
provincial government were established, and those of the federal government extended to B.C.[21] Confederation, therefore, involved an extensive
remaking of state institutions in British Columbia. Part and parcel of this
remaking was the exclusion from the new governmental structures of the
two largest non-European groups: First Nations and Chinese people. Imperialism, coupled with political opportunism, appears to have been the motive for this exclusion.[22] Essentially "British" Columbia was to be for the
British and Anglo-Canadians or those like them, while Others were to be
excluded.[23] Consequently, one of the first acts of the new legislature was to
disenfranchise First Nations people who were then the overwhelming majority of the population, and the Chinese who were a significant proportion
of the non-First Nations population.[24] Over the next seventy-five years this
disenfranchisement was repeatedly reaffirmed at the provincial and federal
levels as well as extended to municipal and school board elections.[25] Between 1871 and 1914 alone, fifteen pieces of provincial legislation excluded
the Chinese from the franchise or from holding public office.[26]

Once these initial exclusions from the institutions of the new province
were effected, first Chinese and later Japanese exclusion tended to assume
dynamics of their own. Between 1872 and 1922, the province enacted over
one hundred pieces of legislation discriminating against the Chinese and
other Asians. The federal government also enacted discriminatory immigration and franchise provisions. At various times, the Chinese were barred
from working on Crown contracts and from working underground in coal-
mines or from holding public office except as official translators. They were
also subjected to discriminatory taxation, licensing procedures and immigration measures, the latter at the provincial as well as the federal levels.[27]

Although these laws were a patch-work, and individual enactments were
often overturned by the courts or the federal government, their overall
thrust was to circumscribe the lives of Chinese residents while making B.C.
state institutions into the preserves of people of European, primarily British descent. To the Chinese people of the province, these laws meant that

British Columbia state institutions and officials were not "for" them, and indeed were often hostile to them.[28]

For example, the legal system was controlled by whites. Disenfranchisement not only ensured that the Chinese could not participate in the enactment of laws, it also prevented them from becoming lawyers and judges, while other legislation barred them from serving on juries. Since anti-Chinese violence was a continual problem for the Chinese during the nineteenth and early twentieth centuries,[29] exclusion meant that the Chinese could not rely on the courts for relief. The courts rarely convicted or gave only minimal sentences to whites who perpetrated violence against the Chinese. Often this was explained on the basis that the Chinese were unreliable witnesses. Chinese accused of crimes, by contrast, were rarely given the benefit of judicial doubt.[30]

Chinese property owners, including well-to-do merchants, were in an especially ambivalent position with respect to British Columbia state institutions. There is some evidence that before Confederation, Chinese property-owners actively participated in the public life of British Columbia. During this era most Chinese were itinerant workers in the gold mining industry, but their numbers included merchants who were among the largest landowners in the area. For example, in 1862, the second largest landowner in the city of Victoria after the Hudson's Bay Company was the Kwong Lee Company.[31] A number of Chinese voted in the first provincial election and in earlier colonial ones,[32] while Chinese merchants in Victoria and New Westminster also participated in public subscription campaigns like that for the Royal Jubilee Hospital, and in the welcoming of new governors and visiting royalty.[33]

After Confederation, official indifference or open hostility towards the Chinese meant that Chinese property rights were far from secure. Chinese property owners could appeal to other property owners, state officials and the courts, but they could not rely upon them for their protection.[34] For example, some whites used the idea that all property owners had certain rights to support the Chinese in their struggle against school segregation in Victoria during 1922-1923. As a 1922 editorial in *The Victoria Daily Colonist* pointed out, "So long as Orientals, or the members of any foreign race, are property owners in British Columbia our municipalities cannot refuse to provide for the education of their children."[35] The notion that Chinese taxpayers had a right to fair treatment did not stop the Victoria School District from singling out Chinese children for segregation.[36]

In this context, it should be noted that the definition of property rights along "race" lines was at the heart of the exclusions established at Confederation. This not only involved imposing Western, specifically British, forms of property on the territory of British Columbia, while marginalizing the practices of First Nations people, it also involved barring First Nations people from the new forms of property. Under the Land Acts of 1866 and 1872, North American aboriginal people were effectively denied pre-emption rights; i.e. unlike "settlers" they were barred from individually claiming or purchasing lands designated as belonging to the crown.[37] Although Chinese property rights were not affected at this point, there were several attempts at limiting them.[38] It was not until 1884, after much of the prime land in southwestern British Columbia which had been frozen in a railway reserve became available for pre-emption, that the Chinese were barred from directly acquiring land from the Crown. In the late nineteenth century, as the economy of the province became dominated by corporations, the Chinese were barred from registering "any Chinese company or association" under the 1897 Companies Act.[39] After World War I, groups such as the Victoria Chamber of Commerce, the Vancouver Board of Trade, and the B.C. Federation of Agriculture spearheaded calls to bar the Chinese and other Asians from owning land.

Not only were their property rights insecure, the Chinese themselves were subject to the harassment and inspection of local health and police officials. Before World War I, Vancouver health officials repeatedly harassed the residents of Chinatown while ignoring abuses elsewhere in the city.[40] In 1906 Vancouver's Chinese Board of Trade, representing the largest Chinese merchant houses of the city, protested to Vancouver City Council that its members

> have been constantly annoyed by what we believe to be an unjustifiable intrusion of certain members of the Vancouver Police Force . . . in the habit of going into our stores and rooms where our families live, showing no warrant whatsoever, nor do they claim any business with us. . . . We are subjected to indignities and discriminating treatment to which no other class would submit and to which *your* laws, we are advised, we are not required to submit.[41]

In many ways, efforts at subjecting the Chinese of all classes to official inspection culminated in the provisions of the 1923 federal Chinese Immigration Act. This act required all Chinese in Canada, native and foreign born, citizen and non-citizen alike, to register with the federal government, and obtain certificates of residence entitling them to remain in Canada. These certificates were subject to inspection without notice and the Chinese were required to carry them with them at all times.[42]

* * *

The response of Chinese merchants to their exclusion from the public realm of British Columbia state institutions was one neither of passive compliance nor futile, but heroic resistance. Although it is apparent that the Chinese often strenuously resisted efforts to extend exclusion (as, for example, was the case with school segregation) and, insofar as they were able, they used the resources of the dominant society to their advantage,[43] their response to exclusion often involved creating their own institutions to take care of their needs. Indeed, the institutional complexities of the Chinese communities of Canada are among their defining characteristics.[44]

These institutions either paralleled those of the dominant society or took traditional Chinese forms. For example, most Chinese in Canada belonged to clan or district associations similar to those of south China and other Overseas Chinese communities. One such district association, composed of people from Toi-san (Taishan) county, was the Ning Yung Yu Hing Tong (Ning Yang Yu Qing Tang) established in Victoria in 1893 and in Vancouver by 1912. By the early twentieth century, Chinese trade associations included labour unions such as the Chinese Shingle Workers Union which actively organized strikes for higher wages and against racist employment practices.[45]

The most important institutions, however, were the Zhonghua Huiguan (lit. "Chinese Association") or Chinese Benevolent Associations (CBAs). Edgar Wickberg has variously described CBAs as umbrella organizations which "stood at the apex of community organizations and spoke for them all and for their membership," and as "the dominant agency of internal control in the community as well as the community's spokesperson to white government and society."[46] The geographer David Chuen-Yan Lai, who has examined the archives of the first CBA in Canada, the Chinese

Consolidated Benevolent Association in Victoria, has gone so far as to describe it as "the de facto Chinese government in Canada."[47] Although this latter characterization seems to be an exaggeration, it is apparent that CBAs exercised a number of local governmental functions within Chinese communities. These functions included resolving internal disputes, policing Chinatowns, organizing welfare functions, and managing collective institutions, including Chinese Public Schools. CBAs were also the principal associations for organizing the defence for Chinese communities as a whole and assisting individuals who were in trouble with the white-controlled legal system or who were facing individual violence or discrimination.[48]

From their inceptions, CBAs were controlled by well-to-do merchants. The first CBA, the Chinese Consolidated Benevolent Association of Victoria, was established in 1884 by several Victoria-based merchants who were then the leading Chinese merchants of British Columbia. They petitioned the Imperial Chinese Consulate in San Francisco for assistance after several thousand Chinese labourers and their camp followers arrived to build the CPR during the early 1880s. This intensified white hostility against the Chinese, created problems of crime and violence which adversely affected Chinese merchants, and by 1883 led to widespread privation among Chinese workers.[49] In their letter requesting assistance, the petitioners noted that Chinese merchants and labourers were both important to the economy of the province and that "the country's officials should welcome the Chinese, but instead are infected with cruel habits even surpassing that seen in recent years in the United States." They complained about "external troubles," including a proposed poll tax on the Chinese and "the enforcement of every kind of cruel law restricting commerce, work and habitation," and noted that "internal troubles" – gamblers, criminals, prostitutes, and privation amongst workers – were also growing.[50] Accordingly they asked for the consulate's assistance in ending discriminatory laws and banning Chinese prostitutes, called for the establishment of a Chinese consulate in Victoria, and urged the formation of a Chinese Association (*zhonghua huiguan*) "to unite the feelings of the multitude."[51] The San Francisco consulate, which the year before had granted a charter for a Chinese association to the leading merchants of San Francisco,[52] responded by sending one of its officials to Victoria. Under his supervision, the Chinese Consolidated Benevolent

Association was established under Imperial charter in 1884, incorporating under provincial statutes the following year.[53]

When first established, the Victoria CCBA nominally represented all Chinese in British Columbia. Its charter provided that "the Association will be commonly held (*gongyou*) by all the Chinese gentry (*shi*), merchants, workers and others, residing in the English territory of British Columbia province," and that its officials would be elected by the membership-at-large.[54] In the 1880s close to one-third of the 15,000 Chinese in the province, including many outside the Victoria area, paid the two dollar levy established by the association as its membership fee.[55]

The CCBA never exercised absolute control over Chinese affairs outside of Victoria, but it was still influential. By the mid-1890s, Vancouver included a number of Chinese merchants of sufficient stature to be able to establish their own Chinese Benevolent Association. The Vancouver CBA, however, did not officially incorporate until 1908. Interestingly, even though this CBA was established in the interests of well-to-do merchants, it could not be funded through a per capita levy because so many Chinese residents in Vancouver had already paid one to the CCBA. Instead, it relied upon the contributions of merchants, and other Chinese associations, as well as a loan from a white businessman, to fund its activities.[56]

The CCBA of Victoria, and later the CBA of Vancouver, could bring considerable sanctions to bear against any Chinese who did not recognize their sway within their immediate areas of control. Since many Chinese labourers, like their white counterparts, used these cities as their bases of operation and locations during the off-season,[57] the associations' influence extended throughout B.C. These sanctions included official ones decided upon by the CBA board of directors such as refusing to act for those who had not paid their membership levies. However, since the principals of the CBA tended to be the leading merchants, other more effective sanctions could also be brought to bear. For example, these merchants included the Chinese agents for trans-Pacific steamship companies.[58] Thus they could refuse to sell tickets to any who could not produce a dues receipt. This method was used during the late 1890s by the CCBA in Victoria to finance a new Chinese hospital. All those leaving the country had to make a two dollar contribution.[59] In later years similar methods were used to fund clan and district associations, which would have their agents waiting on the docks.[60] Since Chinese merchants were often also labour contractors upon whom Chinese workers were dependent for employment and support during the off-season, and since they performed such other functions as forwarding letters and remittances back to families in China, other unofficial sanctions also carried weight.[61]

The creation of a quasi-governmental organization by Chinese merchants to protect their communal interests *vis-à-vis* the dominant society, as well as to ensure their control within their communities, was in many ways an extension of their class position within Chinese society. In late imperial China, a class of scholar/landlords, often called the gentry, were the chief underpinnings of the state. They actively mediated between the relatively small imperial bureaucracy and the population as a whole, and were particularly important in organizing local government on an *ad hoc* basis. Although much has been made of the traditional Confucian hierarchy of gentry, peasants, artisans, and merchants, which regarded merchants as unproductive parasites at the bottom of the social ladder, by the nineteenth century the larger merchants, particularly those of the cities and treaty-ports, were in fact members of the gentry/landlord elite.[62] Well-to-do Chinese merchants in Canada, like those of Victoria and Vancouver, in creating CBAs were by and large continuing traditional gentry roles.[63] Thus the well-to-do Chinese merchants in Canada were "the public" for institutions like the CBA in much the same way that the Chinese gentry was "the public" for imperial institutions.[64]

The importance of CBAs was reflected in the battles that various political-fraternal groups waged in order to control them.[65] The oldest such group was the CKT, which had started in B.C. as an anti-Manchu secret society during the nineteenth century. This organization also provided its members with welfare and mutual support benefits. The CKT was joined in the early twentieth century by the Bao Huang Hui or the Empire Reform Association. This group, which involved many of the largest merchants, was established by the reformers Kang Youwei and Liang Qichao. Sun Yat-sen's revolutionary movement, which eventually became the Kuomintang (Guomindang) or KMT, also became active in British Columbia. All of these groups had links to politics in China, as well as to more local interests. Although their-rank-and-file members included labourers, their leadership circles consisted of merchants of various descriptions.[66] After the 1911 republican revolution in China, struggles for control principally involved the CKT and the KMT. As groups of merchants, and political parties, jockeyed for control of public institutions, the result was a Chinese politics in Canada independent of that of the dominant society.[67]

* * *

Schooling was an important aspect of this formation of Chinese politics and institutions. Chinese schools were not only intended for purposes of cultural retention or language instruction, they also served explicitly political purposes.

Before 1900, there were relatively few second-generation Chinese in British Columbia. The head taxes on Chinese immigration,[68] in conjunction with low wages and widespread anti-Chinese hostility, made it virtually impossible for male Chinese labourers to bring their families to Canada. Only the well-to-do merchants, to whom the head taxes did not apply, were secure enough to bring their wives and dependent children to Canada. The result was that most Chinese families in Canada belonged to the merchant class, as did most children.[69] These merchants, following gentry practices in China, often hired tutors directly from China to instruct their children. Tutors were themselves members of the gentry, who had passed the county level of the Imperial civil service examinations. Those who held such official certificates could always make their living as teachers or tutors. In the nineteenth century, there was also a number of private "schools," but these were likely to have been little more than rooms in the backs of shops or in private dwellings in which clerks working for merchant houses taught basic literacy, accounting, and other skills.[70]

The first formal Chinese school was consequently not established until 1899. In that year, under the auspices of the CCBA in Victoria, the Le Qun Yishu (literally "Happy Multitude Free School") was established on the third floor of the CCBA building on Fisgard Street. Although one of the prime instigators of the school was Lee Mong Kow, the immigration interpreter, the school was organized following extensive discussions within the CCBA and after it had raised three thousand dollars to support the school. The school employed two graduates of the county examinations in China as its teachers, and taught a classical Confucian curriculum similar to that of would-be participants in the Imperial examination system in China.[71] As an *yishu* or "free school," it charged no tuition and was accordingly supported by the CCBA, the charitable contributions of merchants and benefit performances. This school was reorganized in 1908 to accommodate non-English-speaking Chinese students who had been expelled from the Victoria Public School system. This reorganization placed the school under the direct control of the CCBA and modernized its curriculum. In the same era, the school was recognized by and received funding from the Imperial Chinese Ministry of Education, reopening in 1909 at a new site, a block further up Fisgard Street, as the Imperial Chinese School (Daqing Zhonghua Xuexiao), but was renamed the Chinese Public School shortly thereafter.[72]

This school's importance is indicated by its enrolment. From 1908 to 1923, between 43 and 127 new students a year entered in the school.[73] For example, in 1914-1915, it enrolled ninety students in six classes. The four upper classes were held during the evening as they were made up of students who attended the white public schools during the day. The two lower classes were held during the daytime.[74]

A similar Chinese Public School was not established in Vancouver until 1917. In that year the Chinese Benevolent Association in that city raised funds for the school through public subscriptions and benefits, establishing it rent-free in the CBA building. When established, this school was a modern one by Chinese standards. This was evident in the credentials of its teachers, who had degrees from universities, high schools, and normal schools in China, Japan, and Canada. Its curriculum was also organized along modern lines, and included English language instruction.[75] Although this school in the 1930s became the largest Chinese school in Canada under the patronage of the Kuomintang, it operated intermittently during the 1920s due to mounting costs and the decision of its key organizers to return to China.[76]

By the post World War I era, there were a number of schools controlled by political groups and other associations. In 1904 and 1905 respectively, the Empire Reform Association had opened two "Patriotic Schools [Aiguo Xuetang]" in Vancouver and Victoria respectively. This era was one of rapid educational change in China. For example, in 1905 the Qing dynasty abolished the old civil service examination system, while the year before it had established a modern Ministry of Education with a hierarchy of officially recognized schools. The idea that through the appropriate kind of education and training China could gain "the wealth and power" of the West was a popular one in intellectual circles in China. Thus the establishment of the Aiguo Schools which instructed in the "new knowledge" (*xin zhi*) was a logical extension of the association's policies of reform. These schools were still in operation in the 1920s although apparently they had not been in operation continuously.[77] In 1921 and 1922, the CKT established schools in Victoria and New Westminster.[78] In Vancouver, there were several schools controlled by clan and district associations, and by Christian missionaries, as well as night schools for adults.[79] Indeed, in the 1920s and 1930s, as various educational innovations took root among the Chinese in China, the number of Chinese schools proliferated, so much so that their numbers far exceeded the supply of available Chinese children.[80]

The enrolment patterns of these schools suggest that the nature and functions of Chinese schools changed over time. At least during the early part of the twentieth century, they were the most important educational institutions to the Chinese, while the provincial public schools were of secondary importance. By the 1920s, this hierarchy had begun to reverse. Although by the 1920s, most of these schools likely held classes at hours outside of those of the British Columbia public schools, during the first decades of the century some Chinese schools appear to have been day schools. For some time, between 1900 and 1915, the Chinese Public School in Victoria, in its various incarnations, appears to have enrolled more Chinese students than the provincial public schools in the area. For example, when the Le Qun Yishu opened in 1899 it enrolled thirty-nine students, while the Victoria School Board only enrolled fifteen Chinese students in 1900.[81] The following year there were twenty-nine Chinese students in Victoria public schools, but 142 Canadian-born Chinese children living in the city.[82] During the World War I era, the school's junior classes were held during the daytime, while until the early 1920s, it appears that the Chinese Public School in Victoria enrolled more Chinese girls than did the Victoria School Board Schools.[83]

Certainly, successive Chinese governments found the Chinese schools in British Columbia to be worthy of their attentions. Before 1911, overseas Chinese communities were valuable staging areas for revolutionary political organizations. The Imperial Qing government was consequently keenly interested in winning the support of overseas communities and in spying out the activities of their rivals. One manifestation of this interest was a Qing educational delegation which in 1908 visited the Americas to set up schools. The reorganization of the "Chinese School" in Victoria (later called the CPS), required by the exclusion of unilingual Chinese students from the Victoria School Board Schools, neatly fit into their plans. The new school was opened in 1909 with the financial support of the Chinese government. Although this school was mainly concerned with teaching English to students who had been refused admission to the Victoria School Board schools, it followed a curriculum prescribed by Beijing and its teachers were certified by the Chinese Ministry of Education.[84] Indeed, throughout this era, Chinese teachers in the Chinese schools usually held credentials either directly from, or recognized by, Chinese normal schools and universities.

Between 1915 and 1922, the Chinese schools of Vancouver and Victoria were inspected by official Chinese government delegations on at least three occasions. These inspections were conducted by leading Chinese scholars on behalf of the Northern Chinese government, which had official Canadian recognition.[85] Again here, no doubt the motive for these inspections was to win support away from the Southern Kuomintang government. The Chinese delegates in these inspection tours also seem to have been active in selling Chinese government bonds. Nonetheless, the inspections were major events accompanied by official banquets and much speech-making. A particularly warm reception was extended to a delegation headed by the principal of Beijing University, Cai Yuanpei, in 1921. Meanwhile in 1918-1919, the Chinese delegation to the Versailles Peace Conference stopped over in Vancouver and Victoria to inspect the CPS and Aiguo schools and present prize money to the students.[86]

This connection to the Chinese government was further evident in the invitations extended to the Vancouver-based Chinese consuls to present prizes and degrees to graduating students at the CPS in Victoria and schools in Vancouver. Since the CKT supported the Northern government, it is not surprising that such events were reported in its official organ, *The Chinese Times*. But this activity also reflected the role of the consuls as the leading Chinese citizens in British Columbia. Chinese consuls at least had the right of audience with hostile local officials and often acted as a buffer against the dominant society. They were also the ultimate authority figures. On two occasions in 1920 and 1922, the CBA in Vancouver held meetings with all the Chinese students attending Vancouver School Board schools, at which the Chinese consul "explained the rules of the schools" and urged students to obey them in order to forestall school segregation.[87]

Chinese teachers were notable figures in their own right. As the most educated members of the local Chinese communities, they were automatically part of the social elite. Their comings and goings were consequently reported in *The Chinese Times*, as were their other activities. During the summer of 1918, *The Chinese Times* reported on the tour of the province by two teachers from the Victoria CPS, a tour which included a series of banquets for the travelling scholars organized by various associations. In 1921 the teacher from the CKT school in Victoria not only visited Vancouver but also wrote several guest editorials in *The Chinese Times*.[88] His position as a scholar, and therefore presumably an informed commentator, was evident in the fact that one of the editorials was on the rationale behind Canadian immigration policies and the difficulties this occasioned for the Chinese in Canada.

School openings, especially, were public events, even when the schools were sponsored by a particular organization. This was evident when the Qing Consul General in San Francisco came to Victoria to open the new Chinese Public School Building in 1909.[89] But from 1914 onwards, *The Chinese Times* faithfully reported school openings including the speeches of the notables at them. These events seemed to move beyond partisan concerns, as was evident when *The Chinese Times* reported on the participation of the Kuomintang at the opening ceremonies for the CKT school in New Westminster. This was despite the fact that the two groups were inveterate, even deadly, enemies.[90]

All of this activity on the part of Chinese schools, their teachers, sponsoring organizations, and Chinese government officials, faithfully reported in *The Chinese Times*, points to the existence of a collective terrain of common interest to the newspaper's readers. The term sometimes used in the newspaper itself to describe this terrain was *huajie*, meaning "Chinese district" or "Chinese domain."[91] This "*jie*" was not only the creation of *The Chinese Times*, however. Indeed, the paper provides evidence of a broader construction. As the official paper of the CKT, it is not surprising that it reported on the CKT and the activities of its members. However, it also re-ported on the activities of other schools, most of which were not affiliated to the CKT. For example, it reported on the graduation ceremonies of the Guangzhi school in Vancouver, as well as the CPS in Victoria. It also re-ported on the recruitment of Chinese teachers by various clan organiza-tions in Vancouver and Victoria.[92]

* * *

Chinese schools, however, were not only part of a Chinese public in the sense that their activities were covered by the Chinese language press. They were actively involved in forming a Chinese public by inculcating certain habits in the Chinese students themselves. In particular they were con-cerned with anchoring a sense of "Chineseness" in the selves of the stu-dents. Indeed, this appears to have been part of the motivation for the es-tablishment of the first Chinese school in Canada, Victoria's Le Qun Yishu. Quoting an anonymous Chinese, who was probably Lee Mong Kow, the immigration interpreter, the *Victoria Daily Colonist* claimed that the school was created because the Chinese felt, "We are Chinamen wherever we go . . . and find that, in view of the international commercial relations now opening up, it is necessary to have an education in Chinese as well as Eng-lish."[93] Certainly the school was established to provide Chinese children with a sense of their heritage,[94] but the heavy Confucian emphasis of its curriculum and the traditional qualifications of its teachers are suggestive of a desire to instil Confucian morality more than a desire to merely promote cultural retention. At the Le Qun Yishu, students, along with their parents, formally observed Confucius' birthday, including bowing before his por-trait. This Confucian emphasis continued even after World War I. The CPS in Victoria and the one in Vancouver, the Aiguo Schools, and the CKT schools all marked Confucius' birthday with public exercises.[95]

Language instruction also provided a vehicle for instilling an indentity as Chinese in students. Literacy in written Chinese, and the ability to speak standard Chinese languages, were vital elements in becoming "Chinamen wherever we go." Although British Columbia's first generation Chinese mainly originated in the same Chinese province (Guangdong), they spoke several different dialects of Cantonese or even the minority Hakka lan-guage. Individual self-identifications, place of residence in Canada and even occupation were consequently based on place of origin and dialect spoken.[96] People from outside of one's native district who spoke with a different pronunciation often were greeted with hostility. For example, on one occasion Sun Yat-sen was heckled by his audience in Vancouver because he spoke a dialect other than the dominant one there.[97] Lack of a common language was especially difficult in the larger centres. For example, the CPS in Victoria had to conduct its public meetings simultaneously in four languages: Mandarin, standard Cantonese, and two local dialects.[98]

Schooling in Chinese helped to foster a collective identity. Written Chinese had long performed an integrative function in China by allowing those who did not speak the same language to correspond with each other. Literacy in itself was useful to the Chinese in British Columbia because through it one could become aware of what was happening in other districts of the province, which areas were becoming closed to Chinese activities, or which areas were opening up.[99] It also allowed business relations to flourish despite other barriers. Thus by promoting literacy, the Chinese language schools were fostering means of communication which transcended local identities. Chinese language schools also promoted standard spoken Chinese. This primarily involved instruction in standard Cantonese, although Mandarin was also taught. This too fostered a collective identity. For example, standard Cantonese was the language of instruction at the CPS in Victoria, even though most of its students spoke local dialects.[100]

However, these schools were not entirely successful in their objectives of cultural retention. Financial considerations meant that relatively few students were able to complete their courses of study and graduate from the schools.[101] For many second-generation Chinese students, attending Chinese language school was more of an ordeal than a pleasure. This was especially so when classes were organized outside of the hours of the provincial public school. Sing Lim, for example, who attended one of these schools in the 1920s, found the approach of his provincial public schoolteacher to be far gentler than that of his Chinese language schoolteacher.[102] In this respect, Chinese language school may have produced "unintended consequences"[103] by alienating Chinese students from the traditions of China as much as they strengthened them.

Some Chinese language schools also challenged traditional gender roles.

A significant number of girls attended these schools and graduated from them.[104] The presence of so many girls in classrooms was already a departure from established gender roles since traditional Confucian practice did not allow for the schooling of women. The number of girls who made up the graduating class of the CPS in Victoria suggests that the right of girls to an education had gained some recognition from the leading merchants, as in China during the same era. Indeed Susan Yipsang, one of the daughters of a leading Vancouver merchant, started attending the University of British Columbia in 1914-15 and later graduated from Teachers' College, Columbia.[105]

This openness to the education of girls may have reflected the importance of Chinese women to the merchant economy, rather than a weakening of Chinese patriarchy. Since the unpaid labour of Chinese women was particularly valuable to Chinese merchants,[106] and since acting as clerks and the like required some literacy, conservative merchants may have allowed their daughters to attend Chinese schools. However, there certainly did not appear to be any openness to allowing women to participate in the organizational life of the Chinese Benevolent Associations or other groups, although they were sometimes commissioned to perform specific tasks.[107] Thus despite allowing Chinese women access to schooling, the Chinese public sphere in British Columbia remained overwhelmingly male in nature.

* * *

From the above, it is evident that by the early 1920s, the male Chinese merchants of Vancouver and Victoria had created their own institutional networks which were among their principal resources in responding to the dominance of whites and their exclusion from white-controlled institutions. Their lives within these institutions were governed by politics having their roots in China as well as in the conditions of British Columbia. Their actions were judged by an audience of people literate in written Chinese. Chinese schools preserved and perpetuated this domain, at the same time that they contributed some of the principal actors within it. In many ways, this domain was really closer to the institutions and ideologies of the Chinese "state" than the Canadian one.

Whether this merchant public was unique to the Chinese or was found in similar domains within other minority groups in Canada is an unanswered question. It is certainly likely that a similar phenomenon existed among the

Japanese in British Columbia and continues to exist among some First Nations.[108] While it may be that various immigrant groups created institutions such as language schools for their mutual benefit, and that these groups had their own ethnic presses which reported on the activities of political groups oriented towards "the old country," it is doubtful that European immigrant groups had the same kind of relationships to the dominant Anglo-Canadian "public" or to their native states that the Chinese had. In this respect the Chinese public sphere only came into existence after Chinese merchants were excluded from the dominant public. In addition, many activities within the Chinese public sphere appear to have been licensed or condoned to at least some degree by the governments of Canada and China.[109]

It is also interesting to note that the policy of Chinese exclusion adopted by Canadian governments and private institutions did not fundamentally alter this Chinese merchant public. When in 1923 the federal government ended Chinese immigration of all kinds under the Chinese Immigration Act, the Chinese communities of Canada went into decline in terms of their numbers, but their separate institutional lives continued unabated.[110] Having been forced into the margins, the Chinese had created their own terrain for action. White supremacy could keep them out of certain institutions, but in the long run it could not stop them from being actors in the history of Canada. A truly "multicultural history"[111] of British Columbia must recognize this.

Notes

1. This paper was originally presented at the 70th Annual Meeting of the Canadian Historical Association, 3 June, 1991, Queen's University, Kingston, Ontario. Like all academic work, it is made possible by the work of others. In this regard I owe most profound debts to the pioneering efforts of David T. H. Lee, David Chuen-Yan Lai, and Edgar Wickberg. Gerald Tulchinsky and Patricia E. Roy both provided encouragement. Many of the paper's key ideas were formed through discussions with members of the Department of Social and Educational Studies and the Centre for Policy Studies in Education at UBC, several of whom also brought important references to my attention. In particular, I would like to thank Jean Barman, Donald Fisher, Bill Maciejko, Theresa Richardson, and Vincent D'Oyley. I would especially like to thank J. Donald Wilson, who consistently lent me the benefit of his profound historical knowledge and critical insight, and made invaluable corrections to the manuscript. Most of all, this paper would not have been possible without the unstinting support provided by Fran Boyle and the efforts of Elanor Boyle-Stanley and Katherine Boyle-Stanley to remind me what it is to be human. Of course, any errors of omission or commission do not

reflect on any of those who lent assistance, but are entirely my responsibility.

2. As Cantonese was most often the spoken language of the Chinese residents of British Columbia, it is inappropriate to romanize Chinese characters used in B.C. by means of the standard Mandarin *pinyin* system. Therefore, as far as possible, I have followed local usages for the names of organizations and people in the text while providing the *pinyin* romanization in square brackets. However, I have used *pinyin* in the footnotes. The standard in this as in other matters has been set by Harry Con, *et. al.*, Edgar Wickberg (ed.), *From China to Canada: A History of the Chinese Communities in Canada*, Generations Series (Toronto: McClelland and Stewart, 1982). See the glossary of local usages, pp. 272-294.

3. See "Weibu Huaqiao Gongxiao youxing jicheng [Report on the Victoria Chinese Public School's excursion]," *Dahan Gongbao*, 11 July, 1919, 3. *Dahan Gongbao* has began publishing in Vancouver in 1907. Microfilm copies of the paper are only available from 1915 onwards. Access to this publication can be gained through the Chinese Canadian Research Collection at the Special Collections division of the University of British Columbia. This collection contains much of the background research for the Generations Series history of the Chinese, *From China to Canada*. As part of the preparation for this volume, four Chinese speakers read through the newspaper from 1914 to 1970 making notes in English on matters of interest. Their notes can be used as a table of contents for the journal; however, care should be taken in using the resulting translations without reference to the original Chinese. See UBC Special Collections, Chinese Canadian Research Collection (CCRC), Boxes 4-7.

4. On the activities of the CKT and other Chinese "political-fraternal" groups in Canada, see Wickberg, *From Canada to China*, 73-90, 101-117, 157-169. See also Edgar Wickberg, "Chinese and Canadian Influences on Chinese Politics in Vancouver, 1900-1947," *BC Studies* 45 (Spring 1980): 37-55, *passim*.

5. See CCRC, Box 4.

6. The *Victoria Daily Colonist* reported these activities in its "City and District in Brief" column. See "Hold Splendid Outing," *Victoria Daily Colonist*, 10 July, 1919, 6; "Picnic for Members," ibid., 11 July, 1919, 6; "Will Hold Picnic," ibid., 13 July, 1919, 6. See the "News in Brief" column of the *Victoria Daily Times*, for example, "St. Jude's Picnic," *Victoria Daily Times*, 7 July, 1919, 9.

7. My usage of racial categories such as "Chinese" and "white" follows that of early twentieth century sources. These sources treat such categories as "natural" and unproblematic identities. However, the invention and maintenance of such categories is integral to racism. See Robert Miles, *Racism*, Key Ideas Series (London and New York: Routledge, 1989). I explore the problematic nature of such identities in a forthcoming paper, ""Chinamen, wherever we go": Chinese Nationalism and Guangdong Merchants in British Columbia, 1871-1911." Anglo-European attitudes towards "the Chinese" and other Asians have been well documented. The most detailed work is Particia E. Roy, *A White Man's Province: British Columbia Politicians and Chinese and Japanese Immigrants, 1858-1914* (Vancouver: University of British Columbia Press, 1989), although important insights remain from W. Peter Ward, *White Canada Forever: Popular Attitudes and Public Policy Toward Orientals in British Columbia* (Montreal: McGill-Queen's University Press, 1978). Kay J. Anderson, *Vancouver's Chinatown: Racial Discourse in Canada, 1875-1980*

(Montreal and Kingston: McGill-Queen's University Press, 1991) combines theoretical sophistication with a thorough study of local government activities.

8. This point has essentially been made by W. Peter Ward, "Class and Race in the Social Structure of British Columbia, 1870-1939," *BC Studies* 45 (1980): 17-35. For white working class attitudes, see Gillian Creese, "Exclusion or Solidarity? Vancouver Workers Confront the "Oriental Problem"," *BC Studies* 80 (Winter 1988-89): 24-51. That the members of racially oppressed minorities are often well aware of the activities of members of the dominant group, while the latter tend to be unaware of the former, is a point that has been made in a different context by bell hooks, *Feminist Theory from Margin to Centre* (Boston: South End Press, 1985).

9. This is evident, for example, in Ward's usages in *White Canada Forever*. This is not restricted to British Columbia historians. See, for example, the discussion of the division between public and private violence in Judy M. Torrance, *Public Violence in Canada, 1867-1982* (Kingston and Montreal: McGill-Queen's University Press, 1986), 14-16. Bruce Curtis, who cites the creation of a public as an aspect of state formation through early school reform, also does not define the term. See Bruce Curtis, "Preconditions of the Canadian State: Educational Reform and the Construction of a Public in Upper Canada, 1837-1846," *Studies in Political Economy* 10 (1983): 99-121 and *Building The Educational State: Canada West, 1836-1871* (London, Ont.: The Althouse Press, 1988).

10. Jürgen Habermas, *The Structural Transformation of the Public Sphere: An Inquiry into a Category of Bourgeois Society*, Thomas Burger (trans.) (Cambridge, Mass.: MIT Press, 1989), 1. I am indebted to Bill Maciejko for bringing this work to my attention.

11. The terms for the CCBA and CBA are the same in Chinese.

12. While Cantonese and written Chinese were the principal languages of instruction in these schools, they were not solely language schools. The CPS of both Victoria and Vancouver offered English language instruction and many schools offered a full curriculum, including subjects such as History, Geography and even Mathematics and Science, similar to those of elementary schools in China. Hence I refer to them as Chinese schools rather than as Chinese language schools.

13. In this respect the establishment of Chinese schools paralleled the same kind of state-forming activities as those of school reformers in early nineteenth century Ontario. See Curtis, *Building the Educational State*. This issue as well as that of the role of Chinese schools in responding to racism is examined more closely in Timothy J. Stanley, "Defining the Chinese Other: White Supremacy, Schooling and Social Structure in British Columbia before 1923" (unpublished Ph.D. dissertation, University of British Columbia, 1991), esp. 266-318.

14. Habermas, *Structural Transformation*, 5 ff.

15. *Ibid.*, 23-26.

16. My usage of the term "state" is intended to follow that of Philip Abrams, "Notes on the Difficulty of Studying the State [1977]," *Journal of Historical Sociology* 1,1 (March 1988): 58-89, and Philip Corrigan and Derek Sayer, *The Great Arch: English State Formation as Cultural Revolution* (New York: Basil Blackwell, 1985). This is also Curtis' usage. See *Building the Educational State, passim*.

17. The social construction of gender within Chinese communities points to an additional sense in which there was a distinct Chinese public sphere. Habermas discusses this in the context of the Greek *polis, Structural Transformation*, 3-4. This

notion has more recently been developed by feminist scholars as a major aspect of the social construction of gender. See Margaret Stacy, "The Division of Labour Revisited or Overcoming the Two Adams," in Philip Abrams, *et. al.*, (eds.), *Practice and Progress: British Sociology, 1950-1980* (London: George Allen & Unwin, 1981), 172-190 and Eva Gamarnikow, *et. al.* (eds.), *The Public and the Private* (London: Heineman, 1983). On the differing social constructions of gender within Chinese and white communities in North America, see Peggy Pascoe, "Gender Systems in Conflict: The Marriages of Mission-Educated Chinese American Women, 1874-1939," *Journal of Social History* 22, 4 (September 1989): 631-652.

18. For example, in 1915 a Chinese schoolgirl in Victoria, the target of a stoning by a group of white boys, was so seriously injured that she required emergency surgery to save her life. This incident went unreported in the Victoria English language papers, but not in *The Chinese Times*. See "Hua nu beiwu" [Chinese girl assaulted], *Dahan Gongbao*, 26 February, 1915, 3. Indeed, *The Chinese Times* is probably the best source on white supremacist activities during this era. See CCRC, Box 4, *passim*.

19. These issues are developed more fully in Stanley, "Defining the Chinese Other."

20. If many Chinese were "sojourners" and made repeated trips back to the old country, the fact that so did many of British Columbia's Anglo-Canadian "settlers" seems to have escaped notice. There has been some progress in incorporating Chinese activities in the province's history. See, for example, Gillian Creese, "Class, Ethnicity and Conflict: The Case of Chinese and Japanese Immigrants, 1880-1923," in Rennie Warburton and David Coburn (eds.), *Workers, Capital and the State in British Columbia* (Vancouver: University of British Columbia Press, 1988), 54-85.

21. Margaret Ormsby, *British Columbia: A History* (Vancouver: MacMillan of Canada, 1958), 252 ff.

22. On political opportunism as a motive for Chinese disenfranchisement, see Martin Robin, *The Rush for Spoils: The Company Province 1871-1933* (Toronto: McClelland and Stewart, 1972), 54. On imperialism in Canada, see Carl Berger, *The Sense of Power: Studies in the Ideas of Canadian Imperialism* (Toronto: University of Toronto Press, 1970) and Doug Owram, *Promise of Eden: The Canadian Expansionist Movement and the Idea of the West 1856-1900* (Toronto: University of Toronto Press, 1980), especially 125-148. On racism and imperialism, see, for example, Robert A. Huttenback, "No Strangers within the Gates: Attitudes and Policies towards the Non-White Residents of the British Empire of Settlement," *Journal of Imperial and Commonwealth History* I (1973), 271-302.

23. See for example the "private" comments of Dr. John Sebastian Helmcken to the members of the 1885 Royal Commission on Chinese Immigration. Cited by J. A. Chapleau in Canada, House of Commons, *Debates* 1885, 3009. Helmcken reportedly told the Commissioners, "we want you to prevent the influx of Mongolians because we want to be here ourselves, and do not want others to be here." See also the comments with respect to "settlers" and "sojourners" in Edgar Wickberg, Review of *A White Man's Province: British Columbia Politicians and Chinese and Japanese Immigrants, 1858-1914*, by Patricia E. Roy, in *BC Studies*, 88 (Winter 1990-91): 97-100.

24. For population figures, see Ward, *White Canada Forever*, 179.

25. A bill disenfranchising the Chinese and First Nations was passed by the legislature in 1872, but was not signed into law until 1874. See, Patricia E. Roy, *A White Man's Province*, 45. Since the federal franchise was provincially based at the time,

these acts also had the effect of disenfranchising the Chinese residents of British Columbia at the federal level. When the federal government established its own electoral system under the *Dominion Franchise Act* in 1885, Chinese disenfranchisement was re-affirmed. The Act applied to "persons" which it defined as males "excluding a person of Mongolian or Chinese race." *See Statutes of Canada* 1885, Chapter 40, section 2. Another section of this Act disenfranchised all First Nations people west of Ontario. On the significance of this Act in terms of Canadian political history, see Gordon Stewart, "John A. Macdonald's Greatest Triumph," *Canadian Historical Review* LXIII (1982), 3-33.

26. Bruce Ryder, "Racism and the Constitution: The Constitutional Fate of British Columbia Anti-Asian Legislation, 1872-1922," (unpublished ms., 1990), 166. Part of this work is published as "Racism and the Constitution: The Constitutional Fate of British Columbia Anti-Asian Legislation, 1884-1909," *Osgoode Hall Law Journal* 29, 3 (1991): 619-676, however all references below are to the unpublished manuscript. "Race" rather than national origin or citizenship was the basis for these exclusions. See *ibid.*, 1, n. 1, and Peter S. Li, *The Chinese in Canada* (Toronto: Oxford University Press, 1988), 35. With few exceptions these exclusions were upheld by the courts, often on the grounds that as their provisions applied equally to Canadian-born and immigrant Chinese, they were not discriminatory. See Ryder, "Racism and the Constitution," 141-166.

27. Ryder, "Racism and the Constitution," provides the best discussion of B.C. legislation. Roy also provides an excellent discussion. See *A White Man's Province, passim.*

28. Legal exclusion was accompanied by a broader ideological process which represented the Chinese residents of B.C. as "alien" and whites as "native." On this construction in general, see Stanley, "Defining the Chinese Other," 162-207. Officially sanctioned textbooks also fostered it. See Timothy J. Stanley, "White Supremacy and the Rhetoric of Educational Indoctrination: A Canadian Case Study," in J. A. Mangan (ed.), *Making Imperial Mentalities: Socialisation and British Imperialism* (Manchester: Manchester University Press, 1990), 144-162.

29. See, for example, Ward, *White Canada Forever*, 24-25, 37, 44-46, 49, 63-64. For an example in a different context see Cole Harris, "Industry and the Good Life Around Idaho Peak," *Canadian Historical Review* 66, 3 (September 1985): 355 and n. 15.

30. The discriminatory nature of the court system during the building of the CPR is outlined by Patricia E. Roy, "A Choice Between Evils: The Chinese and the Construction of the Canadian Pacific Railway in British Columbia," in Hugh A. Dempsey (ed.), *The CPR West: The Iron Road and the Making of a Nation* (Vancouver: Douglas and McIntyre, 1984), 13-34. *The Chinese Times* regularly reported on court cases in which whites were given minimal sentences for assaults on Chinese. Compare for example the Chinese Canadian Research Collections entries for 12 August, 1915 and 10 June, 1916 with those of 2 November, 1916 and 17 January, 1917 in CCRC Box 4. See also the entry for 13 October, 1919, CCRC, Box 4.

31. Wickberg, *From China to Canada*, 16.

32. Roy, *White Man's Province*, 45.

33. Wickberg, *From China to Canada*, 34-35. The best discussion of Chinese merchants in British Columbia is provided by Paul Yee, "Chinese Business in Vancouver, 1886-1914," (M.A., University of British Columbia, 1983). On the Chinese in British Columbia during this era, see also Jin Tan, "Chinese Labour and

the Reconstituted Social Order," *Canadian Ethnic Studies/Etudes ethniques au Canada* XIX, 3 (1987): 68-88.

34. In this respect it is interesting to note that the federal government had to intervene to pay for the property damage arising from the 1907 anti-Asian riot in Vancouver.

35. "Segregation in Schools," *The Daily Colonist*, 14 October, 1922, 4.

36. On school segregation, see Mary Ashworth, *The Forces Which Shaped Them: A History of the Education of Minority Group Children in British Columbia* (Vancouver: New Star Books, 1979); David Chuen-Yan Lai, "The Issue of Discrimination in Education in Victoria, 1901-1923," *Canadian Ethnic Studies/Etudes ethniques au Canada* XIX, 3 (1987): 47-67 and Timothy J. Stanley, "White Supremacy, Chinese Schooling, and School Segregation in Victoria: The Case of the Chinese Students' Strike, 1922-23," *Historical Studies in Education/Revue d'histoire de l'éducation* 2, 2 (Fall 1990): 287-306.

37. See Robin Fisher, *Contact and Conflict: Indian-European Relations in British Columbia* (Vancouver: University of British Columbia, 1977), 165. On the issue of land title, see Paul Tennant, *Aboriginal Peoples and Politics: The Indian Land Question in British Columbia, 1849-1989* (Vancouver: University of British Columbia Press, 1990).

38. For example, in 1878 legislation allowed officials to seize the goods of those Chinese who could not prove that they had paid a special poll tax.

39. Ryder, "Racism and the Constitution," 177 ff. On the corporate nature of the B.C. economy, see Robin, *Rush for Spoils*.

40. See Kay J. Anderson, ""East" as "West": Place, State and the Institutionalization of Myth in Vancouver's Chinatown, 1880-1980" (Ph.D., University of British Columbia, 1987).

41. Emphasis in the original. Cited in ibid., 171. See also Yee, "Chinese Business," 49.

42. For a discussion of the provisions of the 1923 Chinese Immigration Act, see Cheng Tien-fang, *Oriental Immigration in Canada* (Shanghai: The Commercial Press, 1931), 90-96.

43. For example, Chinese workers made considerable use of workers' compensation. See Wickberg, *From China to Canada*, 135.

44. See, for example, Edgar Wickberg, "Chinese Associations in Canada, 1923-47," in K. Victor Ujimoto and Gordon Hirabayashi, *Visible Minorities and Multiculturalism: Asians in Canada* (Toronto: Butterworths, 1980), 23-31.

45. See Creese, "Exclusion or Solidarity?"

46. Edgar Wickberg, "Chinese Organizations and the Canadian Political Process: Two Case Studies," in Jorgan Dahlie and Tissa Fernando (eds.), *Ethnicity, Power and Politics in Canada* (Scarborough: Butterworth, 1980), 172 and Edgar Wickberg, "Chinese and Canadian Influences on Chinese Politics in Vancouver, 1900-1947," *BC Studies* 45 (Spring 1980): 44.

47. David Chuen-Yan Lai, "The Chinese Consolidated Benevolent Association in Victoria: Its Origins and Functions," *BC Studies* 15 (Autumn 1972): 57. This claim is repeated by Anthony B. Chan, *Gold Mountain: The Chinese in the New World* (Vancouver: New Star Books, 1983), 89.

48. See Wickberg, "Chinese Organizations and the Canadian Political Process."

49. Roy provides the best account of the overall political context of these problems. See "A Choice Between Evils," *passim*. See also Wickberg, *From China to Canada*, 36.

50. David T. H. Lee [Li Donghai], *Jianada Huaqiao shi* [History of the Overseas

Chinese in Canada] (Taibei: Zhonghua Da Dian Bianying She, 1967), 177. Lee reproduces this letter in its entirety. A facsimile of the original letter is reproduced in David Chuen-Yan Lai, "The Chinese Consolidated Benevolent Association in Victoria: Its Origins and Functions," *BC Studies* 15 (Autumn 1972): 53-67. Wickberg has called Lee's work, "the most comprehensive source on the history of the Chinese in Canada," *From China to Canada*, 334.

51. Lee, *Jianada Huaqiao shi*, 178-79.
52. Him Mark Lai, "Historical Development of the Chinese Consolidated Benevolent Association/*Huiguan* System," *Chinese America: History and Perspectives, 1987* (San Francisco: Chinese Historical Society of America, 1987), 13-51.
53. Lee, *Jianada Huaqiao shi*, 176-178.
54. "Constitution of the Chinese Consolidated Benevolent Association," reproduced in Lee, *Jianada Huaqiao shi*, 179.
55. Wickberg, *From China to Canada*, 38.
56. Lee, *Jianada Huaqiao shi*, 195.
57. See Robert A. J. McDonald, "Working-Class Vancouver, 1886-1914: Urbanism and Class in British Columbia," *BC Studies* 69-70 (Spring-Summer 1986): 33-69.
58. See Paul Yee, "Chinese Business."
59. David Chuen-Yan Lai, *Chinatowns: Towns within Cities in Canada* (Vancouver: University of British Columbia Press, 1988), 213-214.
60. *Dahan Gongbao*, 4 September, 1914, 2 and 1 December, 1914, 3. Cited in CCRC, Box 3.
61. On the roles of merchants in forwarding letters and remittances to China, see Wickberg, *From China to Canada*, 35. On the labour contract system, see Li, *The Chinese in Canada* and Gillian Creese, "Class, Ethnicity and Conflict."
62. For the view that merchants were at the bottom of the social ladder in China, while at the top in the new world, see Chan, *Gold Mountain*, 22 and Roger Daniels, *Asian America: Chinese and Japanese in the United States since 1850* (Seattle and London: University of Washington Press, 1988), 25. For an important discussion of the social position of merchants in late imperial Chinese society, see Marie-Claire Bergère, *The Golden Age of the Chinese Bourgeoisie, 1911-1937*, translated by Janet Lloyd (Cambridge: Cambridge University Press, Paris: Editions de la maison des sciences de l'homme, 1986), especially 13-23.
63. For a discussion of continuities between the roles of merchants in South China and British Columbia, see Chee Chiu Clement Ng, "The Chinese Benevolent Association of Vancouver, 1889-1923: A Response to Local Conditions," (M.A., University of Manitoba, 1986). On elite activism in China, see Mary Backus Rankin, *Elite Activism and Political Transformation in China: Zhejiang Province, 1865-1911* (Stanford: Stanford University Press, 1986) and William T. Rowe, *Hankow: Conflict and Community in a Chinese City*, 1796-1895 (Stanford: Stanford University Press, 1989).
64. One must be careful not to carry this analogy too far. What Habermas calls a "rational public," one which used reason to forestall tyranny, did not emerge in China until the twentieth century. Even then, although the Chinese public was strong enough to prevent Yuan Shikai, the prototypical warlord, from re-establishing the imperial system in 1916, it was not strong enough to unify the country. See William T. Rowe, "The Public Sphere in Modern China," *Modern China* 16, 3 (July 1990): 309-329.

65. Wickberg, *From China to Canada*, 101-115.

66. On the origins of these groups, see Wickberg, *From China to Canada*, 30-34, 73-76. On their political machinations, see ibid., passim, and Wickberg, "Chinese and Canadian Influences."

67. This is most striking if one examines the contents of the CKT paper, *The Chinese Times*. See Chinese Canadian Research Collection, Box 4, passim.

68. In 1885 a fifty-dollar immigration head tax was placed on Chinese labourers and their families. By 1904, this tax had been raised to $500. *"Bona fide"* Chinese merchants and their families were specifically excluded from these taxes. The head taxes were abolished in 1923 when Chinese immigration of all types was ended.

69. See, for example, the information on the Chinese population of Victoria supplied by the Chinese Chamber of Commerce to the Royal Commission on Chinese and Japanese Immigration, *Report of the Royal Commission on Chinese and Japanese Immigration* (Ottawa: S. E. Dawson, 1902), 12-13.

70. Lee, *Jianada Huaqiao shi*, 321 ff. On the education activities of the leading Chinese merchant in Vancouver, see *Yeh Ch'un-t'ien xiansheng chuanji* [Biography of Yipsang] (Hong Kong: n.p., [1973]), 6.

71. Lai, *Chinatowns*, 215.

72. The CPS in Victoria is still in operation. Detailed information on the history of this school can be found in Lim Bang, "Weibu Zhonghua Huiguan zhi yuange ji qiaoxiao chuangli zhi yuanqi" [The origins of the Victoria Chinese Consolidated Benevolent Association and the reasons for the creation of overseas schools], in Lee T'ung-hai (ed.), *Jianada Weiduoli Zhonghua Huiguan/Huaqiao Xuexiao chengli qishiwu/liushi zhounian jinian qikan* [Special publication marking the seventy-fifth anniversary of Canada's Victoria Chinese Consolidated Benevolent Association and the sixtieth anniversary of the Overseas Chinese School] (Victoria: Chinese Consolidated Benevolent Association, 1960), Part IV. 1-5. Guan Qiyi, "Jianada Huaqiao jiaoyu shilue," (A short history of Overseas Chinese education in Canada), *ibid.*, Part IV, 17-18. See also "Benxiao xiaoshi," [A history of our school], *ibid.*, Part III, 54-58. See also Lee, *Jianada Huaqiao shi*, 321-324, 329-334.

73. *Jianada Weiduoli Zhonghua Huiguan qikan*, Part V, 26.

74. "Weibu Huaqiao Gongxue baogao ce" [Text of the report of the Victoria Chinese Public School], *Dahan Gongbao*, 13 July, 1915, 1.

75. "Weibu Zhonghua Huiguan Gongli Huaqiao Xuexiao chao sheng guang gao" [The advertisement for students of the Vancouver Chinese Benevolent Association Overseas Chinese Public School], *Dahan Gongbao*, 24 April, 1917, 7.

76. Lee, *Jianada Huaqiao shi*, 334.

77. Lee, *Jianada Huaqiao shi*, 324-329. On educational reform in China during this era, see Marianne Bastid, *Educational Reform in Early Twentieth Century China*, Paul Bailey (trans.) (Ann Arbor: Center for Chinese Studies, University of Michigan, 1988) and Paul Bailey, *Reform the People: Popular Education and Educational Reform in Twentieth Century China* (Vancouver: University of British Columbia Press, 1991). On these schools in the late 1910s, see, for example, "Wenfou – Aiguo Xuetang Tonggao [Vancouver – Patriotic School Notice]," *Dahan Gongbao*, 30 July, 1917, 3. After the 1911 revolution the Empire Reform Association became the Constitutionalist Party. Before 1923, with the exception of the CPS in Victoria, Chinese schools in B.C. operated intermittently. See Stanley, "Defining the Chinese Other," 312-18.

78. "Qinge Xuexiao kai mu zhi chengdian" [Report on the opening ceremonies of the Educate Promising Talent School], *Dahan Gongbao*, 18 July, 1921, 3. See also *ibid.*, 19 March, 1922, cited in CCRC, Box 4.

79. See, for example, "Guangzhi Xuexiao zhi qian xue" [The Broad Knowledge School to move], *Dahan Gongbao*, 23 October, 1922, 3; "Jingcun Xueshi Minguo si nian dier qi xiali kaoshi chengsi" [The results of the second term of the 1915 summer session of the Jingcun School], ibid., 20 July, 1915, 3; and "Huaqiao jiang duo yi xiao xi Zhong Ying wen" [Overseas Chinese get another school to study Chinese and English], *ibid.*, 22 April, 1922, 3.

80. Wickberg, "Chinese Associations in Canada," 25.

81. See "To Exclude the Chinese," *Victoria Daily Colonist*, 10 February, 1901, 8.

82. Royal Commission on Chinese and Japanese Immigration, *Report of the Commission*, 12-13.

83. Stanley, "White Supremacy, Chinese Schooling and School Segregation," 301 ff.

84. Lee, *Jianada Huaqiao shi*, 329-331.

85. Until briefly re-unified under the KMT in the late 1920s, China was divided between a Northern government located in Beijing and the KMT-led government in Canton. The Northern government was the one recognized by the foreign powers and by Canada.

86. See, for example, "Huanying hui zhi renao" [The warmth of the Welcome meeting], *Dahan Gongbao* 3 May, 1918, 3; "Lingshu lai han zhao lu" [Record of delegation's visit], *ibid.*, 2 January, 1919, 2; "Cai Yuanpei Xiansheng zhi cheng kuang" [Mr. Cai Yuanpei's activities], *ibid.*, 7 July, 1921 and "Cai Yuanpei Xiansheng yanshuo ci" [The text of Mr. Cai Yuanpei's address], *ibid.*, 1.

87. "Zhonghua Huiguan zhixun xuesheng jishi" [Memo on the Chinese Benevolent Association instructions to students], *ibid.*, 7 September, 1920, 3 and "Lin Lingshi bugao" [Notice from Ambassador Lin], *ibid.*, 7 November, 1922, 3.

88. See, for example, *Dahan Gongbao*, 22 July, 1918, 3; *ibid.*, 5 November, 1921 and *ibid.*, 1 December, 1921, 1. Cited in CCRC, Box 4.

89. Lee, *Jianada Huaqiao shi*, 329-330.

90. See, for example, *Dahan Gongbao*, 19 March, 1922, cited in CCRC Box 4.

91. See, for example, the editorial "Ben bao zhi zhizhi" [The mission of this newspaper], *Dahan Gongbao*, 17 May, 1918, 1.

92. See, for example, "Guangzhi Xuexiao zhi qian xue" [The Broad Knowledge School to move], *Dahan Gongbao*, 23 October, 1922, 3; "Jingcun Xueshi Minguo si nian dier qi xiali kaoshi chengsi" [The results of the second term of the 1915 summer session of the Jingcun School], *ibid.*, 20 July, 1915, 3; "Weiduoli Huaqiao Gong Xue diyi hui biye tishi" [First graduation ceremony of the Victoria Overseas Chinese Public School], *ibid.*, 22 March, 1915, 3. On clan association schoolteachers, see *ibid.*, 17 November, 1920, cited CCRC, Box 4.

93. "A Chinese School," *Colonist*, 18 January, 1899, 6.

94. Lee, *Jianada Huaqiao shi*, 323.

95. See, for example, the entries in CCRC Box 4, for *Dahan Gongbao* on 13 October, 1917, 2 October, 1918, 8 October, 1920, 11 October, 1920, 29 September, 1921, 20 September, 1921.

96. See David Chuen-Yan Lai, "Home County and Clan Origins of Overseas Chinese

in Canada in the Early 1880s," *BC Studies*, 27 (Autumn 1975): 3-29. See also Wickberg, *From China to Canada*, 7-9, 25-6.

97. See Yun Ho Chang's reminiscences in Daphne Marlatt and Carole Itter (compilers and editors), *Opening Doors: Vancouver's East End*, Sound Heritage Series, VIII, 1 and 2 (Victoria: Minister of Provincial Secretary and Government Services, Provincial Archive, 1979), 40.

98. See "Weiduoli Huaqiao Gong Xue diyi hui biye li shi" [The first graduation ceremony of the Victoria CPS], *Dahan Gongbao*, 23 March, 1915, 3.

99. Stanley, "White Supremacy, Chinese Schooling and School Segregation."

100. *The Chinese Times* reported that "every girl and boy who graduates from the first class can leave behind their local dialects and are fluent in Cantonese when reading and speaking." "Weibu qikao zhuzhong Shenghua Guoyu ying sheng zhi tese," [Special characteristics of the pronunciation of Cantonese and Mandarin at the Victoria end of term examinations], *Dahan Gongbao*, 17 July, 1915, 3. The writer complained that Victoria's Cantonese was not standard as it "suffered from the influence of the students."

101. See Stanley, "Defining the Chinese Other," 314-18.

102. Sing Lim, *West Coast Chinese Boy* (Montreal: Tundra Books, 1979)

103. Brian Simon, "Can Education Change Society?" in J. Donald Wilson (ed.), *An Imperfect Past: Education and Society in Canadian History*, (Vancouver: Centre for the Study of Curriculum and Instruction, University of British Columbia, 1984), 30-47.

104. See the graduation pictures of the Victoria Chinese Public School in *Weiduoli Zhonghua Hui Guan qikan, passim*.

105. Wickberg, *From China to Canada*, 95.

106. Tamara Adilman, "A Preliminary Sketch of Chinese Women and Work in British Columbia 1858-1950," in Barbara K. Latham and Roberta J. Pazdro (eds.), *Not Just Pin Money: Selected Essays on the History of Women's Work in British Columbia* (Victoria: Camosun College, 1984), 53-78.

107. A Mrs. Yip, for example, had been commissioned by the CBA in Vancouver to visit sick Chinese patients in the hospitals. See *Dahan Gongbao*, December 5, 1922, CCRC Box 4.

108. See the account of Japanese newspapers and organizations told by Ryuichi Yoshida in Rolf Knight and Maya Koizumi, *A Man for our Times: The Life History of a Japanese-Canadian Fisherman* (Vancouver: New Star Books,1976). For an example of the continued existence of traditional forms of rule within a First Nation, see Terry Glavin, *A Death Feast in Dimlahamid* (Vancouver: New Star Books, 1990).

109. This is not to deny that there were not certain parallels in the experiences of Chinese immigrants and those from Europe. Compare, for example, the description of the "sojourning" of Chinese "bachelor workers" brought to Canada under the labour contract system found in Chan, *Gold Mountain*, 47-73 and that of Italian male workers imported under the *padroni* system found in Robert Harney, "Men Without Women: Italian Migrants in Canada, 1885-1930," *Canadian Ethnic Studies/Études ethniques au Canada* XI, 1 (1979): 29-51.

110. Wickberg, "Chinese Associations in Canada."

111. Wickberg, Review of *A White Man's Province*, 100.

"The Past of My Place":
Western Canadian Artists
and the Uses of History[1]

JEREMY MOUAT

More than a decade ago Robert Kroetsch asked the simple question, "How do you write in a new country?" In his view this raised some very significant issues:

Our inherited literature, the literature of our European past and of eastern North America, is emphatically the literature of a people who have NOT lived on the prairies. We had, and still have, difficulty finding names for the elements and characteristics of this landscape. The human response to this landscape is so new and ill-defined and complex that our writers come back, uneasily but compulsively, to landscape writing. Like the homesteaders before us, we are compelled to adjust and invent, to remember and forget. . . .

. . . . we both, and at once, record and invent these new places. . . . That pattern of contraries, all the possibilities implied in *record* and *invent*, for me finds its focus in the model suggested by the phrase: a local pride.

The phrase is from William Carlos Williams – indeed those three words are the opening of his great poem, *Paterson*, about Paterson, New Jersey: *a local pride*.

The feeling must come from an awareness of the authenticity of our own lives. People who feel invisible try to borrow visibility from those who are visible. To understand others is surely difficult. But to understand ourselves becomes impossible if we do not see images of ourselves in the mirror – be that mirror theatre or literature or historical writing. A local pride does not exclude the rest of the world, or other experiences; rather, it makes them both possible. It creates an organizing centre. Or as Williams put it, more radically: the acquiring of a local pride enables us to create our own culture – "by lifting an environment to expression."

How do we lift an environment to expression? How do you write in a new country?[2]

Kroetsch's assertion that regional art and literature gives us expression can be seen as a response to the growing uniformity of popular culture, on this continent and around the world. At the same time, as much journalistic commentary emphasizes, globalization is transforming economic relations between nations. The world shrinks, and its population seems intent on marching to the beat of the same drummer. But if the contemporary world is inexorably moving us all toward the same point, our various pasts underline some important differences. This paper examines how three artists have attempted to use history to give expression to a specific western Canadian existence. The following pages will argue that the three reflect the kind of vibrant regional culture which Kroetsch feels is so critical to our lives. Thus their work can be interpreted as a vital antidote to the homogenizing images of contemporary culture, which threaten to rob us of any real sense of ourselves as a distinct society.

The artists discussed here are James Keelaghan, a folk singer; Anne Wheeler, a film maker; and Rudy Wiebe, a novelist as well as an academic. All three have turned to the past for a context in which to situate their work, and have considerable experience in handling historical material. Wiebe, a professor at the University of Alberta, has published a good deal of history, including a compilation of primary sources on the 1885 Rebellion.[3] Wheeler helped to research and write *A Harvest Yet To Reap*[4], a resource book on women's history. Keelaghan only became a professional musician after studying history at the University of Calgary. In addition to their familiarity with history, the three have turned to material which traditional popular history has dealt with in a less than satisfying manner: topics such as the role of women, the experience of Native peoples and the significance of class. Each gives the past of western Canada a specificity and an authenticity that few others – even professional historians – have been able to achieve.

What are we to make of such work? As its subject matter indicates, this is not the blockbuster popular history of Pierre Berton and Peter Newman, nor is it the kind of thing that garners much attention in refereed journals. Academic historians have yet to take fictionalized history very seriously, whether presented in novels, song or on the silver screen.[5] Whatever its status, however, there can be no question that to read Wiebe's *The Temptations of Big Bear*, to watch Wheeler's "Bye Bye Blues," or to listen to Keelaghan sing his songs involves confronting a vivid and living history. This is not the sanitized past presented in television period dramas, series such as "Anne of Green Gables," a glowing place where innocence seems to have been sweeter and actions purer. This is the past where Big Bear tells those in a Regina court room that

> This land belonged to me. When I had it I never needed your flour and pork. Sometimes I was stiff with Indian agents who looked at me as if I was a child and knew less than a child. Before many of you were born I ran buffalo over this place where you have put this building, and white men ate the meat I gave them. I gave my hand as a brother; I was free, and the smallest Person in my band was as free as I because the Master of Life had given us our place on the earth and that was enough for us. But you have taken our inheritance, and our strength. The land is torn up, black with fires, and empty. *You have done this.* And there is nothing left now but that you must help us.[6]

The work of these three artists is best viewed as a celebration of the local and the unique in the face of the dehumanizing and homogenizing trends of an invasive global culture. This is a culture that is necessarily history-less: "A global culture is here and now and everywhere, and for its purposes the past only serves to offer some decontextualized example or element for its cosmopolitan patchwork."[7] Viewed in this way, as a response or counterpoint to the depressing hegemony of global culture, the work of Keelaghan *et al.* is a western Canadian example of a broader trend, the insistence on a specific culture. But within the Canadian context, it needs to be understood regionally: as Frye has noted, the only perspective from which to comprehend the creative imagination.[8]

Regionalism, of course, is not a simple word: it is different things to different people, differences which themselves reflect regional identities. The linguistic and cultural regionalism of the Quebec is no more and no less authentic than the economic and geographical regionalism of the West. Such regionalisms are asymmetrical: as one scholar has pointed out, these are "one-sided polarities . . . a self-designated west but no corresponding east, and a self-conscious French Canada but no parallel English Canada."[9] And from a regional perspective, the work of Wiebe, Keelaghan and Wheeler is evidence of a mature cultural identity in Western Canada. Such a claim can be substantiated by examining this work in some detail; the following pages look in turn at Wiebe's novel, *The Temptations of Big Bear*, Wheeler's film, "Bye Bye Blues," and the songs of James Keelaghan.

* * *

Rudy Wiebe has written a number of novels, as well as short stories and other works, with the explicit purpose of confronting the experiences of those who have lived in Western Canada. He does so with a relentless passion and a clear sense of mission. He once drew a parallel between his efforts and those of V. S. Naipaul:

> He, of course, has with the power of his writing destroyed the "embarrassment" about Port of Spain, something I have not yet achieved with, for example, Steinbach, Manitoba. And if you smiled at that statement, you proved what I am trying to explain: in the fictional worlds of Canada, certain societies are still not really acceptable.[10]

Wiebe has a strong sense of himself as a western Canadian and as a result most of his fiction deals with the Prairie West. Central themes are the encounter between Native and European, the meaning of ethnic identity, and the significance of the Western environment.

More than either Wheeler or Keelaghan, Wiebe is an established figure on the Canadian cultural stage. His first novel appeared in 1962, and in 1973 he won the Governor General's Award for fiction with *The Temptations of Big Bear*. He has received much critical attention, although many regard *The Temptations of Big Bear*, as well as the subsequent (and related) novel, *The Scorched-Wood People*, as his major contribution to Canadian literature. In a brief book on historical fiction, for example, Dennis Duffy argued that *The*

247

Temptations of Big Bear "stand[s] as the culmination of the Canadian historical novel," while George Woodcock has claimed that

> Novels such as Rudy Wiebe's *Temptations of Big Bear* . . . introduce a new
> sense of history merging into myth, of theme coming out of a perception of
> the land, of geography as a source of art. In the process they break time down
> into the nonlinear patterns of authentic memory; they also break down actu-
> ality and recreate it in terms of the kind of nonliteral rationality that belongs
> to dreams.[11]

Some of Wiebe's more recent work has received a less enthusiastic critical response, although his latest book has garnered much praise. Even *The
Globe and Mail* – as will be seen below, not always an admirer of the culture
of the West – was positively effusive, describing it as "quite simply, a wonderful, wonderful book. . . . *Playing Dead* is a piece of evocative prose that
confirms Rudy Wiebe as an outstanding writer . . . whose contribution will
endure."[12]

The Temptations of Big Bear is a long and complex work, one which demands much from a reader.[13] The novel is set in the past of the Canadian
West, from 1876 to 1888. Episodes describe the relationship between the
Cree band of Big Bear and the Canadian officials who sought Big Bear's
assent to the treaty-making process then underway. The climax of the novel
comes at Frog Lake in the spring of 1885, when a number of Europeans
were killed by Big Bear's band. But that is a very simple analysis of what the
novel is "about," since Wiebe regards the past as strange and mysterious
place; at times, unknowable. And to further complicate the story, it has no
central voice: "the novel is composed as a fugue for several narrative voices
of different qualities, each of which emphasizes the tension between references to past and present."[14] The book invites the reader to confront that
complexity rather than offering any one interpretation of the events that it
describes.

Wiebe writes about the past with a respectful diffidence that is both honest and unusual. He tells his reader how the evidence is scattered and contradictory; he pauses to point out the many ironies; and the process of reconstruction often ends with an admission of failure, or at least uncertainty.
His article about the composition of the novel, as well as another describ-

ing a visit to New York to see Big Bear's power bundle, demonstrate the sensitivity that he brought to the historical material at the centre of the work.[15] The quotation earlier in this paper of Big Bear's Regina address serves as a good example of his research and his style. Wiebe's article on the novel describes the difficulties he encountered in trying to find details of Big Bear's defence, in order to compose that passage. As he suggests, these difficulties were instructive:

> though I spent a week in Ottawa doing little else, I could find no trace of his defence in either the Archives or the Department of Justice. So there is nothing left but William Cameron's summary of what Big Bear said, and he concludes with Richardson's answer:
>
> > "Big Bear," said Justice Richardson, and his tone was not unkind, "you have been found guilty by an impartial jury. You cannot be excused from responsibility for the misdoings of your band. The sentence of the court is that you be imprisoned in the penitentiary at Stony Mountain for three years."
> >
> > That's recorded forty years after the fact; this is Nicholas Flood Davin's report in *The Leader*, October 1, 1885:
> >
> > First came Big Bear, who made a long address to the Court, in the course of which he frequently used such language as, "when we owned the country" and he drew the Court's attention to the fact that he being in prison who was to protect his people.
> >
> > Judge Richardson in sentencing him told him that they never owned the land[,] that it belonged to the Queen, who allowed them to use it, that when she wanted to make other use of it she called them together through her officers, and gave them the choicest portions of the country and that, as to his people, they would be looked after as though nothing had occurred. He was then sentenced to three years in the Penitentiary.
>
> How time smears edges; how it liberalizes, softens our motivation![16]

Wiebe has been particularly concerned to articulate a Native voice, to remind other Canadians of the experiences of those people who have been marginalized by the country's history. He does this extraordinarily well; his prose has in places an Old Testament grandeur which seems appropriate to the topic. When this similarity was drawn to his attention, Wiebe commented that "the Biblical prophets and Big Bear had a great deal in common, the sense of a heritage that has been sold out."[17] To draw upon the culture of Native people has become a controversial isssue, but Wiebe emphatically rejects the argument that he is simply another white man appropriating Native culture: "This is my world; I don't have any other country than this. . . . If I grew up in Big Bear's country, he is my ancestor."[18] At the same time, he has been quick to chastise others who have in his view taken liberties with Native peoples. He reacted angrily, for example, to the publication of W. P. Kinsella's *The Miss Hobbema Beauty Pageant* in 1989. Wiebe regarded this collection of stories so offensive as to justify the people of Hobbema taking legal action against Kinsella (a course he recommended that they follow), arguing that if Kinsella "uses an actual place and the actual name of a people, he has the responsibility not to abuse them."[19] An indication of the authenticity of Wiebe's own work may be found in the comment by the Native writer, Maria Campbell, that she sensed the spirit of Big Bear controlling Wiebe, in the speeches of the Cree leader provided in his novel.[20]

History in *The Temptations of Big Bear* is not straightforward nor even all that easy to comprehend. Each of the novel's many voices uses words in a different way, with a different effect. As Big Bear concludes in his speech in that Regina court room,

> A word is power, it comes from nothing into meaning and a Person takes his name with him when he dies. I have said my last words. Who will say a word for my people? Give my people help! I have spoken.[21]

Wiebe leaves the reader profoundly moved, aware of the ignorance reflected in any dismissal of the Prairies as an essentially dull place, "equal parts of Puritanism, Monotony, Farmers, and Depression." Wiebe is committed to raising us out of that ignorance; in an exuberant passage intended to form part of the introductory chapter to *Big Bear*, Wiebe tells how the story emerged from

> the vacuum called history, which in Western Canada is no vacuum at all but rather the great ocean of our ignorance as horizonless as the prairies themselves. . . . For if one is once willing to understand that he is beyond doubt

thoughtlessly treading water on his ancestral past, on the past of his place, and will dare to plunge in, reckless of life and eyes wide open, he finds in that ocean a teeming of wildlife and tamelife and every other kind of life that takes his ordinary breath away. . .[22]

It is that response, that astonishment, that Wiebe elicits in the novel.

* * *

Anne Wheeler has been active in the performing arts for some twenty years. During the last decade she has established herself as one of the leaders in the independent film industry of Western Canada. Wheeler first became involved in films in the early 1970s as a co-owner of Filmwest Associates, a company that aspired "to make western stories, to tell western stories, to the West and to the world."[23] Her first film to reach a large public was released in 1975, the docu-drama "Great Grand Mother," made in association with the National Film Board of Canada. A history of the Prairie West from the perspective of the European women who settled there at the turn of the century, "Great Grand Mother" heralded themes that she would explore over the next fifteen years: the Prairies, women, and the past. "Bye Bye Blues" is thus the culmination of a number of years' work, both in terms of her growth as a director and her interests as a writer: "it combines her search for her roots, both personal and regional, her feminist convictions and her passion for story-telling."[24]

Although acknowledging the help and tutelage of the National Film Board, Wheeler describes herself as a self-taught director. In fact, she tends to perform many of the key tasks – writer, director, producer – for her films, a reflection of her desire to maintain control of the creative process. Her films are her stories (a word she often uses), and Wheeler sees her work as a film-maker as an extension of the role of story-teller in society. She is particularly comfortable with stories that are a mixture of fact and fiction, while emphasizing that "my stories don't have closure. . . . I'm the type of person that tries to make new kinds of stories and to look at things differently than they may have been looked at before." During her formal education, history had seemed to her the most boring of subjects (she has an undergraduate degree in science). Her interest in the past was kindled as she researched the film "Great Grand Mother":

It had been because I can imagine myself there, and that leap of what it would have been like made it fascinating for me. It started with my own grandmother, discovering that she was one of Nellie McClung's best friends, something that had never been told to me before, and I thought that that was extraordinary. . . . I had had no models in terms of history; people like Nellie McClung had never been pointed out to me. . . .

When you do one [film based in the past], you get more interested and you realize how much you don't know, and you go a little further. The more I learned, the more I didn't know, and the more I wanted to know. Very curious person.[25]

"Bye Bye Blues" – made in 1988/89, and her fourth feature film – is a loose reconstruction of her mother's war-time experiences. It is something of a sequel, or parallel narrative, to an earlier film of Wheeler's, "A War Story," made in 1981 with the National Film Board of Canada. Both films are part of what Wheeler describes as "a personal odyssey into understanding my parents and my relationship to them."[26] "A War Story" is a powerful docu-drama based on her father's diaries, describing his experiences as a Japanese prisoner of war. "Bye Bye Blues" is the other story, her mother's world on the home front in Alberta, a woman forced to forge a new life with two children, with little money and a husband lost to the war. To make ends meet and to survive the tedium, the main character (Daisy Cooper) becomes a pianist/singer in a local dance band. At first a rather clumsy amateur, she gradually turns into a professional musician, helped by an American trombonist drawn to her by more than a desire to provide music instruction. Her husband finally returns, however, and Daisy quits the band.

While the plot of the movie can be summarized in a few lines, in fact it is a rich and subtle work, crafted with a sharp eye for detail and beautifully filmed. To dismiss the movie as a catalogue of clichés, as did the reviewer in *The Globe and Mail*, is to insist on viewing it only at the most banal level.[27] His comparison of "Bye Bye Blues" with such superficial fare as Goldie Hawn's "Swing Shift" indicates the intellectual depth that he brought to bear on the movie. Had Jay Scott wanted to engage in a meaningful comparison, the obvious choice would have been John Boorman's "Hope and Glory." As others have pointed out, Scott's review likely guaranteed the commercial failure of Wheeler's movie in Ontario, despite the standing ovation it won when screened at Toronto's Festival of Festivals.[28] The one interesting point to emerge from *The Globe and Mail* review is Scott's inability to see the movie as Canadian or historical; although he contemptuously acknowledges the emotional power of "Bye Bye Blues" ("Hello tear ducts, bye bye brains"), he can only situate the film within the American cultural milieu. To be fair, not all at *The Globe and Mail* shared Scott's assessment. In a column usually devoted to politics, Jeffrey Simpson wrote at length about the movie and its reception in central Canada. He found the film "wonderful," and attempted to reconcile its standing ovation at the Festival of Festivals with the fact that it ran for just two weeks at a Toronto cinema. Simpson ended his column inconclusively, with a question: "will Torontonians, among the most parochial of Canadians despite their pretensions to the contrary, bother with a film made in and about a place as far removed as Alberta?"[29] Western Canadians do not take their cue from central Canada, of course, and audiences have embraced the movie as their own.[30]

The film's real power comes from its sense of authenticity; despite a glowing, at times spectacular, cinematography, it is the attention to detail that draws the viewer into the movie. We begin to care for the women whose lives and relationships are examined:

> the interaction and undercurrents give this seemingly languorous, unhurried movie tension. These lives and values are settled, traditional, but momentarily disrupted. And we're always aware, because of the movie's insistence on a rich social context – that a reckoning or choice is due after the armistice. . . .
>
> "Blues" becomes a lament for those few moments of liberation or love – or even just musicianly camaraderie on stage – that can shine through the seemingly unbroken, inevitable routines of ordinary lives: ties, obligations, the chains of war, class and geography.[31]

At the centre of the movie is Daisy: it is her growth both as an entertainer and as a person that Wheeler is most concerned with charting. But is not a straightforward or simple story, and the movie is true to Wheeler's assertion that her stories do not have closure. Loose ends are not tied, and the viewer is left to draw her own conclusions about Daisy's relationship with the American musician, Matt Gramley. We know that it is a relationship that affected her profoundly: in one of the film's final scenes, Daisy goes to tell Matt that her husband is back and that she will not be moving up to Edmonton with the band the next day; in effect, that she is quitting the band. An angry Matt dismisses her and slams the door in her face, but her sweater is caught in the door. The symbolism might be heavy-handed but it is to the point. Part of her is left with Matt, something she will never get back. In the very last scene of the film, the camera follows the musicians' bus as it heads to the city, away from the small prairie town. The song "Bye Bye Blues" plays, its words underlining Daisy's ambivalence as she tearfully watches her friends exit from her life.

The history disclosed in the film is intimate and personal, in Wheeler's words, "about the unspoken life of women, which hasn't been seen as important."[32] The larger conventional history of the time – the events of the war which decide the fate of Daisy's husband – is subtley folded into the characters' lives and experiences. And we always learn of them secondhand; by radio, in conversation, or through letters. In the course of an evening family card game, for example, the news comes over the radio of the bombing of Hiroshima. "Guess that'll show the Japs," comments one person. Daisy's brother Will, a returned soldier who had lost a leg in the war, responds angrily: "Whole goddam city full of people." We learn not just of the event, but the way in which it is filtered through the experiences of the characters, which in turn informs their reactions to the event. People are at the centre of Wheeler's history.

* * *

James Keelaghan, a Calgary-based folksinger, grew up in a household that was both musically and historically inclined: his father was a veteran of the Spanish Civil War, and had collected folk songs in Ireland before the Second World War. His mother lived through the Blitz in London, and Keelaghan grew up listening to his parents sing. After studying history at the University of Calgary ("I started doing these little historical songs as a cheap excuse for not doing term papers"[33]), he found work as an historical researcher and a musician. By 1988 he was playing the major folk festivals of Canada. With four albums to his credit, he is an established figure on Canada's rich folk scene.

Keelaghan's songs are largely Canadian social history set to music. These vary from a happy-go-lucky trainman's account of a CPR wreck ("Railway Tune") to more sombre works about the murder of marching miners in

Estevan, Saskatchewan in 1931 ("Small Rebellions") and the 1914 Hillcrest mine disaster ("Hillcrest Mine"). What sets his work apart is its subtlety: three minute songs manage to convey more than many a lecture on the same material. Needless to say, they are also reaching a much larger audience. In addition to their lyrical power, his songs ring with Keelaghan's strong voice and an easy familiarity with the folk tradition.

Like both Wheeler and Wiebe, Keelaghan's lyrics draw from his own experiences and link these with more profound issues. This comes across in such songs as "Boom Gone to Bust," where the Depression of his parent's time is juxtaposed to his own knowledge of the 1980s recession:

> My Dad started east some time in the thirties with the On-to-Ottawa men,
> He'd enough of the camps and the dole and the handouts,
> He wanted to work and to tie the loose ends.
> Drifted from factory to foundry to flophouse,
> The war sorted out what mere men could not;
> In Sudbury's forges he worked like a madman,
> His years lost to hunger, Dad never forgot.
> And I headed West when I turned twenty,
> When the factories and foundries had closed.
> And in my mind's eye, I thought I might settle
> Out here where my father was raised and was born.
> I worked as a jughound, a roughneck, a bouncer,
> I worked where I wanted, I drew damn good pay;
> Saw no end to our luck, and so we just pushed it,
> But OPEC and mortgages ate it away.[34]

Such personal experiences are pushed to far broader conclusions by the song's close:

> It seems to me somehow this nation of migrants,
> From father to daughter, from mother to son,
> Must constantly shift from the east or the west,
> Till we run out of work or of places to run.
> Gone now the days when you lived where your parents,
> And their parents before them, were bred and were born;
> Must go where the work is to live any life, boys,
> Bend like a willow to weather the storm. . .[35]

As can be seen, there is a deliberate presentism in his work. Even in a song grounded in a specific event, such as the title song, "Small Rebellions," an account of the march of Bienfait coal miners in Estevan in 1931 which left three of their number dead and many more wounded, Keelaghan is intent on connecting with larger issues:

> I am very serious about relating that song, Small Rebellions, to what happened in Tienanmen Square. . . . The struggle for rights and the struggle for freedom and the struggle for political beliefs, or the struggle to have the right to express your political beliefs, I think is never-ending, and Small Rebellions is about that.[36]

In that album, his second, Keelaghan was particularly interested in confronting the past of the West, and with a specific intent:

> "Small Rebellions" is very much based in prairie geography; the big thing with people in Saskatchewan and Alberta and Manitoba is more than anywhere else in the country, I think we have a real inferiority complex about our history, because there are no landmarks. . . . Because there aren't marvellous stone buildings and things, people think we don't have a history. History for a lot of people seems to be measured in physical structures, and to me it's not; I wanted to deal with some points of history that operate outside of physical structures in a prairie setting.[37]

Like Wheeler, Keelaghan's work has received a mixed response from "the country's national newspaper." For example, *The Globe and Mail*'s review of "Small Rebellions" ignored the content of Keelaghan's songs, commenting only on the form. And at this level, the album was damned with faint praise. The review began: "*Very* small rebellions. Calgary's James Keelaghan is surely the most traditional of the newest generation of Canadian folk singers and songwriters."[38] Audiences have come to their own conclusions: a Keelaghan performance often ends with a standing ovation.

History is almost intrinsic to folk music; the genre is steeped in tradition and memory. Keelaghan's concern with the Canadian past – his use of it as context and meaning for his music – is scarcely unique. Yet his historical songs stand out because they are closely grounded in events, while avoiding temptations to resort to mere narrative or to engage in heavy-handed preachiness. A good example is a recent song concerning the evacuation of

Japanese Canadians from Canada's west coast in 1942; Keelaghan tells the (evidently true) story of a Japanese woman who decided to have her piano pitched off the end of a Steveston wharf rather than see it fall into the hands of others, since all their property was being impounded. In a clever twist, however, the story is told by a sympathetic policeman, who himself struggles to understand the meaning of what is taking place.[39] By contrast, the songs of the late Stan Rogers, the folk musician with whom Keelaghan is frequently compared, tended to focus on the humourous incident or the telling anecdote, to stand outside of a larger and identifiable past.

Keelaghan is by no means the only prairie singer to have reached a broad audience. Others include Connie Kaldor (whose own song "Batoche" is a moving evocation of the 1885 Rebellion), country musicians Ian Tyson and k. d. lang, and the "roots" musicians, Bourne and MacLeod (recent winners of a Juno Award for their debut album "Dance and Celebrate"). The 1990 Vancouver Folk Festival recognised the new wave of talent coming out of Alberta by featuring the province's musicians as one of the highlights of the Festival; it also included a workshop on songs about Canadian history, led by Keelaghan.

* * *

The popularity in Canada of works such as the television production of *Anne of Green Gables*, as well as a host of imported period dramas, suggest that the past can evoke a very positive public response. This invention of an idealized world does not always reflect a desire to produce a marketable commodity for the entertainment industry or to cater to a pervasive nostalgia, of course; the past can be put to innumerable purposes, from selling beer to legitimizing political parties of virtually any ideological stripe. Recently a number of writers have described these ways in which the past has been used, analysing how it is constituted – by whom, for whom, and with what effect – and the ways in which such representations are shaped by the contexts in which they appear.[40] Such discussions often assume that the past has no obvious or direct objective life, maintaining that it is always invented or translated or mediated, for a variety of conscious or unconscious reasons. The argument here is considerably different, shaped not only by the focus on three individuals within a specific regional context, but also by a more optimistic assessment of intent and outcome. The history employed by Wiebe, Wheeler and Keelaghan is part of a process of authentication, of connecting people to the reality of their place. The point, as Eliot put it in a much-quoted poem,

> Will be to arrive where we started
> And know the place for the first time.[41]

The opening section of this paper posed the question of what meaning should be assigned to the work of Keelaghan, Wheeler and Wiebe. We can first of all make clear what this is not: it is not an invented past, a nostalgic and indulgent celebration of a past that wasn't. The father's advice in Keelaghan's "Hillcrest Mine" is scarcely a sanitized version:

> I've heard it whispered in the light of dawn,
> That mountain sometimes moves;
> That bodes ill for the morning shift
> And you know what you're gonna lose.
> Don't go my son where the deep coal runs,
> Turn your back on the mine on the hill,
> 'Cause if the dust and the dark and the gas don't get you,
> Then the goons and the bosses will. . .[42]

Which is not to argue that their work is simply antiquarian chronicling of life in former times; the subjects and themes are chosen deliberately, to illuminate specific dimensions of the Canadian past. This process of selection – with artists as with historians – is neither simple nor straightforward. As Butterfield once observed, we give the semblance of order to the chaos of the past by virtue of what we leave out. Whether consciously or not, writers use their own criteria of significance to determine what is important, and thus what material deserves to be drawn from what is often a very large amount of material.

One confronts traces of the past in many places, in many guises. As Keelaghan suggests, Western Canada does not have the stone buildings of earlier centuries such as those that dot the St. Lawrence basin and other landscapes. Its points of reference have to be consciously sought out to be recovered. Wiebe has recounted the difficulties he confronted in this process of reclamation, in an article describing the genesis of *Big Bear*:

Anyway, it was from reading Cameron in the '50s that I first realized the bush homestead where I was born in northern Saskatchewan probably was traversed in June, 1885, by Big Bear and his diminishing band as among the poplars they easily eluded the clumsy military columns of Strange and Middleton and Otter and Irvine pursuing them; that I first realized that the white sand beaches of Turtle Lake, where Speedwell School had its annual sportsday with Jackpine and Turtleview Schools, right there where that brown little girl had once beaten me in the grade four sprints, a race in which until then I was acknowledged as completely invincible: perhaps on that very beach Big Bear had once stood looking at the clouds trundle up from the north. Of course, thanks to our education system, I had been deprived of this knowledge when I was a child: we studied people with *history* – like Cromwell who removed a king's head, or Lincoln who freed slaves – but I can see now that this neglect contained an ambiguous good. For in forcing me to discover the past of my place on my own as an adult, my public school inadvertently roused an anger in me which has ever since given an impetus to my writing which I trust it will never lose. *All* people have history. The stories we tell of our past are by no means merely words: they are meaning and life to us as *people*, as a *particular* people.[43]

One has to investigate to find, as Wiebe did, the trail of others on the beach of Turtle Lake. Thus Harrison's point about Prairie authors in *Unnamed Country* is wide of the mark: "It is as though they regarded their past as something that must be rediscovered because it has somehow been misrepresented to them."[44] The history of Wiebe and Wheeler and Keelaghan is no more a rediscovery of something that was already known, already in the popular consciousness, than it is invention. Wheeler's comment about the research that she did for her film "Great Grand Mother" is to the point: "so many stories and no one had heard them."[45]

A sense of place is clear in the work of Keelaghan, Wiebe and Wheeler. All three work within western Canada and their work needs to be understood within that context, historically as well as aesthetically. More than forty-five years ago W. L. Morton spoke of western Canada's inability to "accept a common interpretation of Canadian history or a cultural metropolitanism. . . . It has no acceptable alternative to working out its own identity in terms of its own historical experience."[46] Since then there has been a good deal of discussion both in and about the West, listing its grievances, its uniqueness, and so on, discussions which range across the spectrum from the manifestos of separatist political parties through to the papers and published proceedings of academic conferences. Some of this was self-interested posturing, some of it an angry response to the centralist assumptions of the National Energy Program and other discriminatory federal policies. The West continues to prove itself a fertile breeding ground of political parties, but a recent book is right to claim that there is much more than political activism going on in the region and that cultural activity in the West is attaining a new stature and self-confidence.[47] This latter development could well signal the beginning of a more profound "vernacular mobilization" and "cultural politicization" which will be necessary to survive the turbulent years ahead.[48] At the very least, the work of the three artists examined here is evidence that the cultural community in the West is forging the identity referred to by Morton, an inclusive identity which encompasses all western Canadians. With the prospect of the country's federal bonds loosening in the coming years, the need to understand such regional identities will become increasingly important (and the objections of central Canadians to such implicit assertions of difference even less credible[49]).

The emergence of a mature and autonomous cultural community also reflects the end of the West's ingrained deference to imported cultural norms. As in many other areas of the "settler dominions," European cultural expressions in western Canada were until recently essentially derivative, a result of historical experience in an area colonized by Europeans in the later nineteenth and early twentieth centuries. Despite the ethnic diversity of the colonists, the dominant culture was British, and the regional poets, writers and painters of the colonial period employed traditional techniques from "Home" to depict their new world. The product of this mismatch between late Victorian sensibilities and the Canadian west was by and large uninspired and insipid. In a world where the climate was extreme, where speculators made easy fortunes while others were exploited mercilessly by the unrestrained greed of assorted representatives of monopoly capitalism, where the sky was larger than anywhere else in the world, something more than a secondhand Victorian aesthetic was clearly in order.[50]

With virtually all their cultural points of reference on the other side of the

Atlantic, the colonists remained strangers in the land where they lived. The subsequent dilemma was captured by New Zealand's Allen Curnow. In a memorable poem, he described his inability to connect in any meaningful way with the land in which he had been born. As he contemplated the skeleton of an extinct moa, wired erect in a museum in Christchurch, he drew a parallel between his own life in New Zealand and the fate of that giant bird:

> Interesting failure to adapt on islands,
> Taller but no more fallen than I, who come
> Bone to his bone, peculiarly New Zealand's. . . .
> Not I, some child, born in a marvellous year,
> Will learn the trick of standing upright here.[51]

Such an admission of failure could have come as readily from British descendants in other corners of the globe, in the South Pacific, Africa or North America. A common difficulty united them: how to come to terms with this world in which they found themselves, strangers in their homes, at home in a strange land?

This inability to connect the imagination with the environment is plain in the reminiscences of Wallace Stegner and W. L. Morton, as well as in Wiebe's comments quoted on the title page of this paper. All three draw attention to the dichotomy they encountered growing up in the west, the juxtaposition of the literature of England with the overpowering reality of the Prairies. Remembering his early reading in southwest Saskatchewan, for example, Stegner reflected that "What strikes me about this in recollection is not my precocious or fictitious reading capacity, and not the durability of memory, but the fact that the information I was gaining from literature and from books on geography and history had not the slightest relevance to the geography, history, or life of the place where I lived."[52] Resolving this – working out an aesthetic and cultural adaptation to western Canada – has taken a surprisingly long time, although this is equally true of other colonized areas. In central Canada, for example, one can detect an uneasy didacticism in the claim made in the Catalogue accompanying the first exhibition of the Group of Seven in 1920 that "An Art must grow and flower in the land before the country will be a real home for its people."[53] As recently as 1990, Michael Ondaatje wrote that "memoir and history and fiction blend" in Canadian literature; "the past invades us."[54] Robert Kroetsch is the most direct: "we haven't got an identity until someone tells our story. The fiction makes us real."[55]

Canadians share North America with a larger and more powerful English-speaking nation, whose media and culture dominate the continent. The claim that the Yanks have colonized our subconscious is perhaps facile, but borne out by the unthinking adoption of so many American symbols, in Canada as well as Europe.[56] Few cultural domains have survived this imperialist thrust; the most popular (and lucrative) venues, the cinema and television, have proven particularly vulnerable. The efforts of the Canadian state to provide something of a counter-balance to the cultural hegemony of its neighbour have been uneven. Both anglophone and francophone Canadians continually confront absorption, and remain who they are only by deliberate choice.[57] Without such self-consciousness, the survival of Canada is unlikely. It follows that cultural expressions such as those discussed in this chapter have far more than an aesthetic or cultural significance. As Kroetsch claims, they are indeed what makes us real.

Notes

1. I am very grateful to James Keelaghan, Anne Wheeler and Rudy Wiebe – busy people all – for finding the time to speak with me about their work. The paper was written while I was a visiting fellow with the Institute of International Studies at the University of Leeds, and I extend a sincere "thank you" to John Hemery and Alison Moore, who made my time there both pleasant and productive.

2. Robert Kroetsch, "On Being an Alberta Writer: Or, I Wanted To Tell Our Story," Howard Palmer and Donald Smith, eds., *The New Provinces: Alberta and Saskatchewan*, Vancouver: Tantalus Research, 1980, pp. 222-23.

3. Rudy Wiebe and Bob Beal, *War in the West: Voices of the 1885 Rebellion*, Toronto: McClelland and Stewart, 1985.

4. *A Harvest Yet To Reap*, Toronto: Women's Press, 1975.

5. One exception is Dennis Duffy's *Sounding the Iceberg: An Essay on Canadian Historical Novels*, Toronto: ECW Press, 1986, although this work is primarily a survey of the literature it describes.

6. Rudy Wiebe, *The Temptations of Big Bear*, Toronto: McClelland and Stewart, 1973, p. 398; italics in the original. Earlier, Wiebe has Big Bear ask an assembly of government officials intent on treaty-making, and Native leaders, "Who can receive land? From whom would he receive it?" *Op. cit.*, p. 29.

7. Anthony D. Smith, "Towards a Global Culture?" in Mike Featherstone, ed., *Global Culture: Nationalism, Globalization and Modernity*, London: SAGE Publications Ltd., 1990 (a special issue of *Theory, Culture & Society*), p. 177. Similarly: "In the fantasy

culture of the 1980s there is no real history, no real past; it is replaced by an instant, magical nostalgia, a strangely *unmotivated* appropriation of the past." (Elizabeth Wilson, *Adorned in Dreams: Fashion and Modernity*, London, 1985, p. 172). In an earlier book (*The Ethnic Revival*, Cambridge: Cambridge University Press, 1981), Smith recounted the history and meaning of what he terms ethnic nationalism, an excellent analysis of the "broader trend" mentioned in this paragraph.

8. Northrop Frye, *The Bush Garden: Essays on the Canadian Imagination*, Toronto: Anansi, 1971, pp. i-iv.

9. Peter McCormick, "Regionalism in Canada: Disentangling the Treads," *Journal of Canadian Studies*, Vol. 24, No. 2 (Summer, 1989), p. 13. For another useful discussion of the notion of region, see John G. Reid, "Writing About Regions," in John Schultz, ed., *Writing About Canada: A Handbook for Modern Canadian History*, Scarborough: Prentice-Hall Canada, 1990, pp. 71-96, esp. 79-81.

10. Rudy Wiebe, "In the West, Sir John A. is a Bastard and Riel a Saint. Ever Ask Why?" reprinted in *A Voice in the Land*, p. 210; first published in *The Globe and Mail*, 25 March, 1978.

11. Duffy, *Sounding the Iceberg*, p. 74; George Woodcock, "Possessing the Land: Notes on Canadian Fiction," in Woodcock, *The World of Canadian Writing: Critiques and Recollections*, Vancouver: Douglas & McIntyre, 1980, p. 38.

12. Thomas S. Woods, "On the Silent Majesty," (Review of *Playing Dead: A contemplation concerning the Arctic*, Edmonton: NeWest Press, 1989), *The Globe and Mail*, 5 Aug., 1989, C 15. With a good deal of justification, Woods compared Wiebe with Durrell in the review: "*Playing Dead* is to Arctic Canada what Lawrence Durrell's *Reflections on a Marine Venus* is to Rhodes."

13. For extended discussion of *Big Bear*, see *A Voice in the Land*, pp. 126-55; W. J. Keith, *Epic Fiction: The Art of Rudy Wiebe*, Edmonton: the University of Alberta Press, 1981, pp. 62-81; Allen Dueck, "Rudy Wiebe's Approach to Historical Fiction: A Study of *The Temptations of Big Bear* and *The Scorched-Wood People*," in John Moss, ed., *The Canadian Novel: Here and Now*, Toronto: NC Press Ltd., 1978, pp. 182-200; Allan Beavan, "Introduction," in Rudy Wiebe, *The Temptations of Big Bear*, Toronto: McClelland and Stewart, 1973, pp. ix-xv; Susan Whaley, *Rudy Wiebe and His Works*, Toronto: ECW Press, 1987?, pp. 31-37; Duffy, *Sounding the Iceberg*, pp. 71-73. For a fuller bibliography of literature by and about Wiebe, see Whaley, *Rudy Wiebe*, pp. 56-61; there is also much useful information in *The Rudy Wiebe Papers, First Accession: An Inventory of the Archive at the University of Calgary Libraries*, Calgary: University of Calgary, 1986, especially J. M. Kertzer's "Biocritical Essay," pp. ix-xxvi.

14. Whaley, *Rudy Wiebe and His Works*, p. 31.

15. "On the Trail of Big Bear" and "Bear Spirit in a Strange Land ("All That's Left of Big Bear")"; both are reprinted in Keith, ed., *A Voice in the Land*. See also the Native stories in Rudy Wiebe, *The Angel of the Tar Sands and Other Stories*, Toronto: McClelland and Stewart, 1982, especially, "Where Is the Voice Coming From?" pp. 78-87.

16. Rudy Wiebe, "On the Trail of Big Bear," p. 139.

17. In Eli Mandel and Rudy Wiebe, "Where the Voice Comes From," in *A Voice in the Land*, p. 152.

18. Interview with author, 31 Jan., 1991; note also Wiebe's comments in a published interview: "I write about Indians because I grew up in communities where they

were part of the people." (in George Melnyk, "The Western Canadian Imagination: An Interview with Rudy Wiebe," in *A Voice in the Land* , p. 205.)

19. Wiebe quoted in "Kinsella 'ripping off' Indians," *The Globe and Mail*, 8 Dec., 1989, C10. Kinsella responded with an ill-tempered dismissal of Wiebe (a "petty little academic drone") and railed against an unspecified group of literary academics, but one which presumably included Wiebe: "Any one of those guys who attack my work would give his left nut to be in my place, but they won't admit it" (Kinsella quoted in "Colleagues attack motivates Kinsella," *The Globe and Mail*, 21 Dec., 1989, C8). A conversation with Wiebe left me with the impression that Kinsella's analysis was considerably wide of the mark.

20. In Keith, ed., *A Voice in the Land*, p. 151.

21. *The Temptations of Big Bear*, p. 398.

22. From the original introductory chapter to *The Temptations of Big Bear*, deleted prior to publication. Quoted in Rudy Wiebe, "On the Trail of Big Bear," in Keith, ed., *A Voice in the Land*, pp. 136-37.

23. Wheeler, in Jane Evans, "Filmmakers Don't Cry? An Interview with Anne Wheeler," *NeWest Review* (February/March, 1990), p. 16.

24. Gina Mallet, "True Grit," *Homemakers* (March, 1990), pp. 36-37.

25. Interview with author, 6 Nov., 1990, as is the quotation in the text.

26. Wheeler, quoted in Gina Mallet, "True Grit," *Homemakers* (March, 1990), p. 46.

27. Jay Scott, "Catalogue of clichés is interesting read," *The Globe and Mail*, 15 Sept., 1989, C 1. Others, such as *Los Angeles Time* reviewer Michael Wilmington, have been lavish in their praises (see Michael Wilmington, "Wistful Detail Charges 'Bye Bye Blues'," *Los Angeles Times*, 21 Sept., 1990, F 4 & 6).

28. Don Braid and Sydney Sharpe, *Breakup: Why the West Feels Left Out of Canada*, Toronto: Key Porter Books, 1990, p. 58.

29. Jeffrey Simpson, "Singing the box-office blues," *The Globe and Mail*, 12 Jan., 1990, A6.

30. A point also made in Jane Evans, "Filmmakers Don't Cry? An Interview with Anne Wheeler," *NeWest Review* (February/March, 1990), p. 16.

31. Wilmington, "Wistful Detail Charges 'Bye Bye Blues'," *Los Angeles Times*, 21 Sept., 1990, F 6.

32. Mallet, "True Grit," *Homemakers* (March, 1990), p. 37.

33. Keelaghan, quoted in Paul Rodgers, "The Bard of the Bow," *Alberta Report*, Vol. 15, # 33 (1 August, 1988), p. 30.

34. James Keelaghan, "Boom Gone To Bust," words and music, © James Keelaghan.

35. James Keelaghan, "Boom Gone To Bust," words and music, © James Keelaghan.

36. Interview with author, 14 July, 1990.

37. Interview with author, 14 July, 1990.

38. Mark Miller, "Inside the Sleeve," *The Globe and Mail*, 2 April, 1990, C7.

39. "Kirri's Song," on James Keelaghan, *My Skies*, 1993, words and music, © James Keelaghan.

40. James Overton, "A Newfoundland Culture?" *Journal of Canadian Studies*, Vol. 23, Nos. 1 & 2 (Spring/Summer, 1988): 5-22; Ian McKay, "Among the Fisherfolk: J. F. B. Livesay and the Invention of Peggy's Cove," *Journal of Canadian Studies*, Vol. 23, Nos. 1 & 2 (Spring/Summer, 1988): 23-45; E. J. Hobsbawm & Terence Ranger, eds., *The Invention of Tradition*, Cambridge: Cambridge University Press, 1983. For case studies of "invention," see Richard White, *Inventing Australia: Images and*

Identity, 1688-1980, Sydney: George Allen & Unwin, 1981; Colin McArthur, "The dialectic of national identity: The Glasgow Empire Exhibition of 1938," in Tony Bennett, Colin Mercer, and Janet Woollacott, eds., *Popular Culture and Social Relations*, Milton Keynes: Open University Press, 1986, pp. 117-34; and Tony Curtis, ed., *Wales: The Imagined Nation*, Bridgend: Poetry Wales Press, 1986. On the separate (though related) topic of history and nostalgia, see Christopher Shaw and Malcolm Chase, eds., *The Imagined Past: History and Nostalgia*, Manchester: Manchester University Press, 1989. Also relevant here is the section "History, Politics and Classical Narrative" in the Open University reader edited by Tony Bennett, Susan Boyd-Bowman, Colin Mercer, and Janet Woollacott, *Popular Television and Film* (London: British Film Institute, 1981, pp. 285-352), largely a discussion of the BBC television series, "Days of Hope," and Tony Bennett, "The politics of the "popular" and popular culture," in *Popular Culture and Social Relations*, pp. 6-21.

41. "Little Gidding," T. S. Eliot, *Collected Poems 1909-1962*, London: Faber and Faber, 1974, p. 222.

42. "Hillcrest Mine," on James Keelaghan, *Small Rebellions*, 1989, words and music, © James Keelaghan. In June 1914, 189 miners died in an explosion in the Hillcrest Mine.

43. Rudy Wiebe, "On the Trail of Big Bear," in W. J. Keith, ed., *A Voice in the Land: Essays By and About Rudy Wiebe*, Edmonton: NeWest Press, 1981, pp. 133-34. Italics in the original.

44. Dick Harrison, *Unnamed Country: The Struggle for a Canadian Prairie Fiction*, Edmonton: University of Alberta Press, 1977, p. 183.

45. Wheeler, quoted in Jane Evans, "Filmmakers Don't Cry? An Interview with Anne Wheeler," *NeWest Review* (February/March, 1990), p. 16.

46. W. L. Morton, "Clio in Canada: The Interpretation of Canadian History," in A. B. McKillop, ed., *Contexts of Canada's Past*, Toronto: Macmillan of Canada, 1980, pp. 109-10. (Originally published in 1946.)

47. Braid and Sharpe, "Two: My Light Wasn't There," in *Breakup*, pp. 55-74; the reference in the chapter's title is to a remark of Anne Wheeler's, concerning central Canada and its inability to illuminate. The reference to political parties in the text is of course to the populist Reform Party, whose growth has been usefully summarized by Ian Pearson, "Thou Shalt Not Ignore the West," *Saturday Night* (December, 1990): 35-43, 74-75. I am aware that there is a group of people who debate with considerable vigour such notions as whether Canada possesses any indigenous literature. I have found the work of this incestuous and arcane collectivity (in which John Metcalf is prominent) irrelevant; to expand upon this remark would require another paper. My own analysis is similar to that elaborated by George Woodcock in his study of Canadian literature and regionalism (see, for examples, Woodcock, *The World of Canadian Writing: Critiques and Recollections*, Vancouver: Douglas & McIntyre, 1980; Woodcock, *Northern Spring: The Flowering of Canadian Literature*, Vancouver: Douglas & McIntyre, 1987).

48. For a discussion of the process of "vernacular mobilization" and "cultural politicization," see Smith, "Towards a Global Culture?" p. 183.

49. For disparaging comments on a regional approach, see Ramsay Cook, "Regionalism Unmasked," *Acadiensis*, Vol. 13, No. 1 (Autumn, 1983): 137-42, and Lovell Clark, "Regionalism? or Irrationalism?" *Journal of Canadian Studies*, Vol. 13, No. 2 (1978-

79): 119-28. Note however the rejoinders by Buckner ("'Limited Identities' and Canadian National Scholarship: An Atlantic Provinces Perspective," *Journal of Canadian Studies*, Vol. 23, Nos. 1 & 2 (Spring/Summer 1988): 177-98) and Kealey ("The writing of social history in English Canada, 1970-1984," *Social History*, 10, 3 (October, 1985): 347-365). As Buckner points out, "Lurking behind many of the criticisms of regionalism is the belief that regionalism is anti-nationalist and provides an intellectual justification for Ottawa-bashing and the de-centralization of federal powers. . . . A nation may be larger than the sum of its parts but it does have parts and one has to understand them before one can understand the whole" (p. 193).

50. A number of scholars have examined the evolving aesthetic in western Canada; see, for example, Susan Jackel, "Images of the Canadian West, 1872 – 1911," PhD thesis, University of Alberta, 1977; Ronald Rees, *New and Naked Land: Making the Prairies Home*, Saskatoon: Western Producer Prairie Books, 1988; Ronald Rees, *Land of Earth and Sky: Landscape Painting of Western Canada*, Saskatoon: Western Producer Prairie Books, 1984; R. Douglas Francis, *Images of the West: Responses to the Canadian Prairies*, Saskatoon: Western Producer Prairie Books, 1989; I. S. MacLaren, "Alexander Mackenzie and the Landscapes of Commerce," *Studies in Canadian Literature*, Vol. 7, No. 2, 1982: 141-50; I. S. MacLaren, "David Thompson's Imaginative Mapping of the Canadian Northwest, 1784-1812," *Ariel*, Vol. 15, No. 2, (April, 1984): 89-106; I. S. MacLaren, "Retaining Captaincy of the Soul: Response to Nature in the First Franklin Expedition," *Essays in Canadian Writing*, No. 28 (Spring, 1984): 57-92.

51. Allen Curnow, "The Skeleton of the Great Moa in the Canterbury Museum, Christchurch," in *Collected Poems 1933-1973*, Wellington: A.H. & A.W. Reed, 1974, p. 142.

52. Wallace Stegner, *Wolf Willow*, New York: Viking Press, 1955, p. 27; *cf.* W. L. Morton, "Seeing an Unliterary Landscape," in *Contexts of Canada's Past*, pp. 15-25. (Originally published in 1970.)

53. Quoted by Ronald Rees, *Land of Earth and Sky*, p. 44.

54. Michael Ondaatje, "Introduction," *The Faber Book of Contemporary Canadian Short Stories*, London: Faber and Faber, 1990, pp. xvi & xiv.

55. Quoted by Rudy Wiebe, in *A Voice in the Land*, p. 211.

56. A comment by a character in a Wim Wenders film ("Kings of the Road"). I first heard it used by Colin Browne, a B.C. film historian, in his fascinating paper, "The Phantom Ride," presented to the *BC Studies* conference at Simon Fraser University in November, 1988, although since then I have had the opportunity to see Wenders' fine movie.

57. A similar point is made by Gwyn A. Williams; in the following, for example, substitute Canada and Canadians for Wales and Welsh: "Wales is an artefact which the Welsh produce. If they want to. It requires an act of choice. Today, it looks as though that choice will be more difficult than ever before. There are roads out towards survival as a people, but they are long and hard and demand sacrifice and are at present unthinkable to most of the Welsh." – *When Was Wales?*, London: Penguin Books, 1991, p. 304.

Western Canadian History:

A Selected Bibliography

Western Canadian historiography typically approaches the prairie provinces and British Columbia as separate and distinct regions. This brief biographical list bridges that divide by bringing together the literature of the prairie West and what Jean Barman has called "the West beyond the West."

The influence of regionalism in Canadian history is perhaps most graphically illustrated by the fact that there is no general bibliography for the West, although John Herd Thompson's "The West and the North" in *Canadian History: A Reader's Guide, 2: Confederation to the Present*, Toronto: University of Toronto Press, 1994, provides an excellent summary of selected readings for the prairies, B.C. and the North. For more extensive bibliographies, which list books, articles and graduate theses on the West, see Alan F. J. Artibise, *Western Canada since 1870: a select bibliography and guide*, Vancouver: University of British Columbia Press, 1978, and Bruce Braden Peel, *A Bibliography of the Prairie Provinces to 1953 with Biographical Index*, 3rd ed., Toronto: University of Toronto Press, 1994. Also valuable is the *Canadian Historical Review*'s regular bibliographical feature, "Recent Publications Relating to Canada" (organized by topic and region). Provincial bibliographies are another important source. These include Richard A. Enns, ed., *A Bibliography of Northern Manitoba*, Winnipeg: University of Manitoba Press, 1991; Gloria M. Strathern, comp., *Alberta, 1954-1979: A Provincial Bibliography*, Edmonton: University of Alberta Press, 1982; Gloria M. Strathern, *Navigations, Traffiques and Discoveries, 1774-1848, A guide to publications relating to the area now British Columbia* [the first volume of *The Bibliography of British Columbia*], Victoria: University of Victoria, 1970; Barbara J. Lowther, with the assistance of Muriel Laing, *A Bibliography of British Columbia*, Vol. 2, *Laying the Foundations, 1849-1899*, Victoria: University of Victoria, 1968; and Margaret H. Edwards and John C. R. Lort, with the assistance of Wendy J. Carmichael, *A Bibliography of British Columbia*, Vol. 3, *Years of Growth, 1900-1950*, Victoria: University of Victoria, 1975.

There are many historiographical essays but two are especially useful for their interpretive frameworks as well as their lists of relevant literature: Gerald Friesen, "Historical Writing on the Prairie West," in R. Douglas Francis and Howard Palmer, eds., *The Prairie West: Historical Readings*, 2nd ed., Edmonton: Pica Pica Press, 1992; and Allan Smith, "The Writing of British Columbia History," *BC Studies*, 45 (Spring 1980): 73-102. Students interested in the influence of regionalism on western Canadian history will want to consult Richard Allen, ed., *A Region of the Mind: Interpreting the Western Canadian Plains*, Regina: Canadian Plains Studies Centre, University of Saskatchewan, 1973; J. M. S. Careless, *Frontier and Metropolis: Regions, Cities, and Identities in Canada before 1914*, Toronto: University of Toronto Press, 1989; Peter McCormick, "Regionalism in Canada: Disentangling the Threads," *Journal of Canadian Studies*, Vol. 24, No. 2 (Summer, 1989): 5-21; John G. Reid, "Writing About Regions," in John Schultz, ed., *Writing about Canada: a Handbook for Modern Canadian History*, Scarborough: Prentice-Hall Canada, 1990; William Westfall, "The Regional Patterns in Canada and Canadian Culture," in William Westfall, ed., *Perspectives on Regions and Regionalism in Canada, Canadian Issues*, Vol. V, 1983; and Robin Winks, "Regionalism in Comparative Perspective," in William G. Robbins, Robert J. Frank, Richard E. Ross, eds., *Regionalism and the Pacific Northwest*, Corvallis, Oregon: Oregon State University Press, 1983.

A complete synthesis of the Pacific and prairie West has yet to be written although J. F. Conway's *The West: the History of a Region in Confederation*, Toronto: J. Lorimer, 1983, is a good beginning. J. Arthur Lower's *Western Canada, An Outline History*, Vancouver: Douglas & McIntyre, 1983, is dated but still useful. Morris Zaslow's *Reading the Rocks: the Story of the Geological Survey of Canada, 1842-1972*, Toronto: Macmillan Co. of Canada, 1975, is thoughtful if narrowly defined. Gerald Friesen's award-winning book, *The Canadian Prairies: a History*, Toronto: University of Toronto Press, 1987, is the most comprehensive general history of the plains but has been criticized for overlooking women. Jean Barman's *The West Beyond the West: a History of British Columbia*, Toronto: University of Toronto Press, 1991 does the same for B.C. and includes women. Two other general surveys of special note are Morris Zaslow's *The Opening of the Canadian North, 1870-1914* and *The Northward Expansion of Canada*, Toronto: McClelland and Stewart, 1971 and 1988. Zaslow is particularly useful for his treatment of capitalist expansion and resource extraction on the new "investment frontier."

A number of provincial surveys supplement these regional histories. W. L. Morton's *Manitoba, A History*, 2nd ed., Toronto: University of Toronto Press, 1967, remains a respected scholarly work, but should be read with James A. Jackson's commemorative history, *The Centennial History of Manitoba*, Toronto: McClelland and Stewart, 1970. John H. Archer, *Saskatchewan: A History*, Saskatoon: Western Producer Prairie Books, 1980, prepared for that province's seventy-fifth anniversary, is still the most thorough treatment. Howard Palmer with Tamara Palmer, *Alberta: A New History*, Edmonton: Hurtig, 1990, is comprehensive and highly readable. For B.C., in addition to Barman's work cited above, see George Woodcock's *British Columbia: a History of the Province*, Vancouver/Toronto: Douglas & McIntyre, 1990, and Margaret A. Ormsby's encyclopedic *British Columbia, a History*, Toronto: Macmillan, 1958.

The four western provinces also boast scholarly journals devoted wholly or largely to publishing historical research. *Manitoba History, Saskatchewan History*, and *Alberta History* focus entirely on history while *BC Studies* and *Prairie Forum* are interdisciplinary journals. The *Journal of Canadian Studies* has produced relevant special issues, including "British Columbia Aspects," Vol. 25, No. 3 (Fall 1990) and "Western Aspects," Vol. 17, No. 3 (Fall 1982). A thorough treatment of even the most recent works published in these journals is beyond the scope of this essay but students interested in exploring this important source can do so readily through the indexes published by each periodical or in the *Canadian Periodicals Index*.

Published collections of essays, such as this one, are another important source for current work. Typically organized around a central theme, most volumes also provide an introduction, placing the relevant works in an interpretive context. What follows is necessarily a selective list but includes a broad cross section of the available monographs. A number of essays by W. L. Morton – sometimes known as the father of western Canadian history – are collected in A. B. McKillop, ed., *Contexts of Canada's Past: Selected Essays of W. L. Morton*, Toronto: Macmillan, 1980; note also the *festschrift* edited by

Carl Berger and Ramsay Cook: *The West and the Nation: Essays in Honour of W. L. Morton*, Toronto: McClelland and Stewart, 1976. For essays on the West in a national context, see David Jay Bercuson, ed., *Canada and the Burden of Unity*, Toronto: Copp Clark Pitman, 1986, and David Jay Bercuson and Phillip A. Buckner, eds., *Eastern and Western Perspectives: Papers from the Joint Atlantic Canada/Western Canadian Studies Conference*, Toronto: University of Toronto Press, 1981. R. Douglas Francis and Howard Palmer, eds., *The Prairie West: Historical Readings*, 2nd ed., Edmonton: Pica Pica Press, 1992, is a comprehensive collection. Specialized volumes include Henry C. Klassen, ed., *The Canadian West: Social Change and Economic Development*, Calgary: Comprint Pub. Co., 1977; Louis A. Knafla, ed., *Law & Justice in a New Land: Essays in Western Canadian Legal History*, Toronto: Carswell, 1986; Howard Palmer and Donald Smith, eds., *The New Provinces: Alberta and Saskatchewan*, Vancouver: Tantalus Research, 1980; A. W. Rasporich, ed., *The Making of the Modern West: Western Canada since 1945*, Calgary: University of Calgary Press, 1984; Anthony W. Rasporich and Henry C. Klassen, eds., *Frontier Calgary: Town, City, and Region 1875-1914*, Calgary: McClelland and Stewart West: University of Calgary, 1975; Anthony W. Rasporich, ed., *Western Canada: Past and Present*, Calgary: University of Calgary: McClelland and Stewart West, 1975; and Donald Swainson, ed., *Historical Essays on the Prairie Provinces*, Toronto: McClelland and Stewart, 1970. Collections that focus on the Pacific West include Jean Friesen and H. K. Ralston, eds., *Historical essays on British Columbia*, Toronto: McClelland and Stewart, 1976; John McLaren, Hamar Foster, and Chet Orloff, eds., *Law for the Elephant, Law for the Beaver: Essays in the Legal History of the North American West*, Regina: Canadian Plains Research Centre, 1992; Hamar Foster and John McLaren, eds., *Essays in the History of Canadian Law: British Columbia and the Yukon*, Toronto: University of Toronto Press, with the Osgoode Society, 1995; W. Peter Ward and Robert A. J. McDonald, eds., *British Columbia: Historical Readings*, Vancouver: Douglas & McIntyre Ltd., 1981; and Patricia E. Roy, ed., *A History of British Columbia: Selected Readings*, Toronto: Copp Clark Pitman, 1987.

The fur trade West has long been a staple of western Canadian historiography although scholars' questions and perspectives have changed over time. Early works focused on the economic development of the trade including Harold A. Innis's classic account, *The Fur Trade in Canada: an Introduction to Canadian Economic History*, Toronto: University of Toronto, 1970. Arthur S. Morton, *A History of the Canadian West to 1870-71: being a history of Rupert's Land (the Hudson's Bay Company's territory) and of the North-West Territory (including the Pacific slope)*, Toronto: University of Toronto Press, 1973 (first published in 1939), remains useful as a reference work. Less daunting in size is E. E. Rich's *The Fur Trade and the Northwest to 1857*, Toronto: McClelland and Stewart, 1967. Arthur J. Ray's *The Canadian Fur Trade in the Industrial Age*, Toronto: University of Toronto Press, 1990, follows in the tradition of economic history. Ray's earlier work, *Indians in the Fur Trade: Their Role as Trappers, Hunters, and Middlemen in the Lands Southwest of Hudson Bay, 1660-1870*, Toronto: University of Toronto Press, 1974, focuses on the productive role of Native men in the trade. The trade as a social system is explored by Jennifer S. H. Brown, *Strangers in Blood: Fur Trade Company Families in Indian Country*, Vancouver: University of British Columbia Press, 1980, and Sylvia Van Kirk, *"Many Tender Ties": Women in Fur-Trade Society in Western Canada*, Winnipeg: Watson & Dwyer, 1980. Essays in Jacqueline Peterson and Jennifer S. H. Brown, eds., *The New Peoples: Being and Becoming Métis in North America*, Winnipeg: University of Manitoba Press, 1985, explore the implications for the "New Nation" that emerged with the trade. Richard Mackie's *Trading Beyond the Mountains: The British Fur Trade on the Pacific, 1793-1843*, Vancouver: University of British Columbia Press, 1996, describes the trade in the region that later became British Columbia.

Whether or not race relations were as peaceful as fur trade history suggests remains a question for further exploration. Certainly the imposition of white rule which followed the annexation of the Hudson's Bay Company territory and British Columbia's entry into Confederation in 1870-71 signalled a shift in official policy, as Robin Fisher argues in *Contact and Conflict: Indian-European relations in British Columbia, 1774-1890*, 2nd ed., Vancouver: University of British Columbia Press, 1992. Nation-builders sought to control indigenous peoples through the treaty process, the subject of John Tobias's "Canada's Subjugation of the Plains Cree, 1879-1885," *Canadian Historical Review*, Vol. 64, No. 4 (December 1983): 519-48, and Frank Tough's "Economic Aspects of Aboriginal Title in Northern Manitoba: Treaty 5 Adhesions and Métis Scrip," *Manitoba History*, Vol. 15 (Spring

1988): 1-15. Hana Samek, *The Blackfoot Confederacy, 1880-1920: a Comparative Study of Canadian and U.S. Indian policy*, Albuquerque: University of New Mexico Press, 1987, concludes that Canadian approaches were more humane than in the United States but had a similar effect on populations north and south of the border. In her carefully researched *Lost Harvests: Prairie Indian Reserve Farmers and Government Policy*, Montreal: McGill-Queen's University Press, 1990, Sarah Carter traces the ways in which racial prejudice informed Canadian government policy and undermined Native people's efforts to adapt to the new order. As Martin Robin noted, "One cannot excuse a robbery by describing it as orderly" (*The Rush for Spoils*, p. 44).

Métis resistance to marginalization and assimilation has generated a large literature of its own. Two essays that contextualize the historiographical debates on the rebellions and the Métis leader, Louis Riel, are Doug Owram's "The Myth of Louis Riel," *Canadian Historical Review*, Vol. 63, No. 3 (September 1982): 315-36, and George Stanley's "The Last Word on Louis Riel," in F. Laurie Barron and James B. Waldram, eds., *1885 and After: Native Society in Transition*, Regina: Canadian Plains Research Centre, 1986. D. N. Sprague's *Canada and the Métis, 1869-1885*, Waterloo: Wilfrid Laurier University Press, 1988, explores the transition years from fur trade to settlement. Bob Beal and Rod Macleod, *Prairie Fire: the North-West Rebellion of 1885*, Edmonton: Hurtig, 1984, is the most comprehensive treatment of the final armed confrontation.

In the campaign to suppress indigenous peoples, attacks on native cultural institutions were at least as important as military interventions, a point demonstrated by Douglas Cole, *Captured Heritage: the Scramble for Northwest Coast Artifacts*, Seattle: University of Washington Press, 1985, and Douglas Cole and Ira Chaikin, *An Iron Hand Upon the People: the Law Against the Potlatch on the Northwest Coast*, Vancouver: Douglas & McIntyre, 1990. On Indian survival and resurgence, see Barron and Waldram, eds., *1885 and After*; Hugh Brody, *Maps and Dreams: Indians and the British Columbia Frontier*, Vancouver: Douglas & McIntyre, 1981; Celia Haig-Brown, *Resistance and Renewal: Surviving the Indian Residential School*, Vancouver: Tillacum Library, 1987; Rolf Knight, *Indians at Work: an Informal History of Native Indian Labour in British Columbia 1858-1930*, Vancouver: New Star Press, 1978; and J. R. Miller, *Skyscrapers Hide the Heavens: a History of Indian-White Relations in*

Canada, Toronto: University of Toronto Press, 1991. Note however the critical evaluation of some of this work by Robin Brownlie and Mary-Ellen Kelm, "Desperately Seeking Absolution: Native Agency as Colonialist Alibi?" *Canadian Historical Review,* Vol. 75, No. 4 (December 1994): 543-56.

Efforts to control Native peoples were essential to extending Canadian settlement and industrial frontiers. David Hall's two-volume biography on Clifford Sifton, Laurier's Minister of the Interior, Vol. 1, *The Young Napoleon, 1861-1929,* and Vol. 2, *A Lonely Eminence, 1901-1929,* Vancouver: University of British Columbia Press, 1981 and 1985, is a close study of the minister and Liberal government policy. Doug Owram's much praised *Promise of Eden: the Canadian Expansionist Movement and the Idea of the West, 1856-1900,* Toronto: University of Toronto Press, 1980, explains how Euro-Canadians came to see the West as their patrimony ripe for exploitation. "Imperial dreams" stimulated the creation of new institutions, most notably the North-West Mounted Police and railways. R. C. Macleod's *The North-West Mounted Police and Law Enforcement, 1873-1905,* Toronto: University of Toronto Press, 1976, is still the most complete scholarly study of the police. Railway studies are usually uncritical, but for welcome evidence of a new approach, see Frank Leonard, *A Thousand Blunders: The Grand Trunk Pacific Railway and Northern British Columbia,* Vancouver: University of British Columbia Press, 1995. Of the earlier work, John A. Eagle's *The Canadian Pacific Railway and the Development of Western Canada, 1896-1914,* Montreal and Kingston: McGill-Queen's University Press, 1989, is better than most. More critical accounts of the CPR include Robert Chodos, *The CPR: A Century of Corporate Welfare,* Toronto: James Lewis and Samuel, 1973, and David Cruise and Alison Griffiths, *Lords of the Line,* Markham, Ontario: Viking, 1988, although neither adopts a scholarly approach. Two early works on western settlement remain essential reading: Chester Martin's *Dominion Lands Policy,* Toronto: McClelland and Stewart, 1973 (originally published as part of the *Frontiers of Settlement* series, 1938), and W. A. Mackintosh's *The Economic Background of Dominion-Provincial Relations: Appendix III of the Royal Commission Report on Dominion-Provincial Relations,* edited and introduced by J. H. Dales, Toronto: MacMillan, 1978 (written in 1939). Another older book which remains useful is Vernon C. Fowke's *The National Policy and the Wheat Economy,* Toronto: University of Toronto Press, 1957. Tina Loo, *Making Law, Order and Authority in British Columbia,*

1821-1871, Toronto: University of Toronto Press, 1994, is a thoughtful exploration of the uses of the law as a tool of colonization.

Settlement in western Canada was a consequence of immigration from both Europe and Asia, providing the region with a tradition of ethnic diversity. Roberto Perin, "Writing about Ethnicity," in John Schultz, ed., *Writing about Canada*, places ethnicity in a historiographical context. Donald Avery, *"Dangerous Foreigners": European Immigrant Workers and Labour Radicalism in Canada, 1896-1931*, Toronto: McClelland and Stewart, 1979; Howard Palmer, *Patterns of Prejudice: a History of Nativism in Alberta*, Toronto: McClelland and Stewart, 1982; and John Herd Thompson, *The Harvests of War: the Prairie West, 1914-1918*, Toronto: McClelland and Stewart, 1978, explore Ango-Canadian responses to immigration. Useful studies for British Columbia include Patricia E. Roy's *A White Man's Province: British Columbia Politicians and Chinese and Japanese Immigrants, 1858-1914*, Vancouver: University of British Columbia Press, 1989; Kay J. Anderson's *Vancouver's Chinatown: Racial Discourse in Canada, 1875-1980*, Montreal: McGill-Queen's University Press, 1991; and Peter Ward's *White Canada Forever: Popular Attitudes and Public Policies Toward Orientals in British Columbia*, 2nd edition, Montreal and Kingston: McGill Queen's University Press, 1990. Japanese internment during the Second World War remains underexplored in western Canadian history. Two contrasting views are offered by Ann Gomer Sunahara in *The Politics of Racism: The Uprooting of Japanese Canadians during the Second World War*, Toronto: James Lorimer, 1981, and Patricia Roy *et. al.*, *Mutual Hostages: Canadians and Japanese During the Second World War*, Toronto: University of Toronto Press, 1990.

There is also a growing body of literature on specific immigrant communities. The bulk of these studies is published in essay form so that a good place to start is by consulting the extensive bibliographical list in Jean Burnet with Howard Palmer, *"Coming Canadians": An introduction to a History of Canada's Peoples*, Toronto, McClelland and Stewart, 1988. Single studies are also available. Harry Con, Ronald J. Con, Graham Johnson, Edgar Wickberg, William E. Willmott, *From China to Canada: a history of the Chinese communities in Canada*, Toronto: McClelland and Stewart, 1982, is a broad overview, as the title suggests. Ukrainian migrations and settlement are the subject of Myrna Kostash's *All of Baba's children*, Edmonton: Hurtig,

1977, and Manoly R. Lupul's *A Heritage in Transition: Essays in the History of Ukrainians in Canada*, Toronto: McClelland and Stewart, 1982. Frances Swyripa, *Wedded to the Cause: Ukrainian-Canadian Women and Ethnic Identity, 1891-1991*, Toronto: University of Toronto Press, 1992, examines the intersection of gender, ethnicity and region in the shifting identities of these newcomers, and Royden K. Loewen, *Family, Church, and Market: A Mennonite Community in the Old and the New Worlds, 1850-1930*, Toronto: University of Toronto Press, 1993, emphasizes economic adaptation.

Newcomers to the West were also divided by class and social background. Disruption and displacement as a result of 19th and early 20th century economic changes stimulated migrations from Europe and North America at the same time that the investment frontiers attracted land and resource speculation. Social tensions emerged early in the West, with the failure of utopian visions of agricultural settlement, in emerging urban centres, and on booming resource frontiers. Lyle Dick, *Farmers "Making Good": The Development of Abernethy District, Saskatchewan, 1880-1920*, Ottawa: National Historic Parks and Sites, Canadian Parks Service, 1989, and Paul Voisey, *Vulcan: The Making of a Prairie Community*, Toronto: University of Toronto Press, 1988 offer contrasting accounts of agricultural communities. David C. Jones' grim story in *Empire of Dust: Settling and Abandoning the Prairie Dry Belt*, Edmonton: University of Alberta Press, 1987, is summed up in the book's title. Carl A. Dawson and Eva R. Younge, *Pioneering in the Prairie Provinces: The Social Side of the Settlement Process*, Toronto: Macmillan, 1940, is still important, and there are several useful essays in David C. Jones and Ian MacPherson, eds., *Building Beyond the Homestead: Rural History on the Prairies*, Calgary: University of Calgary Press, 1987. John W. Bennett and Seena B. Kohl, *Settling the Canadian-American West, 1890-1915*, Lincoln: University of Nebraska Press, 1995, takes a binational approach using autobiographical material to reconstruct the experience of settlement and community in the Northern Great Plains region. David H. Breen, *The Canadian Prairie West and the Ranching Frontier 1874-1924*, Toronto: University of Toronto Press, 1983, describes the competing pastoral economy. A. A. den Otter, *Civilizing the West: the Galts and the Development of Western Canada*, Edmonton: University of Alberta Press, 1982, is one of the few studies on the role of the entrepreneur in western economic development. Cecilia

Danysk, *Hired Hands: Labour and the Development of Prairie Agriculture, 1880-1930*, Toronto: McClelland and Stewart, 1995, thoughtfully explores the experience of a largely overlooked work force. Jeffery Taylor, *Fashioning Farmers: Ideology, Agricultural Knowledge and the Manitoba Farm Movement, 1890-1925*, Regina: Canadian Plains Research Centre, 1994, explains how educational institutions helped to shape farmers' politics.

Prairie history often focuses on the development of rural agriculture but urbanization and industrial expansion has been equally important to the making of the West, as Martin Robin shows in his two volume provincial history, *The Rush for Spoils: the Company Province, 1871-1933*, and *Pillars of Profit: The Company Province, 1934-1972*, Toronto: McClelland and Stewart, 1972 and 1973. The most comprehensive study of a single prairie city is Alan F. J. Artibise's *Winnipeg: a Social History of Urban Growth, 1874-1914*, Montreal: McGill-Queen's University Press, 1975; for Vancouver, see the long-awaited study by Robert A. J. McDonald, *Making Vancouver, 1863-1913*, Vancouver: University of British Columbia Press, 1996, and the comparative study by Norbert MacDonald, *Distant Neighbors: A Comparative History of Seattle & Vancouver*, Lincoln: University of Nebraska Press, 1987. There are a number of important essays in A. R. McCormack and Ian Macpherson, eds., *Cities in the West: Papers of the Western Canada Urban History Conference, University of Winnipeg, October 1974*, Ottawa: National Museums of Canada, 1975.

The most famous confrontation between capital and labour in Canada took place in Winnipeg. As its title suggests, Norman Penner, ed., *Winnipeg 1919: the Strikers' Own History of the Winnipeg General Strike*, second edition, Toronto: J. Lorimer, 1975, provides first-hand accounts. David Jay Bercuson argues in two well-known books, *Confrontation at Winnipeg: Labour, Industrial Relations, and the General Strike*, Montreal: McGill-Queen's University Press, 1974, and *Fools and Wise Men: The Rise and Fall of the One Big Union*, Toronto: McGraw-Hill Ryerson, 1978, that labour conflict was the inevitable result of harsh conditions in the West. A. Ross McCormack makes a similar case in *Reformers, Rebels, and Revolutionaries: The Western Canadian Radical Movement, 1899-1919*, Toronto: University of Toronto Press, 1977, although his notion of regional exceptionalism is challenged by Robert A. J. McDonald, "Working Class Vancouver, 1886-1914: Urbanism and Class in British Columbia," *BC Studies*, 69-70 (Spring-Summer, 1986): 33-69, and Jeremy Mouat, "The Genesis of Western Exceptionalism: British Columbia's Hard Rock Miners, 1895-1903," *Canadian Historical Review*, Vol. 71, No. 3 (September, 1990): 317-45.

The resource industry has dominated the British Columbia economy so it is not surprising that labour history in that province has attracted much scholarly attention. Recent works include two books by Mark Leier, *Where the Fraser River Flows: the Industrial Workers of the World in British Columbia*, Vancouver: New Star Books, 1990, and *Red Flags and Red Tape: The Making of a Labour Bureaucracy*, Toronto: University of Toronto Press, 1995. The journal *Labour/Le Travail* frequently publishes articles on workers in western Canada, and good essays may also be found in Rennie Warburton and David Coburn, eds., *Workers, Capital, and the State in British Columbia: Selected Papers*, Vancouver: University of British Columbia Press, 1988. More industrial history than labour history, Jeremy Mouat's *Roaring Days: Rossland's Mines and the History of British Columbia*, Vancouver: University of British Columbia Press, 1995, traces the ways in which local, regional and international influences shaped the development of one mining community.

The influence of gender in the making of Western Canada is less well understood and until recently women have been largely invisible in the historiography. Thankfully, a number of edited essay collections have now appeared and these typically include useful introductions and bibliographies. See Mary Kinnear, ed., *First Days, Fighting Days: Women in Manitoba History*, Regina: Canadian Plains Research Centre, University of Regina, 1987; Catherine A. Cavanaugh and Randi R. Warne, eds., *Standing on New Ground: Women in Alberta*, Edmonton: University of Alberta Press, 1993; Gillian Creese and Veronica Strong-Boag, eds., *British Columbia Reconsidered: Essays on Women*, Vancouver: Press Gang Publishers, 1992; Barbara Latham and Cathy Kess, eds., *In Her Own Right: Selected Essays on Women's History in B.C.*, Victoria: Camosun College, 1980; and Barbara K. Latham and Roberta J. Pazdro, eds., *Not Just Pin Money: Selected Essays on the History of Women's Work in British Columbia*, Victoria: Camosun College, 1984. There are also several important essays on Canadian women in Susan Armitage and Elizabeth Jameson, eds., *The Women's West*, Norman: University of Oklahoma Press, 1987.

In addition, Alison Prentice *et. al.*, *Canadian Women: A History*, Toronto: Harcourt, Brace, Jovanovich, 1988, provides a broad overview for the four western provinces. Susan Jackel, ed., *A Flannel Shirt and Liberty: British Emigrant Gentlewomen in The Canadian West, 1880-1914*, Vancouver: University of British Columbia Press, 1982, and Margaret A. Ormsby, ed., *A Pioneer Gentlewoman in British Columbia: The Recollections of Susan Allison*, Vancouver: University of British Columbia Press, 1976, reprint middle-class women's accounts of settlement. A similar book is Georgina Binnie-Clark's *Wheat and Woman*, with an introduction by Susan Jackel, Toronto: University of Toronto Press, 1979, which tells of one woman's homesteading efforts in turn-of-the century Manitoba. Elaine Leslau Silverman uses oral history to look at a more diverse population in *The Last Best West: Women on the Alberta Frontier, 1880-1930*, Montreal: Eden Press, 1984. Nanci L. Langford, *"Home Was Never Like This": The Gendered Identities of Prairie Homestead Women*, Regina: Canadian Plains Research Centre, 1996, explores the lives of seventy-eight adult women who settled on the prairies between 1880 and 1930. Sara Brooks Sundberg, "Farm Women on the Canadian Prairie Frontier: The Helpmate Image," in Veronica Strong-Boag, Anita Clair Fellman, eds., *Rethinking Canada: The Promise of Women's History*, Toronto: Copp Clark Pitman, 1991, challenges the standard view of women's supportive role in agriculture, and Marjorie Griffin Cohen, *Women's Work, Markets, and Economic Development in Nineteenth-Century Ontario*, Toronto: University of Toronto Press, 1988, includes prairie women in her reconsideration of agricultural production. Veronica Strong-Boag, "Pulling in Double Harness or Hauling a Double Load: Women, Work and Feminism on the Canadian Prairie," *Journal of Canadian Studies*, Vol. 21, No. 3 (Autumn 1986): 32-52, focuses on the 1920s and 1930s. The recent publication of Mary Hallett and Marilyn Davis's full length biography of Nellie McClung, *Firing the Heather*, Saskatoon: Fifth House, 1993, and Randi R. Warne's *Literature as Pulpit: The Christian Social Activism of Nellie L. McClung*, Waterloo: Wilfrid Laurier University Press, 1993, together offer a good beginning to students interested in the prairies' most well-known woman activist. For a biography of a lesser-known B.C. activist, see Irene Howard's *The Struggle for Social Justice in British Columbia: Helena Gutteridge, the Unknown Reformer*, Vancouver: University of British Columbia Press, 1992. Serious analysis of

masculinity in Western Canada has only just begun, but see Morris
Kenneth Mott, "Manly Sports and Manitobans, Settlement Days to World
War One," Ph.D. thesis, Queen's University, 1980, and Cecilia Danysk's
chapter in this volume.

As the following list shows, political histories of Western Canada emphasize regional identity and the politics of discontent. Walter D. Young, *Democracy and Discontent: Progressivism, Socialism and Social Credit in the Canadian West*, second edition, Toronto: McGraw-Hill Ryerson, 1978, looks at
the development of radical parties on the prairies and in B.C.. This theme
is also the focus of the essays in George Melnyk, ed., *Riel to Reform: protest in
Western Canada*, Saskatoon: Fifth House, 1992. W. L. Morton, *The Progressive Party in Canada*, Toronto: University of Toronto Press, 1967, explains
how the wheat economy shaped prairie protest in the 1920s as do Paul F.
Sharp, *The Agrarian Revolt in Western Canada: A Survey Showing American
Parallels*, New York: Octagon Books 1971, and David Laycock, *Populism and
Democratic Thought in the Canadian Prairies, 1910-1945*, Toronto: University
of Toronto Press, 1990. For a comparative analysis of farmers' political
movements, see Robert C. McMath, Jr., "Populism in Two Countries:
Agrarian Protest in the Great Plains and Prairie Provinces," *Agricultural History*, Vol. 69, No. 4 (Fall 1995): 517-46. Roger Gibbins, *Regionalism: Territorial Politics in Canada and the United States*, Toronto: Butterworths, 1982, is a
comparative approach to regional identity, while his *Prairie Politics and Society: Regionalism in Decline*, Toronto: Butterworths, 1980, remains a good survey through to the 1960s and 1970s. John Richards and Larry Pratt, in *Prairie Capitalism: Power and Influence in the New West*, Toronto: McClelland and
Stewart, 1979, compare the political influence of the re-emergence during
the 1970s of provincial entrepreneurship in Saskatchewan and Alberta. The
resurgence of western alienation is explored by Don Braid and Sydney
Sharpe, *Breakup: Why the West Feels Left Out of Canada*, Toronto: Key Porter
Books, 1990; David Kilgour, *Uneasy Patriots: Western Canadians in Confederation*, Edmonton: Lone Pine Publishing, 1988; and Larry Pratt and Garth
Stevenson, eds., *Western Separatism: the Myths, Realities & Dangers*, Edmonton: Hurtig, 1981. George Melnyk, *Beyond Alienation: Political Essays on the
West*, Calgary: Detselig Enterprises Ltd., 1993, reprints articles from this
ongoing debate.

Among published studies on provincial politics, the thirty-six year reign of Social Credit in Alberta has attracted particular attention. Alvin Finkel's comprehensive *The Social Credit Phenomenon in Alberta*, Toronto: University of Toronto Press, 1989, argues that the party's radical origins were eclipsed during Aberhart's second term. Two early but still worthwhile studies are C. B. MacPherson's *Democracy in Alberta: the Theory and Practice of a Quasi-Party System*, Toronto: University of Toronto Press, 1953, and John Allan Irving's *The Social Credit Movement in Alberta*, Toronto: University of Toronto Press, 1959. The prevailing views about Social Credit are challenged in Edward Bell's *Social Classes and Social Credit in Alberta*, Montreal: McGill-Queen's University Press, 1994, on the basis of the author's analysis of voting patterns in the 1935 and 1940 provincial elections. L. G. Thomas's *The Liberal Party in Alberta: A History of Politics in the Province of Alberta, 1905-1921*, Toronto: University of Toronto Press, 1959, together with Carl Betke's "Farm Politics in an Urban Age: The Decline of the United Farmers of Alberta after 1921," in Thomas, *Essays in Western History*, are still the best accounts of the early years in that province. David E. Smith's *Prairie Liberalism: The Liberal Party in Saskatchewan, 1905-1971*, Toronto: University of Toronto Press, 1975, and Barry Wilson's *Politics of Defeat: The Decline of the Liberal Party in Saskatchewan*, Saskatoon: Western Producer Books, 1980, together tell of the rise and fall of the party in that province. S. M. Lipset's *Agrarian Socialism: The Cooperative Commonwealth Federation in Saskatchewan; A Study in Political Sociology*, 2nd ed., New York: Anchor, 1968, is still required reading. On political change in Manitoba, Gerald Friesen's "Homeland to Hinterland: Political Transition in Manitoba," Canadian Historical Association, *Historical Papers/Communications historiques* (1979): 33-47, is a thoughtful overview while Nelson Wiseman, *Social Democracy in Manitoba: A History of the CCF-NDP*, Winnipeg: University of Manitoba Press, 1983, explores the influence of the political left. The essays in James Silver and Jeremy Hull, eds., *The Political Economy of Manitoba*, Regina: Canadian Plains Research Centre, 1990, and David Leadbeater, ed., *Essays on the Political Economy of Alberta*, Toronto: New Hogtown Press, 1984, reflect more recent debates. Despite its reputation for flamboyant politicians, B.C. has not been well-served by political historians, although one exception is Robin Fisher's *Duff Pattullo of British Columbia*, Toronto: University of Toronto Press, 1991.

Compared to the United States, the Canadian West has never had an enduring influence on the national imagination, but the region has nonetheless inspired a rich literary and artistic history. R. Douglas Francis, *Images of the West: Responses to the Canadian Prairies*, Saskatoon: Western Producer Prairie Books, 1989, details the shifting perceptions of the prairie West. Edward McCourt's *The Canadian West in Fiction*, Toronto: Ryerson Press, 1970, rev. ed., is dated but still useful; Dick Harrison, *Unnamed Country: the Struggle for a Canadian Prairie Fiction*, Edmonton: University of Alberta Press, 1977, is required reading, as is Laurence Ricou, *Vertical Man, Horizontal World: Man and Landscape in Canadian Prairie Fiction*, Vancouver: University of British Columbia Press, 1973. For British Columbia, see Douglas Cole's article, "The Intellectual and Imaginative Development of British Columbia," *Journal of Canadian Studies*, Vol. 24, No. 3 (Autumn 1989): 70-79. Ronald Rees, *Land of Earth and Sky: Landscape Painting of Western Canada*, Saskatoon: Western Producer Prairie Books, 1984, and *New and Naked Land: Making the Prairies Home*, Saskatoon: Western Producer Prairie Books, 1988, introduces prairie painters, showing how they have reinterpreted the landscape. For British Columbia, see Maria Tippett and Douglas Cole, *From Desolation to Splendour: Changing Perceptions of the British Columbia Landscape*, Toronto: Clarke, Irwin, 1977, as well as the numerous studies of Emily Carr (Maria Tippett's *Emily Carr: A Biography*, Toronto: Oxford University Press, 1979, is a good place to start). A number of works analyse the Native art of the Pacific coast; for an introduction to this complex topic, see Bill Holm, *Northwest Coast Indian Art: An Analysis of Form*, Seattle: University of Washington Press, 1965, and Wilson Duff, *Images: Stone: B.C.: Thirty Centuries of Northwest Coast Indian Sculpture*, Toronto: Oxford University Press, 1975.

Students of the Canadian West might be interested in exploring the lively debate sparked by the "new western history" in the United States. Works of particular interest include Patricia Nelson Limerick's *The Legacy of Conquest: the Unbroken Past of the American West*, New York: W. W. Norton & Company, 1987; William G. Robbins, *Colony and Empire: the Capitalist Transformation of the American West*, Lawrence: University Press of Kansas, 1994; Richard White, *"It's Your Misfortune and None of My Own": A New History of the American West*, Norman: University of Oklahoma Press, 1991;

and Donald Worster, *Under Western Skies: Nature and History in the American West*, New York: Oxford University Press, 1992. In addition to these monographs, the following essay collections provide helpful introductions to "new western" themes: William Cronon, George Miles, Jay Gitlin, eds., *Under An Open Sky: Rethinking America's Western Past*, New York: W. W. Norton & Co., 1992, and Patricia Nelson Limerick, Clyde A. Milner II, and Charles E. Rankin, eds., *Trails: Toward a New Western History*, Lawrence: University Press of Kansas, 1991. Finally, two striking books of historical images from the American West have appeared: William H. Truettner, ed., *The West As America: Reinterpreting Images of the Frontier, 1820 – 1920*, Washington: Smithsonian Institution Press, 1991, and Jules David Prown *et. al.*, *Discovered Lands, Invented Pasts: Transforming Visions of the American West*, New Haven: Yale University Press, 1992.

Reflecting on the transformation of his home province, Manitoba, W. L. Morton in 1970 pointed to the place of imagination in the "material reshaping of the land" (see his "Seeing an Unliterary Landscape," reprinted in *Contexts*, cited above). Our own "post-colonial" age is more critical of what Morton and so many of his generation saw as "the elegant undress of the wild landscape" yet, as even this brief bibliographical list shows, his question concerning the crucial interplay of "man's intended purposes" and the material and cultural reshaping of the country remains at the core of our common project. As new, more diverse voices join the debate, we gain fresh insight into the complexity of how the West was made.

CATHERINE CAVANAUGH

JEREMY MOUAT